WORLD® AIR POWER
JOURNAL

Aerospace Publishing Ltd
AIRtime Publishing Inc.

Published quarterly by
Aerospace Publishing Ltd
179 Dalling Road
London W6 0ES
UK

Cutaway drawings copyright
© Mike Badrocke/Aviagraphica

ISSN 0959-7050
Aerospace ISBN   1 86184-002-0
                  (softback)
                  1 86184-003-9
                  (hardback)
Airtime ISBN   1-880588-07-2
                  (hardback)

Published under licence in USA and
Canada by AIRtime Publishing Inc.,
USA

Editorial Offices:
WORLD AIR POWER JOURNAL
Aerospace Publishing Ltd
3A Brackenbury Road
London   W6 0BE   UK

Publisher: Stan Morse
Managing Editor: David Donald

Editors: Robert Hewson
         David Donald

Sub Editor: Karen Leverington

Editorial Assistant: Tim Senior

Origination by Chroma Graphics
Printed in Italy by Officine Grafiche
        de Agostini

Correspondents:
General military: Jon Lake
USA Washington: Robert F. Dorr
USA Southwest: Randy Jolly
Europe: John Fricker
Russia/CIS: Yefim Gordon
Asia: Pushpindar Singh
Canada: Jeff Rankin-Lowe
Argentina: Jorge Nunez Padin
Chile: Patrick Laureau

The publishers gratefully acknowledge the assistance
given by the following people:

Mike Moss (US Naval Airforces Atlantic, Public Affairs),
Lieutenant Commander Larry Slade (US Navy), Doug
McMurrach (Lockheed Martin). Commander Hnarakis,
Lieutenant Peterson and Lieutenant Westendorf (VF-103),
Lieutenent Thomas Baker (VF-41) for their time and
assistance with the F-14D 'Bombcat' briefing.

Mr Tim Lewis (DCPRO Strike Command), Captain
Claire Lucas (AGC/PIO BFFI), Wing Commander Rich
Jones (OC Air Wing), the personnel of No. 78
Squadron, including Squadron Leader Mark Beardsmore
(OC), Flight Lieutenant Peter Quick (OC 'A' Flt), Flight
Lieutenant Andy Barr (OC 'B' Flt) and Flying Officer
Ian Henning, Squadron Leader Roger Dickinson (OC
1312 Flight), the personnel of 1435 Flight, and Flight
Lieutenant Geoff Wilson and his No. 216 Squadron
crew, for their invaluable assistance and warm hospitality
during the preparation of the *Falklands Garrison* article.

Thanks, for contributions large and small, are due to:
Apache fliers CW3 (P) Robert D. Mitchell, Major
Morgan M. Lamb, Captain Thomas J. Hadel, CW2 Mike
'Crash' Croslin, CW2 Brian K. McFadden, Major
Wayne A. Sauer, CW2 Bobbie S. Bass and CW3
Michael Champion. Ft Rucker PAO: Major James
Yonts. Public Information Specialists: Sergeant Carla
Porter, Bill Hayes, Ted Walls, and Ken Holder at
Ft Rucker, Master Sergeant William T. Powell at
Ft Hood, and Jack Coffey at FORSCOM. The author is
also grateful to Lindsay Peacock and Doug Richardson,
authors of the AH-64 volume in the Combat Aircraft
series, published by Salamander Books Ltd.
    Thomas M. Ring, who contributed the US Army unit
details, would like to point out that he is a resident of
Houston and not Dallas, as previously stated.
    Finally, a special acknowledgement is due to the
'Outlaws' of the 7th Cavalry, who made bad times better
– thanks again.

The authors of the Zimbabwe Air Force feature would
like to thank all the officers and men at the Air Force of
Zimbabwe Headquarters, Manyame and Thornhill Air
Force Bases. In particular they would like to
acknowledge the help and enthusiasm of Air Marshall
Shiri, Air Vice Marshall Harvey, Air Commodore Vinyu,
Group Captains Marangwanda, Mhlanga, Moyo, Sqn
Leaders Chasakara, Govere, Goremusandu, Sibanda,
Magwa, Gwata, Nyagweta, Mandaba, Manyange,
Dhabha, Atkins and Chikonzo, and Flight Lieutenants
Zvobgo, Ncube, Magama and Masakadza. Without their
contributions this article could not have been written.

**World Air Power Journal is a
registered trademark in the
United States of America of
AIRtime Publishing Inc.**

**World Air Power Journal is
published quarterly and is
available by subscription and
from many fine book and hobby
stores.**

**SUBSCRIPTION AND BACK
NUMBERS:**

**UK and World (except USA and
Canada) write to:**
Aerospace Publishing Ltd
FREEPOST
PO Box 2822
London
W6 0BR
UK

**(No stamp required if posted in
the UK)**

USA and Canada, write to:
AIRtime Publishing Inc.
Subscription Dept
10 Bay Street
Westport
CT 06880, USA
(203) 838-7979
Toll-free order number in USA:
1 800 359-3003

**Prevailing subscription rates are
as follows:**
Softbound edition for 1 year:
$59.95
Softbound edition for 2 years:
$112.00
**Softbound back numbers
(subject to availability) are
$16.00 each, plus shipping and
handling. All rates are for
delivery within mainland USA,
Alaska and Hawaii. Canadian
and overseas prices available
upon request. American Express,
Discover Card, MasterCard and
Visa accepted. When ordering
please include card number,
expiration date and signature.**

U.S. Publisher:
Mel Williams
Subscriptions Director:
Linda DeAngelis
**Charter Member Services
Managers:**
Geetha Shirol
Zoë Williams
Retail Sales Director: Jill Brooks
Shipping Manager: E. Rex Anku

WORLD AIR POWER ®
JOURNAL

CONTENTS

Military Aviation Review

International

More Eurofighter delays

Top-level ministerial pressure late in 1996 from the UK on the German government had failed to achieve any funding allocations in Bonn's 1997 budget plans for the Eurofighter production investment phase. In an earlier statement, the chairman of the Parliamentary defence committee in Bonn said that while Germany needed the Eurofighter, public spending cuts to qualify for the single European currency in 1999 meant that funding was a problem, which could delay plans to start production.

Still more economies were threatened to Germany's 1997 defence budget, in addition to recent cuts of DM200 million ($131.55 million) to DM46.4 billion ($30.53 billion), in Bonn's frenetic efforts to qualify for European monetary union. Spain followed Britain's September lead on 21 October 1996 with a production commitment for its 87 required EF 2000s. In contrast to Spain's Pts25 billion ($195 million) 1997 defence budget loan allocations for its production investment phase, DASA was still trying to bridge the gap in funding for continuation of its share of the Eurofighter R&D programme in 1997.

Some DM6.5 billion ($4.295 billion) has already been spent by Germany on Eurofighter R&D. The Finance Ministry in Bonn, however, resolutely refused to offer more than DM100 million ($66 million) in the FY1997 defence budget, increasing to DM350 million in FY1998 and DM600 million in the following year, against DASA's request for DM392 million ($259 million) in the current fiscal year. Similar funding gaps apply each year until 2000, by which time only DM1.9 billion will have been allocated, against DASA requests totalling DM3.7 billion.

In mid-November 1996, a German Defence Ministry official said that finances were so tight that there was no room for manoeuvre, leaving open the question of who would pay the difference between allocations and requirements. The Ministry has denied any reduction in Luftwaffe requirements for 180 Eurofighters, including 40 multi-role ground-attack variants.

While some German industry sources hinted that further EF 2000 funding delays might be manageable if the government gave a firm commitment to continuation of the programme, BDLI and DASA president Manfred Bischoff said that deferring a production investment decision until after 1 January 1997 would invalidate previous costings. Late in 1996, however, it became clear that no production investment decision could be expected from Germany before the spring of 1997.

In London, UK Defence Secretary Portillo said that more delays in the EF 2000 programme were to be "greatly regretted". They would inevitably make the aircraft more expensive, and damage its competitiveness. They would not be fatal, however, and he did not think that "Eurofighter was heading for the rocks." At a ministerial meeting in London in December 1996, State Secretary Simon from Germany nevertheless joined his opposite numbers, including Signor Brutti from Italy, Señor Morenes from Spain, and UK Defense Procurement Secretary James Arbuthnot, in confirming the expectation of the four partner governments of completing their national approval processes to start the next phases of the programme in 1997.

The MoD said that, following this decision, it was expected that intergovernmental MoUs would be concluded to expedite further work on the production investment, production and support phases. This would lead to contracts, with Eurofighter and Eurojet as prime contractors.

Italy – the fourth partner in Eurofighter – is also experiencing funding problems for its 121 aircraft, with options on another nine. Ironically, on 12 November the UK joined, with Italy, the embryonic Bonn-based agency formed by France and Germany to promote and organise joint European arms production projects. Britain's membership of the joint arms agency followed assurances

On 14 January 1997 the first mission-equipped EH Industries Merlin HAS.Mk 1 for the Royal Navy (RN02/ZH822) flew for the first time from Westland's Yeovil factory. The navy has 44 on order for the ASW role, for service from Type 23 frigates, aircraft-carriers and RFA vessels.

from the original partners that participation would not imply a blanket European preference in weapons procurement, or exclude the purchase of US arms if they offered better value.

McDonnell Douglas loses JSF

The Boeing and Lockheed Martin teams were short-listed in November 1996 as the preferred contenders for the US$218.8 billion multi-service/multi-role Joint Strike Fighter programme. This was a temporary setback for British Aerospace, as partner to McDonnell Douglas/Northrop Grumman, whose design submissions were rejected. For the JSF STOVL version, these were based on the use of a discrete 17,000-18,000-lb (75.6-80.07-kN) thrust GEA-FXL lift-fan engine being developed jointly by Rolls-Royce and its Allison Division, teamed with General Electric, to augment the Pratt & Whitney YF119-100 propulsion turbofan with an axisymmetric pitch/yaw balanced-beam thrust-vectoring system.

Following the JSF down-selection decision on 16 November, US Defense Department contracts worth $718.8 million have been awarded to the Boeing team, and $661.8 million to Lockheed Martin, for construction of two prototypes each of conventional and STOVL versions, to fly by 1999-2000. After extensive fly-off evaluations, the eventual winner stands to receive contracts in 2001 for up to 2,036 conventional JSFs for the USAF and 300 carrier versions for the USN, plus 642 STOVL versions for the USMC and 67 for the Royal Navy, for delivery from 2007.

BAe was not expected to remain for very long outside the JSF R&D programme, in which the UK has a $200 million investment accompanying the RN's requirements. Approaches to BAe earlier in the programme for technical co-operation on the part of Boeing and Lockheed Martin were resumed almost immediately when the UK company lost its MDC JSF commitments. Canada, Denmark, the Netherlands and Norway were also planning to join the JSF consortium at the lowest 'informed customer' level, with no design requirement inputs, in late 1996.

Budget cuts affect European helicopter programmes

Drastic economies in European defence budgets have led to major cuts and delays in the joint development and production plans for the Eurocopter Tiger attack helicopter and the NH Industries NH 90 transport/utility and naval helicopter. German protests over French proposals in 1996 to cut Tiger procurement by almost 50 per cent to only 120 eventually resulted in France's originally planned 215 total remaining unchanged, as was Germany's 212. Production investment for the DM10 billion ($6.6 billion) programme was deferred by about a year, and planned delivery schedules stretched from proposed service entry in 2001.

From its originally planned 726 orders, including 182 naval versions, the NH 90 has now been reduced to 647, costing an estimated $12 billion. France has reduced its requirement from 220 to 160, and Germany from 272 to 243. Italy, however, is unique in increasing its NH 90 needs from 214 to 224, resulting in the second largest share in the programme. Dutch requirements remain unchanged at 20 NFH 90 naval frigate helicopters, with a target fly-away unit cost of $29 million at 1994 values. This compares with $18 million for the TTH 90 tactical transport helicopter version.

The first of five prototype NH 90s planned – PT1 – first flew at Marignane on 18 December 1995. It will be re-engined in summer 1997 from its 2,100-shp (1565-kW) Rolls-Royce/Turboméca RTM322-01/9 turboshafts, as specified for the French requirements, to 2,040-shp (1520-kW) Alfa Romeo/General Electric T700-T6Es, for the Italian examples. Engine selection was still awaited by Germany and the Netherlands late in 1996. NH 90 deliveries (particularly NFH 90s to Germany and Holland) are now due to start in 2003, three years after the original target date.

Europe

AUSTRIA:

Fighter decision postponed

In the last meeting of the Defence Council, held on 10 December 1996, an agreement was reached regarding massive procurements for the mechanised troops of the Austrian army (e.g., 114 MBT Leopard 2A4s, among other items). The costs for the entire package are about Sch6 million (about $550 million).

No decision was made about the demand for a follow-on aircraft to replace the ageing Saab 35OE Draken. This political decision was postponed to 1998 due to the chronically under-funded Austrian defence budget, which has been exhausted by the other procurements. This could create a gap in Austrian air defence capability because retirement of the Draken will start in 2000, and there is no other aircraft in inventory that could be used for air policing and air defence. After signing a contract for a replacement aircraft, it will still be five to six years until the first of them join the wings. To prevent such a gap, the decision about aircraft type must be made not later than 1998; however, there is little hope of this happening because a decision will not be made before the next Parliamentary elections, scheduled for 1999. The political decision which led to Draken took about 15 years. Evaluations are currently being completed by the OeLk of such types as the Dassault Mirage 2000-5 and JAS 39 Gripen, as well as the Lockheed Martin F-16C/D and MDC F/A-18C/D. Talks have also been held with other European countries of similar political alignments, including Finland and Switzerland, which both operate Hornets, concerning mutual technical and logistic support arrangements.

Austrian army helicopter to protect outer border of EU

The Austrian army will keep the eastern border of Austria under airborne surveillance and will protect it against illegal frontier crossings, to meet Schengen treaty requirements. Austria does not have special border troops such as the German Bundesgrenzschutz, and the Austrian Ministry of the Interior has insufficient numbers of helicopters (which in any case are not equipped for large-scale surveillance operations). Therefore, the Ministry of the Interior has requested assistance from the Ministry of Defence. It is primarily the Bell OH-58B Kiowa and the SA 316B Alouette which will be used for the surveillance operations. The section of the border that will be patrolled is the western section running from the 'corner' of Austria/Czech Republic/Germany to the 'corner' of Austria/Italy/Slovenia. Due to a demand for surveillance flights during the night, the helicopters have been equipped with NVGs.

BOSNIA:

New air base construction

Although its deputy army chief claims Bosnia has no (fixed-wing) aircraft, IFOR officials are concerned about the half-completed construction of a new airfield with a 4000-m (13,123-ft) runway 20 miles (32 km) from Sarajevo. This, claims General Jovan Divjak, is 'just for helicopters', including the first 15 of a planned 50 surplus UH-1Hs from US military aid.

BULGARIA:

More MiG-29s sought

Alone among most ex-WarPac countries – including the Czech Republic, Hungary, Poland and Romania, which are interested in obtaining Western combat aircraft – the Bulgarian air force (BVVS) was finalising in late 1996 long-term plans for the acquisition of 12 more MiG-29s from Russia. They would supplement 18 MiG-29s and four two-seat MiG-29UB combat trainers delivered to Bulgaria in 1990, subject to satisfactory negotiations for a barter deal, which would also include 100 surplus Russian T-72 main battle tanks.

The second batch of 'Fulcrums' would be new and upgraded multi-role MiG-29SMs, supplied and equipped to operate with air-to-surface missiles including Vympel/Molniya Kh-29TEs (AS-14 'Kedge') and free-falling KAB-500KR bombs, both employing TV-guidance.

CROATIA:

New equipment moves

The expanding Croatian air force (HRZ), which has its HQ in Zagreb in the former Yugoslavia, operates mostly ex-Soviet types such as the MiG-21bis, An-32, Mi-24, Mi-8/17 and An-2. Recent aircraft deliveries have included the first three of possibly up to 10 Pilatus PC-9 turboprop tandem trainers. They are equipping a new flying training school at Zemunik, and are expected to be followed by more Western equipment. This includes 10 Bell Textron 206B-3 JetRanger light helicopters ordered in late 1996 for Croatian military use, from a $15 million contract, including training and technical support. Delivery was due between January and March 1997, with the aircraft slated for training and liaison roles. Croatia is also interested in acquiring Western infantry SAMs to supplement its ex-Soviet SA-7s, SA-2s, SA-9s, SA-13s and S-300s, and has been evaluating such missiles as Mistral and Stinger. Truck-mounted Swedish Saab RBS 15

SAMs are already operated by the Croatian navy.

The first of 11 PZL Swidnik W-3As arrived in the Czech Republic in September 1996. The fleet will be based at Prague-Kbely, Plzeň and Přerov. One is assigned to the VZLU (research and testing institute) at Prague-Letňany.

FRANCE:

Defence economies affect equipment deliveries

Now that the dust has settled from arguments over the recent defence budget cuts, and the scaled-down five-year defence plan for 1997-2002, the main changes affecting French military aviation concern further delays in Dassault's Rafale combat aircraft programme. Despite the limited remaining airframe lives of Aéron-avale's dozen or so F-8E(FN) Crusaders, the first 12 Rafale Ms will not enter service until 2002, three years after the new carrier *Charles de Gaulle* is commissioned in July 1999. The ship therefore will begin operations with only upgraded Super Etendards (undertaking additional interception roles) and two Northrop Grumman E-2Cs instead of the planned four. The French navy is also due to lose one of its two current carriers in September, when *Clemenceau* will be retired following completion of *Foch*'s refit.

Rafale C service entry has now been delayed until 2005, although efforts are being made to operate an initial batch of 10 at an earlier date to clear the way for export sales. According to the French Parliamentary defence committee, the Armée de l'Air will be operating 140 Rafale Cs by 2015, supplementing remaining deliveries from earlier Mirage 2000 orders. These include 30 2000B two-seat combat trainers; 124 Mirage 2000C interceptors, of which 37 are being upgraded to 2000-5 standards

A special scheme was applied in mid-1996 to this Transall C.160D to commemorate the 35th anniversary of LTG 63. The unit also painted up one of its UH-1Ds.

A new Tornado unit came into being with the establishment of a German training unit at Holloman AFB. The badge worn by the Tornados is based on that of the state of New Mexico.

Two KLu F-16 units which celebrated their 45th anniversaries in 1996 were 311 and 312 Squadrons, which both fly from Volkel. The 312 Sqn aircraft (left) is seen on the flight line of the KLu's training detachment at Goose Bay.

between 1997 and 2000, the first being delivered in 1997 for service trials with the CEAM at Mont-de-Marsan; 86 (formerly 90) two-seat 2000D conventional ground-attack versions; and 60 tactical nuclear-strike Mirage 2000Ns armed with ASMP stand-off missiles.

Funding has been included in the 1997 defence budget for an upgraded and more stealthy ASMP Plus, with about twice the 350-km (189-nm) range of the existing version, to arm Rafale Cs in the nuclear roles from about 2008. The tanker support force of 11 Boeing C-135FRs will now be supplemented by only two ex-USAF KC-135CRs, similarly upgraded with CFM56 turbofans, in 1997. Although no funding has been allocated for the Future Large Aircraft, the French requirement for 52 remains unchanged, and the government has promised down-payments to cover most R&D costs when programme totals and national participation have been finalised.

Following earlier disbandment of the Mirage IVP nuclear strike squadron, the French strategic deterrent force will comprise only four nuclear submarines each carrying 16 new Aérospatiale M-51 SLBMs with six independent warheads by 2010. The 18 3500-km (1,889-nm) S-3D ICBMs of the AA's strategic missile wing were formally deactivated at their Plateau d'Albion site on 15 September 1996.

GERMANY:

More Lynx orders

GKN Westland was awarded contracts worth DM312.5 million ($204 million) in October 1996 for the acquisition by German naval aviation (Marineflieger) of seven Super Lynx Mk 88A ASW/ASV helicopters. From 1999,

they will supplement 16 ASW-only Sea Lynx Mk 88s remaining in German naval service from earlier deliveries. They are planned to be upgraded to Super Lynx standards, similar to those of the Royal Navy's HMA.Mk 8s, when defence budget funding becomes available.

Upgrades include Gem 42 turboshafts, composite main rotor blades, GMAv Sea Owl FLIR and a 360° Seaspray Mk 3 search radar, conferring additional anti-surface vessel capabilities with BAeD Sea Skua AShMs. Overall Lynx orders now total 370 from a dozen customers.

Military aircraft cuts

Defence economies and spares problems are forcing the Heeresflieger to withdraw over 50 of its 176 Bell UH-1D utility helicopters in 1997. They will be cannibalised to extend the operating lives of the remaining 124 until their scheduled replacement by TTH-90 helicopters from about 2003. Other casualties of German budget cuts are two of the four ex-Interflug Airbus A310-304 twin-turbofan transports which the Luftwaffe was to have taken over in the past few months, although the first two were delivered in summer 1996.

GREECE:

Aircraft procurement plans

Funding for 60 combat aircraft – presumably refurbished ex-USAF GD F-16A/Bs – and four Boeing E-3 AWACS aircraft, among other Hellenic air force re-equipment, plus seven Boeing CH-47 Chinooks, 10 more MDH AH-64 Apaches, and eight observation helicopters for the army, is

included in a Dr3,800 billion ($16 billion) long-term defence modernisation programme announced by the Greek government in November 1996. Allocations are also included for major avionics upgrades of the air force's 76 MDC F-4E and 25 RF-4E Phantoms, for which competing tenders from DASA in Germany and Rockwell are now being evaluated.

Both F-4E proposals centre on replacement of the original Westinghouse APQ-120 fire-control radar with a new digital multi-mode unit to operate AIM-120 AMRAAM active-radar homing medium-range AAMs. DASA's submission is based on its now-completed improved combat effectiveness (ICE) programme for the licence-built Hughes APG-65 radar with a Litef digital fire-control computer, Honeywell H-423 laser inertial platform, GEC-Marconi Avionics air data computer and other new 1553B databus-linked systems. Rockwell is offering a similar avionics package based on an F-16-type Westinghouse APG-68(V) radar.

The Greek air force has an associated F-4 requirement for up to 25 laser-designator pods, for which GMAv's TIALD, Lockheed Martin's LANTIRN and Rafael's LITENING systems are competing, with compatibility also required for Greek F-16s and A-7 Corsairs. McDonnell Douglas has recently estimated that about 950 of its F-4 Phantoms are still in service with nine countries, together with 260 or so active A-4 Skyhawks. The F-4s are forecast to remain operationally effective until at least 2015, and MDC has recently reached agreement with US Derco Aerospace Inc. and Kitco Inc. to supply spare parts and components to keep both types flying into the next century.

ITALY:

C-130J negotiations progress

AMI plans for acquiring 16 to 18 C-130J Hercules 2 tactical transports

were nearing finalisation late in 1996 following the visit of an Italian delegation, led by Defence Minister Beniamino Andreatta, to Lockheed Martin's Marietta production plant. Delivery of the first AMI C-130Js are planned for 1998, to start replacing the 14 C-130Hs delivered from 1972, which are operated by 50° Gruppo of 46° Brigata Aerea from Pisa.

MALTA:

More Alouettes acquired

Two Aérospatiale SA 316B Alouette III light helicopters formerly operated by the Royal Netherlands air force (Klu) have recently been bought for $295,000 for the Air Squadron's 2nd Regiment of the Armed Forces of Malta. They will supplement three similar helicopters transferred from Libya in the 1980s, which entered Maltese service after long-term storage from December 1992, following refurbishment in France.

NETHERLANDS:

First attack helicopters for air force

In the afternoon of 13 November 1996 the first Dutch AH-64 Apaches arrived at Gilze-Rijen air base. Twelve AH-64As have been leased from the US Army, serving as an interim solution until the 30 AH-64Ds will be delivered in 1998. The dozen AH-64As will equip 301 Squadron of the Taktische Helikopter Groep (THG, Tactical Helicopter Group) based at Gilze-Rijen. The Apaches were flown by US Army pilots from the US Army base at Illesheim, Germany, since the Dutch Apache pilots are all in the USA. One US Army CH-47D came along to ferry the pilots back to Germany.

Fokker 50s delivered

Formal acceptance took place at Eindhoven on 22 November 1996 of the first of two twin-turboprop Fokker 50 transports to replace a pair of Fokker F27s operated by No. 334 Sqn for VIP and government use. The second F50 was delivered in December, to supplement a twin-turbofan Gulfstream G.IV and a Fokker 70 in the KLu's VIP

Rarely seen in Europe are the Fokker F27MPAs of the KLu's 336 Squadron. They are based at Hato in the Netherlands Antilles for patrol missions in the Caribbean.

flight, plus four twin-turboprop Fokker 60U utility transports.

PORTUGAL:

More F-16s purchased

The Portuguese air force has negotiated the FMS purchase in Washington of 25 ex-USAF GD F-16s, costing $258 million, as a follow-on to 1995 deliveries of 17 Block 15 F-16As and three two-seat F-16Bs. The new contract also includes five spare F100-PW-220E engines, engine upgrades, and other spare parts, and represents a programme unit cost of $10.32 million. Some $30-40 million may be spent on modernising the FAP F-16s prior to delivery, expected to start in 1997.

ROMANIA:

F-16 procurement planned

Although no orders had been placed by late 1996, a decision in principle to buy 'a small number' of F-16 Fighting Falcons as MiG-21 replacements was announced during an October 1996 visit to Washington by Romanian Foreign Minister Teodor Melescanu. Preliminary discussions on Romanian F-16 plans have already been reported with Lockheed Martin, and form part of Bucharest plans to join NATO.

Romanian F-16 interest appears to be in new, rather than surplus ex-USAF aircraft now being offered in refurbished form for about $7 million each. FY97 costs of six new Block 50/52 F-16s for the USAF equate to $25.8 million each.

Israeli contracts extended

Elbit Defence Systems in Israel has received a $35 million extension of the $300 million contract to upgrade 110 Romanian air force MiG-21M/MF fighters by 2001. Elbit has also received another contract, worth about $100 million, for the installation of armament and associated systems in Romanian IAR-330 Puma helicopters by 2001, in conjunction with IAR, for attack roles.

SLOVAKIA:

Ka-50 export customer?

Russia is using arms transfers to help pay off its original $1.2 billion trade deficit with Slovakia, which since 1994 has received 14 MiG-29s, including a two-seat combat trainer version, to supplement its original 10 transferred from the Czech Republic. CFE agreements currently limit Slovakia to 115

In October 1996 the first Swiss air force F/A-18C completed its first phase of weapon tests. They were undertaken at NAWC Patuxent River, and included the launch of AIM-9 Sidewinders (illustrated). On 3 October, the first Swiss-assembled F/A-18D made its first flight, piloted by Res Schmid and Bernhard Berset.

The Kamov Ka-52 made its show debut at Aero India '96 after its rapid completion. The two-seater is being offered to the Indians, and was displayed carrying Vympel R-73 air-to-air missiles. The comprehensive sensor fit includes chin, underfuselage, roof- and mast-mounted antennas/sights.

combat aircraft, plus 25 attack helicopters, but increases in the latter totals are now being sought by the government in Bratislava, to supplement its Mil Mi-24s by the possible acquisition of co-axial single-seat Kamov Ka-50s.

Having built 12 pre-production Ka-50s and the prototype Ka-52, the Progress factory at Arsenyev, in the Primorki region, is about to fly its first production Ka-50. This is planned to have uprated TV3-117VMA-SB3 turboshaft engines, each developing 2,500 shp (1865 kW). Target sales price is $15 million, fly-away. Maximum take-off weight of the Ka-52, also claimed to be in production, is now quoted by Kamov as 10400 kg (22,930 lb), compared with 9800 kg (21,600 lb) for the Ka-50. Performance is claimed to be virtually unchanged from the Ka-50, apart from a small decrease in hover ceiling to 3600 m (11,811 ft).

SWEDEN:

New support aircraft

Recent equipment deliveries have included the first of six production Saab 340B (S 100B) Erieye twin-turboprop AEW aircraft (c/n 342, 10002), followed by a second example in November 1996, for initial service trials from Malmen air base. Deliveries will be completed in 1999. Two Gulfstream G.IVs delivered in August 1995 are being equipped in Sweden as S 102Bs with Elint and other specialised avionics, to replace the Tp 85 Caravelles of F16M.

SWITZERLAND:

First Swiss-assembled Hornet flies

The first of 32 MDC F/A-18C/D Hornet multi-role fighters (F/A-18C J-5002) being assembled by the Swiss Aircraft and Systems Company for the Swiss air force made its initial flight at Emmen on 3 October. All but the first

two of Swiss orders costing $2.6 billion for 26 F/A-18Cs and eight two-seat F/A-18D combat trainers are being completed by SASC by 1999, following initial examples of each variant from McDonnell Douglas in St Louis.

TURKEY:

F-5 upgrade plans

Submissions were invited late in 1996 for a two-phase upgrade of 48 Turkish air force (THK) Northrop F-5A/B fighter-bombers and combat trainers, involving both structural and avionics refits. They are required for extended service as lead-in trainers for the F-16C/D and other combat aircraft, following contractor selection from competitive evaluation, in mid-1997.

After prototype testing, F-16-type digital avionics, including head-up and multi-function cockpit displays, INS/GPS, mission and air data computers, HOTAS, and data transfer and video recorder systems, are planned for installation in 20 Northrop F-5As and eight two-seat F-5Bs, plus 14 Dutch licence-built NF-5As and six NF-5Bs, from contractor kits at the THK's Eskisehir maintenance base. Structural upgrades to replace fatigue-lifed components would be undertaken by Turkish Aerospace Industries (TAI) near Ankara.

Turkish helicopters

Orders worth $150 million for a second batch of 10 Bell AH-1W Super Cobra attack helicopters, which would have doubled the Turkish army aviation inventory of this type, have now been cancelled following US disapproval of Turkey's Kurdish policies. Discussions have been continuing,

however, for the possible purchase of four to six Boeing CH-47D heavy-lift helicopters costing up to $100 million. They would represent an initial batch towards total Turkish requirements for up to 16. Turkey was also expected to sign a February 1997 agreement to purchase four SH-60 Seahawks.

UNITED KINGDOM:

RN AEW Sea King upgrade contracts

Initial MoD contracts were awarded in October 1996 for the planned radar and mission systems avionics upgrade of the Royal Navy's 10 Westland Sea King AEW.Mk 2A shipborne airborne early-warning helicopters. Racal Radar Defence Systems was selected as prime contractor for the £90 million Staff Requirement (C) 6131 programme, which mainly concerns replacement of the AEW Sea Kings' original Thorn Searchwater surveillance radar, mounted in a swing-down pod on the right rear fuselage, with a similar upgraded pulse-Doppler system. A new Racal Avionics central tactical system with twin colour displays and an RLG INS/GPS is also included, together with a JTIDS (Link 16) datalink.

Having taken over Thorn's radar interests, Racal Radar Defence Systems will supply the new and lighter-weight Searchwater 2000 for the RN's proposed Sea King AEW.Mk 7. This radar is an AEW version of the Searchwater 2000 maritime patrol surveillance system selected for the RAF's Nimrod 2000 programme, using a new high-power transmitter and advanced pulse-Doppler signal processing, and will increase Racal's total contract for these two radars to over £150 million.

Racal will be responsible for all aspects of the Sea King AEW.Mk 7

upgrade, including equipment supply, installation, aircraft modification and certification, and provision of an extensive logistic support package. Logica will develop the JTIDS Link 16 processing, with GKN Westland Helicopters undertaking required airframe modifications and acting as aircraft design authority.

This represents a second stage upgrade for the RN AEW Sea Kings, which began receiving Have Quick II secure speech communication radios and a new IFF system in 1995. Three Sea King HAS.Mk 5s will be converted with the AEW.Mk 7 upgrades as development aircraft, followed by seven of the current AEW.Mk 2As. The Spanish navy, with three Search-water-equipped AEW SH-3 Sea Kings, is also interested in the RN's upgrade programme.

Privatised military helicopter training contracts

Britain's FBS consortium was selected by the MoD in October 1996 to operate a new combined services helicopter basic training school at RAF Shawbury, through contracts worth £400 million over a 10-year period from April 1997. FBS is a joint-venture partnership between Cobham's Flight Refuelling Ltd, Bristow Helicopters and SERCo Defence Ltd, all with extensive experience of working with the UK defence forces.

The Defence Helicopter Flying School (DHFS) is being established as part of the MoD's Private Finance Initiative for cost-savings in UK military operations through commercialisation of support services. Combined service helicopter pilot and navigator training at the DHFS will take over existing basic RAF/RN rotary-wing instruction at Shawbury, and similar courses which will continue at the Army Air Corps (AAC) centre at Middle Wallop. It will train 230

aircrew students per year, including about 180 pilots, with savings of more than £77 million anticipated over the next 15 years.

FBS proposes to operate 38 MoD-owned Eurocopter AS 350BA Squirrel single-turboshaft and nine Bell Textron 412 twin-turbine helicopters at the DHFS, which would be staffed by 76 military and 45 civilian flying instructors. After modification to MoD specifications by Bristow at Redhill and FRA at Hurn, the AS 350s and Bell 412s will replace 79 veteran Westland Gazelle and Wessex AAC and RAF helicopters currently used for service training.

They will be maintained by the consortium to civil airworthiness standards, while FBS will also provide most of the ground school and support facilities. Flight simulators and training ground aids will be the responsibility of SERCo. The DHFS will allow service helicopter pilots, mostly from the AAC, to train on more modern equipment as a prelude to continued conversion to the Lynx, Puma, Chinook and Sea King, to be followed by such new operational types as the Apache and Merlin at service units.

YUGOSLAVIA:

More MiG-29s?

Discussions have been reported with Russia by the Air and Air Defence Forces of the Yugoslav Federal Republic, which includes Serbia and Montenegro, concerning the possible acquisition of up to 20 more VPK-MiG MiG-29s, plus associated weapons and equipment. As new aircraft from undelivered ex-Soviet orders, they would augment much earlier deliveries of 14 MiG-29s and two two-seat MiG-29UB combat trainers. Their quoted cost of $400 million would be offset against Russian trade debts to the former Yugoslavia of around $1.2 billion.

Slovenia's Pilatus PC-9s have recently been upgraded with wiring/plumbing for underwing hardpoints to allow the carriage of fuel tanks or armament. The aircraft now wear three-tone tactical camouflage, new two-digit codes and revised national insignia.

having difficulty working out the deal to acquire the Black Hawks to replace Bell 212s that are deemed too expensive to operate and maintain. Israel previously received 10 used Black Hawks from the US government free of charge.

JORDAN:

F-16 training

Defence co-operation agreements recently concluded with the Turkish government will result in some RJAF pilot training on Jordan's 16 leased F-16A/Bs being undertaken in Turkey. In return, Jordanian bases will be made available for Turkish air force training exercises, in which RJAF units will also take part. Other joint training will be undertaken by the RJAF with units from the Gulf States, as well as from the UK, France and the US.

When delivered to the RJAF from 1997, the F-16s will be based at Azraq, 120 km (75 miles) east of Amman. The base's infrastructure is being expanded, again with FMS funding, at a cost of $80 million. The 12 F-16As and four F-16Bs, refurbished and upgraded at an FMS cost of $140 million, have been leased for five years for $5 million.

QATAR:

Qatari arms package

British Aerospace was nominated prime contractor to the UK government on 17 November for the management and long-term technical support of a new UK arms package agreement worth £500 million ($835 million) with the Gulf state of Qatar. In addition to a dozen or more BAe Hawk trainers, a memorandum of understanding between the two

governments, signed in Doha by UK Defence Secretary Michael Portillo, covered the provision of GKN Piranha armoured personnel carriers, Shorts Starburst close-range air defence missiles, and Vosper Thorneycroft 46-m (150-ft) patrol vessels.

The planned UK arms orders represent the second stage of a defence agreement involving technical and military assistance signed in London in April 1996 by Portillo and his Qatari opposite number, Sheikh Hamed bin Jassem al-Thani. Precise details of the British equipment to be ordered have not yet been specified, but Qatar is known to have been interested in a small number of BAe Hawk 100 lead-in fighter trainers to supplement or replace the six Dassault/Dornier Alpha Jets currently employed in similar roles.

SAUDI ARABIA:

Second-batch Tornado deliveries

Delivery of the second batch of 48 Tornado interdictor-strike fighters (s/n 7201 onwards) started on 3 October 1996 with formal acceptance at Warton. They were ordered in January 1993 through the Al Yamamah II arms programme for a reported cost of $6 billion. The new Tornados double Saudi procurement of the IDS version, some of which appear to be equipped for tactical reconnaissance to RAF GR.Mk 1A standards.

Middle East

EGYPT:

Equipment orders and deliveries

New EAF equipment orders reportedly include two twin-turbofan Gulfstream IV-SP transports from Gulfstream Aerospace for VIP and government use. Deliveries were expected to start late in 1996 of a second batch of 12 MDH AH-64A Apache attack helicopters to the EAF, increasing its overall total to 36.

ISRAEL:

More fighters sought

Although delivery to Israel is due to start in 1997 of the 25 MDC F-15I strike-fighters ordered in 1994-95, a similar $2 billion or so has been ear-

marked from 1998 for the acquisition of new combat aircraft to replace 50 upgraded F-4E Phantom 2000s and some older F-16A/Bs early in the next century. Procurement will continue to be via the annual $1.8 billion US military aid allocations, which will effectively limit selection to the latest production versions of the F-15, F-16 and F/A-18.

More Israeli Black Hawks?

Israel is quietly seeking a short-term US government-backed loan to pay for up to 14 Sikorsky UH-60 Black Hawk utility helicopters required by the Israeli air force for missions in Israel and southern Lebanon. Because Israel has overspent Foreign Military Sales (FMS) money on F-15I Eagle fighters and other items, Jerusalem is

Far East

CAMBODIA:

Upgraded MiG-21s arrive

Delivery was scheduled late in 1996 to the Royal Cambodian air force of its first four MiG-21bis 'Fishbed' fighters after upgrading by Israel Aircraft Industries Lahav division to MiG-21 2000 standards. Four more are expected in 1997, and funding is being sought to modify the remaining 11 to

IAI's similar standards. Upgrades include new digital 1553B avionics featuring a head-up and a multi-function cockpit displays, an INS/GPS, air data computer, IAI tactical datalink, Western UHF/IFF systems, a new control column with HOTAS functions, interfaces for Western armament, and a new one-piece windscreen. Also included in the $80 million upgrade contract are weapons such as the Python 3 air-to-air missile, and the MBT Griffin laser-guided bomb. Further upgrades are being made by IAI of eight Aero L-39ZA trainers for Cambodia.

This BAC One-Eleven 500 has been fitted out as a radar testbed by GEC for the Defence Research Agency. It made its first flight in its new guise in November 1996.

Right: RAF trainers are receiving white wingroots and wingtips as a refinement to the gloss-black trainer scheme adopted recently. Shown here is a Hawk from Valley.

CHINA:

AWACS sought for new fighter forces

AF/PLA acquisition of 50 Sukhoi Su-27 advanced multi-role fighters, plus a \$1.2 billion licensed production agreement for Shenyang to produce 120 from Russian components over a three-year period, followed by 80 more from indigenous parts at up to 20 per year, has been accompanied by an associated AWACS requirement. This is for at least four, and possibly up to 20, airborne early-warning and control systems aircraft for integration with a new air defence ground environment system.

China has reportedly been evaluating proposals for the Russian Vega-equipped Beriev A-50U 'Mainstay', Britain's GEC-Marconi Avionics Argus 2000 mission systems equipment from the cancelled AEW Nimrod programme, and Israel's similar IAI/Elta Phalcon phased-array radar. A decision in principle now appears to have been taken in favour of the Israeli radar, ESM and associated equipment, for installation in an Ilyushin Il-76 'Candid' four-turbofan transport.

Up to 10 Il-76s are believed to be already operating with the AF/PLA, and IAI has been negotiating with Russia for the purchase of an additional example for its proposed \$250 million Phalcon prototype conversion. Details of this do not yet appear to have been finalised, but initial indications are that up to three Elta EL2075 radar antenna arrays will be dome-installed rather than conformal, as in the original Boeing 707 Phalcon. These three arrays would allow 360° coverage from triangular deployment in a fixed rather than rotating dome, as used in the A-50, thereby minimising aerodynamic complications.

Surveillance radar for Y-8?

In a \$50 million Chinese navy maritime patrol aircraft programme, the possible installation of Racal's Searchwater surveillance radar and associated systems is being considered in up to half a dozen An-12-derived Shaanxi Y-8 four-turboprop transports. The original maritime patrol Y-8X (previously Y-8MPA) featured a Litton APS-504 radar.

Su-27 delivery details

Following earlier deliveries from 27 June 1992 of 22 Komsomolsk-built single- and four two-seat Su-27SK/UBs, believed to be known locally as J-11/JJ-11s, the AF/PLA was reported to have received 11 of a second batch of 24, including three of six two-seat Su-27UBs, at Suixiu air base on 25 July 1996. Like Wuhu, in Anhui Province, where the first batch of the AF/PLA Su-27s are reportedly based with the 3rd Air Division, Suixiu is believed to be protected by some of China's three batteries of Fakel S-300PMU (HQ-10) Patriot-type air defence missiles purchased from Russia.

Licence-built Chinese Su-27s are expected to be equipped with retractable air-refuelling probes, which require an associated aerial tanker fleet. This will probably be based on the Russian Il-78 'Midas', or similar Il-76 conversions, although a few AF/PLA Xian H-6 (Tu-16) twin-jet strategic bombers have previously been modified for tanker roles.

Rosvoorouzhenye officials claim that China is interested in a third batch of 55 Su-27s, apparently in addition to its licensed production agreement for this type. Chinese interest has also been reported in the carrier-based Su-27K (Su-33) version, although Beijing defence officials maintain that no finance has been allocated for an aircraft-carrier in the current five-year military budget plans.

INDONESIA:

New equipment receipts

Recent equipment deliveries to the Indonesian air force (TNI/AU) have reportedly included two ex-USN MDC A-4T Skyhawk two-seat combat trainers from former AMARC storage in the US, and six Transall

Another RAF squadron number was revived on 1 November 1996 when the Sea King HAR.Mk 3 type conversion unit (SKOCU) at St Mawgan was redesignated as No. 203 (Reserve) Squadron. The squadron badge consists of a winged seahorse, from its days stationed in the Arabian Gulf. The unit's previous incarnation was as a Luqa (Malta)-based Nimrod squadron, disbanded in 1977.

C.160NG twin-turboprop tactical transports, the latter previously operated locally by Pelita Air Services in civil roles. In the same category are five ex-UAE DHC-5D Buffalos acquired in part-exchange for IPTN CN.235Ms, of which three are for Indonesian army aviation (TNI-AD) and two for the navy (TNI-AL).

More twin-turboprop transports, although in a lighter category, are being sought by the TNI-AL in the form of 20 AsTA/GAF N22/24 Nomads retired by the Australian Army Aviation Corps in 1995. These would supplement the 18 N22SB/SL Searchmaster versions acquired by the TNI-AL from late 1975 for coastal patrol and general transport.

TNI/AU Chief of Staff Air Vice Marshal Sutria Tubagus has confirmed a forward-planning Indonesian requirement for AWACS aircraft, to supplement the three Boeing 737-2X9 Surveillers currently used for maritime patrols of the South China Sea. AVM Tubagus said that Riau, near Singapore, and Pontianak, on Borneo, will be developed as main bases for the TNI/AU BAe Hawk 100s and 200s to defend the natural gas resources of the Natuna Islands in the South China Sea.

JAPAN:

Procurement plans

Procurement of the Mitsubishi-built MFC F-15J Eagle by the Japanese Air Self-Defence Force recently ended with completion of the last of 169 single-seat versions and 44 F-15DJ two-seat combat trainers ordered since 1978. Funding has also finished for the JASDF's Fuji T-5 turboprop trainer, after the 35th example, and the

JMSDF's Kawasaki/Lockheed P-3 Orion programme, with 110 ordered.

FY1997 Japanese Defence Agency requests comprise 65 new aircraft costing \$2.9 billion, although further defence economies are likely to cut these numbers. JASDF proposals, with final FY1996 totals in parentheses, comprise nine (11) Mitsubishi F-2 strike-fighters; 13 (nine) Kawasaki T-4 advanced trainers; four (three) Raytheon/Hawker U-125A SAR aircraft; three (one) Mitsubishi/Sikorsky UH-60J transport helicopters; and one (three) Gulfstream U-4 VIP transports.

JGSDF helicopter purchase proposals comprise one (one) Fuji/Bell AH-1S HueyCobra; five (nil) new Kawasaki OH-X scouts; six (four) Mitsubishi/Sikorsky UH-60JAs; three (seven) Fuji/Bell UH-1Js; and two (two) Kawasaki/Boeing CH-47JAs; plus three Beech King Air 350 light fixed-wing twins. FY1997 JMSDF aircraft funding is for two (one) Shin-Maywa US-1A SAR amphibians; seven (eight) Mitsubishi/Sikorsky SH-60J ASW Seahawks; two (three) UH-60J Black Hawks; and two (nil) Kawasaki/MDH OH-6DA helicopters.

KAZAKHSTAN:

More MiG-29s?

According to the UN Arms Register, 12 combat aircraft, presumably MiG-29s, were exported by Russia to the air force of Kazakhstan in 1995. Four older fighters of unspecified type were accepted by the Russian government in part exchange. Russian arms sales in 1995 totalled \$2.7 billion, and were estimated to increase to at least \$3.6 billion in 1996.

REPUBLIC OF KOREA:

New aircraft requirements

While still taking delivery of a second batch of 120 licence-built Block 52 F-16s, following earlier procurement of 40 Block 32 versions, the Republic of Korea air force is stepping up evaluations of possible replacements through its $10 billion F-X combat aircraft programme. This will involve procurement of 120 or so new fighters for delivery from 2002, for which such aircraft as the Dassault Rafale, Eurofighter and JAS 39 Gripen are being evaluated, although the MDC F-15E, in either single- or two-seat configuration, is apparently the current RoKAF preference.

Sukhoi is also heavily promoting the thrust-vectored Su-37, which despite its early stage of development was flown to and at the recent Korean air show, and/or earlier Su-35 variants. The RoK's defence, logistic and technical support ties with the US, however, strongly favour either an F-15E 'Strike Eagle' variant, or possibly even the $70 million Lockheed Martin F-22. Russian promotion in Korea includes the Patriot-class Antey S-300 (SA-10 'Grumble) SAM/ABM system.

Other RoKAF requirements include four AWACS aircraft, for which considerations had narrowed late in 1996 to two Boeing 767-based proposals from Boeing, using a Westinghouse AN/APY-2 radar in a ventral dome, and from IAI, featuring a 360° version of its Phalcon conformal phased-array system, with an additional tailcone installation. A third submission has been made to the RoKAF by Saab and Ericsson of their Erieye phased-array AEW system mounted on a Saab 2000, adding five onboard radar operators, for which selection is expected in 1998.

That year is now forecast as the likely date for a launch decision on the proposed $1.6 billion Samsung/Lockheed Martin KTX-2 transonic trainer/light fighter programme, which has been delayed from its planned July 1997 go-ahead. This is attributed to disagreements between the industrial partners on cost and work shares, which threaten government financial support for the programme in Seoul, and may extend the planned prototype first flight date to 2001. Initial service of the 100 aircraft required was planned for 2005. Delays were also reported in late 1996 in the RoKAF's planned five-year lease of 30 USAF Northrop T-38As as interim trainers, because of their refurbishing costs.

RoK Army Aviation is considering replacements for its 70 or so Bell AH-1S attack helicopters, with initial requirements for 18 gunships in the Apache class by the turn of the century. Evaluations are being made of other types, including the Eurocopter Tiger, but MDH's AH-64 remains RoKAA's attack helicopter datum.

MALAYSIA:

Helicopter evaluations narrowing

Large-scale helicopter procurement plans for the Malaysian armed forces are currently concentrated mainly on a new gunship for the recently-formed army aviation wing, and an ASW/ASV helicopter to replace the navy's dozen or so Westland Wasps. For the army requirement, evaluations are being made of all the main international attack helicopters, including the Bell AH-1W, MDH Apache, Eurocopter Tiger, Kamov Ka-50, and Denel Rooivalk. Selection is expected to narrow following a recent memorandum of understanding for defence co-operation signed by Malaysia and South Africa.

This follows earlier military co-operation agreements between South Africa's Denel arms group and Malaysian companies, including one with Airod for possible co-production and technical support of Rooivalk and Puma-derived Oryx helicopters to fulfil gunship roles. A pre-production Rooivalk has already been demonstrated in Malaysia, and the new MoU is expected to follow earlier negotiations with quotations to supply both types to its armed forces. The SAAF order for 12 Rooivalks was an essential preliminary to export sales, although it is currently threatened by recent severe cuts in South African defence spending to less than R10 billion ($3.96 billion), plus devaluation of the rand.

The Malaysian navy's final choice between its short-listed Kaman SH-2G Super SeaSprite and the Westland Super Lynx is expected in mid-1997, and the latter is reportedly favoured on technical grounds. Although initial orders may be restricted to only about six helicopters, the RMN has a longer-term requirement to equip its 27 planned new patrol vessels with similar types.

Having lost another of its 30 or so Sikorsky S-61A Nuri SAR and transport helicopters at sea last October, the RMAF is intensifying its evaluations of possible successors. RMAF plans were confirmed in November for the purchase of two Sikorsky S-70A Black Hawk helicopters for VIP use, and there has been speculation that up to 40 could follow to fulfil the S-61 replacement requirement. Evaluations are also being made of the Bell 412, Eurocopter Cougar, and EH101.

PHILIPPINES:

Fighter acquisition plans

Sixty-five billion pesos ($2.48 billion) has now been allocated to the Philippine air force (PhilAF) in the 15-year armed forces modernisation programme, from which about $240 million is earmarked for 18 zero-time Block 15 ex-Pakistani F-16A/Bs or similar surplus USAF aircraft offered by Washington. All would require mid-life upgrades, but would still be cheaper than new F-16s and F/A-18s also offered by the US, or other new fighters.

The PhilAF has also been negotiating a barter deal with Canada, however, to acquire up to 18 Canadair/Northrop CF-5 fighter-bombers. They are priced at about $75 million, but the Philippine government has been discussing (with the US Triton Systems Corporation, as agents) the possibility of granting long-term gold and copper mining rights in its Batong Buhay region rather than paying cash.

The CF-5A/Ds are being handled by Bristol Aerospace, which was nominated by the Canadian government in March 1995 to dispose of 60 airframes rendered surplus by defence economies. Thirty-six of them had been upgraded but undelivered by Bristol with new MDC CF-18 Hornet avionics, apart from radar, for lead-in fighter training. If agreement on the proposed deal is reached, the Philippine government may opt for its own upgrade, through Bristol, of some of the remaining CF-5s.

SINGAPORE:

New F-16 procurement

Twelve new-build Lockheed Martin Block 52D F-16C/Ds are to replace from 1999 the nine F-16A/B Fighting Falcons on long-term lease from the USAF by the Republic of Singapore air force (RepSAF) for operational training at Luke AFB, Arizona. Through an unpublicised lease-purchase deal with Lockheed Martin, these aircraft will also supplement other RepSAF F-16s. They comprise eight similar F100-PW-229-powered F-16Cs and 10 F-16D combat trainers ordered in July 1994 but not yet delivered, plus the surviving three F-16As and four two-seat F-16Bs from four each originally received by Singapore in 1988.

Overseas deployment plans

Continuing RepSAF training arrangements with Australia because of Singapore's airspace limitations, a squadron of 12 AS 532UL Super Puma (Cougar) helicopters is to be based until at least December 2012 at Oakey, near Brisbane, HQ of the Australian Army Aviation Centre. Up to $A35 million ($27.5 million) has been allocated by Singapore for the necessary support infrastructure to be installed by late 1998 at Oakey, to be manned by 250 RepSAF personnel. Apart from advanced training, the Super Pumas are expected to provide airlift support for Singapore army exercises held in eastern Australia.

This latest training agreement with Australia, which also includes reciprocal air-refuelling exercises, follows Singapore's transfer of jet pilot training on 27 RepSAF SIAI-Marchetti S.211s to RAAF Pearce, Western Australia. Singapore also plans to base two of its four Boeing KC-135A air refuelling tankers, now being upgraded to KC-135R standard with CFM56 turbofans, at March AFB, CA, for crew training when completed.

TAIWAN:

New equipment orders

After prolonged negotiations, a letter of offer and acceptance was signed by the Taiwanese government late in 1996 for four Lockheed Martin C-130H-30 stretched Hercules. With a single Hercules ordered by the Japanese Air Self-Defence Force, these are

The Aero India '96 show at Yelahanka provided views of the ALH (advanced light helicopter) seen above, with the fifth prototype on display. This is the first of the naval variants. Also on show was the first HS748 AEW conversion (below), which is known as the ASP (aerial surveillance platform).

the last C-130Hs off the Marietta production line, where output changed solely to the C-130J in October 1996. RoCAF C-130H orders now total 21, including another four delivered in 1993-94.

The Republic of China became the 19th customer for the Hughes Stinger RMP man-portable surface-to-air missile, with a recent $420 million FMS order for 1,299 missiles and 74 truck-mounted Avenger multiple launch systems. Deliveries will be completed in 1997-98. Procurement is also planned by Taiwan of upgraded Raytheon Patriot PAC 2 Plus SAM/ABMs, for deployment of the first three batteries by 1999.

Southern Asia

INDIA:

MiG-21 upgrade delays

Delays of up to two years are reportedly anticipated in implementing the $314.3 million contract signed in March 1996 by the Indian government with the VPK MIG MAPO group, to upgrade 125 MiG-21bis fighters for the IAF, with options for 50 more. Apart from an initial Rs5 billion ($140 million) deposit, shortfalls in previously agreed Indian Defence Ministry payments for the initial stages of the programme are blamed by the Russians for the lack of progress.

Continued Indian indecision concerning the proposed upgrade standard, based on MIG MAPO's updated MiG-21-93 project including installation of the Phazotron Kopyo pulse-Doppler X-band fire-control radar and new cockpit systems from Sextant Avionique, have also contributed to delays of at least nine months in prototype conversion. This involves the modification by late 1996 by the Sokol factory at Nizhni Novgorod, as prime contractor, of two IAF MiG-21bis with the upgrade systems originally planned. A 27-month development programme is then due to follow, after which HAL was scheduled to convert the remaining aircraft in the contract at Nasik from Russian kits by 2001.

German Alpha Jets for AJT requirement?

A long-awaited solution for India's urgent advanced jet trainer (AJT) requirement could be forthcoming, if recent IAF discussions with the German government for the acquisition of 50 surplus Luftwaffe Alpha Jets prove successful. IAF requirements for 80 advanced trainers, first formulated in 1984, have been scaled down to 66 in recent years because of defence economies. Allocations of $88 million to initiate procurement in the 1995-96 military budget had to be transferred to meet maintenance and support commitments.

As a low-cost interim AJT measure, the IAF has been scouring Eastern Europe for 16 surplus two-seat MiG-21UM combat trainers for about $1.8 million each, having insufficient funds to buy its short-listed BAe Hawk, Dassault/Daimler-Benz Alpha Jet or MiG-AT. German inability to sell its long-withdrawn tactically-equipped Alpha Jets elsewhere has now led to them being offered to India for a reported $250 million in a package deal, including some spares and technical support equipment, which could represent a cost-effective solution for IAF AJT requirements. The urgency of these is reflected in the reported loss of 74 IAF aircraft through accidents since early 1994.

PAKISTAN:

More K-8 trainers delivered

As the sole customer nominated to date for the NAMC K-8 basic jet trainer, the PAF is reported to be receiving more than 30 so far produced at the Nanchang factory, following the initial evaluation batch of six delivered in 1994. They are being operated by the PAF Air University at Risalpur, alongside ageing ex-USAF Cessna T-37s, but further procurement is likely to be limited following recent completion by AlliedSignal of its contract with NAMC for the supply of 58 TFE371s for the K-8 programme.

This still awaits orders from China's AF/PLA, expected some time in 1997, almost certainly with an alternative non-Western powerplant such as the Progress/ZVL DV-2 used in the Aero L-59. Exports could then follow to such Chinese military aircraft clients as Bangladesh, Iran, Myanmar, Sri Lanka and Zimbabwe.

Orion delivery

The US government has ended its embargo on the delivery to Pakistan of three Lockheed P-3 Orion Update II.5 patrol aircraft rolled out in September 1990 and paid for by Pakistan long ago. In January 1996, the US Congress passed the Brown amendment which had the effect of cancelling a previous item of legislation, the Pressler law, which had held up the P-3s because of US displeasure with Pakistan's nuclear weapons programme. The trio of Orions had been kept in storage at the US 'boneyard' at Davis-Monthan Air Force Base, AZ. In 1996 they were prepared for shipment and ferried to Pakistan, where they will carry out anti-submarine patrol operations at Karachi, flown by crews trained by US Navy Squadron VP-30 'Pro's Nest' at NAS Jacksonville, FL. The Pakistani Orions differ from standard Update II.5 aircraft in having communications suite, navaids and ALR-66(V)2 ESM system more characteristic of the Update III, and for this reason are sometimes known by the unofficial designation Update II.75. The aircraft are BuNos 164467/164469, Pakistani Navy numbers 26/28.

Seen at Gifu air base is the first two-seat XF-2B. The aircraft carries four dummy ASM-2 anti-ship missiles underwing and two dummy AAM-3 air-to-air missiles on the wingtips. Both missile types and the aircraft are products of Mitsubishi Heavy Industries.

Australasia

AUSTRALIA:

BAe Hawk selected

After a long evaluation, the British Aerospace Hawk 100 was finally selected in November 1996 by the RAAF to replace its Aermacchi MB.326Hs with new lead-in fighter trainers for its $A1 billion ($790 million) Project Air 5367 requirement. The Hawk version chosen, in preference to the Aermacchi MB.339FD, will have upgraded cockpits and equipment, based on the layout of Australia's F/A-18 Hornets. A mock-up incorporating redesigned Hawk 100 cockpits consolidating F-18-type HUDs, head-down displays and HOTAS was completed by BAe some time ago, and has been exhibited at several international air shows.

The RAAF Hawk order will involve 35-40 aircraft, the final number depending on assessment and cost estimates of the training task. BAe will complete the first 12 in the UK from mid-1999, to enter RAAF service by January 2000. The rest will be assembled in Australia from mainly Brough-built components by a local consortium headed by BAe's Australian subsidiary. Hawker de Havilland is building Hawk stabilators, rudders and ailerons, which will be incorporated in the final assembly stage, followed by flight-testing, by Hunter Aerospace at Newcastle, next to the RAAF's Williamtown F/A-18 base. QANTAS will undertake Adour

Another participant in the Yelahanka show was this licence-built MiG-27M. The HAL production line ended in 1996, and VPK-MAPO (Mikoyan) is offering an avionics upgrade to the aircraft now in service. An upgraded Russian aircraft was displayed by VPK-MAPO.

Seen at the Zhuhai air show was this NAMC (Nanchang) A-5C, believed to be part of an order for the Pakistan air force. The A-5C differs from Chinese Q-5s by having some Western equipment, including Sidewinder-capable pylons and Martin-Baker PKD10 ejection seats.

GAIC (Guizhou) is the source of two-seat FT-7s. This FT-7P is a Westernised export version (as sold to Pakistan), incorporating new avionics. FT-7Ps also differ from other FT-7s by having two underwing pylons on each side instead of one.

Left: Seen prior to delivery at Nanchang, this line-up of NAMC K-8s are in air defence fit, with PL-7 missiles underwing and a centreline gun pod. The K-8 was developed with 25 per cent funding from Pakistan, and the first deliveries have been made to the PAF.

assembly and support, while more work will be completed by Air Flite and other Australian companies.

Current Hawk 100s operated by Abu Dhabi, Indonesia, Malaysia and Oman are powered by the 5,845-lb (25.6-kN) Rolls-Royce/Turboméca Adour Mk 871 turbofan, but precise details of the RAAF powerplant version are still being finalised. Alternative installation of the 6,300-lb (28.02-kN) ITEC F124-GA-400 turbofan proposed by McDonnell Douglas and AlliedSignal for their T-45 submission was rejected by the RAAF in 1996, and this project was suspended after a single 90-minute initial test flight to 25,000 ft (7620 m) at St Louis on 7 October 1996.

AWACS tenders invited

Four US companies received requests for tenders late in 1996 from the Australian government for its $A1.2 billion ($944.5 million) Project Air 5077 requirement, also known as Project Wedgetail, for at least four AWACS aircraft required by the RAAF from about 2002. Boeing, Lockheed Martin, Northrop Grumman and Raytheon E-Systems are bidding to become potential prime contractors, for final selection by 1999.

Boeing is proposing a twin-turbofan B.737-700 with a Northrop Grumman electronically-scanned adaptive phased-array radar; the latter company is also linked with Lockheed Martin to provide an E-2C-style dorsal APS-145 radar on the C-130J. Lockheed Martin and Northrop Grumman are offering another C-130J option with a 360° Ericsson phased-array S-band radar, while Raytheon is teamed with Elta. The latter programme is based on used Airbus A310 airframes, each fitted with a phased-array radar in a non-rotating

Sentry-style radome.

These aircraft will form part of a new and integrated national air defence ground environment organisation, within Project Air 5333, and known as Australian Air Defence System 2000 (AADS 2000). This will also include three new ground-based radars for the associated Project Air 5375 requirement, to integrate these and a dozen or more other air defence elements, including the Jindalee over-the-horizon long-range ground radar, through a new communications and datalink network.

NEW ZEALAND:

C-130 ECM contract

Five Lockheed C-130Hs operated by the Royal New Zealand air force are to be equipped with defensive aid subsystems by Raytheon E-Systems of Dallas, TX, from a $NZ14.5 million ($10.22 million) Defence Ministry contract. One of the RNZAF Hercules is currently being fitted with a prototype installation of radar and missile approach warning systems, plus chaff/flare dispensers, plus cockpit armour in the US, after which kits will be supplied by Raytheon E-Systems for installation in New Zealand.

New Mistral order

Contract negotiations were being finalised late in 1996 by the New Zealand government with MATRA of France for the purchase of 23 Mistral short-range surface-to-air missiles, plus a dozen launchers and seven day/night thermal imaging sights costing $NZ22.75 million ($16 million). They will equip the first air defence missile troop of the New Zealand army for initial training.

Africa

MOROCCO:

US Cessna T-37s supplied

The survivors of 15 long-serving Fouga Magister armed basic jet trainers of the Royal Moroccan air force (FRAM) have recently been supplemented by 14 surplus USAF Cessna T-37Bs delivered through a US military aid programme. They are being operated by the FRAM's Ecole de Pilotage at Marrakech, alongside FFA AS 202 Bravos, Raytheon/Beech T-34C Turbo Mentors and Mudry aerobatic lightplanes.

ZAMBIA:

Y-12 transports from China

Recent equipment deliveries to the Zambian air force have included another three Harbin (HAMC) Y-12(II) light turboprop transports, as a follow-on to earlier deliveries of at least two. Several other African countries have received small numbers of Y-12s for military use, including three for the air force of Eritrea and two for the Tanzanian Ministry of Defence.

South America

ARGENTINA:

More US aid prospects

Talks began late in 1996 in Washington for the acquisition by Argentina of more surplus US military equipment to help re-equip the cash-strapped national armed forces. US State Department arms policies towards Latin America are expected to lift the current ban on supplying advanced military equipment, allowing a follow-on to Argentina's $285 million Lockheed Martin contract now in progress for the provision and joint upgrade of 36 MDC A-4M Skyhawks.

Under discussion is a US arms transfer package which could include another eight to 12 unmodified A-4Ms for spares, plus six to eight ex-USN Lockheed P-3A/B Orion maritime patrol aircraft requested for the navy, 11 more Grumman OV-1D Mohawk twin-turboprop ground-attack aircraft for the army, and eight to 12 Bell UH-1H Iroquois utility helicopters for each of the three armed forces.

BRAZIL:

New fighter plans

Replacements for the FAB's Dassault Mirage IIIBRs and Northrop F-5E/F fighters are initially being sought from requests for information issued late in 1996 by the Brazilian air force for its new F-X BR all-weather radar-equipped multi-role combat aircraft requirement. Between 72 and 149 of the new fighters, including 12 and 24 two-seat combat trainer versions, respectively, would be required for FAB service from about 2004. They would be selected from such types as the Dassault Mirage 2000-5 or Rafale, Eurofighter EF 2000, JAS 39 Gripen and MiG-29, plus the Lockheed Martin F-16 and MDC F/A-18 if they are then released for Latin American export.

Requests for proposals are planned for issue in March 1998, followed by final selection and award of a development contract a year later, for a prototype first flight by spring 2001.

Resplendent in low-visibility grey scheme and high-visibility No. 76 Squadron markings, and fitted with the rarely-seen underwing fuel tanks, this is one of the three PC-9s used by the RAAF for FAC training at RAAF Williamtown. These aircraft have replaced the Commonwealth CA-25 Winjeel, which finally retired on 30 June 1995. In addition to the extra fuel for longer endurance, the FAC PC-9s have upgraded radios and a smoke marker ejector.

Brazilian industry expects to be involved in large-scale component production and possible assembly from offset contracts sought through the F-X BR programme. Similar participation is planned in the proposed upgrade of the FAB's 49 Northrop F-5E/Fs to extend their operating lives to around 2015.

COLOMBIA:

Helicopter expansion

Congressional FMS notifications by the Pentagon in late 1996 included the proposed supply to Colombia of 12 Sikorsky UH-60 Black Hawk transport helicopters, armed with twin door-mounted M60D machine-guns, costing $169 million. They would join 10 Black Hawks already in FAC service, and six more being delivered. The new UH-60s will operate alongside the Colombian National Police anti-narcotics division, which will also receive at least 11 ex-US Army Bell UH-1H utility helicopters from US aid programmes, supplementing 20 supplied earlier to the FAC for similar roles.

Orders have also been placed through the Russian Rosvoorouzhenye arms export agency for 10 Mil Mi-17 transport helicopters, costing only $40 million, for Colombian military use. Delivery was expected by late 1996.

PERU:

Russian deliveries confirmed

Earlier reports of former Soviet combat aircraft deliveries to Peru from Belarus have now been confirmed as comprising 12 MiG-29 fighters, including a couple of two-seat MiG-29UBs, and 14 Sukhoi Su-25s for ground-attack, plus associated weapons. They were reportedly taken from Belarus inventories of about 83 MiG-29s and 87 Su-25s, which have exceeded Conventional Forces Europe treaty limitations. After conversion training of Peruvian military personnel in Belarus, the first MiG-29s were airlifted to Peru in chartered Antonov An-124s in late 1996, together with air-to-air missiles which were thought to include close-combat Molniya R-60s (AA-8 'Aphids') and medium-range Vympel R-27s (AA-10 'Alamos'), operated in conjunction with helmet-mounted sights.

In bringing a new level of combat capabilities to Latin America, these weapons evade the US embargo (now under review) on the supply of advanced military equipment and technologies to this area, to minimise potential arms races.

31-year operational career of the standard, carrier-based medium attack aircraft. The occasion was the return of the Enterprise Battle Group from a Mediterranean cruise. The last Intruder was the final ship of 14 in VA-75 'Sunday Punchers' to be launched from USS *Enterprise* (CVN-65) as Carrier Air Wing 17 came home from the cruise. The final Intruder to leave a carrier deck was A-6E 162179 side no. 501, piloted by deputy CAG Captain Bud Jewett, with VA-75 squadron commander Commander James 'Gigs' Gigliotti as bombardier-navigator. Earlier, VA-196 'Main Battery' made the final West Coast Intruder launch. Both squadrons will disestablish on 1 February 1997.

Middle East build-up

The US Navy presence in the Persian Gulf region was boosted when USS *Enterprise* (CVN-65) passed through the Suez Canal on 14/15 September 1996 to join USS *Carl Vinson* (CVN-70) on station. The arrival of the *Enterprise*, together with the reduction in the level of tension following the withdrawal of Iraqi forces from Kurdish areas, permitted the *Carl Vinson* to be relieved and returned home.

During early September the majority of USAF KC-135s, RC-135s and E-3s of the 4409th Operations Group (Provisional) were moved to their new rotational facility at Prince Sultan Air Base at Al Kharj from Riyadh, Saudi Arabia. Al Kharj is a huge new base located in a remote area of desert 60 miles (100 km) to the southeast of Riyadh, and is expected to house, in due course, the remainder of the US combat and support forces currently operating from Dhahran. The Royal Saudi Air Force E-3 Sentries and KE-3 tankers are also expected to move to Al Kharj. The move will enable all US Air Force based operations in Saudi Arabia to be centralised at one location, although other branches of the US military will perform temporary

duty elsewhere in the Gulf. The move was intensified by the terrorist attack on a barrack block at Dhahran on 25 June which left 19 USAF personnel dead and others injured. The $200 million cost of the move was to be shared by both governments.

Pacific Air Forces has begun to provide aircraft for Operation Southern Watch. Wild Weasel-dedicated F-16Cs from the 35th FW at Misawa AB, arrived at Dhahran during September.

USAF units deployed to Middle East locations as Air Expeditionary Forces on at least two occasions in 1996. In April a dozen F-15Cs of the 94th FS, 1st FW from Langley AFB, VA, together with 12 68th FS, 347th Wing F-16Cs from Moody AFB, GA and six 389th FS, 366th Wing F-16Cs from Mountain Home AFB, ID deployed to two bases in Jordan. The deployment was supported by four KC-135Rs from the 96th ARS, 92nd ARW from Fairchild AFB, WA. The AEF was established primarily to fill the 'carrier gap', whereby USAF combat elements replaced some of the capabilities of a full carrier air wing. The squadrons were in residence in Jordan for 10 weeks, with air and ground personnel rotated from their home bases. The AEF finally came to an end at the end of June when the aircraft staged home with refuelling stops at Moron AB, Spain and Lajes in the Azores. The next provisional composite wing, which was the third in the series and was designated as the 4417th Air Expeditionary Force (Provisional), began at Doha in Qatar at the beginning of July, involving 12 F-15Cs of the 33rd FW from Eglin AFB, FL, 12 F-15Es of the 335th FS, 4th FW from Seymour Johnson AFB, NC, and six F-16Cs of the 78th FS, 20th FW from Shaw AFB, SC. The aircraft arrived in Qatar from the USA, with the cells of F-16Cs and F-15Es flying directly to the Middle East from their home bases.

WC-130J for AFRes

A single WC-130J, scheduled for delivery in August 1997, will join the 815th WRS, 403rd Wing at Keesler AFB, MS, which is part of the Air Force Reserve. An additional four examples have been funded from the FY 1997 budget, with three of them currently under construction by Lockheed Martin at Marietta. The AFRes hopes eventually to receive 12 WC-130Js to replace the WC-130Hs currently in service, which are close to 30 years old.

North America

CANADA:

Transport conversion programmes

Two of the Canadian armed forces' four ex-airline Airbus A310 freight transports may be converted for multi-role operations, with the addition of aerial tanker equipment, from proposals with an estimated cost of over $C30 million (£14 million). The A310s are required to replace the two Boeing 707-320Cs in current Canadian air force use for tanker roles, which are due for retirement in April 1997. Another CAF Airbus A310 is equipped solely for passenger transport.

Two L-100-30 stretched Hercules civil cargo aircraft – the last off the Marietta production line – are being modified to full C-130 military standards by CAE Aviation Ltd of Edmonton, Alberta, on behalf of

Lockheed Martin Aeronautical Systems for the Canadian Forces. The $C4.2 million ($3.12 million) contract is due for completion by 31 March 1997, and the new Hercules will supplement nearly 30 remaining C/KC-130E/Hs in CAF service from 36 originally delivered.

UNITED STATES:

Last Intruder launch

The US Navy carried out the final carrier launch of a Grumman A-6 Intruder on 19 December 1996, ending the

As the serial number might suggest, this is the Presidential transport of Venezuela. The aircraft is a Boeing 737-2N1 Advanced, first delivered in 1976. Other VIP transports are a DC-9-15, Learjet 24D and two Gulfstreams, all serving with Escuadrón 41.

Canada's two remaining Boeing CC-137s are shortly to retire. The aircraft (of 437 Sqn) are configured for both tanking (with Beech 1800 pods) and transport.

US reconnaissance to have increased budget

The Department of Defense is to significantly increase the budget for reconnaissance operations in FY 1997, to enable higher quality intelligence to be available to US commanders. Many of the programmes involved are highly classified, with details not being released, although it is known that the 55th Wing at Offutt AFB, NE will receive two extra RC-135W Rivet Joint aircraft. The two aircraft in question are currently being converted by E-Systems at Greenville, TX, and are reported to be former 55th Wing command support aircraft (CSA). The wing operated three CSA types earlier in the decade, including NKC-135A 55-3119, C-135A 60-0378 and C-135B 62-4130. In addition, C-135B 62-4125 was operated by the 55th Wing in the support role during the early 1990s. It is quite likely that 62-4125 and 62-4130 are the two aircraft involved in the conversion programme. They are both in the same production batch as the six existing RC-135Ws, and are fitted with Pratt & Whitney TF33-P-5 engines which incorporate thrust reversers. These same powerplants are fitted to the six existing RC-135Ws, but not to the RC-135U and V models, which have TF33-P-9 engines lacking thrust reversal capability. It has already been announced that the RC-135 fleet is to undergo conversion involving the fitment of CFM F108-CF-100 turbofan engines in place of the TF33s currently installed. No aircraft has yet been seen with the new powerplants installed, although the first is expected to emerge imminently.

Funding will also be available for the two SR-71s to continue operations with Det 2, 9th Wing at Edwards AFB, CA throughout FY97. The two SR-71s have recently adopted tailcode 'BB' in line with the remainder of the unit's aircraft. SR-71 operations were halted due to legal obstacles during the latter part of FY 1996, although the funding of the programme for FY 1997 largely overcame these difficulties. Another three RC-7B Airborne Reconnaissance-Low aircraft are to be added to the current fleet.

Money has been made available to develop the tactical reconnaissance pod for the F-16, and an enhanced sensor suite is to be acquired for the U-2S. The Navy will receive an increased budget to enable enhancements to be incorporated into the capabilities of the EP-3E Aries Elint versions of the Orion, and the ES-3A Shadow Sigint versions of the Viking. No details of the budget involved have been made available.

E-8 J-STARS news

The static park at the Farnborough air show in September 1996 was dominated by the first production E-8C J-STARS to be delivered to the 93rd Air Control Wing at Robins AFB, GA. The 93rd ACW has replaced tailcode 'JS' with 'WR' for Warner Robins, the home base. The aircraft was assigned to the recently formed 12th Air Command and Control Squadron, and was displaying '93 ACW' across the tail for the commander, together with a multi-coloured fin band consisting of blue, yellow, green and red rectangles. The four colours represent each of the squadrons assigned: green for the 12th Airborne Command and Control Squadron, red for the 16th ACCS, blue for the 93rd Operational Support Squadron, and yellow for the 93rd Training Squadron. The 12th and 16th ACCS will be the two operational units, with the training squadron using aircraft as required, probably drawn from the other two. The 93rd OSS will have no aircraft, as its duties are strictly support.

The first production aircraft is 92-3289, delivered to the unit during the summer. The aircraft has production number P1 and construction number 19622, having previously served as a Boeing 707-320B with Qantas. The aircraft is actually the fifth J-STARS, having been preceded by the two E-8A prototypes 86-0416 (ex-N770JS) and 86-0417 (ex-N8411), which were the two aircraft hurriedly

prepared for duties in Operation Desert Storm. The sole YE-8B (88-0322) was to have been the first production standard aircraft, but was placed in short-term storage with AMARC at Davis-Monthan AFB, AZ, arriving in primer. The aircraft left soon afterwards, taking up the civilian allocation N707UM. The first pre-production E-8C example was 90-0175, which has spent much of its career to date on trials work with Northrop Grumman at its Melbourne, FL facility. It was this aircraft, together with E-8A 86-0417, which were flown from Frankfurt/Rhein Main Air Base, Germany from December 1995 to monitor activities in Bosnia. The two aircraft were assigned to the 4500th J-STARS Squadron (Provisional) while detached to Europe. The aircraft returned to Melbourne on 29 March, having flown 97 operational missions.

The next five production aircraft will be P2 to P6, serials 92-3290 (c/n 19295), 93-1097 (c/n 19296), 94-0284 (c/n 19293), 94-0285 (c/n 19442), and 95-0121 (c/n 20016). A number of other former civilian airframes are due for conversion to E-8C standard, including c/n 18949 (ex-JY-AEC), c/n 19628 (ex-N780JS), c/n 19294 (ex-G-EOCO), c/n 20316 (ex-HR-AMF), c/n 20319 (ex-Canadian air force 13705), and c/n 20495 (ex-JY-ADP). As will be readily apparent, the airframes chosen have been obtained from a variety of civilian and military operators from all over the world. Most, if not all, have been or are in storage with AMARC before being returned to airworthy condition for the flight to Lake Charles, LA to commence conversion.

The J-STARS fleet was temporarily grounded from 1 July 1996 due to the discovery that defective rivets had been used by the manufacturer during conversion. Each aircraft had the defective components replaced and was returned to service in a short space of time.

B-2 update

The Air Force is well on the way to receiving its full complement of 20 B-2As, with half this number delivered to the 509th BW at Whiteman AFB, Missouri, by the latter part of 1996. In addition, the six aircraft from the first batch, which were intended to perform much of the development

work, have also been delivered. The majority of these development aircraft will eventually be reworked and assigned to the 509th BW. The six aircraft were ordered from 1982 with serials allocated as 82-1066 to 82-1071, even though the funding arrangement was spread over several years. The aircraft were constructed as Block 10 configuration, with some being upgraded to Block 20 standard.

Aircraft numbers seven through to 20 are the production versions which commenced delivery to Whiteman AFB in December 1993. All have been named after a specific state, with most receiving their name at a ceremony hosted by military and civil dignitaries at an appropriate facility. Details of the order book and deliveries are as follows: 88-0328 *Spirit of Texas* delivered 31 August 1994, 88-0329 *Spirit of Missouri* d/d 17 December 1993, 88-0330 *Spirit of California* d/d 7 August 1994, 88-0331 *Spirit of South Carolina* d/d 30 December 1994, 88-0332 *Spirit of Washington* d/d 30 October 1994, 89-0127 *Spirit of Kansas* d/d 17 February 1995, 89-0128 *Spirit of Nebraska* d/d 28 June 1995, 89-0129 *Spirit of Georgia* d/d 14 November 1995, 90-0040 *Spirit of Alaska* d/d 24 January 1996, 90-0041 *Spirit of Hawaii* d/d 11 January 1996, 92-0700 *Spirit of Oklahoma* d/d 3 July 1996, first Block 20 airframe, 93-1085 unnamed as yet d/d 15 May 1996, 93-1086 scheduled for delivery in 1996, and 93-1087 due in October 1997 to complete the production cycle.

Aircraft allocated serials in FY 1988, 1989 and 1990 were all planned as Block 10 configuration, while those of 1992 and 1993 are Block 20, except the final airframe which was to have been the only example constructed to Block 30 standard. However, all the aircraft from 90-0040 have been upgraded during manufacture to the latest standard. Block 10 aircraft were to be capable of carrying either B83 nuclear bombs or 16 Mk 84 2,000-lb conventional munitions. Block 20 involved an upgrade with a GPS-aided targeting system coupled with a GPS-aided munitions guidance capability to enable the B-2 to have an early, interim, near precision strike capacity. The aircraft was to have been capable of carrying 16 of these GPS-guided weapons and could also house the B61 nuclear bomb. The final version is Block 30, which has the full precision-guided munitions capability including provision for 16 JDAMs housed on a rotary launcher in the bomb bay. Other types of munitions which will be compatible are Mk 82 500-lb bombs, as well as cluster munitions such as the sensor fused weapon, the M117 750-lb bomb, and Mk 62 aerial mines. Block 30 also incorporates fully operational defensive and offensive avionics, a sophisticated mission planning system, and additional operat-

End of an era: deck crew from USS Enterprise manhandle AA 501 (BuNo 162179), a VA-75 A-6E, on to the catapult for the Intruder's final deck launch. The final shot took place off Norfolk on 19 December 1996.

ing modes compatible with the synthetic aperture radar. Aircraft 88-0329 is being upgraded already to Block 30 standard and should be returned to Whiteman AFB at the end of 1997. The remainder will be upgraded subsequently.

US bolsters anti-drug smuggling enforcement

The US government is to bolster the detection of drug smugglers by donating a large number of surplus aircraft and helicopters to Central and South American nations. The value of the military equipment involved, which comprises C-26A/B Metros and UH-1H Hueys, is $112 million. Colombian recipients of the equipment include the police with a pair of C-26A/Bs and an unspecified number of UH-1Hs, and the military which will receive three C-26A/Bs and a batch of UH-1Hs. Peru will be allocated four C-26A/Bs, while Venezuela will receive two C-26A/Bs. The Eastern Caribbean States – Antigua, Barbados, Bermuda, Dominica, Grenada, St Kitts and Nevis, St Lucia and St Vincent and the Grenadines – will acquire a pair of C-26A/Bs. Mexico is to become heavily involved in the detection of smugglers in the Gulf of Mexico, and will be provided with four C-26A/Bs and 53 UH-1Hs. The value of the Mexican equipment is $37 million.

Ten former Air National Guard C-26As were stored at Rickenbacker International Airport, OH for several months during 1996, and most likely will be among the aircraft involved in the transfer. The majority of the equipment should have been delivered to their respective new operators by October 1996. The aircraft will probably have been modified with the fitment of detection equipment to aid their capabilities. The Colombian military is also in the process of planning to receive a dozen UH-60 Black-hawks valued at $107 million, also to be employed in anti-drug operations.

The USAF has mounted a sizeable effort to detect drug smugglers crossing from South to North America. Among these are a contingent of aircraft operating from Howard AFB, in the Panama Canal Zone, including an E-3 Sentry from the 552nd ACW at Tinker AFB, OK which orbits known flight paths to identify low-flying aircraft containing drugs flown by smugglers. A pair of active-duty KC-135Rs operates to provide air refuelling to the Sentry and to an EC-130E signals intelligence aircraft

Following earlier thrust-vectoring work with the General Electric F110-powered F-16 MATV, Lockheed Martin has completed fitment of a Pratt & Whitney F100-PW-100 engine with a low-observable (note sawtooth) vectoring nozzle for 1997 flight trials. The nozzle also has reduced IR signature and increased life. Here the F-16 LOAN (low-observable axisymmetric nozzle) aircraft is seen during ground runs.

from the 193rd SOS of the Pennsylvania ANG. The 192nd Reconnaissance Squadron at Reno Cannon International Airport, NV also provides support with one of their photo recon-naissance 'Pacer Coin' C-130Es, which house a camera system in the lower fuselage. The Army, Navy, Coast Guard and Customs Service all make use of Howard AFB for various purposes, including the detection of drug smugglers.

At least 10 Air National Guard support C-26Bs, strategically located around the USA, have assumed an anti-drug smuggling role with the fitment of a large oval pod beneath the fuselage at the wingroot. The aircraft operate from bases in the southern United States, next to the Mexican border, adjacent to the Gulf of Mexico, or along the Eastern Seaboard.

Fort Worth JRB to expand

At at Fort Worth Joint Reserve Base, TX are the 457th FS operating the F-16C/D under the Air Force Reserve, and VMGR-234 flying the KC-130T (formerly located at NAS Glenview, IL). They are the only resident units at present, although the facility is to see large-scale construction of facilities during 1996 and 1997 in readiness for the arrival of the reserve elements located at NAS Dallas. They include VF-201 equipped with the F-14A, VMFA-112 with the F/A-18A, the 181st AS/Texas ANG flying the C-130H, and a large contingent of US Army Reserve helicopters. The base will also house a second US Marine Corps Reserve F/A-18A unit when VMFA-124 reforms (formerly at NAS Memphis, TN).

Tactical airlift to rejoin AMC

The Air Force has reversed its earlier decision and will shortly transfer some of the active-duty C-130 Hercules fleet that performs the tactical airlift role from Air Combat Command (ACC) back to Air Mobility Command (AMC). AMC was responsible for these aircraft when the Command was formed in June 1991, but transferred them to ACC on 1 October 1993. The result was the application by the units of tailcodes, fin-tip

squadron identification stripes, and the serial presented in tactical style with the fiscal year and last three digits displayed on the tail. The reassignment is expected to take place throughout FY 1997. Directly affected are the 7th Wing at Dyess AFB, TX with two squadrons of C-130Hs, and the 314th AW at Little Rock AFB, AR with three squadrons of C-130Es and one with the C-130H. The two Dyess-based squadrons will become tenants, with a parent group organised to assume control. The entire operation at Little Rock AFB will be transferred to Air Education and Training Command (AETC), as the unit has the primary duty of training aircrew to fly the C-130. The unit will continue to perform a number of worldwide airlift roles, and will continue to rotate squadrons to support United Nations-backed humanitarian duties. Responsibility for daily running of the base at

F-16 testing continues apace at Lockheed Martin's Fort Worth plant. Shown above is a USAF Block 50 aircraft with a brake chute fitted. The USAF is evaluating the chute as a means to reduce brake wear. Below is an experimental aircraft with an entirely new intake fitted, thought to be for radar cross-section reduction. The new intake includes a bulge underneath the aircraft, suggesting a serpentine, compressor face-shielding inlet.

Little Rock will also be switched from ACC to AETC.

ACC also has airlift squadrons assigned to composite units at Pope AFB, NC under the 23rd Wing and at Moody AFB, GA as part of the 347th Wing. Initially, the C-130Es of the 52nd AS at Moody will also have tenant status, although a centralisation would seem inevitable. At Pope AFB, the 23rd Wing will become part of AMC, with the two squadrons of A-10s being in residence as tenants.

ACC currently is responsible for the huge number of airlift C-130s operated by the Air National Guard (ANG) and Air Force Reserve (AFRes), and would assume direct control of individual squadrons in the event of them being mobilised for active duty. This responsibility will also be assumed by AMC, involving 11 AFRes and two dozen ANG C-130 units. They would be expected to apply markings appro-

The coveted 'WW' tailcode, previously assigned to the F-4Gs of the 561st FS before their retirement, is now worn by the F-16 Block 50s of the 35th Fighter Wing at Misawa AB, Japan. The wing's aircraft are equipped with the HTS system and HARM missiles to qualify them for Wild Weasel status.

The US Navy conducts torpedo tests at its AUTEC (Atlantic Underwater Test and Evaluation Center) facility. Two civilian-registered Sikorsky S-61Ns operate from Andros Island in the Bahamas for torpedo recovery and for transport tasks around the range.

priate to their new gaining command, resulting in the elimination of more than 30 tailcodes. The 154th Training Squadron of the Arkansas ANG at Little Rock AFB trains reservist C-130 crews, and would become part of AETC if mobilised.

The US-based fleet of active-duty C-21A Learjets currently assigned to Air Combat Command, Air Education and Training Command, Air Force Space Command and Air Mobility Command are to be transferred to AMC in an effort to streamline operations. Those operated by USAFE and PACAF are unaffected by the change, while the four operated by the 201st AS with the District of Columbia ANG will remain *in situ* until replaced by the Israeli Aircraft Industries Astra SPX VIP, designated as C-38As.

Goodwill visits to CIS

The US Air Force undertook goodwill visits to bases in Russia and the Ukraine during the summer of 1996. A KC-135R of the 319th ARW from Grand Forks AFB, ND flew to Melitopol Air Base in the Ukraine in mid-July for a three-day exchange with the resident transport regiment, which operates a mixed complement including the An-12 'Cub', An-22 'Cock' and Il-76 'Candid'. Personnel from both nations were provided with orientation flights in each other's aircraft. Between 5 and 9 August the 3rd Wing from Elmendorf AFB, AK deployed four F-15C/Ds to Murom Air Base, Russia. The deployment was supported by a 437th AW C-17A and a 60th AMW KC-10A, although the latter only routed as far as Spangdahlem, where it remained with two more F-15s which acted as air spares. One of the Eagles was piloted by the Commander of the 11th Air Force, Lieutenant General Lawrence E. Boese. The visit to Russia followed a successful visit by Su-27s to Elmendorf AFB in 1995.

Joint Navy/Air Force training expansion

The first USAF T-1A Jayhawk to be assigned to the joint flying training operation at NAS Pensacola, FL was delivered to VT-4 on 1 May. Ten

T-1As are scheduled to be assigned to VT-4 and VT-10 at NAS Pensacola to conduct the intermediate navigator training phase, thereby releasing additional Navy T-39Ns to the advanced phase, which is conducted by VT-86.

By the summer of 1996 the Air Force had established four, and the Navy five, fixed-wing training squadrons to teach basic flying or navigational skills to students from all branches of the military. The Air Force units involved are the 8th FTS, 71st FTW at Vance AFB, OK with the T-37B; the 32nd FTS, 71st FTW and 52nd FTS, 64th FTW at Reese AFB, TX, both with the T-1A; and the 562nd FTS, 12th FTW at Randolph AFB, TX operating the T-43A. The latter squadron currently has a commanding officer from the Navy. Navy squadrons performing joint training are VT-3 at NAS Whiting Field, FL with the T-34C; VT-4 at NAS Pensacola with the T-1A, T-34C and T-39N; VT-10 at NAS Pensacola with the T-2C, T-34C and T-39N; VT-31 at NAS Corpus Christi, TX operating the T-44A; and VT-86 at NAS Pensacola with the T-2C and T-39N.

J57-powered C-135 retired

The Air Force retired the last operational C-135 powered by Pratt & Whitney J57 water-injected turbojet engines. The aircraft involved was NKC-135A 55-3128, which had been employed by the 452nd Flight Test Squadron of the 412th Test Wing at Edwards AFB, CA for many years performing anti-icing trials by spraying supercooled water droplets from the flying boom onto test aircraft flying in the tanker's slip stream. A much reduced usage, coupled with the necessity for the aircraft to undergo a $2 million depot-level maintenance, resulted in the NKC-135 being declared uneconomic and retired for storage to AMARC on 20 May 1996.

Unit news

Detachment 1 of the 9th Reconnaissance Wing at RAF Akrotiri, Cyprus received its complement of two U-2S models during February 1996, becoming the second overseas unit to operate the re-engined aircraft.

The 23rd Wing at Pope AFB, NC officially relinquished the F-16C/D from service with the 74th FS when the last aircraft departed on 11 July 1996 for transfer to the 27th FW at Cannon AFB, NM. The squadron has transitioned to the OA/A-10A, joining the 75th FS.

The first two B-1Bs of the 34th BS, 366th Wing to be permanently transferred to Mountain Home AFB, ID from their present home at Ellsworth AFB, SD were moved on 22 August 1996. Another pair relocated in September, with all 11 due to have taken up residence with the parent wing by March 1997.

The 21st Fighter Squadron was reformed at Luke AFB, AZ under the 56th FW on 1 October 1996 to train Taiwanese air force pilots who will operate modified, new-build Block 20 F-16A/Bs. The project will last for three years initially, with aircraft operating in full USAF markings.

The 6th Air Base Wing at MacDill AFB, FL was redesignated as an air refuelling wing prior to assuming control of the 91st ARS, which officially moved from Malmstrom AFB, MT on 1 October 1996. The unit operates the KC-135R.

The 64th Airlift Squadron was deactivated at O'Hare IAP, IL during the summer of 1996, with its C-130Hs being distributed to other units.

The consolidation of F-14 Tomcat operations from NAS Miramar, CA to NAS Oceana, VA is scheduled for completion by June 1997. The first squadron to move from Miramar was VF-2, which officially took up residence at Oceana on 1 April 1996. It was followed by VF-211 in August 1996, and a VF-101 det in October. VF-11 and VF-31 followed in November 1996, with just VF-213 remaining. The latter is due to vacate Miramar by May 1997.

The first two joint US Air Force-US Navy EA-6B Prowlers squadrons, VAQ-133 and VAQ-134, have both applied tailcode 'NL'. VAQ-134 deployed to the Far East during mid-1996 and was scheduled to return home in January 1997, having been replaced by VAQ-133. The third joint squadron is VAQ-137, which was commissioned in October 1996 and is due to make its first carrier deployment aboard CVN-73/USS *George Washington* early in 1997.

VMFA-235 was decommissioned at NAS Miramar on 14 June 1996. VMFA-451 at MCAS Beaufort, SC is due to be axed in 1997.

Two naval reserve heavy-lift helicopter squadrons are both to transition from the RH-53D to the CH-53E. HMH-769 at MCAS El Toro, CA commenced conversion during the summer of 1996, with HMH-772 at NAS Willow Grove, PA due to transition in 1997. HMH-769 moved to El Toro from NAS Alameda, CA during 1996. The only other resident unit at Alameda was HM-15, which relocated to NAS Corpus Christi, TX in April 1996. Alameda officially closed its runway operations on 30 June 1996, with the facility due to shut completely on 27 April 1997.

VP-92 at NAS Brunswick, ME is to receive five P-3Cs from VP-68, together with the handful of EP-3Js operated by VP-66 at NAS Willow Grove. Eventually a new reserve squadron will be formed to operate the EP-3Js, together with the EP-3Es of VQ-2 which will move to NAS Brunswick from NAS Rota, Spain.

Surplus equipment transfers

The US government has agreed to supply surplus equipment to several overseas air arms; much of the equipment is held in storage with the Aerospace Maintenance and Regeneration Center (AMARC) at Davis-Monthan AFB, AZ. A pair of refurbished C-130Bs was due to have been delivered to the Romanian air force in October 1996, with another two being received by December 1996. They are the first surplus US transport aircraft to reach the former Warsaw Pact. The Lebanese government was to have received a second batch of 16 UH-1Hs during the summer of 1996 to join those delivered in 1995. Israel should also have received 14 surplus UH-1s by the end of 1996. The Chilean air force was expecting to acquire a dozen former US Army UH-60As during 1996 and 1997 from funding provided by the United Nations in payment for peacekeeping duties.

The Bosnian government should have received 16 former Army National Guard UH-1s by November 1996, with the helicopters being prepared for delivery at Hunter AAF,

On 1 October 1996 the 6th Air Base Wing at MacDill AFB, Florida, became the 6th Air Refueling Wing. At the same time base control changed from ACC to AMC. The 91st ARS, previously with the 43rd ARG at Malmstrom, is now part of the new organisation, flying the KC-135R.

The HH-1N serves with the US Navy in small numbers on base rescue flights, with Antarctic squadron VXE-6 and on single-aircraft detachments to assault ships. This aircraft is assigned to the NWTS at China Lake, California, for rescue duties around the weapons range.

GA in September 1996. The helicopters have been overhauled by ATCOM and the transfer was managed by Lockheed Martin. The Jordanian air force was also the recipient of 17 UH-1Hs late in 1996, to join 18 already in service.

Jordan signed the formal agreement with the Department of Defense to lease surplus F-16s under the Peace Falcon programme. The agreement covers a five-year, no-cost lease of 12 F-16As and a single F-16B, all of which have exceeded 75 per cent of their life expectancy of 4,000 flight hours. In addition, the lease covers three F-16Bs at the low cost of $4.64 million, together with a $215 million letter of offer and acceptance covering future structural modifications and engine reliability upgrades. Jordanian pilots were due to commence flight training at either Luke AFB or Tucson IAP, AZ in January 1997, with the 16 aircraft involved due to be delivered between December 1997 and February 1998.

The Portuguese air force has requested the purchase of 25 surplus F-16A/Bs which – together with additional engines and associated equipment – will be valued at $258 million. The Portuguese request is the first to be considered under a new export policy which values secondhand aircraft at considerably less than originally planned under the Coalition Force Enhancement programme. Under the CFE scheme the cost per unit of secondhand F-16s would have been only slightly less than obtaining brand new equipment, therefore not producing the desired effect of disposing of surplus equipment and generating funds.

The Singapore air force hopes to initially locate two of its four KC-135Rs at March AFB, CA for crew training, and to develop air refuelling techniques for their F-16 pilots in training at Luke AFB.

F/A-18F carrier trials

A McDonnell Douglas F/A-18F Super Hornet made the type's first landing on an aircraft-carrier aboard USS *John C. Stennis* (CVN-74) on 18 January 1997. The aircraft was 'F-1', the first two-seater built. The carrier trials of the Super Hornet began after flight testing was briefly suspended in December 1996 when an aircraft experienced a compressor stall during supersonic flight in one of its two General Electric F414 engines.

AL-1 laser attack aircraft

Boeing was chosen in November 1996 to construct a single 747-400F transport as the YAL-1A, service test prototype of the AL-1 attack aircraft. The prototype will be delivered after fitting out with a laser system by TRW plus optics and fire-control systems designed by Lockheed Martin, and will join the US's theatre missile defence effort. The USAF plans to acquire at least six AL-1As for Air Combat Command, each capable of firing up to 30 five-second laser 'shots' using its onboard supply of chemicals. The AL-1A's laser weapon is charged with achieving a range of 185 to 360 miles (297 to 579 km) and must be aimed and fired only while the aircraft maintains a steady bank. The 747/laser combination is scheduled to take to the air in 1999 and is expected to destroy a boosting theatre ballistic missile in a test by autumn 2002.

V-22

The long-stalled Bell-Boeing CV-22 Osprey, the special-operations version of the tilt-rotor aircraft, is now back on track. A $490 million contract will enable the manufacturing team to modify the ninth EMD V-22 prototype into the first production-representative CV-22, slated to fly in 1999. The CV-22 will be a simplified version of the aircraft once contemplated. It will differ from the Marine Corps' MV-22 transport in having Texas Instruments APQ-147D terrain-following/terrain-avoidance radar, a new radio countermeasures radar

jammer, and a receive-only satellite terminal for intelligence data.

JPATS designation

The turboprop Raytheon/Pilatus PC-9 Mk II trainer for the US Air Force and Navy has been designated T-6A. The first US Air Force squadron is scheduled to become operational at Laughlin AFB, TX in August 2001. Two military pilots, Lieutenant Mike Floyd, USN and Captain Stu Farmer, USAF, began a qualification, test and evaluation programme with Raytheon Aircraft (formerly Beech) in September 1996 to qualify the aircraft according to the services' joint operational requirements. The evaluation is scheduled to continue through 1998.

Predator squadron

The 11th Reconnaissance Squadron at Nellis Air Force Base, NV took over operations of the Predator UAV (unmanned aerial vehicle) from the US Army on 3 September 1996. The squadron, which reports to Air Combat Command, had been flying Predator missions over Bosnia since May 1996. The Predator is flown by a rated pilot who, although on the ground, handles controls and talks with air traffic controllers as if he were aboard the aircraft. The payload opera-

tor, an enlisted photo-imagery specialist, sits near the pilot and operates the UAV's three sensors: electro-optical for video images, infra-red to pick up heat concentrations, and synthetic aperture radar to distinguish figures through clouds. The USAF is purchasing 10 Predators at $3 million each. Flight operations are carried out at Nellis's Indian Springs Airfield.

Navy helicopters

The US Navy launched its Helicopter Master Plan on 1 November 1996 with announcement of its planned purchase of a CH-60 naval demonstrator based on the US Army UH-60L Black Hawk. The Navy plans to acquire 134 CH-60s for combat support, vertical replenishment (VertRep) and search and rescue duties. The service also intends to turn over the Military Sealift Command VertRep task to a civilian contractor, transferring about 32 helicopters for operations to and from MSC logistics ships, and to upgrade all of its 270 SH-60B, SH-60F and HH-60H Sea Hawks to multi-mission SH-60R standard. The Plan would enable retirement of the Vertol CH-46 Sea Knight fleet, in addition to allowing Reserve forces to replace their last SH-2Gs and SH-3s. So far, funds have been made available only for the single CH-60 demonstrator.

The sole EC-130V was originally developed for the US Coast Guard anti-drug smuggling mission, and used a standard C-130H airframe and E-2C Hawkeye radar system. The USCG programme was not proceeded with, and the aircraft is now used for testing by the USAF's 514th TS, 545th TG, based at Hill AFB. It retains full USCG colour scheme and serial 1721, but is now designated an NC-130H.

BRIEFING

Chengdu F-7MG

Making yet more of the MiG-21

For three decades, the Chengdu J-7 has been one of the most obvious examples of the Chinese military aviation industry and is now that industry's number one export. Developed at a slow, but steady, pace since its first flight on 17 January 1966, the J-7 (J/*Jianji*-Fighter, number seven) began life as nothing more than a reverse-engineered MiG-21F-13 with a partial copy of the original R-11F-300 turbojet, the WP-7 (WP/*Wopen*-engine jet). While other attempts at developing indigenous Chinese combat aircraft have failed or faded away, the J-7 continued its very gradual evolution. It has become the sole choice for those nations who feel they need an agile, unsophisticated but Mach 2-capable, day fighter/interceptor and either cannot afford, or are politically barred from, anything else.

In Volume 7 of *World Air Power Journal* we presented a detailed review of the J-7's development history and export career, as the F-7.

The radical new wing design of the F-7MG is obvious from this view. Arranged around it are 30-mm cannon rounds, 57-mm rockets (front) and HF-7C rocket pods (back), PL-2, PL-3, PL-7 and PL-5 (on rails) AAMs plus NORINCO 250-kg and 500-kg GP HE bombs.

At that time is seemed as if the improved J-7II/F-7M was at last about to give way to full-scale development of the J-7III – an only slightly-less obsolete copy of the MiG-21MF 'Fishbed-J'. Chengdu first flew the prototype J-7III on 26 April 1984 and the chief advantages it offers over previous J-7s are the inclusion of the JL-7 fire control radar and a more powerful WP-13 (broadly similar to the R-13-300) powerplant. The J-7III has entered limited service with the People's Liberation Army Air Force – PLA(AF) – but not to the same extent as the J-7II, nor has it been exported.

Part of the reason behind this was a 1987 agreement between Chengdu and the US Grumman Corporation to develop the Super-7 (originally Sabre 2), a radical upgrade and overhaul of the J-7 complete with a new wing, radar nose, single-piece canopy and much improved avionics, weapons and engines. The Super-7 would allow Chengdu, and Chinese industry, to stop merely tinkering with outdated designs and would put it on the first rung to developing more modern combat aircraft. Like many other Western joint ventures ongoing at that time, all US work on this project was terminated in the wake of the Tiananmen Square massacre of 1989. CATIC (China National Aero Technology Import and Export Corporation), the supervisory body which oversaw the entire Chinese aviation industry, and its successor AVIC (Aviation Industries of China), continued to work on the programme with Pakistani collaboration. The Super-7 design that emerged in model form closely resembled today's models of the FC-1 multi-role fighter, but ultimately the Super-7 programme itself was abandoned.

In its place came a return to the J-7 and a further modified version dubbed J-7E/F-7E. As announced in 1994/95, the J-7E utilised the J-7II airframe, rather than the J-7III, but mated it with an entirely new wing design – which radically altered the familiar lines of the aircraft. The new wing was a double-delta design to improve handling and manoeuvrability in the low-speed regime. The aircraft had four underwing pylons, upgraded air-to-air missiles and some improved cockpit avionics. However, while some preliminary drawings and outline specifications were released, and oblique references made to the new fighter, no concrete evidence of its existence existed until November 1996.

That month, China hosted its first international air show and aviation trade exhibition – Air Show China '96 – at the coastal town of Zhuhai, in Guangdong Province, southern China. The show boasted a wide range of Chinese aviation and space technology with a sizeable line-up of Chinese-built aircraft and missiles on display. Taking pride of place in the main exhibition hall, and in the flying display, was a hitherto unknown F-7 variant, the Chengdu Aircraft Industrial Corporation's (CAC) F-7MG, which is the true current form of the F-7E/J-7E. The J-7E was once reported to have made its maiden flight in 1990 and to have entered PLA(AF) service in 1993/94. Chengdu officials stated that aircraft similar to the F-7MG were in PLA(AF) service, but that the two (export-intended) F-7MGs present at the show were the only two that had been built, so far. The date for its maiden flight was given as 1993, although it was unclear whether this related to the export-dedicated version alone. Interestingly, an aircraft clearly marked as an F-7MG appeared in a CATIC photo released in 1995 (see *World Air Power Journal*, Volume 22), but was positioned in a such a way as to be indistinguishable from the F-7Ps (P/Pakistan) surrounding it.

The F-7MG is intended for the export market and it is uncertain whether J-7s of this standard are already in PLA(AF) service – though it is likely that at least small numbers are.

The F-7MG is based on the F-7M airframe. The F-7M (dubbed Airguard) is in turn an upgraded version of the J-7II with new avionics, including a HUD/WAC, fire control radar, air data computer, IFF and navaids – all sourced from the UK's GEC-Marconi Avionics. According to one Chengdu representative, the 'M' in F-7M signifies 'Marconi'. The 'G' in the F-7MG designation derives from the Chinese character 'Gai', meaning improved. Production aircraft, delivered to export customers, will most likely be designated as F-7MGAs, F-7MGBs, F-MGPs, etc. (Chengdu has said that customers can call the aircraft anything they like, so long as they buy them!)

The first and most obvious difference between the F-7MG and all previous versions of the aircraft is its new double-delta wing, which CAC claims to have designed and developed completely independently. The forward section of the wing retains the original leading-edge sweep of 57°. The new outboard section has sweep of only 42°, while the trailing edge of this outboard section is tapered. Wingspan is increased by 1.17 m (3 ft 10 in) compared to the J-7II, and area by 1.88 m² (20.2 sq ft), providing an overall increase in wing area of 8.17 per cent. Combined with this are new automatic leading- and trailing-edge flaps which give the F-7MG a sustained turning rate of 16° per second at 1000 m (3280 ft), 11° per second at 5000 m (16,400 ft) and 8° per second at 8000 m (26,250 ft). Using a formula that combines the improvements in radar, engine and wing, Chengdu claims that, compared to any other variant, the F-7MG boasts a 43 per cent increase in integrated manoeuvrability', an 83.9 per cent in 'close-in combat effectiveness' (when combined with its improved armament), a 10 per cent increase in operational radius, a 30 per cent decrease in take-off run, a 28.6 per cent

Above: This F-7MG flew during the Air Show China '96 display with wingtip smoke generators. It was difficult to discern from its brief displays whether the F-7MG offered any significant performance enhancements.

Right: The F-7MG's cockpit is a marked improvement over previous F-7/J-7s and features two GEC-Marconi Avionics colour displays.

decrease in landing run and a 24 per cent increase in climb rate (in afterburner, from a standing start). The original wing, optimised for high speed at high altitude, has been replaced by a larger wing with a lower loading that greatly aids low-speed, low-altitude manoeuvring and performance as a whole.

Improvements over previous variants of the J-7 are not merely aerodynamic. Chengdu has worked closely with GEC-Marconi Avionics (GMav) and AlliedSignal to improve the F-7MG's avionics, radar and cockpit layout. The Super Skyranger Radar (SSR), supplied by GEC-Marconi Avionics, is a small, affordable multi-mode radar that can be accommodated in the F-7MG's centrebody intake and the limited avionics space in front of the cockpit. Super Skyranger has been specifically developed for use in small aircraft (particularly the MiG-21) and Chengdu has referred to the SSR as the 'Short Skyranger' to underline their satisfaction with its compact size. Previously, the F-7M (exported to Bangladesh, Iran, Myanmar, Zimbabwe and Pakistan, as the F-7P Airguard) has been fitted with the basic GMav Type 226 Skyranger. Reportedly, Italy's Fiar had been contracted to supply Grifo-7 fire control radars for future F-7 developments and to replace the Skyranger, but GEC-Marconi Avionics now appears to be secure in its relationship with Chengdu.

The I-band Super Skyranger has a maximum look angle of ±30° with its fixed antenna, but on the

Right: The F-7MG's Super Skyranger radar fits neatly into the intake centrebody and is compact enough not to be hampered by the limited avionics storage space in the aircraft's nose. This multi-mode, pulse-Doppler radar is integrated with the F-7MG's HUD/WAC system – all supplied by GEC-Marconi Avionics.

F-7MG this is limited to ±20°. Super Skyranger operates in two basic engagement modes – guns and missiles – and has a maximum range of 15 km (9.3 miles) for missiles and 5 km (3.1 miles) for guns. Minimum range against a target in a guns attack is 300 m (984 ft) and 150 m (492 ft) for missiles. Air combat radar modes include HUD search (field of view), vertical search and boresight. In air-to-air modes, the SSR offers range-while-search and single-target-track functions. The SSR can perform simple air-to-ground ranging functions and also has its own built-in test facilities. The radar allows

look-down shoot-down engagements and is optimised for HUD/WAC aiming as it is linked via an ARINC 429 digital serial link to the air data computer. The highly-ECM resistant SSR will even provide HUD steering data for off-boresight missiles. Super Skyranger is currently under flight test with the F-7MG.

The F-7MG's HUD/WAC, a Type 856, is supplied by GEC-Marconi Avionics and the HUD video recording system is also UK-built. Flanking the HUD are a Chinese-supplied ECM/counter-measures panel (left) and RWR display (right). A chaff/flare fit is

Chengdu stated that two aircraft have been built to F-7MG standard and at Air Show China '96 a second example – CAC 0142 – was on display in the main exhibition hall.

part of the F-7MG's baseline equipment fit. Low down on the instrument panel are two side-by-side colour CRT displays, which function as the primary ADI and HSI indicators. A Chinese AD3 400 HF/VHF radio or AlliedSignal 908/9 radio can be fitted, according to customer preference, as can VOR/DME/ILS, TACAN or GPS. Chengdu has displayed a GEC-Marconi Avionics air data computer, while stating that the equipment on board the F-7MG can be either Chinese-sourced or supplied by the UK's Smiths Industries. Smith Industries also supplies the F-7MG's radar altimeter. A Chinese-built ADF system is supplied as standard, but a more compact Western equivalent (such as AN/ARN-149) would be preferred. The pilot has HOTAS controls and an overall working environment that is a great improvement over Chengdu's basic F-7s, and even the F-7P. Some of the changes made to the F-7P have been retained in the F-7MG. For example, the control stick has been shortened by 50 mm (1.96 in) and two rear-view mirrors incorporated in the canopy. A CAC zero-zero ejection seat is presently fitted, although this might be replaced by the Martin-Baker Mk 10L, as fitted to the F-7P. The single-piece canopy hinges to the rear and Chengdu has said preliminary studies

to include a bubble-canopy for the F-7 have been undertaken. Should any customer demand such an improvement, the new canopy could be added on the production line within 12 months.

The F-7MG has two Type 30-I belt-fed 30-mm cannon. The standard ammunition supply on all previous F-7 models has been just 60 rounds per gun. Like the F-7M/P, the F-7MG has four underwing pylons and a centreline hardpoint. Its basic air-to-air armament is two PL-7, MATRA R.550 Magic or AIM-9P

Sidewinder AAMs, carried on the inboard pylons. Four AIM-9Ps plus a single 500-litre (110-Imp gal) centreline fuel tank can be carried for maximum combat persistence. Two AAMs and three fuel tanks can be carried but the drag/weight penalties of this configuration probably outweigh the benefits of the additional fuel. For ground-attack missions, the F-7MG can carry four HF-7C rocket pods, or two rocket pods and three 500-litre fuel tanks, or four pods and one 800-litre (176-Imp gal) centreline

tank. The same combination of weapons and fuel tanks can also be applied to Mk 82 or 500-kg (1,000-lb) bombs. For ferry flights, the F-7MG can travel with two underwing 500-litre tanks and one centreline 800-litre tank.

The F-7MG has a combat radius of 850 km (530 miles) on a hi-hi-hi air superiority mission carrying two PL-7 AAMs and two 500-litre drop tanks. On a hi-lo-hi combat mission, with five minutes combat at low-altitude, this decreases to 490 km (305 miles). On a lo-lo-hi ground-attack sortie the F-7MG's combat radius with two Mk 82 bombs and two 500-litre tanks is 550 km (345 miles). On a lo-lo-lo close air support mission, this is reduced to 420 km (260 miles).

At Air Show China '96 a Chengdu spokesman was keen to point out that the F-7MG was available for export now, while acknowledging that the world 'was at peace' and that this was not necessarily good for business. In early 1996 the F-7MG was flown by a foreign pilot from the air force of a likely customer, and there were certainly plenty of other F-7 users and potential customers from Iran, Libya and Tanzania attending Air Show China '96 – both in and out of uniform. Chengdu acknowledges that the greatest impediment to the F-7MG at present is its outdated WP-13F turbojet. Representing only a slight improvement from the original WP-7 engine, the WP-13F is a mid-range thrust powerplant that Chengdu is keen to replace. Discussions with Rolls-Royce and Saturn (Lyul'ka) were acknowledged, but progress is consistently hampered by the small size of the F-7's airframe, which has prevented any meaningful advances. Chengdu is keen to pitch the F-7MG as a lead-in fighter trainer for more advanced combat aircraft, such as the F-16. Getting the aircraft to a standard where it could truly be considered as such is a major goal for the company. Some changes that have been made, such as the redesign of the stores management system from four panels to one, represent a step in the right direction – integrating additional Chinese and Western weapons will be another.   **Robert Hewson**

This F-7MG is arrayed in front of a long line-up of what appear to be Chengdu F-7Ps. Pakistan is an obvious customer for the F-7MG, and may take delivery in 1997.

Chengdu F-7MG
Specification
Type: single-engined interceptor/fighter
Powerplant: WP-13F twin-spool eight-stage axial flow turbojet, rated at 33.83 kN normal, 20.02 kN maximum and 29.36 kN in afterburner
Length, overall: 14.885 m (48.83 ft)
Wingspan: 8.32 m (27.29 ft)
Wing area: 24.88 m² (267.81 sq ft)
Height: 4.103 m (13.46 ft)
Empty weight: 5292 kg (11,666 lb)
Normal take-off weight: 7540 kg (16,622 lb), with two AIM-9P AAMs
Maximum take-off weight: 9100 kg (20,061 lb)
Maximum indicated speed: 1200 km/h (745 mph, 648 kt)
Minimum indicated speed: 210 km/h (130 mph, 113 kt), in level flight

Maximum Mach number: 2.0
Maximum climb rate: 195 m/s (38,400 ft/min)
Operational ceiling: 17500 m (57,414 ft)
Absolute ceiling: 18000 m (59,055 ft)
Operational radius: hi-hi-hi air superiority mission with five minutes combat time in full a/b 850 km (528 miles), with two AIM-9P AAMs, three 500-litre (132-US gal, 109-Imp gal) external fuel tanks; lo-lo-hi attack mission 550 km (342 miles), with two Mk 82 bombs and two external fuel tanks
Take-off distance, maximum: 700 m (2,296 ft)
Landing distance, maximum: 700 m (2,296 ft)
Operational g limit: 8g

Shenyang J-8IIM 'Finback'

Another attempt at the second generation

Since the Shenyang J-8 was last featured, in detail, in *World Air Power Journal* (Volume 3) the programme has moved on – as have China's efforts to field a credible, modernised air force. The J-8 was once the shining star of China's indigenous military aviation industry, but the project has been hindered by major technical hurdles and outflanked by political developments. Today the J-8 is only one of at least three ongoing Chinese programmes to build a modern family of combat aircraft, all of which are being assisted by outside firms, to some degree or another.

The J-8 has the longest pedigree of any of these and is already in service, to a limited degree, with the People's Liberation Army Air Force. The original unsuccessful J-8 'Finback-A' fighter, which resembled nothing more than a large twin-engined MiG-21, can trace its history back to 1964. The J-8 and subsequent all-weather J-8I led to the redesigned and streamlined J-8II 'Finback-B', which first flew in 1984. Limited production of this aircraft was followed by the joint US-Chinese Peace Pearl programme whereby Grumman and Shenyang initiated a major modernisation attempt, primarily to equip the J-8II with modern avionics, radar and weapons systems. The Tiananmen Square massacre ended this venture and left the J-8 in limbo. Against this background China began to vigorously diversify its military aviation industry and seek other avenues, abroad, for assistance to develop more modern aircraft.

Chief among these is the long-heralded CATIC (Chengdu) J-10, an aircraft still shrouded in secrecy but widely held to be based on Israeli technology developed during IAI's Lavi programme of the 1980s. Western-generated artists' impressions of the J-10, including those most recently issued by US government sources, show a delta-winged, canard-equipped airframe which closely resembles the Lavi, first flown in 1986. For an aviation industry hitherto based almost solely on revamping obsolete Soviet designs of the 1950s, the J-10 represents a major step forward, leap-frogging as it does several decades of R&D. Like much of Israel's cutting-edge defence tech-

nology, the Lavi was backed by US funding, and objections to the transferral of such sensitive technology have been the cause of subdued but insistent US criticism of Israeli links with China. Russian firms have also bid to be involved in the J-10: Saturn/Lyul'ka is believed to have supplied AL-31F turbofans to power the single-engined prototype, and Phazotron's Zhuk multi-mode radar is a leading candidate for inclusion. The status of the J-10 is the subject of much debate. A first flight was predicted for 1996 and some sources allege that the prototype was then lost during trans-sonic flight tests later that year – others insist that the J-10 has not even reached the roll-out stage.

The other, more publicly-acknowledged design under development is the CATIC (Chengdu) FC-1. The FC-1 is intended as a lightweight multi-role combat aircraft, initially for the Chinese and Pakistani air forces, but later for the export market. Design assistance has been provided by the Mikoyan Design Bureau (the FC-1 echoes the MiG-33 fighter design), and Klimov has supplied the RD-93 (RD-33 derivative) powerplant. Western firms including GEC-Marconi, Thomson CSF/Sextant and Sagem are bidding to supply onboard systems such as the INS, SMS and air data computer. The FC-1 will be equipped with a pulse-Doppler, multi-mode radar and here the field is still open, with the GEC-Marconi Blue Hawk, a derivative of the Thomson RDY, Fiar Grifo-7 and Phazotron's Super Komar in the running. The FC-1 has been widely shown in model form, and at Air Show China '96 CATIC showed a representative cockpit mock-up of the aircraft fitted with a GEC-Marconi wide-angle raster HUD. Chengdu and GEC-Marconi now have an established

tradition of co-operation with the F-7M/MG programme and the UK firm is seen as front-runner for any deal on the FC-1. The FC-1's maiden flight had been expected in 1997, but this has been pushed back to 1998, at the earliest. Wrangling between China and Pakistan on the K-8 trainer project has not helped smooth the way for the FC-1, and Pakistan is now insisting that China must not only speed up the FC-1 programme but also make a firm commitment to acquire the type.

Another Chinese project of which little has been heard recently is the Xian JH-7 all-weather attack aircraft. Intended as a Q-5 'Fantan' replacement, the twin-engined JH-7 was revealed in model form in 1988, powered by Xian WS9 (Rolls-Royce Spey 202) turbofans. A maiden flight was declared to be imminent but, since then, nothing has been reported. Against this background the J-8 remains one of very few visible symbols of the Chinese military aviation industry's

This photograph reportedly depicts the first flight of the J-8IIM. Whether this aircraft is a rebuilt J-8II, or even carried any J-8IIM systems (such as radar), is unclear.

Above: This inert PL-9 AAM does not have the IR seeker head or laser fuze seen on other PL-9s on exhibit at Air Show China '96.

Above: The PL-3 is the last of the 'Atoll'-derived AAMs developed in China. A larger warhead and forward fins differentiate it from the PL-2.

Like previous J-8IIs, the J-8IIM has a twin-barrelled 23-mm Type 23 cannon installation in a belly fairing, just aft of the nose-gear.

It was the appearance of the Vympel R-27R (AA-10 'Alamo') on the J-8IIM that highlighted the real advances made with this variant.

The Shenyang J-8IIM is unlikely to be operational with the PLA(AF) yet, but the type has already been linked to a major pending Chinese arms export deal with Iran.

progress and, despite the many question marks that still surround the aircraft, it seems to indicate that progress has been slow and unspectacular.

The major difference between the J-8IIM and its predecessors is the integration of Russian-supplied radar and weapons that may, at last, make the J-8 a useful combat aircraft. For the first time on a Chinese military type, the J-8IIM was displayed at Air Show China '96 with a BVR missile – the Vympel R-27 'AA-10 Alamo'. The version carried by the J-8IIM was the basic semi-active radar homing R-27R. The R-27R is believed to have a range of approximately 50 km (30 miles) with a 39-kg (86-lb) expanding rod warhead. The R-27R entered service with the Soviet air force in the mid-1980s and has been widely exported since then. It represents the first quantifiable BVR missile to be associated with a Chinese aircraft, but this is not to suggest that China has ignored developing its own medium-range AAMs.

Also displayed at Air Show China '96 was the LY-60(N) missile, a virtual replica of Alenia's Aspide, believed to be in Chinese service as a mobile SAM, with an air-launched version imminent. Aspide technology was handed over to China during Aeritalia/Alenia co-operation with Nanchang on the Q-5M/A-5M upgrade from August 1986. In its air-launched form (the PL-11) the LY-60 has been mooted as the primary armament for the FC-1. A missile believed to have been based on the Aspide/Sparrow, PL-10, was previously proposed as the primary armament for the J-8, but only rough drawings were ever seen. With the appearance, in public, of the LY-60, the weapon's Italian roots are revealed. The Aspide family was developed from the AIM-7E Sparrow by Selenia (now part of the Alenia conglomeration), and has been built in ground-launched, air-launched and naval versions. An active radar version, IDRA, which evolved into the (less-expensive) Aspide Mk 2

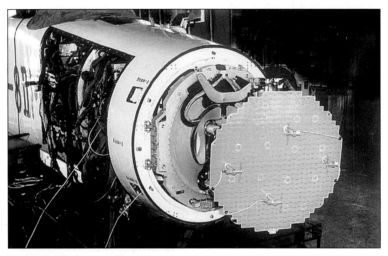

Above: The Phazotron Zhuk-8II radar fits neatly into the nose of the J-8IIM. It is unclear what type of (Chinese) radar it replaces.

Left: The LY-60(N) SAM may well pave the way for an Aspide-based BVR AAM for deployment on the J-8IIM and other Chinese fighters, such as the J-10 and FC-1.

entered development in the late 1980s, and it is this version that the LY-60 most closely resembles. There has never been a formal disassociation between Alenia and Nanchang on the Q-5M project, but it has been reported that plans to supply the Aspide to the PLA (AF) had fallen through. Development of the LY-60 family has obviously continued and the missile must still remain an option for the J-8IIM. Russian sources have also indicated that the Vympel R-77 'AA-12 Adder' will also be supplied for the J-8IIM. The addition of such weapons, even to an aircraft as basic as the J-8, no longer allow it to be disregarded as a threat and provides China with a second BVR fighter alongside its Su-27s.

For close-in combat the J-8IIM can carry the full range of Chinese built IR-homing short-range AAMs. These include the 1960s vintage PL-2 and PL-3 (based on AA-2 'Atoll' copies), the PL-5 (based on hybrid AA-2/AIM-9 Sidewinder technology), the PL-7, first seen in the mid-1980s (and based on the MATRA R.550

Magic), and the very latest PL-9. The PL-9 integrates elements of late-model Sidewinder design, such as the tail 'rollerons' and double-delta forward fins, with an airframe closer in size to that of the (wider) R.550. Like the LY-60 it was first revealed as a ground-launched system, in 1989. Today, its developer Luoyang Optoelectro Technology Development Centre (LOEC) promotes the PL-9 as "an advanced third-generation air combat IR missile with advanced and well-designed aerodynamic configuration, capable of high manoeuvrability." PL-9 has a stated range of 5 km (3 miles) and minimum firing range of 500 m (1640 ft). The missile is 2.9 m (9.5 ft) in length, 15.7 cm (6.18 in) in diameter, weighs 115 kg (253 lb) and has a manoeuvre limit of 35g. LOEC also states "(the) IR seeker with cooling system has counter-countermeasures capability against background radiation clutter and high sensitivity. With advanced terminal technique, the missile can be guided to the optimal position and achieve the most efficient lethality." The PL-9 appears to be

fitted with a laser proximity fuse and the seeker head reportedly uses targeting logarithms to seek out the most vulnerable elements of the aircraft before detonating – as do contemporary Western AAMs. LOEC has a 20-year history of IR-detector design, for military and civil purposes, and has a range of wide-spectrum, large active-area IR sensors in development and manufacture. The PL-9 is attributed with "high acquisition and off-boresight firing capability", which would be a distinct advantage when fired from the decidedly unagile J-8. LOEC has also developed a helmet-mounted sight which, if claims that it rivals Russian developments in this field are true, would be a major asset to the J-8IIM or any Chinese combat aircraft.

The real key to the J-8IIM's improved air-to-air combat capability is its Phazotron Zhuk multimode radar, the first such system to enter service on a Chinese-built aircraft and dubbed 'Zhuk-8 II' by its Russian manufacturer. While Zhuk-8 II is slightly downgraded in comparison to the Zhuk-27, as fitted to the Sukhoi Su-27, it nevertheless represents a major step forward for China and one which Chinese industry must increasingly be in a position to produce itself. According to Phazotron's own documentation, the Zhuk-8 II has virtually all the air-to-air and air-to-surface modes of its Russian equivalents. For use against airborne targets the Zhuk-8 II boasts a range-while-scan capability in look-up and look-down modes, a track-while-scan capability to follow 10 targets while simultaneously engaging two, and a range of close-in air combat modes (vertical scan, HUD search, wide-angle and bore-sight). The Chinese radar does not have a TFR capability. Phazotron claims a TWS capability of eight targets while simultaneously engaging four for the Zhuk-27. In air-to-ground modes both synthetic aperture radars provide identical real beam ground-mapping and Doppler beam-sharpening modes, 'enlargement/freezing' capability, GMTI/tracking modes, air-to-surface ranging and navigation modes. Angular coverage for the Zhuk-8 II ranges from ±20° to ±60° to ±90° in azimuth and two to four bars in elevation – the same as the Zhuk-27. Peak power for both sets is 5 kW and average power 1 kW. Both radars have a claimed MTBF of 120 hours. The Zhuk-8 II is 10 kg (22 lb) lighter than the -27, weighing in at 250 kg (551 lb). Its detection capability is less advanced than the Zhuk-27, translating into a reduced (forward) range of 80 km (50 miles) compared to 100 km (220 miles) for the Russian radar. Aft range for the Zhuk-8 II is 40 km (25 miles) compared to 55 km (34 miles).

The Zhuk-8 II improves the J-8IIM's ground attack capability, although no public statements have been made about the supply of improved (Russian) air-to-ground armament to China. Shenyang has only displayed the aircraft carrying standard Chinese-built dumb bombs and rocket pods. These include NORINCO low-drag 250-kg, 500-kg and 1000-kg GP bombs and 57-mm HE rocket pods. An anti-shipping capability, using the Ying-Ji 1 (Eagle Strike 1) YJ-1/C-801 ASM, is also claimed. The J-8IIM has an internal gun, the 23-mm Type 23-3 twin-barrelled cannon, which is belly-mounted with an ammunition pack of 200 rounds. The aircraft has seven hard-points: three under each wing, and one ventral station which is stressed for the highest weights. The outer wing stations are plumbed for fuel tanks and the two inner stations are used chiefly for AAM carriage.

On a hi-hi air combat mission, with a Mach 0.8 transit at 11000 m (36,000 ft) to the target and five minutes combat fuel reserves, the J-8IIM has a combat radius of 1000 km (620 miles), with an unspecified warload. At 500 m (1,640 ft) this range is reduced to 350 km (220 miles). A notional combat air patrol, with only 10 minutes on station and five minutes combat fuel, allows the J-8IIM a radius of action of 600 km (375 miles). For lo-hi air-to-ground missions, with a Mach 0.74 transit, the J-8IIM has a combat radius of 500 km (310 miles) with five minutes combat fuel and a Mach 0.8 transit back to base.

In the cockpit, Shenyang has made some changes to the 1960s-era avionics, and chief among these is the addition of a new Chinese-built HUD and HOTAS controls. An autopilot with low-altitude pull-up and stability augmentation functions has been added. Onboard systems, including the RWR, stores management and radar combat modes, are linked through an ARINC-429 databus to the aircraft's fire control computer. TACAN navigation equipment has been installed along with a Xian INS/GPS system. A single mono-

The J-8IIM has only been shown with loads of 'dumb' ordnance. China is believed to have PGMs and airborne designation systems in advanced stages of development.

chrome 'MFD' display and associated control buttons have been mounted high on the instrument panel, above the standard 'clockwork' instruments, to the left of the HUD. In a similar position, to the right of the HUD, is the RWR display. Shenyang claims a datalink system is fitted to the J-8IIM. To drive this new equipment the onboard (AC) electrical system has been boosted from a 6-kVA system to twin 15-kVA generators. For self-defence, the aircraft has a 360° RWR system with antennas on the fin and chaff/flare dispensers.

The first (rebuilt) J-8IIM flew on 31 March 1996 and an unknown number have been built to date. It is not even certain if a full standard J-8IIM has been completed. Chinese sources have variously described the design as intended for the PLA(AF) and exclusively for export. Hampered by an ageing airframe and obsolete engines, the J-8IIM represents the last attempt at wringing some value from a project which, after all, has provided employment for over 30 years. The addition of much improved weapons and avionics represents a dramatic increase in capability for an aircraft which was not considered to be a credible threat from its inception. The impetus behind the J-8IIM is obviously China's ongoing procurement of the Su-27 and the looming licence-production deal being bartered with Sukhoi. With new-found access to such technol-ogy, it makes sense to integrate it with indigenous designs to gain a better understanding of 'how things work'. The J-8IIM lags far behind the Su-27 in terms of capability – China's acquisition of the Su-27 ultimately brings with it a major shift in the balance of air power in the region – but the J-8IIM will at least be a 'testbed' for Chinese-developed technolo-gies which were previously beyond the country's grasp. This in turn means that China will never again be restricted to a choice between fickle foreign suppliers and inadequate indigenous military technology. With the J-10, and others, waiting in the wings, the J-8IIM may yet turn out to be the first stepping stone to true Chinese air power.

Robert Hewson

Specification
Shenyang Aircraft Corporation J-8IIM
Type: twin-engined all-weather interceptor/fighter with secondary ground-attack capability
Powerplant: two Liyang WP-13B turbojets, rated at 47.1 kN (10,584 lb) dry, 68.67 kN (15,430 lb) reheat
Length overall: 21.389 m (70.17 ft)
Height overall: 5.41 m (17.74 ft)
Wingspan: 9.344 m (30.65 ft)
Wing area: 42.2 m² (454.25 sq ft)
Empty weight: 10371 kg (22,864 lb)
Normal fuel load: 4200 kg (9,259 lb)
Normal take-off weight: 15288 kg (33,704 lb)
Maximum take-off weight: 18879 kg (41,620 lb)
Service ceiling: 18000 m (59,055 ft)
Rate of climb: 224 m/s (44,100 ft/min) to 1000 m (3,280 ft) at Mach 0.9; 160 m/s (31,500 ft/min) to 5000 m (16,404 ft) at Mach 0.9
Maximum range: 1900 km (1180 miles)
Take-off speed: 330 km/h (205 mph; 178 kt)
Take-off distance (with reheat): 630 m (2,067 ft)
Landing speed: 300 km/h (186 mph; 164 kt)
Landing distance (with brake-chute): 900 m (559 ft)

The LOEC helmet-mounted sight (HMS)

While HMS systems are receiving growing attention from Western manufacturers, relatively few nations have yet to place them in service. Russian systems such as the Su-27's NSts-27 (NSc-27) and the MiG-29's Shch-3YM-1 have no real Western parallel (except perhaps in Israel). At Air Show China '96, the Luoyang Electro-Optical Equipment Research Institute of AVIC revealed its first helmet-mounted sight (HMS) system, which was declared to be operational. The Chinese HMS is a lightweight bracket-mounted system that uses a single small sighting reticle and a pair of cockpit-mounted 'head-tracking' sensors. The system is claimed to offer off-boresight engagement capability (coupled with LOEC's PL-9 AAM) and an ARINC 429 interface.

Specification:
Field of view: azimuth ±60°
pitch ±40°
Accuracy: <0° 35'
Head Movement range: forward and back 180 mm (7.08 in)
left to right 400 mm (15.7 im)
up and down 200 mm (7.87 in)
Weight: 0.2 kg/0.44 lb (added to head)
Power consumption: total 27V DC/20 W

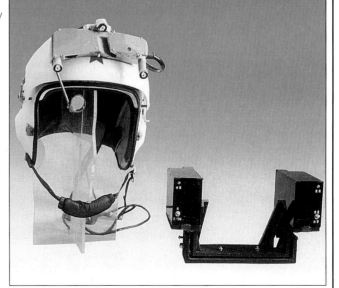

Changhe Z-8, Harbin Z-9 and Changhe Z-11

Curious Chinese helicopter developments

At Air Show China '96, the China aviation industry put on a show of force, displaying to the public virtually every type of military and civil aircraft currently in production in China. Except, that is, for helicopters, which were represented solely by the Harbin Z-9A Haitung (Dolphin). The Z-9A is certainly the most sophisticated helicopter under development in China, being a licence-built version of the Aérospatiale (Eurocopter France) SA 365N1 Dauphin. The Z-9A is touted as a military/civil multipurpose helicopter suitable for such tasks as passenger transport, off-shore support, air ambulance, search and rescue, and survey. In China, however, it is being built principally for the People's Liberation Army as a troop transport and anti-tank helicopter. The aircraft on display at the show carried a stylish red, white and blue finish,

but other photos seen at Zhuhai showed the Z-9 in wrap-round grey/green camouflage. Assembly of an initial batch of 50 Z-9s, equivalent to the AS 365N/N1, began in the mid-1980s – the last of these were built as Z-9As (N1), with an increase in the amount of local components used. The current production version, which first flew on 16 January 1992, is the Z-9A-100, which is still not entirely 100 per cent Chinese built. The engines are built under licence by South Power Corporation as the 734-shp (546-kW) WZ-8A.

The aircraft on show at Zhuhai, a Z-9A-100, had an interesting mix of AS 365N1 and N2 design features. The Chinese helicopter had the tail assembly of the N2 attached to an N1 fuselage. The AS 365N2 has 11 (wider-chord) blades in its tail rotor compared to the 13 blades in the N1. The N2's tail is all composite,

whereas the N/N1 tail was composite but with a metal fenestron assembly. The N2 has fixed undercarriage doors which the N1 and the Z-9A-100, it seems, do not.

It was China's other helicopter manufacturer, Changhe Aircraft Industries, that was conspicuous by its absence. The lack of aircraft on display by Changhe was made all the more pronounced by the evidence on its company stand in the exhibition hall of a hitherto completely unpublicised Chinese helicopter, the Changhe Z-11. It was described as a 'light multi-purpose helicopter'. A handful of photographs appeared in brochures with virtually no accompanying information – nor were any Changhe representatives inclined to comment on the project. The Z-11 appears to be intended, initially, as a military type, and all aircraft seen to date have been wearing the colours of the PLA.

It is clear that the Z-11 is based on the Aérospatiale/Eurocopter AS 350 Ecureuil/AS 550 Fennec, but Eurocopter is not yet ready to comment on this. The sparse details available at Air Show China

'96 stated that the Z-11 has an empty weight of 1256 kg (2769 lb), a (maximum) take-off weight of 2200 kg (4850 lb) and a cruising speed of 240 km/h (149 mph). Its maximum range was given as 598 km (372 miles) and ceiling as 5250 m (17,224 ft). Further details released after the show stated that the single-engined Z-11 is powered by a 685-hp (510-kW) Liming WZ-8D. Additional performance figures included a range of 600 km (373 miles). One source reported that the Z-11 had been under study since 1991 and obtained final go-ahead in 1994, with Sikorsky acting as technical consultant. This seems surprising, as the Z-11 clearly has its roots in a Eurocopter design and Changhe has close ties with the Franco/German firm. The same source also announced that the Z-11's first flight (at company headquarters in Jiangxi province) took place on 26 December 1996. This fact is at odds with photographs of two airborne aircraft, released by Changhe, in November 1996. Interestingly, press reports in Hong Kong during early 1996 suggested that the PLA forces moving into the former RAF airfield at Sek Kong would be operating "Dauphins (Z-9) and Ecureuils."

Changhe's more public helicopter project, the Z-8 (a licence-built Sud-Est/Aérospatiale Super Frelon), continues its leisurely production and development phases.

Robert Hewson

Above and right: The Changhe Z-11 helicopter was quietly unveiled at Air Show China '96, with little comment on its obvious Eurocopter origins.

Left: The Harbin Z-9A-100 has many features of the SA 365N/N1 Dauphin, such as its undercarriage doors, combined with the very different tail design of the SA 365N2.

Left and above: The Changhe Z-8 (based on the radar-equipped SA 312Ja Super Frelon) is now in operational service with the Chinese navy. A transport version, with a rear loading ramp, has been developed in parallel. Changhe has also demonstrated water landings with the Z-8.

Northrop Grumman F-14 'Bombcat'

Attack Tomcat sharpens its claws

Taking another large step towards improving the strike capabilities of its F-14 fleet, the US Navy has deployed its first Tomcat squadron (VF-103) with the proven Lockheed Martin LANTIRN (Low Altitude Navigation and Targeting Infra-Red for Night) system. The addition of this laser guidance system to the F-14 allows the Tomcat to undertake autonomous long-range precision strike missions, day or night, while retaining its air-to-air combat capability and reducing the need for fighter escorts.

Designed in 1969 by Grumman Aerospace (now Northrop Grumman), the F-14 was envisioned from the start, by its creators, as a multi-role aircraft. With 10 external hardpoints, the Tomcat was to carry a wide variety of air-to-air and air-to-ground ordnance and continue defending the fleet in much the same way as its predecessor, the F-4 Phantom. The Navy, more concerned with the threat of Soviet long-range bombers, emphasised the fighter's long-range intercept and fleet defence capabilities. As a result, the AWG-15 air-to-ground attack system was incorporated into the F-14, but remained neglected for almost 20 years.

In 1987, the Navy's focus began to shift to multi-role aircraft as the F/A-18 became a common sight on US carriers. With this shift, the Naval Operational Advisory Group (OAG) issued a recommendation that the US Navy could no longer afford costly single-mission aircraft. Furthermore, the OAG also recommended that the F-14 community should begin to utilise its latent attack capabilities. During 1988, the Navy's Operational Test and Evaluation Force (primarily VX-4 at NAS China Lake) undertook separation tests with various air-to-ground stores on the F-14.

Testing began with the standard Mk 80 series of GP bombs and continued with cluster munitions, such as the Mk 20 Rockeye, and various training rounds. Air-to-ground stores are carried between the engines in an area commonly referred to as 'the tunnel', on modified Phoenix pallets. Bomb racks based on the F/A-18's horizontal ejector racks gave way to a BRU-32

bomb rack fitted into an ADU-703 adapter. This combination can then be fitted to all four Phoenix pallets in the tunnel. For training exercises involving the Mk 76 25-lb training round, the BRU-42 ITER (a modified triple ejector rack), is fitted to the BRU-32. This combination is usually only fitted to the two forward Phoenix pallets.

By 1990, the F-14 'Bombcat' began to be integrated into the battle group as VF-24 'Renegades' and VF-211 'Checkmates' became the first fleet squadrons to drop bombs from the F-14 in August of that year. Unfortunately for the Tomcat community, the programme had not reached a level where the Navy could allow the F-14s to utilise their new-found

Right: This VF-41 'Black Aces' F-14A is seen launching from the USS Theodore Roosevelt during Operation Deliberate Force, soon after VF-41 became the first Tomcat squadron to ever attack ground targets in anger.

Below: A 'Jolly Rogers' F-14B shows off its mixed-load capability, carrying AIM-9s (on stations 1A), an AIM-54 (on 1B), an AIM-7 (on 4), and a Mk 82 bomb (on station 3). Two GBU-12 LGBs could be carried on stations 3 and 6.

'Bombcat' weapons can be carried in 'the tunnel', on modified Phoenix pallets. However, TARPS-capable F-14s cannot carry LANTIRN.

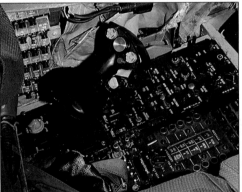

Above and left: The most significant change to the rear cockpit of the 'Bombcat' is the addition of the 8 x 8-in (20 x 20-cm) programmable tactical information display (PTID) which can display radar and LANTIRN information for the RIO. The PTID's side-stick hand controllers (left) were originally manufactured for the A-12 programme and withdrawn from storage for the 'Bombcats'.

talent in the war with Iraq just five months later. As the Iraqi air force fell victim to USAF F-15s (and a pair of self-escorting Navy F/A-18s), the Tomcat community found itself on the sidelines, escorting strike packages whose path had been cleared by the Air Force fighters and performing reconnaissance missions into some of the most heavily defended areas in Iraq for CENTCOM.

After the war, F-14 squadrons continued their work-ups with an ever-growing air-to-ground arsenal. The Navy's test and evaluation squadrons continued to test drop various stores and soon began trials with laser-guided bombs (LGBs) in order to clear them for use by fleet squadrons. The GBU-16 1,000-lb LGB was among the first approved for the F-14 in 1994. VF-103 'Sluggers' wasted no time incorporating this weapon into its inventory. On 2 May 1994, two F-14s from the 'Sluggers' delivered three Paveway II GBU-16s on the Capo Frasca bombing range on the coast of Sardinia while Air Wing 17 Intruders and Hornets 'lased' the targets for direct hits.

In the autumn of 1995, VF-41 'Black Aces' found itself patrolling the skies over Bosnia. Deploying from the USS *Theodore Roosevelt* in mixed sections with F/A-18s from VFA-87, the Tomcats carried a variety of A/G ordnance, including GBU-16s, in support of IFOR. The situation on the ground soon deteriorated enough that IFOR commanders ordered coalition air strikes against Bosnian-Serb targets in Bosnia. This time the Tomcat would not be left on the sidelines. On 5 September two 'Black Aces' Tomcats, descending from high altitude in 50° dives, delivered their GBU-16s against an ordnance facility, marking them as the first F-14 squadron to deploy air-to-ground stores in combat. Their F/A-18 wingmen used the AAS-38A NITE Hawk system to designate the targets for the F-14s before commencing their own attacks. VF-41 Tomcats delivered a total of 24,000 lb (10900 kg) of ordnance during Operation Deliberate Force, including 10 GBU-16s by five aircrew, on Serbian targets. The Tomcat community had finally proved what it could not during the Gulf War: the F-14 is indeed a capable strike platform.

Only the lack of a laser designator/targeting system prevented the Tomcat from achieving its full potential as a strike aircraft, but VF-103 was well on its way to deploying such a system to make the Tomcat a truly independent,

multi-role aircraft. The project began in the summer of 1994 when Lockheed Martin representatives visited NAS Patuxent River, Maryland, to perform structural testing on the F-14's wing and fuselage stations for a modified version of the LANTIRN Targeting System (LTS). Shortly thereafter, Fighter Wing Atlantic was directed to demonstrate the capability of the Tomcat/LTS combination. In early 1995, Lockheed Martin, together with Fairchild and Litton, funded the $1.5 million modification of the demonstration aircraft from VF-103. At NAS Oceana, Northrop Grumman carried out the necessary modifications to enable the aircraft to carry LANTIRN.

The Tomcat's LTS uses a modified version the US Air Force's AN/AAQ-14 targeting pod, used by its F-15E and late-block F-16s, while omitting the AN/AAQ-13 navigation pod. Incorporation of the latter would have caused a need for extensive modification to the aircraft's software, while at the same time escalating the cost and delaying the deployment of the system. A global positioning system (GPS) has been added to the pod, making the Tomcat the first aircraft with this unique capability. The GPS receives satellite navigational data through an antenna in the aircraft's spine, providing the aircrew with an accurate position, target location in GPS co-ordinates, and range to target. Also added is an inertial measuring unit (IMU). The IMU measures variables in velocity, pitch, and yaw to stabilise the FLIR's line of sight (LoS). By incorporating the IMU into the pod, it uses those velocity variables inherent in the pod to create a more stable image. On aircraft such as the F-15E, the system uses an IMU located in the aircraft's fuselage, measuring variables inherent in the airframe and different from those of the pylon-mounted FLIR, affecting accuracy. Together the GPS and IMU form what is called the integrated targeting system (ITS), combining data from both parent systems into a single hybrid solution. This gives the Tomcat's LTS the ability to stabilise the FLIR's line of sight beyond the capabilities of any current system, greatly improving accuracy.

The heart of the LTS is of course its FLIR and laser designator. The FLIR has a field of regard (FoR) of 150° in any direction

This VF-41 F-14A, 'Fast Eagle 101', is seen on the deck of the Roosevelt on 5 September 1995 about to undertake the F-14's first bombing mission against the Bosnian Serbs.

Right: This sequence of photographs shows the first GBU-16 launch (made by Commander Hnarakis and Lieutenant Commander Slade) by a VF-41 F-14 against the Vieques Island range.

from the centred-forward position. Its only limitation is to the left, where the FLIR line of sight impacts the fuselage. There are two fields of view (FoV) available to aircrew – wide (5.87°) with x4:1 magnification, and narrow (1.68°) with x10 magnification. The latter gives the Tomcat's LTS a keen edge over the F/A-18 Hornet's NITE Hawk system's narrow FoV and x4 magnification, in the long-range acquisition and identification of targets. There is also an 'expand' view available with a x20 magnification, an electronic enhancement of the narrow FoV. This mode is extremely pixelated, yet helpful for precise positioning of the targeting laser. The laser has two wavelengths, 1.56 microns for training and 1.06 microns for combat. The pod also contains its own computer with all GBU ballistics data and has limited interface with any of the aircraft's systems. Mounted on the starboard shoulder station 8B, the

A VF-143 'Pukin Dogs' F-14A drops a 1,000-lb Mk 83 AIR retarded bomb during early 'Bombcat' trials. LANTIRN has now transformed the F-14's once-limited attack capability.

LANTIRN targeting pod receives data from the AWG-15 and AWG-9 weapons systems through a MIL-STD 1553 databus. The latter must be added to all F-14As and Bs in the right wing glove, but the F-14D is already configured with a MIL-STD 1553 databus. The pod then sends only FLIR imagery with targeting data to a modified display in the rear cockpit.

The 8x8-in programmable tactical information display (PTID) replaces the circular target information display (TID) in the radar intercept officer's (RIO) cockpit. The new display is capable of presenting both radar and LANTIRN information. Using separate controls the RIO can adjust the contrast and intensity of whichever system requires his attention, enabling a

rapid change from air-to-air and air-to-ground modes. The incorporation of the PTID also allows the recording of FLIR imagery and radar data for later analysis. This capability was not previously available to the F-14 community and is a powerful training tool. A control panel installed on the left side of the rear cockpit – in addition to a hand control originally manufac-

This F-14B from VF-103 'Jolly Rogers' (the former 'Sluggers') is carrying a LANTIRN AN/AAQ-14 targeting pod (LTS) and an AIM-9M Sidewinder.

Left: This NAWC (AD) F-14A is seen test dropping two 1,000-lb GBU-16 LGBs during February 1994, after the Tomcat had been cleared to drop Mk 80 series GP bombs.

tured for the now cancelled A-12 project – allows the RIO to command all LTS functions in a variety of mission profiles.

During a pre-planned strike mission, aircrew will navigate to the target area using GPS and the aircraft's own inertial navigation system (INS). The RIO will then acquire the target by pointing the FLIR at a GPS reference point (latitude, longitude and elevation), providing the pilot with steering commands overlaid on the FLIR imagery on his vertical display indicator (VDI). This is the pilot's primary attitude indicator and also displays information from the television camera system (TCS). There is no LTS data presented on the HUD. The pilot will continue to follow the steering commands until

the release point and drop the LGB as the RIO continues to designate the target with the laser. Bomb damage assessment is recorded by the FLIR sensor as the weapon reaches the target. Two modes are commonly used in identification and prosecution of targets of opportunity. In the 'cue to HUD' mode, a pilot conducting a visual search may identify a possible target. The RIO is then requested to select the 'cue to HUD' mode for the LTS. This positions the FLIR line of sight to a position in the HUD field of view. The pilot manoeuvres the aircraft, positioning the target in the HUD. The RIO can then acquire and identify the target in the FLIR. In the 'snowplow' mode, the FLIR line of sight is set at -15°. If a possible target enters the FLIR's field of view, the RIO will initiate an area track, centre and identify the target.

Weapons load-outs vary, yet according to VF-103 aircrew a typical configuration for most (Bosnian) missions included an AIM-9M and AIM-7M on stations 1A and B, respectively, port shoulder; external fuel tanks on stations 2 and 7, engine nacelles; GBU-16 1,000-lb LGBs on modified Phoenix pallets,

This VF-14 aircraft is seen firing a salvo of 5-in Zuni rockets off the Virginia coast in August 1996. (The 5-in Zuni is being withdrawn in favour of 2.75-in rockets.) The Tomcat community is receiving a Zuni capability as a result of its emerging foward air controller (airborne) (FAC(A)) mission.

stations 3 and 6, between the engine nacelles, forward; an AIM-7 on station 4, between engine nacelles, aft; and an AIM-9 and the LANTIRN pod on stations 8A and B, respectively, starboard shoulder. During late March and early April 1995, Commander Hnarakis and Lieutenant Commander Slade of VF-103 demonstrated the capabilities of the modified F-14 by conducting a total of 40 sorties, deploying laser-guided training rounds and inert GBU-16s. The final demonstration sortie involved dropping live GBU-16s on the Vieques Island range, east of Puerto Rico. Weapons scored direct hits on their targets. Following the successful conclusion of the demonstration phase of the programme, Lockheed Martin received a preliminary contract in June. A formal $46 million contract was awarded on 11 November 1995.

VF-103 soon began preparation and training of aircrew, with the goal of having the squadron operational with the system before its deployment in June 1996. It was also during this period that VF-103 dropped its 'Slugger' identity and took up the skull-and-crossbones insignia of the now-decommissioned VF-84 'Jolly Rogers'. In doing so, VF-103 preserved a 50-year-old naval aviation legacy. By spring 1996 the new 'Jolly Rogers' had received five modified aircraft and had begun to develop tactics for employing the LTS. The 'Jolly Rogers', ready to integrate their system and tactics into air wing operations, embarked aboard USS *Enterprise* for a two-week joint fleet exercise with the Royal Navy. From 26 April through 17 May 1996, aircrew repeatedly demonstrated the capabilities of the new 'Bombcat', at times even designating targets for LGB-carrying Sea Harriers from HMS *Illustrious*.

On 26 June 1996, the 'Jolly Rogers' once again embarked aboard USS *Enterprise* for a six-month deployment. The squadron by then was fully operational with 14 aircraft, nine of these being modified with LANTIRN. Of the nine LTS-configured Tomcats, six were also fitted with the MXV-810 'Cat's Eye' NVG system, further expanding on the F-14's night-attack capabilities. The remaining five aircraft were configured with the TARPS. During the six-month deployment, VF-103 employed the LTS in several ancillary missions.

Forward air controller (airborne) has been a mission mostly associated with the USMC F/A-18D, yet the F-14 community has been undertaking this mission since 1995, although only in daylight. For VF-103's FAC(A) trained aircrews, the addition of LANTIRN and NVGs allowed them to operate at night. Over Iraq, 'Jolly Rogers' aircrew soon employed the LTS in reconnaissance missions, detecting SAM batteries that the Iraqi army had hoped to save by relocating them. Once found, the RIO used the FLIR to lock onto the SAM battery, and GPS co-ordinates for the target were then recorded.

The LTS also enhances the Tomcat's air-to-air role. The FLIR may be used as a means of visually acquiring targets at long range, allowing aircrew to perform a positive raid count before entering weapons range. The FLIR's FoV is also greater than that of the TCS and may be operated at night,

allowing a greater flexibility in operations. Close air support, surface search, and target hit assessment (post-strike) can also be performed by the LTS-equipped Tomcat. 'Jolly Rogers' F-14s were also in high demand by Air Wing 17's strike leaders, which tasked the Tomcats with the highest priority targets during training exercises and contingency planning. This tasking, according to Commander Hnarakis, CO of the 'Jolly Rogers', is the ultimate sign of success for the new Tomcat as the system's potential was fully recognised. With the conclusion of VF-103's deployment, Grumman's concept of a multi-role Tomcat has finally been realised, yet expansion of the system's potential is already in the planning stage. The Tomcat fleet is due to receive the ANVIS-9 NVG system as a replacement for the MXV-810. The new system provides a wider field of view, a x3 increase in light amplification, and lower cost, pos-

sibly allowing all LTS-configured F-14s to receive the new system. The Tomcat may also be the first aircraft to deploy the Joint Direct Attack Munition (JDAM) and Joint Stand-Off Weapon (JSOW). Both systems use GPS to guide the weapons to their targets. If there is a need to obtain a target's GPS co-ordinates through onboard sensors, the Tomcat is the only aircraft currently available with a GPS system able to reprogramme these weapons.

Twenty-seven years after the type's first flight, the F-14 is undertaking a new mission that has given it an extension on life. With the retirement of the A-6 Intruder, and the F/A-18E/F still several years from service, the LANTIRN-equipped Tomcat is the only aircraft in the fleet available to battle group commanders that is capable of carrying out the long-range surgical strike mission.

Jose M. Ramos

Greek Armed Forces

Elliniki Polimiki Aeroporia

Taktiki Aeroporikis Dynamis (Tactical Air Force)

110 PM Larissa

337 MPK 'Fantasma' will continue to operate the F-4E until 2010, since the EPA has chosen to modernise 40 F-4Es from FY 1972 and 1977. The upgrade will be done by DASA, which will modernise the Greek F-4Es to a similar standard as the F-4F ICE aircraft. Since 337 MPK has an air defence task, it has a forward operating location (FOL) at 130 Sminarchia Machis Limnos, situated in the northeastern Aegean.

The reconnaissance assets of 348 MTA 'Matia' were boosted with the delivery of 29 former Luftwaffe RF-4Es from 1992. Before that, the squadron comprised only four operational RF-4Es, painted in the jungle colours. The former Luftwaffe Phantoms are easily recognised by their 'lizard' camouflage. According to 348 MTA pilots, the dark camouflage is effective against the Greek landscape in the autumn and winter and when flying at low level over the dark blue sea. An advantage of the former Luftwaffe RF-4Es is their capability to carry and deliver ground attack armament.

The Block 30 F-16s, currently in use with 111 PM at Nea Agchialos, will be used to reactivate 347 MPK at Larissa to become the first new Greek F-16 squadron in June 1997. 347 MV 'Perseos' was a former A-7H operator at Larissa and was disbanded in July 1992.

349 MAI 'Kronos' received former 341 MAI F-5s in 1993. This increase in F-5A/Bs led to a transfer of all 12 NF-5s to 343 MAI at Thessaloniki. 349 MAI operates F-5A/Bs and the RF-5A, which is used as a regular F-5A from Larissa and from a FOL at 134 SM Santorini, situated in the centre of the southern Aegean. The two F-5 squadrons perform the daylight air defence role with the approximately 70 survivors of the original 150 delivered, and are nominated to convert to the F-16. In late 1997/early 1998, 'Kronos' will become the second new F-16 squadron, also equipped with the current Block 30 F-16s of 111 PM. Relocation of 349 MAI to 113 PM Thessaloniki will take place before the summer of 1997 in order to clear the hardened shelters for the expected F-16s of 347 MPK.

In mid-1996 370 MEE was deactivated, followed by a transfer of its T-33As to 221 MEE at 115 PM Souda.

111 PM Nea Agchialos

341 MAI 'Assos' operated F-5s with diverse colour schemes until it was deactivated in late 1993. The F-5s were divided between 343 MAI and 349 MAI. The former also took over the F-5 SMET task of 341 MAI. In the summer of 1996, the EPA expressed a need for an additional 80 F-16s; they were to have been used USAF F-16A/Bs currently stored at the AMARC in Arizona. These F-16A/Bs would equip the reactivated 341 MPK, among three others squadrons.

However, in November 1996 Prime Minister Simitis presented the Defence Spending Proposal for the next decade, which comprised the purchase of 50 new F-16C/Ds instead of 80 used F-16A/Bs. They will be Block 50 or Block 52 F-16s and are planned to be delivered around 2000. 341 MPK will be reactivated then and be equipped with the F-16. When 341 MPK achieves IOC, it is intended to relocate it to 113 PM at Thessaloniki. Until then, all 37 EPA Block 30 F-16C/Ds (three have been written off since 1989) will be operated by 330 and 346 MPK, both based at Nea Agchialos. The new Block 50 F-16s will be delivered to these two units, which will transfer their Block 30 F-16C/Ds to 347 and 349 MPK.

In 1996 the capacity of the F-16s was boosted by an order of 84 AGM-88B HARM and 50 AIM-120B missiles. EPA staff have shown interest in buying 20 to 25 laser-designator pods for the F-16, which must also be compatible with the A-7. Offers are expected from GEC-Marconi (TIALD), Lockheed Martin (LANTIRN) and Raphael (LITENING).

The Greek F-16s defend the whole of Greece from centrally situated Nea Agchialos, as well as from several FOLs. One of the most active FOLs is 115 PM Souda, on Crete.

113 PM Thessaloniki

In late 1993, 343 MAI 'Asteri' received a number of F-5A/Bs, including several former Royal Jordanian AF examples painted in desert colours. The unit also assume the SMET role from 341 MAI. In 1994 all 12 NF-5s were received from 349 MAI at Larissa. Plans of summer 1996 foresaw 'Asteri' becoming an F-16 squadron, equipped with its share of the 80 former USAF F-16A/Bs intended to be purchased. Since, under the Defence Spending Proposal of November 1996, new F-16s will not be delivered until 2000, 343 MAI will continue to operate the F-5 for a few more years. Before the summer of 1997 349 MAI is expected to relocate from Larissa to 113 PM. Thessaloniki will then become the last Greek F-5 base.

The C-47s of 355/1 STM at Sedes are the oldest aircraft in service with the EPA today, and are expected to be operated into the next millennium. The oldest Dakota is former RAF C-47B KK156, build in 1943 and delivered to Greece in 1949. This C-47 is still performing well as a target-towing aircraft. Four other Dakotas remain operational, of the original 80, including 49622 which is the sole remaining Dakota of those which served with 13 Sminos, the Greek C-47 flight which was deployed to the Korean War. One C-47 is detached to 110 PM to serve as a VIP transport in the ATA flight.

114 PM Tanagra

At Tanagra 38 Mirage 2000EG/BGs are currently shared by 331 'Aegeas' and 332 MPK 'Geraki'. The EPA satisfaction with the Mirage 2000 resulted in a request for another 10 Mirage 2000s in the Defence Spending Proposal of November 1996. To defend the western part of the central Aegean, 114 PM has a Mirage 2000 FOL at Skiros.

Since, under the Defence Spending Proposal of November 1996, new F-16s will not be delivered until 2000, 342 MPK 'Sparta' will continue to operate the Mirage F1CGs. 342 MPK shares a central Aegean FOL with 349 MAI F-5s at 134 SM Santorini. The four T-33As of 366 SEE are still operated by 114 PM.

115 PM Souda

Since 1975 the A-7H has been operated by 340 'Alepou' and 345 MV 'Lailaps'. In July 1992 115 PM received the T/A-7Hs of the deactivated 347 MV from Larissa. After more than two decades of service about 45 of the original 60 A-7Hs remain operational, as well as five TA-7Hs.

From the more than 150 T-33As delivered to the EPA from 1951, about 30 remain operational; almost all T-33s are now stationed at Souda. 222 MEE is tasked with target towing, mainly for the nearby NAMFI (NATO Missile Training Centre) range but also for gunnery exercise. For target-towing purposes, 222 MEE is equipped with three surviving Dayglo-painted T-33As. In mid-1996 the T-33As of the disbanded 370 MEE were transferred to 222 MEE at Souda. With the 'T-bird' fleet boosted to 18 operational T-33As, plus some in reserve, 221 MEE expects to operate the type for a few more years; both loss rate and maintenance costs of the type are low.

116 PM Araxos

All Starfighters had disappeared from Araxos by June 1993; 30 of the type in the best condition (20 F-104G, six RF-104G, four TF-104G) have been placed in storage, and the remaining F-104s were dumped at 132 SM Agrinion. As an interim solution to the hiatus which resulted at Araxos between the F-104s' withdrawal and the (delayed) delivery of the A-7E Corsairs, 115 PM deployed a number of A-7Hs. Although referred to as 347 MV in the past, it was actually a 115 PM detachment. In April 1993 the first A-7E Corsairs arrived at Araxos. Modernisation of the TA-7Cs took place at the US Naval Air Depot at Jacksonville and the two-seat Corsairs were redelivered to Greece as TA-7Hs. Currently, 116 PM is equipped with 32 A-7Es and four TA-7Hs, operated by 335 MV 'Tigreis' and 336 MV 'Olympus'. Hellenic Aerospace Industries has stored 16 A-7Es and four TA-7Cs for spare parts, and eight to 10 of them are expected to be brought to operational status before mid-1997.

117 PM Andravida

339 MPK 'Ajax' has a primary ground-attack task and initially operated the SEA jungle-painted F-4Es. Since 1993 these Phantoms have been repainted in Aegean Blue, a process that finished in 1996. The FY 1972 and 1977 F-4Es of 339 MPK will receive an upgrade by DASA, bringing them to a similar standard as the F-4F ICE aircraft. Following this modernisation the Greek Phantoms are expected to be operated until 2010. 338 MPK 'Aris' continues to operates all former US Air National Guard F-4Es, which will remain in the USAF Hill Gray II colour scheme for the air-defence role.

Above: 334 MPK is based at Iraklion with the Mirage F1CG for the defence of Crete. This aircraft carries an AIM-9P Sidewinder.

Right: 349 MAI flies the F-5A/B in the daylight air defence role, but also has a few RF-5As which are flown as fighters.

Araxos houses two units of ex-US Navy A-7Es, aircraft from 335 MV being shown. TA-7H trainers converted from TA-7Cs are also on charge.

Carrying a dart target for aerial gunnery practice is an F-4E from 337 MPK at Larissa. These aircraft are being upgraded to ICE standard.

Tactical reconnaissance resources have been swelled by the delivery of 29 ex-Luftwaffe RF-4Es to 348 MTA at Larissa.

This Dakota is on the strength of 355/1 STM but is detached to 110 PM to serve as a VIP transport for Tactical AF headquarters.

The main transport fleet of 356 MTM was swelled in 1992 by the addition of five ex-USAF C-130Bs. The unit also flies YS-11s.

Some F-5As have received a new three-tone camouflage scheme. In addition to the main bases at Larissa and Thessaloniki, F-5s also operate from a FOL at Santorini.

126 SM Iraklion

Since 1977 334 MPK 'Thalos' has been based at Iraklion, equipped with the Mirage F1CG and tasked with the air defence of Crete. As the Mirage F1CG is only armed with the AIM-9P Sidewinder and the gun, it can not dogfight with Turkish F-16s. Therefore, the 111 PM FOL at Souda has to scramble its F-16s for interceptions. Another problem for 334 MPK is that Iraklion is an international airport, and commercial traffic is so dense during the high season that the unit has had to delay and even cancel missions.

Diikissi Aeroporikis Ipostirixis (Air Support Command)

112 PM Elefsis

During late 1995 355 MTM 'Ifaistos' received four ex-Slovenian (i.e., Yugoslavian) AF CL-215s, bringing the total number of Canadairs to 16. Slovenia transferred the CL-215s to Greece on the condition that the EPA would assist in fire-fighting in Slovenia when needed. 355 MTM's Dornier fleet has shrunk from the 15 Do 28Ds delivered in 1985 to five in 1996. The Dorniers are not loved by 355 MTM because

they are too slow and too noisy, but with no replacement in sight the Do 28D will have to soldier on. Until at least the year 2000 the main transport squadron – 356 MTM 'Iraklis' – will continue to operate two or three NAMC YS-11As, of the original six delivered in 1981. The YS-11As are used along with the 11 C-130H Hercules, the numbers of which were augmented in 1992 by five former USAF Lockheed C-130Bs. The latter are still painted in the European One camouflage and three remain operational today. The Hercules fleet is expected to grow even more, as the Defence Spending Proposals of November 1996 mention the purchase of six transport aircraft. The sole Grumman Gulfstream I was struck off charge in 1995 and was transferred to the EPA museum at Dekelia after 31 years of service.

Although thought to be withdrawn from use in 1990, one of the two AB 206 JetRangers is still operated by 358 MED 'Faethon' for VIP transport; it flies just enough to stay operational. Five AB 212s are also used for VIP transports. The main task of 358 MED is search and rescue, which it undertakes with 15 AB 205As. In addition to Elefsis, some examples are detached to the EPA bases of Araxos, Kalamata, Nea Achgialos and Souda, as well as on the islands of Chios, Limnos and Rhodos.

Dekelia

One could expect the Bell 47 helicopter to be withdrawn from service soon, but the opposite is true. The survivors of the 25 examples delivered in 1971 – Bell 47Gs and OH-13Hs – remain in service with 359 MAEDY. About five are still operated in the liaison and agricultural role, and are expected to continue to be flown into the next millennium, as the helicopters are useful and operational costs are low. Further crop-spraying tasks of the 359 MAEDY are performed with a dozen Grumman AgCats and about 20 PZL M-18A Dromaders.

The Diikissi Aeroporikis Ipostirixis is likely to be boosted with an early warning division in the next decade, as the November 1996 Defence Spending Proposal mentioned the purchase of three AEW aircraft. The preferred type is the Grumman E-2C Hawkeye.

Kratiko Ergostatio Aerosfakon

The Kratiko Ergostatio Aerosfakon (KEA, State Aerospace Industry) is the maintenance centre for the EPA and is situated at the Athens-Hellenikon airport. KEA is responsible for the maintenance of propeller-driven aircraft like C-47, Do 28, YS-11 and T-41D, as well as the helicopter types Bell 47, AB 205 and AB 212. Jet aircraft like the T-33, T-37 and F-5 are also overhauled at KEA.

The most advanced type which undergoes maintenance at KEA is the F-4E. The more modern aircraft – A-7, Mirage F1, Mirage 2000, F-16, T-2, P-3, CL-215 and Navy helicopters – are the responsibility of HAI at Tanagra.

CFSE treaty

Although having been placed in open storage since the early 1980s, the F-84Fs have officially been listed by the EPA as fighter aircraft. The total number of EPA aircraft exceeded CFSE treaty limits, so in September 1995 the Thunder-streaks stored at Preveza (Aktion) and Athens-Hellenikon were destroyed. It remains to be seen if the 30 stored Starfighters at Agrinion will survive when the new F-16s arrive in Greece.

Diikissi Aeroporikis Ekpedefsis (Air Training Command)

Dekelia

At the Skoli Ikarus at Dekelia, aptitude tests are performed by 360 MEA with five (not four) Grob 103 Twin Astir gliders, as is basic training with 19 Cessna T-41D Mescaleros.

Kalamata 120 PEAM

Since 1964 primary jet training has been performed with 34 Cessna T-37B/Cs by 361 MVE Mystras. In the mid-1980s replacement plans for the T-37 were abandoned, as they were in early 1995 when the EPA showed interest in 60 former Luftwaffe Alpha Jets. The Defence Spending Proposal of November 1996 included plans for 20 trainers, expected to be a turboprop like the PC-9, or more T-37s.

Elliniki Polimiki Aeroporia

UNIT	TYPE
110 PM, Larissa	
337 MPK 'Fantasma'	F-4E
348 MTA 'Matia'	RF-4E
349 MAI 'Kronos'	F-5A/B, RF-5A
ATA flight	C-47 (det from 355/1 STM)
111 PM, Nea Agchialos	
330 MPK 'Keraunos'	F-16C/D
346 MPK 'Iason'	F-16C/D
Det 358 MED	AB 205A
112 PM, Elefsis	
353 MNAS 'Albatross'	P-3B
355 MTM 'Ifaistos'	CL-215, Do 28D
356 MTM 'Iraklis'	C-130B/H, YS-11A
358 MED 'Faethon'	AB 205, AB 206, AB 212
113 PM, Thessaloniki	
343 MAI 'Asteri'	(N)F-5A/B
355/1 STM	C-47 (based at Sedes)
114 PM, Tanagra	
331 MPK 'Aegeas'	Mirage 2000EG/BG
332 MPK 'Geraki'	Mirage 2000EG/BG
342 MPK 'Sparta'	Mirage F1CG
366 SEE	T-33A
115 PM, Souda	
340 MV 'Alepou'	T/A-7H
345 MV 'Lailaps'	T/A-7H
222 MEE	T-33A
Det 358 MED	AB 205A
116 PM, Araxos	
335 MV 'Tigreis'	A-7E, TA-7H
335 MV 'Olympus'	A-7E, TA-7H
Det 358 MED	AB 205A
117 PM, Andravida	
338 MPK 'Aris'	F-4E
339 MPK 'Ajax'	F-4E
126 SM, Iraklion	
334 MPK 'Thalos'	Mirage F1CG
Dekelia	
360 MEA	T-41D, Grob 103
359 MAEDY	AgCat, Dromader, Bell 47
120 PEA, Kalamata	
361 MVE 'Mystras'	T-37B/C
362 MPE 'Nestor'	T-2E
363 MEE 'Danaos'	T-2E
Det 358 MED	AB 205A

Elliniki Polimiko Naftikon

In late 1996 only one operational HU-16B of 353 MNAS Albatross remains of the dozen Grumman Albatrosses delivered in 1969. The final Albatross is a former ECM platform which was stripped of its electronic equipment in summer 1996. It will be withdrawn from service before the end of 1996. In 1995 the first of four P-3As was delivered to HAI, and were to be used for ground instruction training and spare parts while the actual flying would be performed with four P-3Bs. Later this order was changed to six P-3Bs.

The first P-3B was officially handed over to the EPN on 31 May 1996, and arrived at Elefsis in June. It was a US Navy standard grey-camouflaged P-3B with toned-down Greek roundels and flag, but also had the EPN anchor logo flanked by 'P' and 'N' (for Polimiki Naftikon) painted on the nose. The EPN logo was short-lived, however; the EPA, which operates the aircraft for the Navy, considered it to be unacceptable and it was overpainted within two weeks of the aircraft's delivery. The EPN has already expressed its wish to provide the pilots for the Orion, to make it an all-Navy crew, but the EPA has resisted this idea.

The Greek Orion pilots and crew are currently being trained by former US Navy employees who are now working in a civilian firm. By late 1996 four P-3Bs had been delivered to 353 MNAS, and the squadron should be fully equipped by early 1997.

Diikissi E/P Naftikon (Navy Helicopter Command)

In 1994 the EPN took charge of the S-70B-6 Aegean Hawk, which is a hybrid of the SH-60B Sea Hawk and SH-60F Ocean Hawk operated by the US Navy. This helicopter is a LAMPS (Light Airborne Multi-Purpose System) platform which combines all possible tasks of the earlier helicopter types of the Diikissi Elikopteron Naftikon. The most important difference from the US Navy variants is the ASW system. The other helicopter type operated by the DEN is the AB 212, of which there are eight AB 212ASWs and two AB 212EWs.

The SH-60B/Fs employ a towed MAD and the S-70B-6 is equipped with a Bendix AN/ASQ-18(V)3 active dipping sonar for ASW. An Eaton AN/APS-143(V)3 pulse compression surveillance radar is used, which is compatible with the NFT Penguin Mk 2 Mod 7 anti-ship missile (the US Navy Sea Hawks are armed with Mk 46 or Mk 50 torpedoes). The first S-70B-6, with serial PN-51, was handed over to the EPN in October 1994 in the USA. The first three S-70B-6s were originally planned to be shipped to Greece by the end of 1994 but this batch was delayed, and the first Aegean Hawks arrived in Greece in the second half of 1995. The helicopters were unloaded at the EPN reserve heliport at Amfiali, where the S-70B-6s were assembled and flown to their base at Kotroni. With the arrival of the Aegean Hawks the new S-70 Sminos (Flight) was formed at Kotroni, and in the summer of 1995 the first mission was flown. The fifth and final Aegean Hawk was flown to Kotroni in February 1996.

With the arrival of the high-tech Aegean Hawk, the DEN's training programme had to be adjusted. In May 1996 a new DEN unit was established. At the Skoli E/P Naftikon (SEPN, Naval Helicopter School), a student can qualify for the Alouette III after 87 flight hours and two months of ground school, while the AB 212 student clocks 157 flight hours combined with three months of ground school. Experienced Alouette III pilots become Aegean Hawk pilots after about 65 flight hours; a novices will have to undergo a total of 42 flight hours and two months of ground school with the Alouette III, followed by 63 hours in an AB 212 plus three months of ground school. The differences between the controls and instruments of the Alouette III and the S-70B-6 have proved to be extensive, and the remaining two Alouette IIIs will be flown in the trainer role until the airframes' last hours.

In late 1996 the EPN approved new patches for the S-70 flight and the school. The patch of the S-70 Sminos depicts a wave of the Aegean Sea, which is also a stylised rendition of the head of a hawk. Below it is the powerful NFT Penguin Mk 2 Mod 7 anti-ship missile. The new Skoli E/P Naftikon patch shows a seabird holding schoolbooks and dropping a torpedo.

Liminiki Astonomia (Coastguard)

The Greek Coastguard, which currently operates two Cessna 172RG Cutlass and two SOCATA TB 20 Trinidad aircraft, has plans to extend its fleet with three to four aircraft. The type has not been specified but will be a turboprop with VFR-IFR capability.

Elliniki Polimiko Naftikon

UNIT	TYPE
DEN Kotroni	
Alouette III Sminos	Alouette III
AB 212 Sminos	AB 212ASW, AB 212EW
S-70 Sminos	S-70B-6
SEPN	all types

The PZL M-18A Dromader is the main agricultural aircraft in use with 359 MAEDY, partnering the Grumman AgCat.

Above: Grob 103 Twin Astirs are used by 360 MEA for screening duties. The unit also flies T-41Ds for primary training.

Right: 359 MAEDY's crop-spraying fleet at Dekelia includes around five elderly Bell 47Gs. Note the spray bars beside the nearest helicopter.

There is some dispute over who should operate the recently arrived P-3B Orions. They are currently flown on behalf of the navy by the air force's 353 MNAS at Elefsis.

The Greek Coast Guard currently flies two Cessna 172RGs and two TB 20 Trinidads (illustrated) on coastal patrol work.

Each of the four army battalions has Cessna U-17A/Bs for observation, liaison and training. These are from 2 TEAS.

Left: An AB 212ASW flies in company with an S-70B-6 Aegean Hawk. Five of these aircraft are in service, able to carry the Penguin anti-ship missile.

Above: Alouette IIIs are mainly flown by the navy at Kotroni as trainers with the SEPN. The aircraft are fitted with nose radar for observer training.

The recently modified CH-47DGs serve with 3 Lokos of 2 TEAS. The aircraft all wear standard US Army dark green.

Elliniki Aeroporia Stratou

The Defence Spending Proposal presented by Prime Minister Simitis in November 1996 made reference to the purchase of up to nine CH-47D Chinook transport helicopters. The EAS has expressed the wish to receive another 10 Apaches but they were not listed in the last Defence Spending Proposal.

In June 1995 the first Apache was shipped to Greece, with the 20th and last arriving in December 1995. The Greek AH-64A fleet is under the command of the 1 Tagma Epidolkon Elikopteron (TEEP, Attack Helicopter Regiment) based at 1 TEAS at Stefanovikio. This Army Aviation base in northeastern Greece is a logical home base for the Apache, as it is close to Thrace, which borders Turkey. That country possesses a relatively large number of main battle tanks and – since Greece generally has mountain-ous terrain – a Turkish armoured attack can only be executed via the relatively flat soil of Thrace.

The 10 Greek army CH-47C Chinooks underwent a modification programme at Boeing in Philadelphia during 1992 and late 1995. The update brought the Chinooks to CH-47DG standard, comprising more powerful engines, enlarged fuel capacity, composite rotor blades and new avionics, including NVG. After modernisation the Chinooks lost their wild desert camouflage and all are now painted in the standard US Army dark green.

The 16 artillery-spotting and observation AB 206As of the EAS were withdrawn from active service in 1996. The observation task is now performed with the 25 surviving Cessna U-17 Skywagons.

René van Woezik

Elliniki Aeroporia Stratou

UNIT	TYPE
SAS Stefanovikio	
1 Lokos	NH-300C
2 Lokos	UH-1H
3 Lokos	U-17A/B
4 Lokos	Aero Commander 680FL
1 TEAS Stefanovikio	
1 Lokos	AB 205A, UH-1H
2 Lokos	AB 205A, UH-1H
3 Lokos	U-17A/B
1 TEEP	AH-64A
2 TEAS Megara	
1 Lokos	AB 205A, UH-1H
2 Lokos	AB 205A, UH-1H
3 Lokos	CH-47DG
4 Lokos	U-17A/B
5 Lokos	AB 212, C-12C
3 TEAS Alexandroupoli	
1 Lokos	AB 205A, UH-1H
2 Lokos	AB 205A, UH-1H
3 Lokos	U-17A/B

British Air Power Down South

1435 Flight Tornados wear the Falklands crest on the forward fuselage.

Left: Helicopters are vital for transporting men and materiel around the Falkland Islands. The Chinook is the island workhorse, able to transport large numbers of troops or move heavy loads with ease.

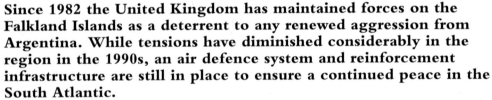

Since 1982 the United Kingdom has maintained forces on the Falkland Islands as a deterrent to any renewed aggression from Argentina. While tensions have diminished considerably in the region in the 1990s, an air defence system and reinforcement infrastructure are still in place to ensure a continued peace in the South Atlantic.

In the early hours of 1 April 1982, 800 Argentine Marines came ashore in the Port Stanley area of East Falkland. With the airfield secured, Fuerza Aérea Argentina C-130s began landing the troops of the 25th Infantry Regiment. By mid-morning the British Governor, Rex Hunt, was forced to surrender and the Argentine Operación Rosario had been successfully completed. For the next 74 days the Falkland Islands were to have a new official name: Islas Malvinas. Quite apart from the professional skills, unquestioned bravery and, on occasion, good fortune demonstrated by the British forces, the campaign to retake the Falkland Islands will also be remembered as a masterpiece of logistic supply. Shipping an army big enough to oust a dug-in force of over 10,000 troops across 8,400 miles (13520 km) of ocean in such a short time, with the nearest available land base nearly 4,000 miles (6440 km) away, was one of the great military feats of recent times.

In the evening of Monday, 14 June 1982, General de Brigada Mario Menendez surrendered the Argentine forces on the Falkland Islands to Major General Jeremy Moore, RM. The brief and fierce war was over, but with victory came a new set of responsibilities. Under the terms of the surrender, Argentina did not revoke its claim to the islands, and it

became immediately clear that British forces would have to stay put in the Falklands as long as their sovereignty was challenged. Throughout the 1980s an uneasy peace reigned over the South Atlantic, a peace which held largely due to the deterrent effect of the strong UK forces which remained. In 1990 the Madrid Agreement saw Argentina and the United Kingdom return to a more normal footing, with some air transport services, diplomatic relations and other key international ties restored. However, the question of the sovereignty of the Falklands/Malvinas was not resolved, a situation which remains today.

It is hoped that such a stalemate can be ended one day, but in the meantime both the civil governments and military are continuing to normalise relations between the two countries. The islanders themselves wish, for the time being, to remain as part of a UK Crown Colony, despite attempts by Argentina to woo them with large sums of money. It would be naïve to suggest that the sovereignty question was the only reason the UK and Argentina went to war: with possession of the Falklands rides right of access to a sizeable slice of the Antarctic continent. Rich fishing waters and recent oil finds have further enhanced the economic attractiveness of this otherwise remote archipelago.

A penguin and captured Argentine weapons greet new arrivals at Mount Pleasant Airfield. The first formality consists of a briefing on the dangers of unexploded mines and cluster bomb munitions.

Geographically, the Falklands are a group of over 700 islands some 150 miles (240 km) from east to west and 80 miles (130 km) from north to south. The 4,700 sq miles (12175 km²) of land area are dominated by the two main islands: East and West Falkland. The former has a hilly main region in the north, joined by a narrow isthmus at Goose Green to the glacially-scraped lowlands of Lafonia. The administrative centre and largest town, Port Stanley, and the main communications centres are on East Falkland. Altogether more remote, West Falkland is mostly hilly, and has only a few small communities, Fox Bay being the most important. There are few roads in the islands, although more are being constructed, so the principal means of travel are by air or sea. FIGAS (Falkland Islands Government Air Service) runs a fleet of PBN Islanders from its base at Port Stanley to many short grass strips

Spearheading the Falklands air defences are the four Tornado F.Mk 3s of 1435 Flight. These undertake a 24-hour QRA alert tasking from the main military base at Mount Pleasant, having replaced Phantom FGR.Mk 2s in mid-1992. The aircraft usually fly armed with Sky Flash and Sidewinder AAMs, and only carry drop tanks for ferry flights back to the UK.

Right: Sea Kings have been familiar sights around the Falklands since the start of the 1982 war. No. 78 Squadron operates a pair for rescue duties and secondary transport duties.

located at the settlements as the principal means of transport around the islands.

Quite apart from the harsh terrain and remoteness of the islands, the biggest problem to air operations is posed by the weather, which is notoriously changeable. "Four seasons in one day" is an oft-heard quote on the islands, while the more cheerful put it another way: "Don't like the weather? Just wait half an hour." In the squadron crewrooms one window will have the label 'Today's Met' – the adjacent window has the label 'Tomorrow's Met'. Wind is present to some degree or another all day, all year, but it can come from almost any quarter, and is rarely of lesser strength than a sturdy breeze. Blizzards, driving rain and hill fog add their own problems to the mix. Forecasting is made difficult by the lack of land stations elsewhere: for 180° from the north through east to the south, there is only the station on South Georgia to provide any reports of approaching weather.

Island defence

The defence of these windswept islands is funded entirely by the UK Ministry of Defence, although it is hoped that in the future, when projected oil revenue starts flowing, the island government may make a contribution. The military units on the islands are under the control of Commander, British Forces Falkland Islands (BFFI, locally pronounced 'biffy'), who also sits on the FI government, albeit in a non-voting capacity. The role of BFFI is to provide a deterrent force against attack from the Argentine mainland, 300 miles (485 km) away at its nearest point, and to provide the infrastrucure for rapid reinforcement should the need arise.

Above: The volcanic mountains of Ascension provide a dramatic backdrop as No. 216 Squadron's sole TriStar C.Mk 2A refuels at Wideawake airfield.

Left: No. 216 Sqn uses the passenger-only TriStar C.Mk 2/2As on the Falklands run. The stop-over at Ascension is around 90 minutes; the total flying time from Brize Norton to the Falklands is 15 to 16 hours.

Below: A No. 216 Sqn crew takes its TriStar south from Ascension. The southern half of the Falklands run is usually flown by a crew based at Wideawake on rotation from Brize Norton.

Argentine air bases which provide the clearest threat are BAM Rio Gallegos on the southernmost tip of mainland Argentina, 428 nm (492 miles; 792 km) from Port Stanley and being built up as an FAA Mirage base, and BAN Almirante Quijada (Rio Grande) on Tierra del Fuego, a naval base 381 nm (438 miles; 705 km) from Stanley but one which has been run down since the war. Other Argentine bases in the area include BAN Ushuaia, a small naval airfield on Tierra del Fuego, BAM Comodoro Rivadavia to the north, and the civilian airfields at Santa Cruz, San Julian and Puerto Deseado, all of which were used during the war.

At the time of the conflict, Britain unilaterally imposed the TEZ (Total Exclusion Zone) of 200 miles (322 km) radius around the islands, and this formed the basis for the immediate post-war defence structure. Today a more complex system is in use, comprising no fewer than five different zones. The largest is the FOCZ (Falklands Outer Conservancy Zone), a circle with a 200-mile radius from the geographic centre of the island group. Further in is the FICZ (Falklands Interim Conservancy Zone), 150 miles (241 km) from the central point. This is the chief area for policing, both for the military and the civil fishery patrols (a

licence is required to fish within the FICZ – a healthy source of income for the FI government). There is an airspace control zone (CTRZ), which extends 150 miles (241 km) westwards and 75 miles (120 km) to the north, south and east. This is Class D airspace and flight planning is required to enter it. In 1990, the Madrid Agreement added the ENA (Exercise Notification Area) 50 miles (80 km) out from the coast, in which the operations of military aircraft must be notified to the other side, and the corresponding 15-mile (24-km) MNA (Maritime Notification Area) for military ships. Although instances of military forces operating within these limits are rare, the framework exists to build confidence in each side's military operations in the area.

Island supply

Just as it was in the war, one of the most impressive facets of today's Falklands operation is the logistic support from the United Kingdom. It was obvious at the end of the war that, if the British were to stay in the islands as a permanent deterrent for any length of time, new facilities had to be constructed to handle the logistics supply. The Hercules air bridge could not go on forever. Accordingly, sites

were studied for the location of a new RAF station, with a long, wide runway that could handle wide-body jets, while bulk cargo would need a deep-sea shipping terminal, preferably close to the airfield. The locations chosen were Mount Pleasant for the airfield, around 30 miles (48 km) by road from Port Stanley, and the nearby Mare Harbour for shipping traffic. RAF Mount Pleasant opened as such in 1984, allowing the various flights deployed to the islands to congregate at one base, greatly easing the operational logstics.

Virtually all cargo now arrives in the Falklands via ship through Mare Harbour, while most personnel are transported by air. The use of Ascension Island as a stop-over for both ships and aircraft was vital to the prosecution of the war, and remains so in supplying the garrison and for stockpiling supplies, such as aviation

For 10 years from the end of the war, Falkland skies were patrolled by the Phantom. One of the last four aircraft was preserved at Mount Pleasant, resplendent in the markings of 1435 Flight and fitted with an SUU-23 cannon pod.

fuel, which may be required in the event of a Falklands reinforcement.

Life for the military on the Falklands revolves around 'Timmy'. Twice-weekly TriStar flights from Brize Norton are the lifeblood of the garrison, bringing in new personnel and returning those from their stint 'down South'. The flight is eagerly awaited by those completing their four-month tour of duty. Welcoming parties gather to wave in the ariving TriStar, while good-natured abuse and humorous – yet usually less than polite – signs from those left behind mark its departure. Twice a week, the lead item on the local radio news is that the TriStar has left Ascension safely and is to arrive on time.

In 1982 the RAF had no wide-body long-range transport capability, a disadvantage exposed by the Falklands conflict. To remedy the situation the RAF purchased six TriStar 500s from British Airways and had them converted by Marshall of Cambridge to either K.Mk 1 tanker/passenger transport status or similar KC.Mk 1 with cargo door. The first of these flew in its new guise for the first time on 9 July 1985. The 500 was the last of the TriStar production variants, featuring an increased-span wing and shortened fuselage for true inter-continental range. This capability was put to full use on the Falklands run.

Three further TriStar 500s were also acquired, from Pan Am. Designated C.Mk 2s, these aircraft lack any tanker equipment and the inflight refuelling probe of the Mk 1. Two went into service as passenger-only troopers, while the third was earmarked for K.Mk 2

conversion with wing-mounted Mk 32 HDUs. This plan was cancelled, and the aircraft became a C.Mk 2A. This, too, has a passenger-only cabin, with seats for 248, but has different avionics. It has an additional INS compared to the C.Mk 2, and has had the troublesome digital autopilot replaced by an analog unit, like that fitted to the Mk 1s. The two C.Mk 2s will be brought up to this standard so that all of the RAF's nine TriStars will have similar flight deck instrumentation.

Passenger service

When Mount Pleasant opened in 1984 the TriStar fleet was not yet in service, and the passenger service was undertaken by British Airways Boeing 747s under contract. As the reformed No. 216 Squadron received sufficient TriStars, these were put on to the route. Due to their passenger-only configuration, only the C.Mk 2/2As are used on the South Atlantic service, which departs from RAF Brize Norton twice each week. The outbound flight leaves in the late evening, arriving at Ascension Island

after about eight hours. The UK-Ascension run was previously flown by Hercules or VC10, the latter usually requiring a fuel stop at either Dakar in Senegal or Banjul in the Gambia. These two destinations are the primary divert airfields for the TriStar's Brize-Ascension leg, which routes out over Portugal, across the Canaries and then tracks the West African coast before heading south to Ascension.

Ascension Island is a volcanic formation in the middle of the Atlantic, a few hundred miles south of the Equator. Room was found to thread one runway between the barren volcanic hills on the south of the island to create Wideawake Airfield, which is the centre of military operations on the island. The United States maintains a major Sigint listening post, with regular supply flights by military transports. Although Wideawake has only one runway, and is close to some high and rugged mountains, air operations are rarely a problem. Unlike the Falklands, the weather is generally good, and the wind virtually never more than 20° from the direction of the runway. Any bad

A TriStar C.Mk 2 overnights at Mount Pleasant before heading north again. In the background is another aircraft normally associated with Brize Norton: the 1312 Flight VC10 on detachment from No. 101 Squadron.

weather usually clears through rapidly, and the TriStar will normally hold rather than immediately divert if a landing is not possible when it arrives.

After about 90 minutes on the ground at Wideawake, the TriStar continues its journey south with a fresh crew. No. 216 Sqn dispatches a complete TriStar crew to Ascension on a two-week *roulement*. During their deployment the crew flies three or four trips down to the Falklands and back. On leaving Ascension, the TriStar flies roughly parallel to the South American coastline down to the Falklands, the flight taking 7 to 7½ hours. During this time the crew keep in contact with civilian controllers as they pass along the continent, and with RAF controllers by using the HF 'company' frequencies. If the atmospheric conditions are right, the crew can sometimes pick up Mount Pleasant when they are climbing out of Ascension, quite a feat over nearly 4,000 miles.

For the second leg there are divert airfields in Brazil and at Montevideo in Uruguay. Due to political sensitivities, the latter is also the designated divert for Mount Pleasant. This requires the TriStar to arrive in the Falklands with sufficient fuel to fly all the way back up the coast to 'Monte' should a landing be impossible. In turn this cuts into the payload that can be carried on the second southbound leg. If the weather at Montevideo turns bad, the TriStar will turn back to Ascension even if the weather in the Falklands is fine.

The highlight of the journey south occurs when 'Timmy' is nearing the Falklands. For a few minutes the based Tornados formate on the TriStar and escort it in, having used it for intercept practice. The flight arrives in the early afternoon local time, providing the crew with sufficient rest before taking the aircraft back to Ascension the following day. Often escorted out by the Tornados, the northbound flight

does not suffer from the divert problems of the inbound flight. After arriving back at Wideawake in the evening for a fuel stop and crew slip, the TriStar then flies through the night back to Brize Norton.

No. 216 Sqn runs the Falklands flight on a scheduled basis, and civilians may purchase tickets at a standard commercial rate, although seat allocation priority is given to key military personnel. The service on board is excellent by military standards. For a civilian passenger there is one other way to reach and leave the islands. Once a week there is a service from the mainland, operated by the Chilean airline DAP, using a Boeing 727. This routes into Mount Pleasant via Punta Arenas from the Chilean capital, Santiago, which is a terminus for a British Airways service from London.

'Purple' force

BFFI is a truly 'purple' (i.e. tri-service) force, combining the assets of Army, Navy and Air Force into one garrison centred on Mount Pleasant Airfield. The total military force numbers around 2,000 personnel, or one for each islander. This is regarded as the minimum needed to staff a credible 24-hour deterrent. HQ BFFI has representatives of all three services on the staff, including an RAF officer of at least group captain rank, and all messing and accommodation is tri-service. The 'purple' nature of the garrison was further reinforced by the renaming of RAF Mount Pleasant as Mount Pleasant Airfield (known universally as MPA).

Left: One of 1435 Flt's Tornados peels away in afterburner from the regular intercept of the inbound TriStar. This practice is popular with islanders travelling on the transport, and provides the Tornado crews with regular intercept training.

Below: Ground crew prepare a Tornado for an engine test. A sizeable engineering staff ably supports the QRA operation.

BFFI consists of various subordinate units, one of which is the Air Wing. Under the control of the Officer Commanding, Air Wing are 10 units and around 450 personnel. In addition to the OC, there are six headquarters staff. The RAF component is responsible for the air defence of the islands with both air and ground units, search and rescue, maritime surveillance, intra-theatre transport and for supporting the air transport effort between the islands and the United Kingdom.

To enable these tasks to be met the RAF has in-theatre four Tornado F.Mk 3s, two Sea King HAR.Mk 3s, two Sikorsky S-61s operating under civilian contract, two Chinook HC.Mk 2s, one Hercules C.Mk 1P, one VC10 K.Mk 4 and ground-based missile and radar units, supported by a sizeable engineering organisation which not only maintains the based aircraft but also any transient traffic, notably the TriStar flights. A 24-hour air traffic service is provided, in line with the QRA tasking, and a large fire service is provided, chiefly to cover any incidents involving the TriStar.

Ground-based units

Cornerstone of the air defence of the Falklands is the FIADGE (Falkland Islands Air Defence Ground Environment). This has three main radar sites situated strategically around the islands on high ground, one on East Falkland and two on West Falkland. In addition to the obvious task of tracking aircraft within the control zone and providing early warning of aircraft further out, the radars are also able to perform maritime surveillance thanks to their elevated positions and proximity to the sea. One acts as the CRC (Command and Reporting Centre).

SHORAD (short-range air defence) is handled by an RAF Regiment's Rapier unit, known as the RRS (Resident Rapier Squadron). In 1996 the Rapier batteries received the latest Field Standard C equipment, far more capable than the FS-B used previously. Although easily relocatable, the Rapiers are usually deployed around the MPA area to protect the main garrison, airfield and deep-sea anchorage at Mare Harbour. With the unrestricted airspace around the Falklands, the Rapier units can perform live firings over the sea. Similarly, the Navy can also undertake high-seas gunnery with live ammunition. The

Army has the Onion live-firing range on East Falkland, which became the final resting place for many of the wrecked aircraft from the war.

Air defence

In the immediate aftermath of the 1982 conflict, air defence of the islands was provided by a mix of Sea Harrier FRS.Mk 1s and Sidewinder-equipped Harrier GR.Mk 3s, which operated from carriers, the Port San Carlos FOB (Forward Operating Base – known as 'Sid's Strip' or 'HMS Sheathbill') and later RAF Stanley. At the latter base work was undertaken to extend the 4,100-ft (1250-m) runway with a further 2,000 ft (610 m) of AM2 matting to allow RAF Phantoms to assume the air defence mantle. Even with the extension, runway arrester gear was used to stop the heavy fighters on landing.

On 17 October 1982 the first of nine No. 29 Squadron Phantom FGR.Mk 2s arrived at Stanley to take over the air defence of the Falklands. The Sea Harriers of 809 Naval Air Squadron returned home, while the HarDet Harrier GR.Mk 3s resumed ground attack duties, later becoming 1453 Flight and serving at Stanley until the opening of Mount Pleasant in 1985, whereupon they were withdrawn. No. 29 Sqn's PhanDet lasted until 30 March 1983, No. 23 Sqn personnel arriving to take over the Phantom aircraft. The PhanDet was renumbered as No. 23 Squadron on 1 April, the unit's red and blue vertical bars surviving to this day as part of the current air defenders' markings.

Falklands Garrison

Above: A single VC10 K.Mk 4 is detached to MPA to provide air defence refuelling support. While at MPA, the aircraft is operated by 1312 Flight, having replaced the recently-retired Lockheed Hercules C.Mk 1K tankers.

Right: One of many reminders of the Falklands War, this Pucará was one of those disabled at Pebble Island by 'D' Sqn, 22 SAS. It resides at MPA, along with a former CAB601 UH-1H, pending display at a museum in Port Stanley.

With the opening of the full-size runway at RAF Mount Pleasant, the Phantoms could leave behind the potential perils of arrested landings, while the crews could enjoy the greater comfort of a purpose-built alert facility. No. 23 moved in during 1985/86, with the complement having been reduced to four aircraft. The squadron disbanded on 30 October 1988, a new No. 23 Squadron standing up the following day at Leeming, to operate the Tornado F.Mk 3 (today it is at Waddington with Sentry AEW.Mk 1s). On the same day, 1 November, the four Phantoms in the Falklands became 1435 Flight. With Phantoms fast disappearing from squadron service in the early 1990s, it was only a matter of time before Tornado F.Mk 3s were deployed as replacements, this occurring in July 1992. Three of the Phantoms were scrapped but one was saved and put on display outside the passenger terminal building at Mount Pleasant.

'Quietly Rotting Away'

Today the four Tornado F.Mk 3s continue the work of their predecessors, the tasking being to provide a 24-hour air defence coverage of the airspace around the islands. A QRA (Quick Reaction Alert) is maintained with two aircraft. These are held at high readiness to enable them to launch rapidly to investigate unidentified or unauthorised air movements in the control area. Any scrambles are notified by the Master Controller at the CRC. Real scrambles are extremely rare, and usually involve wayward civilian aircraft.

Accommodation for the Tornados is provided amid the sizeable shelter complex, and in common with most alert operations the two mission-ready aircraft are housed in shelters with taxiways leading straight on to the end of the runway. The shelters – known as 'houseys' – are not hardened, but are surrounded by large earth revetments for protection. In addition to the QRA building, the flight has a well-equipped engineering/operations facility in the shelter area. The QRA facility offers some comfort for the on-duty crews: a kitchen, bedrooms and a recreational area are provided. A key feature of the facility is obviously the communications system which links the building to the CRC, the tower and other operations and command centres.

A scramble begins with the notification from the CRC and a siren sounding in the QRA facility. The crews run to their aircraft, using a tunnel through the earthworks to rapidly access the 'housey'. The aircraft are maintained with full fuel and a standard missile load of Sky Flash MRAAMs and four AIM-9L Sidewinder SRAAMs, with the cannon also armed. External fuel tanks are virtually never used during FI operations apart from during aircraft change-overs. Umbilicals are connected to the aircraft to provide immediate ground power, and the crew will start one engine as soon as they reach the aircraft to begin the launch sequence. Aligning the inertial navigation system takes the longest time to accomplish, but once up and running the aircraft can quickly taxi the few yards to the runway. The 'housey' has opening doors at the rear as well as the front, allowing internal engine starts and the use of sizeable amounts of power when leaving the shelter without damaging it.

Crews are drawn from all of the UK-based F.Mk 3 squadrons, and are posted to Mount Pleasant for five weeks. The flight is usually manned by five crews with a squadron leader as OC. The length of QRA alert for each crew is 24 hours, one crew being replaced at 8.00 in the morning and the other at 7.30 in the evening. Daytime training flights are undertaken regularly (including those involving the QRA jets), and a full practice scramble is usually unleashed on the unsuspecting crews once a month. The aircraft are drawn from the UK fighter pool, but are usually basic standard aircraft.

During World War II it was 1435 Flight (established in 1941 as the Malta Night Fighter Unit) which had inherited the traditions of Malta's unofficial 'Fighter Flight'. For two weeks during mid-1940, this ad hoc unit had by itself valiantly defended the key Mediterranean island against the Italian air force, using the only machines available at the time: four stored Navy Sea Gladiators. These were later named Faith, Hope, Charity and Desperation, although some controversy exists over the derivation of these names. Notwithstanding the veracity of the story, the Tornados maintain the popular traditions by wearing the codes 'F', 'H', 'C' and 'D', and by carrying a red Maltese cross on the fin. The fuselage markings consist of the Falklands shield with the blue and red bars (inherited from No. 23 Squadron) on either side.

Tanker alert

As the air defence Tornados do not fly with external tanks, a vital part of the QRA operation is the provision of inflight refuelling. As detailed below, in the months following the end of the war tanking assets were provided by the Hercules detachment at RAF Stanley (later at Mount Pleasant). The Hercules C.Mk 1K was a versatile aircraft, for although the tanker conversion involved sealing the rear ramp and fitting four auxiliary fuel tanks inside, it was available for some transport tasks, and could also undertake the maritime reconnaissance role. However, by 1996 the tanker Hercs had been worked so hard that they were ready for retirement. In March the fleet was withdrawn from use, its place in the Falklands being taken by the VC10.

One VC10 K.Mk 4 is currently assigned to 1312 Flight at Mount Pleasant, drawn from No. 101 Squadron at RAF Brize Norton. The aircraft and ground crew are on a four-month rotation, while the aircrew change over every six weeks. Two crews are assigned to 1312 Flt, along with 21 ground personnel.

Primary role for the VC10 is QRA support for the Tornados. A 24-hour alert is

The 1312 Flight VC10 operates from the main ramp at MPA. The K.Mk 4 variant is the most cost-effective version of the 'Ten' for MPA operations, due to a combination of divert considerations and the high landing weights possible.

The Hercules is a valuable vehicle to the Falklands garrison, being able to undertake a variety of tasks. These include maritime reconnaissance, SAR top cover, emergency casevac and supply-dropping.

maintained, hence the two crews required for the aircraft. Readiness states vary but are sufficient to fully support the fighters in any scenario. If the VC10 is not launched in direct support of the Tornados, it remains on alert should the weather take a turn for the worse. Launching the VC10 allows the Tornados to hold until the weather improves.

Secondary roles include the continued training of the Hercules and Tornado aircrews in the art of refuelling, and to support the Hercules in maritime reconnaissance, either by performing the mission if the Hercules is required elsewhere or by refuelling the aircraft during the long maritime missions around South Georgia. The aircraft remains an option for emergency medevac work, although its commitment to the QRA mission is of such high priority that any emergency would have to be very severe to take the VC10 away from the vicinity of the islands.

The K.Mk 4 is the most recent of the pure tanker VC10 conversions and, unlike the preceding K.Mk 2 and K.Mk 3, does not have extra cylindrical fuel tanks in the main cabin. It also retains insulation in the rear of the cabin, making it of more use in an emergency transport role. The aircraft in the Falklands is configured with two high-speed baskets on the wing-mounted Mk 32/2800 refuelling pods for the Tornados, which routinely refuel at about 280 kt (322 mph; 518 km/h), and a low-speed basket on the centreline Mk 17B HDU for the Hercules, which receives at speeds between 230 and 250 kt (265 and 288 mph; 426 and 463 km/h). There are no set refuelling areas in the Falklands, although the Tornados usually tank in the vicinity of Swan Island in Falkland Sound. With virtually no airspace restrictions, refuelling altitudes are kept down to about 5,000 ft (1525 m).

Converted from ex-British Airways Super VC10s, there are five K.Mk 4s in service with No. 101 Squadron, and it is the chosen variant for service with 1312 Flight. The principal reason for this is that the K.Mk 4 has a much higher maximum landing weight than the other tanker models, in turn allowing the aircraft to land with far greater fuel loads. This is of benefit in the Falklands as the designated diversion base is Montevideo in Uruguay, around 1,000 miles (1600 km) to the north.

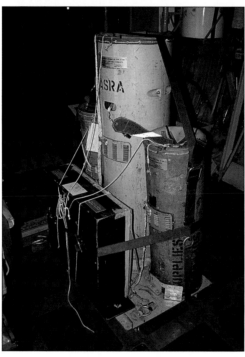
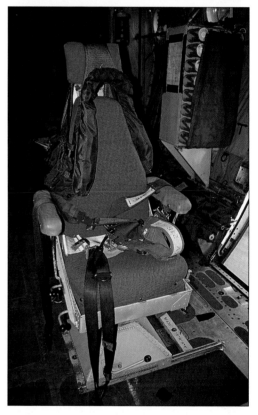

For the SAR role the 1312 Flt Hercules carries two sets of ASRA equipment (above), and is fitted with observer chairs in the paratroop doors (right) for long searches.

The K.Mk 4 can take off with sufficient fuel for the normally short mission and enough reserves to reach Montevideo safely, and then land back routinely without having to dump any fuel. 1312 Flt recognises that, in certain respects, the VC10 is not as good an aircraft for this mission as the Hercules tanker was – it is less versatile, has tighter crosswind limitations, is more

expensive in fuel and requires yet another spares supply and maintenance infrastructure – but the VC10 performs its primary QRA mission perfectly well, and offers multi-point refuelling, a much faster transit to an intercept area, keeps up with the Tornados better if they are involved in a long pursuit, and can refuel them at a more comfortable speed.

'Albert'

On 24 June 1982 a Hercules C.Mk 1P of the Lyneham Transport Wing became the first fixed-wing RAF aircraft to land at the reopened Port Stanley airport after the war. Throughout the conflict 'Fat Albert' had been a vital part of the 8,400-mile (13520-km) air bridge from the UK, air-dropping supplies on inflight-refuelled flights from Ascension, one of which reached a record 28 hours 4 minutes endurance. Between 14 and 29 August the Stanley runway was closed for repair and extension, and the

South Atlantic regulars are the two Lynx HAS.Mk 3ICE helicopters. Parented by 815 NAS, the pair flies from the Antarctic ice patrol ship HMS Endurance, and is seen here visiting Ascension.

Above: The two Sea King HAR.Mk 3s which equip No. 78 Squadron's 'B' Flight are drawn from a fleet of six Falklands-fit aircraft in the UK. The assigned squadron codes are 'Sx', but aircraft in-theatre have only the common first letter applied ('S'); the individual code letter would be applied when required.

Left: The badge of No. 78 Squadron is a twin-tailed tiger – when it was authorised the squadron was flying the Tiger-engined, twin-finned Whitley bomber.

Below: The Falklands Sea King fit adds extra avionics and mountings for a defensive gun. The grey scheme is more combat-worthy than the yellow of UK-based SAR aircraft.

(principally the HMS *Leeds Castle*), and on occasion by helicopters such as the Sea Kings or Navy Lynxes. Every six months a Nimrod detachment is sent to the Falklands to conduct MRR sorties across the area.

Occasional Hercules sorties are launched to the UK Dependency of South Georgia and the South Sandwich Islands to patrol those waters. South Georgia lies around 950 miles (1530 km) to the east of the Falklands, with the South Sandwich chain a further 500 miles (805 km) beyond. During the 1982 war, Argentina put troops ashore on South Georgia, and from late 1976 a small military party had illegally held Southern Thule in the South Sandwich Islands. The latter force was not evicted until a few days after the end of the war in the Falklands.

A secondary activity is to support the Falkland Islands Government fishery patrols out to the FICZ, which are undertaken using two patrol vessels and two civilian-registered Britten-Norman Defenders. During its patrols, the Hercules uses its weather radar to spot ships, and can then investigate anything suspicious by dropping down for a look. Argentine vessels are given a suitably wide berth (500-ft/152-m) altitude and ½-mile/800-m) separation) to avoid the Hercules appearing in any way threatening, but fishing vessels are approached much closer.

South Georgia supply

In the 'load-dumping' role the Hercules is used for a supply run to South Georgia every six weeks. There is no airfield, and the principal settlement, Grytviken, nestles under steep cliffs in the Cumberland East Bay. This requires the Hercules to air-drop the supplies into the harbour. The process is more difficult than might be imagined, for the Hercules has to perform a 180° turn to avoid the cliffs. Several drop runs are made on each visit, the Royal Marine party on South Georgia rescuing the supplies by boat.

The Hercules is also the vehicle of choice for any emergency transport requirements, such as medical evacuation or compassionate leave. These flights generally terminate at Montevideo or occasionally Rio de Janeiro, from where the patient or relative can be flown by civilian carrier back to the UK. Using the Hercules for these flights rather than the VC10 preserves the QRA capability of the latter. Besides, the Hercules is also better equipped to handle stretcher cases. Very rarely the Hercules is called away on emergency medevac missions to Antarctica, mainly using the dry runway at the Chilean Teniente Rodolfo Marsh base.

With its long endurance and onboard equipment, the Hercules is ideal for long-range SAR missions, and it is occasionally impressed into this role. It has the equipment to be able to home in on SAR beacons, and can use its radar to locate vessels in distress. Visual searches are also performed, and the Falklands-based aircraft is unique among the RAF fleet in being fitted with two chairs bolted to the floor next to the paratroop doors. Observers manning these chairs can watch the oceans through the open doors, the numbing effects of a potential multi-hour search pattern in freezing conditions being partially offset by some sheepskin padding!

Depending on the rescue scenario, once the survivors have been located, the Hercules can either call in a helicopter or ship to pick them

Hercules returned to non-stop trips, although an air snatch system was devised to pick up mail. With the runway repaired the Hercules again flocked to Stanley, and a detachment was established to serve the needs of the forces in the islands.

Aircraft assigned were a mixture of probe-equipped C.Mk 1Ps and tanker-configured C.Mk 1Ks. Four (later increased to six) of the latter were hastily ordered during the war to provide additional refuelling assets on the air bridge, but although the first conversion first flew on 8 June 1982, none saw service during the conflict. However, they proved extremely valuable in support of the Falklands garrison, refuelling both transports coming to and from Ascension, and also for supporting the air defence fighters.

On 20 August 1983 the Hercules detachment was officially designated 1312 Flight, previous

incarnations of this unit being a Dakota operator in 1944-45 and an Abingdon-based Hastings user in 1954-57. In 1985, 1312 Flt joined other Falkland Islands air assets at RAF Mount Pleasant, and in March 1996 the C.Mk 1K was withdrawn from use, leaving just one C.Mk 1P with the flight. 1312 Flight describes itself as 'Gas Pumpers, Load Dumpers' and the squadron leader in command can be drawn from either the VC10 or Hercules communities. To describe the role of the Hercules as simply 'load-dumping' is far from the truth, for the single aircraft has a wide variety of missions to perform.

Primary among the roles is that of MRR (Maritime Radar Reconnaissance). The priority is to patrol the ENA area every two days to locate and track any military shipping activity. The Hercules is augmented in the maritime role by the land-based radars and by military vessels

Both Sea Kings and one of the Chinooks are seen on the No. 78 Sqn ramp at MPA. One of the Sea Kings is always maintained at a high SAR readiness state, the other acting as back-up or performing secondary transport tasks.

Above: A Sea King takes off from a hilltop REBRO site on West Falkland while a Chinook slings in a load behind. The Sea King provides a useful support helicopter (SH) function to augment the larger Chinook.

up or drop ASRA (Air-Sea Rescue Apparatus) sets. The ASRA set is packed in three canisters which are dropped from the paratroop doors, and contains an inflatable dinghy, food, water-proof clothing and the like. Two ASRA sets are always carried on board the aircraft, whatever its mission, and the dropping of them is routinely practised back in the UK prior to a crew deploying 'down South'.

On rescue missions the Hercules also provides top cover for the dedicated rescue Sea Kings. It carries marine band radio, and provides a communications relay platform across wide distances. When several agencies are involved in a search, it undertakes the scene-of-search command role. At long distances from land, the Hercules is vital in locating survivors first owing to the limited range and search endurance of the Sea King. A well-publicised rescue in 1996 of a family attempting to sail round the world highlighted this: with time of the essence due to increasingly bad weather and mounting seas, the Sea King had barely enough fuel to reach the stranded vessel and return safely even though it already had a precise positional plot from the Hercules. Wihtout that plot the family stood little chance of survival.

Manning the Hercules detachment is a Lyneham Transport Wing-wide responsibility, whereas it used to be the province of Nos 24

One of No. 78's Sea Kings transits across the Falkland Sound, the body of water which separates the two main islands. The terrain below is typical: treeless coastal mountain/moorland liberally covered with rocky outcrops.

and 30 Squadrons. The single aircraft is flown by one crew, who rotate every six weeks, and is suppprted by a ground party of 13, who rotate every three months. In normal operations the aircraft is airborne every other day to perform its ENA reconnaissance patrols.

No. 78 Sqn

Mount Pleasant's only numbered squadron is No. 78, which operates the military helicopters: Sea King and Chinook. With a proud history as a home defence fighter unit in World War I and Bomber Command unit (with Whitleys and Halifaxes) in World War II, No. 78 was employed on transport tasks in the post-war years, flying the Dakota, Valetta, Pioneer, Twin Pioneer and Wessex in the Middle East. After disbandment at Sharjah in 1971, the squadron lay dormant until 1 May 1986, when it was resurrected to take over the operations of the RAF's two helicopter flights then operating in the Falklands. The squadron leader in command of the squadron is alternately drawn from the Sea King and Chinook communities, and the 'boss' is required to complete a conversion

course on the other type prior to taking up his six-month posting. The aircraft are heavily tasked, and there are normally just three crews on the squadron. The leader's ability to fly either type is very important.

Sea King

In its 'Pinger' (ASW HAS.Mk 5), 'Pinglie' (transport-configured HAS.Mk 2) and 'Junglie' (commando HC.Mk 4) forms, the Westland Sea King was one of the workhorses of the Falklands War. During the conflict only one RAF aircraft was brought into play, a HAR.Mk 3 dispatched to Ascension Island for utility transport and SAR work. However, in August 1982, three grey-painted and suitably modified aircraft from No. 202 Squadron's 'C' Flight were dispatched south on board the MV *Contender Bezant* to establish a Falklands detachment. Their duties were to perform SAR (search and rescue) and general transport, relieving the hard-pressed Navy helicopters which had remained after the end of the war.

Disembarking on 25 August 1982, and continuing to operate as 'C' Flight, the three-helicopter detachment set up at Navy Point, a fuel storage depot on the north side of Port Stanley harbour. On 20 August 1983 the detachment was redesignated as 1564 Flight, and in 1985 made the move to Mount Pleasant. The following year it was brought together with the Chinook detachment to reform No. 78 Squadron. The Sea King operation became 'B' Flight of the new squadron, and currently operates two aircraft.

The primary role of the Sea King is to provide military SAR (search and rescue) coverage. No. 78 Sqn keeps an aircraft on readiness 24 hours a day, 365 days a year. During daytime (i.e. when there is military flying), the aircraft is held at RS15 (Readiness State, 15 minutes), but this readiness state drops to RS60 during the night. The second role is to provide SAR cover to the civilian fishing fleet, and also a medevac capability for the islanders. The Sea King can undertake fire-fighting duties, and is can augment the Chinook on general transport duties.

Falklands Garrison

When equipped with the **Sims Rainmaker** bucket, the **Chinook** provides a valuable fire-fighting tool. Shown above is the set-down procedure: the aircraft displaces to one side of the bucket in a low hover before landing clear of it, while at right the full 1,000 Imp gal (4540 litres) of water is released. The bucket is refilled in a hover from any stretch of water deep enough in which to submerge it.

A Chinook lifts APFCs from one of the two forward operating locations on West Falkland. Heavy cargo is usually ferried around the islands by ship prior to the final lift into place by Chinook.

A total of six Sea Kings in the RAF fleet is fitted out for Falklands operations. The 'Falklands fit' comprises additional avionics, ability to mount GPMGs (General Purpose Machine-Guns) and the all-over grey paint scheme unique to these machines. At any time two aircraft are in-theatre, being changed over by sea every 15 months. The two flying crews are on an 8-week *roulement*, while groundcrew serve for four months.

In the SAR role the Sea King HAR.Mk 3 offers a six-hour endurance and is fully equipped for operations in all weathers. NVGs (Night-Vision Goggles) are regularly worn, and the helicopter's automatic transition system allows it to descend and enter a stable hover at 50-ft (15-m) altitude. The search radar is the primary sensor, and can put the aircraft within 200 ft (60 m) of a vessel. As described earlier, the Sea King often works with the Hercules on long-range SAR operations.

In the Falklands the crews receive a lot of practice working with ships, including deck landing and winching. This can include winching from submarines. The two aircraft fly about 80 hours a month, of which some 30 per cent are for crew training. The capability does exist for the Sea King to undertake emergency trips to the mainland or South Georgia. For the former, a HIFR (Helicopter InFlight Refuelling) from a ship is required, while to reach South Georgia the Sea King has to land on the RFA *Grey Rover*, or other suitable vessel, and sail for some while before the island falls in range. This latter scheme is virtually never used, as the Chinook can reach South Georgia in one hop, but the capability does exist.

Partnering the Sea King in the No. 78 Squadron roster is the Chinook, the packhorse of the islands. The saga of 'Bravo November', the only one of four Chinooks to survive the sinking of the MV *Atlantic Conveyor*, has passed into Falklands War folklore. The second Chinook to reach the islands did so on the day of the Argentine surrender, and a further five arrived within days. Operating from the Port San Carlos FOB, the Chinooks were immediately made busy in the massive clear-up operation, and also in keeping the wheels of supply well greased. Large amounts of aviation fuel were moved ashore while permanent facilities were installed at Stanley airport. The minimal cargo handling facilities at Port Stanley were augmented by Chinooks lifting ashore containers, while in the opposite direction travelled returning troops, war trophies and damaged helicopters. The Chinook was in the Falklands to stay.

Known unofficially as the ChinDet, the Chinook detachment was initially manned by No. 18 Sqn at Odiham. On 23/24 March 1983 the unit left Port San Carlos and moved to a new location at Kelly's Garden, close to San Carlos settlement. In line with the other Falklands detachments, it received a flight number on 20 August 1983, becoming 1310 Flt. A penguin was adopted as its badge. It also moved to Mount Pleasant, and became 'A' Flight of No. 78 Sqn on the unit's reformation.

Currently there are two aircraft on charge, although one is officially an in-use reserve. Only one Chinook crew is assigned to No. 78 Squadron, and they work hard during their stay on the islands. The chief task for the Chinook is medium lift in support of a variety of agencies. The FIADGE air defence network relies on the Chinook to resupply its mountain-top sites which are virtually unreachable by any other form of transport (the sites do have Haglund BV all-terrain vehicles for local transport). Fuel,

A Falklands detachment for a Chinook crew provides a welcome opportunity to practise low-level flying, and also to undertake deck lifts, usually lifting **ISO** containers. Water is never far away, so immersion suits are regular attire.

food and a host of other supplies reaches these locations by Chinook, as do construction materials. The sites suffer during the long Falklands winter, and a major repair effort is undertaken each spring to make good the storm damage. Other hill-top sites such as REBRO (RElay BROadcasting) stations are also supplied by the Chinook.

Other support is for the SHORAD Rapier batteries, these being resupplied and relocated using the Chinook, while the type can be called upon to lift heavy items for the Royal Engineers during construction work. The aircraft also flies in support of the infantry company during its exercises, and can be used to transport the ground Quick Reaction Force if the need arises. In a land bereft of roads, the Chinook is used to carry just about anything that its broad shoulders can lift. Tasking usually reaches over 60 hours per month.

Water-bombing

Secondary tasks include fire-fighting. For this, the Chinook carries a 1,000-Imp gal (4540-litre) Sims Rainmaker bucket which can be refilled from any stretch of water deep enough to take it. Fire is not a major worry in the Falklands, although in dry periods peat fires can threaten settlements and installations. The Sea King also has a fire-fighting capability, although its bucket can only carry 350 Imp gal (1325 litres). Another secondary role for the Chinook concerns South Georgia, as the helicopter is the only quick way of getting an injured person away from the island. The flight requires the fitment of three ERTs (Extended Range Tanks) in the cabin, which gives a range of about 1,000 nm (1,150 miles; 1850 km), and also requires the use of the Hercules to scout ahead for weather reconnaissance as there are no diverts. The Chinook can be called upon in time of emergency or for special needs by the civilian government. Its long range and large

Above: A Chinook crew displays the helicopter's exceptional agility for one so large. Note the open hatch and gantry attachment for a central underslung load (similar additional attachments are mounted fore and aft). No. 78 Sqn was the first unit to receive operational HC.Mk 2 aircraft. This updated version has T55-L-712F engines, new APU, FADEC equipment, revised defensive avionics and many other improvements. The all-over dark green paint offers a low IR signature.

Right: A Chinook clatters at low level across typical Falklands terrain. In good weather the mountains and valleys offer no special problems, but the notorious weather often results in crews drawing heavily on their skills and experience. The absence of large population centres, and the attendant lack of ambient light, also makes nocturnal NVG work particularly challenging.

capacity could also be brought into play during a SAR emergency, although the strong down-draught from the rotors and lack of radar do not make it an ideal tool. Furthermore, the cabin is not protected against saltwater corrosion like that of the Sea King, and any sea rescue would pose maintenance nightmares as the aircraft would have to be stripped out and washed down thoroughly afterwards.

In March 1994 No. 78 Squadron became the first RAF unit to get the improved Chinook HC.Mk 2 variant. For combat operations this can be armed with M60 or M134 Minigun armament, the latter providing either 2,000 or 4,000 rounds per minute suppressive fire capability. The aircraft has armour, and is fitted with the Sky Guardian defensive counter-measures suite. Regular use is made of night-vision goggles, the islands proving a tough training ground for their use due to the lack of artificial light and the fact that the sky is difficult to discriminate from the ground during low-level NVG terrain-following.

In the Falklands the Chinook operates with ships far more frequently than elsewhere, for much of the cargo and equipment is moved

Left: The radar and REBRO sites on the hilltops are supplied exclusively by helicopter, requiring skilful flying in the face of the strong winds prevalent throughout the year. Here a 'hooker' from the JHSU removes fuel 'bollocks' from under a Chinook during a routine resupply tasking.

Opposite page: In addition to its resupply tasks, the Chinook is also the vehicle for carrying the rapid reaction infantry force. Note the mechanical countermeasures dispensers on either side and winch to starboard.

around the islands by ship. The MV *Saint Brandan*, based at Mare Harbour, is used to transport materiel as close as it can get to its destination before the Chinook comes along to lift it from the deck to its final delivery point. This saves a considerable effort in slinging cargoes all the way from Mount Pleasant, as underslung loads severely eat into the Chinook's range. Much of the shipborne cargo is containerised, while fuel is carried in APFCs (Air Portable Fuel Cells), known to all as 'bollocks'. The excellent range of the Chinook allows it to perform several taskings within one sortie. Occasionally there are more pleasant tasks to undertake, for instance taking parties of servicemen on R&R visits to wildlife reserves such as Sealion Island.

'Hookers' and 'Erics'

Assisting the operations of the helicopters, in particular the Chinook, are personnel from the JHSU (Joint Helicopter Support Unit), otherwise known as the 'hookers'. They are positioned at various locations around the islands to provide ground support for the helicopters, principally to hook and unhook underslung cargoes, and also to train others to perform the tasks. Although based at MPA, the helicopters are also regular visitors at Port Stanley airfield, and there are two permanent refuelling sites on West Falkland, one in the north and one in the south. A regular store of fuel at these landing sites allows the helicopters to continue a long tasking in West Falkland without the long transit back to MPA for fuel. The refuelling locations are conveniently close to the West Falkland FIADGE radar sites, and also have berthing for coastal shipping. For other specific purposes, for instance a long construction haulage tasking, a temporary refuelling site can be created using APFCs.

In addition to the aircraft of No. 78 Squadron, BFFI also has two Sikorsky S-61Ns available, these being leased under civilian contract from Bristow Helicopters. These have been long-term servants of the military in the islands, and are known affectionately as 'Erics' (after Eric Bristow, a well-known Cockney darts player). The S-61Ns are flown under full CAA regulations and operate from the same hangar as No. 78 Squadron. They are used for passenger-only transportation of military personnel around the islands, often being referred to as BFFI's bus service. The experience of Bristow's pilots in flying on oil exploration and rig transport services in appalling weathers worldwide made them a natural choice for the contract.

Operations by all of the helicopters are tasked by one cell. 'Helimovs' is the agency which receives requests from the many customers within the military, prioritises them and then assigns a helicopter asset. This turns into a daily tasking sheet for each of the crews, including the Bristows pilots. It is usually issued the evening before. Within the tasking there is room for No. 78 Sqn to meet its own ongoing training requirements.

Caretaker base

Although the role of BFFI and its air assets is to send a clear message of deterrence, for the benefit of both Argentina and the islanders, it also acts in a 'caretaker' role. Clearly the construction of MPA, Mare Harbour and the surrouding infrastructure was designed to provide the ability to rapidly reinforce the islands' defences in time of tension. The cluster of aircraft shelters at MPA suggests the ability to deploy sizeable numbers of tactical aircraft to the theatre and undertake operations from the moment they arrive. Certainly the capability to have Tornados, in both air defence and attack/anti-ship forms, in the Falklands with very little notice is a key part of BFFI's deterrence value.

Life for the Falkland Islanders changed dramatically with the 1982 war. Another sea change is forecast following the discovery of a potentially large oilfield to the north of the islands. Until Argentina renounces its claim to the islands, one thing which will not change is the presence of BFFI. Just as the 1982 campaign demonstrated, the long-term British presence is the clearest indication of the UK's resolve to keep the Falklands British, while representing an ongoing triumph of logistical planning over the harsh realities of geography. **David Donald**

Above: Two Sikorsky S-61Ns from Bristow Helicopters operate on a long-term contract on behalf of the Ministry of Defence, providing passenger transport around the islands for British personnel. The aircraft are equipped with radar and are operated under full civil regulations.

Left: The two 'Erics' – named Slains (G-BCLD) and Diamond (G-BFMY) – are maintained in the same hangar as the No. 78 Sqn aircraft and the operations of both are integrated by one movements staff. Bristow Helicopters has a fleet of 15 S-61Ns, three of them being used for rescue work under the HM Coastguard banner at Sumburgh, Stornoway and Lee-on-Solent.

AH-64A/D Apache and AH-64D Longbow Apache

The Apache is the world's premier attack helicopter. Its long, and sometimes controversial, early history was crowned by a combat record in Operation Desert Storm which swept away any lingering doubts about the Apache's supremacy – doubts which none of its crews shared. Once a product of Hughes Helicopters and then McDonnell Douglas, the Apache is today the responsibility of the Boeing Corporation. To them now falls the responsibility of fielding the AH-64D Longbow Apache, an attack helicopter so advanced it will revolutionise the future battlefield.

AH-64 Apache and Longbow Apache

Above: A total of 821 (excluding prototypes) AH-64As was delivered to the US Army, between January 1984 and April 1996. The first operational unit reached IOC in July 1986. Since then the Apache has led the field in terms of battlefield helicopter technology and tactics. As the massive Soviet threat which the Apache was designed to defeat declined, the AH-64A and its crews have had to adapt to new 'security' roles – in a world far less politically and militarily 'certain' than the Cold War era.

Above right: The AH-64D Longbow Apache transforms the combat capability of the basic AH-64A and ushers in a new era of the 'omnipotent' battlefield helicopter. The AH-64D substantially improves upon the AH-64A's already staggering reputation as a tank killer, while adding effective anti-air and SEAD capability to the same airframe.

Opposite page, right: The best defence for any combat helicopter is agility and this was a watchword throughout the Apache's early developmental days at Hughes Helicopters. Despite its size, the AH-64 boasts a reputation for manoeuvrability that was once unequalled.

At 02:37:50, in the early darkness of 17 January 1991, First Lieutenant Tom Drew thumbed the radio switch in the pilot's seat of his AH-64A and initiated Operation Desert Storm with the laconic words "party in 10." Today it is a fact well-known, but still worth repeating, that the first shots of the war against Iraq were fired not by US Air Force F-117s, 'Secret Squirrel' B-52s or Tomahawk-toting US Navy vessels, but by AH-64A Apaches of the 101st Airborne Division, US Army. On that first night, eight Apaches operating as Task Force Normandy headed north from Al Jouf in Saudi Arabia, over the border and through the Iraqi front line, to destroy two key air-defence radar sites inside Iraq. First with Hellfires, and then with rocket and gun fire, the two teams of Apaches obliterated the Iraqi positions in a mission that would prove to be the template for all subsequent AH-64 operations in Desert Storm – supremely effective and deadly accurate.

There is no denying that the Task Force Normandy operation, planned and executed by Lieutenant Colonel Dick Cody and the men of the 1st Battalion, 101st Aviation Regiment, 101st Airborne Division, was the long-awaited vindication of the AH-64 as a weapon, in its first true combat test. The Apache and its crews had come in for more than their fair share of criticism since the first AH-64s were fielded in 1986. Teething troubles – some serious, some not – led to damaging speculation and Congressional scrutiny that proved, to the Apache community, that mud sticks. Furthermore, the personnel of the 15 Apache battalions deployed to the Gulf, along with their friends and families at home, had to suffer the assault of a prime-time American current affairs programme which damned the aircraft and forecast doom for those about to go to war in it. None of their prophecies came true. As recorded below, the AH-64 had an exceptional operational debut and notched up many firsts for US Army aviation, and for the combat helicopter as a whole. In Operation Desert Storm the Apache finally proved its claim to be the best attack helicopter in the world, a claim which no-one could begin to dispute, except perhaps those involved with the AH-64D Longbow programme.

This is not to say that the Apache is invincible, and one need look no further than the success of TF Normandy to discern some of the weaknesses that still hinder the AH-64A. While the Apaches performed with finesse their task of killing their first night targets, it is an unpalatable

fact (for some) that they could never had found those targets without the help of USAF AFSOC Pave Low III MH-53Js which led the Apache teams to the right place with their GPS and TFR systems. The Apache's own navigational fit was simply not up to the job. As an aircraft of the 1970s the Apache is an analog, not a digital, warrior. The mission-planning effort required for any Apache mission today, let alone one as important as TF Normandy, is immense, because every eventuality must be foreseen, sketched out and planned on paper before the aircraft are in the air. Apaches fight as a team and if the cohesion of that team is lost, so is the mission. More than most, Apache crews know the truth of von Clausewitz's maxim that 'no plan survives contact with the enemy'. This places immense strain on the crews, who have to call on the skill and experience gained from hundreds of hours of training. Communication of new ideas or new intelligence is difficult, if not impossible, after launch, so Apache crews have to fly and fight in one of the most stressful combat environments imaginable, hoping that all the answers have been worked out before the shooting starts.

This will soon change. At present, the US Army is in the early stages of fielding the AH-64D Longbow Apache, a combat helicopter for the digital battlefield of the 21st century. These are not mere buzz-words. The US Army is probably further ahead than any other branch of the US armed forces in planning to make maximum use of new technology in weapons, sensors, intelligence gathering and C^3 (command, control, communications) on the future battlefield. Army aviation and McDonnell Douglas have designed the Longbow to fight and win the intelligence war, which again is not an empty phrase but one which describes a combat situation where the AH-64D crew will be all-seeing, all-knowing and all-powerful. That, at least, is the plan. Before examining the Apache of the future we should discuss the Apache of the present, and why it is the benchmark against which all others are measured.

Although the lineage of the attack helicopter in United States service can be traced to Southeast Asia, the roots of the Apache lie firmly in Europe. The Bell AH-1G Huey-Cobra had a highly successful combat career in Vietnam after its introduction in August 1967. The Hughes BGM-71 TOW (Tube-launched, Optically-tracked, Wire-guided) missile ultimately gave the sleek 'Snake' unprecedented hitting power against armoured targets, coupled with secure stand-off ranges (though initial results of airborne TOW firings in Vietnam were poor). In Europe, where the 'real' war would be fought, the arrival of the AH-1 paved the way for the second generation of US attack helicopters that would be firmly dedicated to killing Soviet tanks in Germany. However, the AH-1 was originally only a stop-gap – developed in haste to cover delays in the Army's 'big plan' for armed helicopters.

Prehistory of the AH-64

After the successful debut of the armed UH-1, the US Army initiated the Advanced Aerial Fire Support System programme to develop a new combat helicopter for gunship, escort and fire support tasks. The result was a 1966 contract with Lockheed to develop 10 prototypes of the immense AH-56A Cheyenne. The Cheyenne was one of countless aircraft which appear as a footnote to the story of others but deserve an entire account of their own. It was conceived not as a manoeuvrable armed helicopter for nap-of-the-earth (NoE) flying, but as a large weapons platform for Vietnam-era gun and missile attacks. The Cheyenne had a General Electric T64 turboshaft driving a four-bladed main rotor, coupled with a conventional tail rotor and a decidedly unconventional pusher propeller at the end of the tailboom. The first AH-56A made its maiden flight on 21 September 1967, chalked up a startling maximum speed of 220 kt (407 km/h, 253 mph), and in January 1968 the US Department of Defense signed a contract for an initial batch of 375. The Air Force took issue with the Army for

acquiring this 'close-support aircraft'. The first prototype crashed on 12 March 1969 (killing the pilot), technical delays and hitches abounded and, finally, the advent of the shoulder-launched SAM, in the shape of the SAM-7 'Grail' (9K32 Strella-2), sealed the fate of the Cheyenne. To survive from then, any new helicopter would have to

Above: Lockheed's AH-56 Cheyenne was an over-complex design that was ultimately defeated by the small infantry SAMs that emerged in the late 1960s. As a result the Cheyenne became just a museum exhibit.

Right: In 1972 Lockheed became one of the five bidders for the Army's Advanced Attack Helicopter (AAH) competition with its proposed CL-1700. Owing much to the Cheyenne, the CL-1700 was one of the more unwieldy AAH designs.

The Boeing AAH

Right: Boeing's AAH entrant featured a novel side-by-side, yet staggered, cockpit arrangement offering "four eyes forward to find and fight," as the brochure put it. Ironically, Boeing is now at the helm of the AH-64 Apache.

Right and below right: When the winners of the AAH initial evaluation were announced it was not surprising that Bell was selected as one of the two finalists. The wooden mock-up that Bell first produced was completely camouflaged; even the blades were painted. In contrast, the two prototypes wore an overall drab green scheme. Bell's YAH-63 design drew on all the company's experience with the AH-1 HueyCobra. It was beaten into the air by its Hughes rival, by a single day, in September 1975. The YAH-63 had an unhappy development and one of the two flying prototypes was lost in a crash. The other prototype, like the Cheyenne before it, survives today as an exhibit in the US Army Aviation Museum, at Ft Rucker, Alabama.

operate at less than tree-top height and be supremely agile. What was needed was a gunboat and not an ironclad, and so the US Army retired to generate another specification.

The space left by the cancellation of what might have been up to 1,000 Cheyennes still needed to be filled. With a eye on the Central European front, the US Army's next requirement coalesced around an aircraft that would better the AH-1 in terms of range, performance and firepower which still being manoeuvrable enough to fly NoE missions through, around and under forests, hills and power lines. The AH-1/TOW combination was still the best available and held the line in Europe for a decade, but it obviously could be improved.

Birth of the AAH

In August 1972 the official Request for Proposals (RFP) for the Advanced Attack Helicopter (AAH) was announced. It specified an aircraft that would cruise at 145 kt (269 km/h, 167 mph) with a full load of eight TOW missiles (or a minimum expendable ordnance load of 1,000 lb/ 454 kg) for a mission duration of 1.9 hours. Performance demands were set, surprisingly, in (Middle Eastern) terms of 4,000 ft (1220 m) altitude at an ambient temperature of 95° F (35°C). By way of comparison, conditions for 'NATO hot day' operations were defined as 2,000 ft (610 m) at 70°F (21°C). Maximum speed was to be 175 kt (323 km/h, 201 mph) and maximum vertical rate of climb 500 ft/min (152 m/min). The new helicopter would have to have operational g limits of +3.5 and -1.5 and be structurally resistant to hits from 12.7-mm armour-piercing incendiary rounds. In addition, the rotorhead (and the entire aircraft) had to remain flyable after a hit from a 23-mm high-explosive incendiary shell, the then-standard Warsaw Pact AAA calibre. A sign of the prescience of these requirements is that they would not be seen as unreasonable, or inadequate, today. The SAM threat to the aircraft was perhaps even a higher priority and the AAH would have to prove that its IR signature, and thus its vulnerability to shoulder-launched infantry SAMs, could be reduced to an acceptably low level. Such passive countermeasures would be backed up by chaff/flare dispensers. Crew survivability was placed at a premium – far too many crews had been lost in Vietnam in fragile helicopters. The AAH crew must be able to survive a crash at 30 mph (48 km/h) – a vertical impact of 42 ft/s (12.8 m/s) – with a forward speed of 15 kt.

Of course the key to survivability on the battlefield would be to allow the AAH to kill its targets outside the air defence envelope that could be expected around an advancing armoured column. The alarming Israeli experience of the 1973 Yom Kippur war showed that this might no longer be possible when faced with Soviet weapons such as the ZSU 23-4 Shilka radar-directed mobile AAA system or SA-8 'Gecko' and SA-9 'Gaskin' mobile SAMs. The TOW missile was becoming progressively less able to outreach these defences and its method of employment left the launch aircraft exposed for an unacceptable length of time.

Bell's rival and the YAH-64

While this issue was emerging as a serious challenge to the AAH concept, the US Army was faced with five competing submissions for the new helicopter – from Bell, Boeing-Vertol (teamed with Grumman Aerospace), Hughes, Lockheed and Sikorsky. Bell Helicopter Textron, not surprisingly, saw itself as the front-runner. It had amassed the most relevant experience of any of the competitors and its resultant YAH-63 (Bell Model 409) had the appearance of a thoroughbred. Boeing-Vertol, whose YUH-61A design was about to go head-to-head with Sikorsky for the US Army's UTTAS transport helicopter fly-off, offered a large AAH design, reminiscent of the Cheyenne, with some unusual features. It had a reversed tricycle undercarriage, podded engines, four-bladed rotor and large forward fuselage. The crew sat in tandem, but in

separate off-set cockpits. Lockheed, determined not to be left behind after the success, and failure, of the Cheyenne, developed the Cheyenne-lookalike CL-1700, powered by a Lycoming PLT-27 engine. Sikorsky (which would ultimately win the UTTAS competition in December 1976 with the UH-60 Blackhawk) came up with a development of the S-67 Blackhawk – however, like Boeing-Vertol, the ongoing UTTAS competition made it an unlikely candidate for AAH victory.

The final competitor was Hughes Helicopters, of Culver City, California. Hughes Helicopters was founded on 14 February 1934 by the great Howard R. Hughes Jr, as the aviation division of his Hughes Tool Company. Hughes had supplied the much-loved and respected OH-6A Cayuse, the 'Loach', to Army aviation units in Vietnam, where the type had proved to be a very tough and reliable performer, even though substantial numbers were lost in combat. For the AAH competition Hughes looked first to its OH-6 experience and took that type's small size and damage-tolerant structure as its guiding principles. An OH-6-inspired design soon proved to be far too small to meet the Army's AAH requirements and so Hughes's designers proffered the angular and awkward-looking Model 77 which, to the US Army, became the YAH -64.

Defining the future battlefield

As planning for the AAH competition advanced so, too, did US Army doctrine for the attack helicopter, as a concept and a weapon. The philosophy during the 1960s and 1970s had been one of 'whoever brings the most to the party wins' – victory in battle would be decided by the size of the force one side could apply to the battlefield. By the 1970s advancing technology – and clear Soviet numerical superiority – transformed this credo to 'win at night'. The interim Army aviation solution, the AH-1/NVG combination, was not proving successful in Europe. The Cobra had only maps rather than Doppler navigation, limited comms, limited reach and limited combat effectiveness. The emergence of the doctrine of 'active defence', where units would move laterally along the battlefield to reinforce each other, defined the AAH as an aircraft that must be able to conduct regimental operations at night. The objective was for an attack helicopter regiment to be capable of destroying an armoured corps. As a result, the AAH fell into line with other Army battlefield systems destined for

service in the 1980s (and then under development), such as the XM1 which became the Abrams MBT and the MICV which became the M2 Bradley IFV. The AAH became a platform for electro-optical sensors that would allow it to locate, identify and target the enemy in darkness when their combat performance was rightly seen as degraded, and then engage them from concealed positions. As the AAH competition progressed so did the development of this system, the heart of the Apache, which emerged under the unrevealing acronym of TADS/PNVS.

On 22 June 1973 the US Department of Defense announced that the Bell YAH-63 and Hughes YAH-64 had been chosen as the AAH competitors. This launched Phase 1 of the competition whereby both firms would build and fly two prototypes, plus a Ground Test Vehicle (GTV) for a competitive fly-off in mid-1976. Following the Phase 2 evaluation and selection, it was anticipated that an initial order for 472 aircraft would be awarded in late 1978/early 1979. Hughes confidently predicted that its aircraft would have a flyaway cost of not more than $1.6 million, in 1972 dollars. Bell's YAH-63A drew heavily on its AH-1G experience and was essentially a scaled-up HueyCobra which retained Bell's trademark twin-bladed, 'teetering' rotor. Like the YAH-64 it was powered by a pair of 1,500-shp (1117-kW) General Electric YT700 turboshafts – an engine choice virtually dictated to the two manufacturers for commonality with the UTTAS (Utility Tactical Transport Aircraft System) helicopter. The YAH-64 followed the same configuration, though without the same

Hughes Helicopters responded to the AAH competiton with a design based on its egg-shaped OH-6. The 'Loach', a nickname derived from its LOH (Light Observation Helicopter) designation, was a Vietnam stalwart much respected by its crews. OH-6s were used as FACs and light gunships, and their losses were heavy – one wry saying at the time had it that 'the target is marked by the burning Loach'. However, Hughes's designers respected its structural integrity enough to use it as their starting point. All OH-6 developments soon turned out to be too small to make an effective AAH, so Hughes's engineers ultimately produced the Model 77. The mock-up (above) differed from the prototypes (top) in several respects, but is clearly the ancestor of the Apache. Note the original TOW missile pods on the mock-up.

Above: AV-02 (73-22248) was the first YAH-64 to fly. The first to be built (AV-01/73-22247) served its whole life as the GTV (Ground Test Vehicle). AV-02 is seen here soon after its first flight with the original T-tail configuration and mid-set rotor. Several tailplane configurations were tested, including reversing the 'arrowhead' tailplane and adding end-plate fins.

Top right: AV-03 (73-22249) is seen here with a revised tail configuration, featuring the low-set stabilator adopted for production AH-64s. For a period AV-05 flew with no horizontal stabiliser.

Above right: AV-02 flew with a (red) instrumentation boom on its earliest flights. It also carried a dummy gun under its nose, to maintain the YAH-64's centre of gravity.

Below: This photograph of dummy Hellfires fitted to AV-03 provides a clear view of the actuated trailing-edge flap originally fitted to the YAH-64's stub wings.

sleekness of form, sharing Bell's stepped tandem cockpit, widely-spaced podded engines, stub wings, narrow tailboom and nose-mounted sensors. It differed through its tailwheel undercarriage arrangement (versus a tricycle one), four-bladed main rotor and unfaired gun installation set well back under the fuselage. The YAH-63's cannon was located above and in front of the sensor turret. In the Bell design the pilot sat in the front seat (the direct opposite of the AH-1G), but not so in the YAH-64. Hughes positioned its pilot aft on the principle that by sitting just 2 ft (60 cm) forward of the rotorshaft he would be more attuned to shifts in pitch and angle of rotation – a useful aid to ultra-low-level flight.

The definitive YAH-64 mock-up did not appear until late in 1973, and Hughes soon refined some elements of it still further. Chief among these was the addition of a revolutionary new gun, the single-barrelled XM230A 30-mm Chain Gun® cannon designed by Hughes Aircraft Corporation. It is worth pointing out at this stage that the YAH-64's manufacturer – Hughes Helicopters – was by then a division of the Summa Corporation, while Hughes Aircraft Corp. (which had not built an aircraft for 20 years) was a separate entity, although both owed their existence to Howard Hughes. The YAH-63 was fitted with the three-barrelled General Electric XM188 30-mm cannon, which also was originally specified by Hughes. Ongoing research at Hughes convinced its AAH designers that the Chain Gun® concept offered sizeable advantages over previous aircraft guns, chiefly light weight and resistance to stoppages, and Hughes rushed its development in parallel with that of the YAH-64. Another change made to the mock-up by July 1975 was the revised canopy, which had previously been curved and less heavily framed. The revised canopy used flat-plate transparencies to reduce the problem of glint (curved transparencies will reflect light in a number of planes and for an increased length of time compared to a smaller flat surface). Framing of the canopy was also made more pronounced, dividing the cockpit glass into seven distinct sections.

The YAH-64 consortium

The Hughes AAH entry was widely perceived as a conservative one, avoiding the complicated design features and advanced material techniques that dogged the Cheyenne. Its lightweight aluminium, conventional skin-and-stringer airframe design, rugged straight-forward power train and simple rotor system were tailored to meet the Army's design-to-cost requirements. A team of 12 major sub-contractors was formed to provide expertise in areas where Hughes was lacking and to cut costs. All were allowed the freedom to develop the solution to problems in their particular area of expertise, while meeting Hughes' basic criteria. These firms included Bendix Corporation's Electric Fluid Power Division, responsible for design/fabrication of drive shafts, couplings, electrical power systems. Bertea Corporation: hydraulic systems. Garrett Corporation: design/fabrication of IR suppressors, integrated air systems. Hi-Shear Corporation: crew canopy/escape system. Litton Precision Gear Division: main transmission, engine nose gear boxes. Menasco Manufacturing Inc: landing gear. Solar Division, International Harvester Corporation: APU. Sperry Flight Systems Division: auto-stabilisation system. Teledyne Ryan Aeronautical Division: fabrication of airframe structure. Teledyne Systems: design assistance for fire control computer. Tool Research and Engineering Corporation, Advanced Structures Division: main/tail rotor. Precision Products Division, Western Gear: intermediate/tail rotor gear boxes. Of all the above probably the most significant contribution was made by Teledyne Ryan, which not only supplied major sections of the airframe but later facilitated the demanding initial production schedule that had a major effect on the early days of the Apache.

By June 1976 Hughes had begun ground tests with AV-01 (Air Vehicle), the prototype. This aircraft would be tasked with all the preliminary power tests, but AV-02 would be

the first to fly. In fact AV-01 never flew and served as Hughes's *de facto* Ground Test Vehicle. In contrast, Bell had already run a dedicated YAH-63 GTV in April of that year and its apparent lead in the programme forced Hughes to hurriedly accelerate its work. The first YAH-64 succeeded in beating the YAH-63 into the air by a single day, on 30 September 1975. Pilots for the YAH-64's 38-minute maiden flight (delayed for several hours after the port starter unit failed) were Robert G. Ferry and Raleigh E. Fletcher. It was then Bell's turn to suffer delays as the YAH-63 experienced gearbox problems induced by its high-speed transmission. Gene L. Colvin and Ronald G. Erhart's maiden flight in the YAH-63 had ended after only 2½ minutes, when the aircraft began to experience main rotor vibration. Two more flights were made on that day, totalling 10 minutes, but vibration problems persisted on later flights. Hughes launched AV-03 on its maiden flight on 22 November 1975 (by which time AV-02 had logged 35 flying hours), while Bell's second aircraft followed on 21 December. Pilots for the maiden flight of Hughes's AV-03 were Morrie Larsen and Jim Thompson. Hughes conducted all ground and air tests at Palomar Airport, Carlsbad, California. The flight test programme entailed 342.6 hours between September 1975 and 31 May 1976 before the AAH competitor was handed over to the Army's integrated flight evaluation programme at Edwards AFB. A further 125.5 hours of flying ensued in Army hands, from 16 June, plus 384.4 hours of associated ground tests. The Army's senior Apache test pilot, Colonel Robert L. Stuart, later became the first astronaut to spacewalk (from the Space Shuttle) without using a tether.

Bell's transition to service testing did not go smoothly. On 4 June 1976, while being flown by an Army pilot in the front seat and a Bell pilot in the rear – just prior to its scheduled handover on 16 June – the number two prototype YAH-63 crashed. The accident was traced to a tail rotor drive shaft failure during high-load, sideways flight. Both crew survived but the aircraft was destroyed, and so Bell desperately scrambled to make its GTV airworthy for the US Army.

Sensor systems and Hellfire

The Army test programme was not concerned merely with the AAH aircraft but also with the TADS/PNVS (Target Acquisition and Designation Sight/Pilot's Night-Vision Sensor) suite which was being developed for it. As in the AAH competition, there were two firms vying for this contract – Martin-Marietta and Northrop, which both submitted their proposals on 27 November 1976. Both systems were broadly similar, combining a FLIR and electro-optical sensors in a rotating ball turret mounted on the aircraft's nose. The Martin-Marietta system provided a

permanent FLIR for the pilot above the nose faring, but Northrop's design was retractable. TADS/PNVS evaluation would be an important part of the Phase 2 evaluation of the AAH winner.

Before revealing which of the two designs would be the winner, the Army announced a major change in the AAH specification, one which must have caused dismay to all concerned at the time but which set the seal on the Apache's future as the most lethal helicopter on the battlefield. In 1972 the requirement had been for an aircraft armed with eight basic TOW missiles that had a maximum range of 3000 m (9,843 ft), in day or night. By 1973 this had been modified to include the extended-range XRTOW with its 3750-m (12,303-ft) range. By 1975 the shortcomings of TOW were acknowledged and a replacement weapon was introduced for AAH. This was the Rockwell Hellfire (HELicopter-Launched, FIRE-and-forget), a laser-guided anti-tank missile which promised effective engagement ranges in excess of 6 km (3.7 miles). The unproved, and then unbuilt, Hellfire had a development history that stretched back to the early 1960s, but the risks inherent in its adoption were wisely seen to be less serious than allowing the AAH programme to proceed with inadequate weaponry. On 6 January 1976 the Army System Acquisition Review Board approved the adoption of Hellfire, and this decision was recommended to the Defence Systems Acquisition Review Council on 26 February. Hughes Aircraft Corporation and Rockwell International were both awarded contracts for Hellfire engineering development, with a single contract to be awarded as a result. The decision to integrate Hellfire added five months to the AAH RDT&E schedule, and $49.6 million. It was expected to add, in 1976 terms, $6,000 to the price of each AAH (a figure which later turned out to be impossibly low) but would provide a quantum leap in penetration capability compared to the TOW and Shilleleagh missiles then in service. On 8 October 1976 the Hellfire development contract was awarded to Rockwell International.

Above left and right: As the competition to build the AAH airframe progressed, so too did the competition to supply the TADS/PNVS primary mission sensor. The two rival designs, built by Martin Marietta (left) and Northrop (right), are seen here displayed in front of a YAH-64. Directly above is a view of the unsuccessful Northrop design, mounted on an a testbed aircraft. The chief difference between the Northrop design and its rival was the former's pop-up pilot's FLIR (PNVS) mounted above the nose. Northrop did not develop independent FLIR and DVO turrets in the TADS, but (perhaps unwisely) combined them in a single 'ball' mounting.

Top: All the early prototypes (this is AV-01) flew with representative FLIR housings. When the definitive TADS/PNVS was fitted, the cheek fairings were extended to accommodate the avionics. Note also the long grab handle beside the cockpit which was deleted on production AH-64s.

Phase 2 proposals were submitted in two parts: technical and management portions on 31 July 1976, and cost proposals on 16 August. Details were discussed, debated and disputed with the Army programme managers for four months before each manufacturer submitted its final Phase 2 proposal on 22 November. On 10 December 1976, having reviewed the evaluation results, the Secretary of the Army announced that the Hughes YAH-64 was the winner of the AAH competition. Factors which counted against the YAH-63 included doubts about the damage tolerance of its twin-bladed rotor and the small footprint of its tricycle landing gear, which left the aircraft unstable on the ground. Some claimed that Bell's existing production commitments had made it a likely second choice, as the US Army had no wish to interfere with ongoing AH-1 production. Hughes had met the Army's performance demands in all but one area. The YAH-64's maximum speed was 196 kt (362 km/h, 225 mph) compared to the ultimate goal of 204 kt (377 km/h, 234 mph). The rate of climb achieved by the prototypes was 800 ft/min (244 m/min), twice the original requirement, and the Phase 2 aircraft were expected to achieve 1,100 ft/min (335 m/min). Weapons demonstrations were conducted twice – 1,176 rounds were fired by the XM230 Chain Gun® during forward flight at angles up to 90°, and 184 2.75-in rockets were launched from the hover and at forward speeds of up to 130 kt (241 km/h, 150 mph). The streamlined TOW pods developed for the AAH were also test flown, but they subsequently were replaced by a yet-to-be designed Hellfire launcher. These weapon tests brought about a further success for Hughes – the Army's adoption of the M230 as the YAH-64's onboard gun.

Main rotor redesign

There had been some problems during the Phase 1 evaluation. Perhaps the most alarming of these was described by Hughes thus: "Apparently adequate rotor to canopy clearance was provided within this dimension (the requirement to limit vertical height to allow transportation by the C-141 airlifter), however, during flight testing it was found to be inadequate under sever manoeuvring conditions. In fact, under one extreme condition, it was possible to demonstrate an interference of the non-structural trailing edge of the blade with the corner of the canopy." In short, during negative-g (-0.5 g) pushovers the aircraft hit its own blades. The rotor masts on the two flying prototypes were lengthened by 9.5 in (24.3 cm) to allow safe operations up to -0.4 g, the first aircraft flying in this revised configuration on 9 February 1976. The rotor mast was subsequently lengthened by an additional 6 in (15.24 cm) for production aircraft to permit NoE flight to the design limit of -0.5 g, even in a 54-kt (100-km/h, 62-mph) headwind. On the other hand, during NoE evaluations one crew hit the tail wheel hard enough to burst the tyre, but no 'tailboom bounce' back into the main rotors occurred.

A build-up in blade vibrations as the rotor system entered the high-speed regime led to a redesign of the blade tips, which were swept back. The refined tip design reduced noise and increased the AH-64's maximum speed, exceeding the Army's goals. The flat-plate transparencies on the side of the cockpit were rounded, to add stiffness and reduce vibration-induced 'drumming' caused by the frequency of the rotor system.

Black Hole IR suppressors

The YAH-64 had a predicted primary mission weight of 13,200 lb (5988 kg) but the prototypes exceeded this by about 1,000 lb (454 kg). This figure was significantly reduced through the redesign of the all-important IR-suppression system. Hughes had originally developed an engine-driven cooling fan system which mixed surrounding air with exhaust efflux. This was replaced with Hughes-designed Black Hole IR-suppressors, using a

newly-developed material known as Low Q. The Low Q liner absorbs heat from the exhaust and radiates it slowly into the airflow surrounding the nacelle. Exhaust flow through each duct is used to draw ambient air into the dynamic section of the helicopter, cooling the transmission – via the oil heat exchangers – and the two engines. The fan system drew the equivalent of 50 hp (37 kW) from the 1,536-shp (1143-kW) T700-GE-700 turboshafts, so its removal, coupled with the addition of the lighter (and far less complex) Black Hole system, amounted to a saving of 400 lb (181 kg) in airframe weight. The bulk of the remaining weight saving came through changes in the tail design. This was achieved through a revision of the prototypes' T-tails (a process detailed elsewhere), but not their transformation to the low-set configuration intended for production aircraft. This lightweight tail, coupled with the extended rotor head, became known as the Mod 1 package.

Phase 2 proceeds

The $317.6 million Phase 2 contract called for the building of three production-standard AH-64s, conversion of the two prototypes and GTV to this standard also, and complete weapons and sensor system integration. The 50-month Phase 2 flying programme began on 28 November 1976, although an AH-64 production decision was not expected until May 1980. Notwithstanding, Hughes made the decision to commit to the massive expansion of its production facilities that would be needed to cater to the AAH. The Army's stated initial requirement now stood at 536 aircraft. Hughes began to issue long-lead materials contracts, recall laid-off staff and lease an additional 157,000 sq ft (14585 m²) of factory space. Its partners were faced with similar decisions. Hughes instigated a computerised management control system to its 'Team to the AAH' programme, one in which the Army was very interested. Flight tests continued to be conducted at the Palomar facility, using the gunnery range at the nearby MCAS Camp Pendleton. Full-scale weapons tests were conducted by the Army at the Yuma proving ground, while some Army flight test activity was carried out at Edwards AFB. Environmental testing was conducted at the indoor controlled climate facilities at Eglin AFB, Florida, and icing tests were conducted at Moses Lake, Washington.

All initial Phase 2 activity was limited to the AH-64 GTV, on which every design change was extensively tested.

As a result, only 21 months of the 56-month programme (financial hiccups had forced its extension) remained when the first flight of the modified AV-02, now in production configuration, took place on 28 November 1977. Pilots Bob Ferry (Hughes's chief experimental test pilot) and Morrie Larsen (dedicated AAH test pilot) logged 9.1 hours in 10 flights on that one day alone. After 50 hours of GTV Pre-Flight Approval Tests (PSAT) intended to check out the transmission and gear box systems, AV-04, the first true AH-64, was cleared to fly on 31 October 1979. Bob Ferry and Jack Ludwig were at the controls for the 18-minute maiden flight, which was the first made with a redesigned low-set all-moving tailplane, dubbed the stabilator.

Above: Phase II testing revealed problems with the AH-64's rotor tips. As a result, the blade tips were swept back, leading to a reduction in compression loads and overall noise signature.

The dramatic desert scenery around the Apache production plant at Mesa, Arizona, has provided a spectacular backdrop for many AH-64 photos. One of the pre-production aircraft is seen here skirting a nearby peak.

Opposite page, top: Early rocket tests were conducted with Mk 40 rockets, which have now been replaced in the inventory by Mk 66s, as seen here.

Opposite page, bottom: Hellfire testing began in 1980 and the problems encountered delayed actual missile production until 1982. Initial tests were undertaken in clear desert conditions and some doubts were expressed as to how the missiles would perform under European conditions. As a result, a trial was held in 1981 involving eight shots fired in fog, smoke, dust clouds and rain. Two missiles failed to hit their targets and the Army had to admit that under some conditions Hellfire would not be 100 per cent reliable.

Hellfire tests began in April 1979, initially from an AH-1 fitted with a trial Airborne Target Acquisition Fire Control System (ATAFCS). AH-64 tests were conducted at Camp Pendleton. Initially, missiles were fired (by AV-02) unguided from the critical upper inboard station on the left wing, This station was almost in direct line with the tail rotor so the possible effects of rocket plume and associated debris were a cause of concern, which proved groundless. While these early tests provided useful basic information, true weapons tests could not proceed without a complete onboard weapon guidance and fire control system. The two competing TADS/PNVS systems were installed on the AH-64 prototypes – AV-02 carried Martin-Marietta's system and AV-03 Northrop's. A competitive fly-off between the two sensor fits, at the Yuma Proving Ground, was scheduled for December 1979 after the preliminary guided missile test shots. The first of these autonomously-

guided Hellfire tests was made by AV-02 in October 1979. Within a month Hellfires were scoring self-guided bullseyes on 10-ft x 10-ft (3-m x 3-m) targets. TADS-guided Hellfire tests were part of the overall Armament and Fire Control Survey (A/FCS) test programme, during the early stages of which the AH-64 test fleet passed the 1,000 flying hours mark. The addition of the full-standard fire control system went hand-in-hand with the Mod 2 changes to the AH-64 which added to the prototypes the long cheek fairings of AV-04, and all subsequent aircraft.

In December 1979 AV-05 made its maiden flight, followed by the last of the Phase 2 batch of three aircraft, AV-06, on 16 March 1980. This final aircraft was the first to fly with the definitive stabilator design and extended (by 10 in/25 cm) tail rotor. By April 1981 the prototypes had amassed over 1,000 flying hours. Performance milestones included a new top speed for the AH-64 of 206 kt (381 km/h, 237 mph) achieved in a dive by AV-04 with a further refined tail rotor design, and manoeuvres of +3g. In April 1980 a crucial landmark in the AAH story was reached with the selection of the Martin-Marietta TADS/PNVS for production. A two-month fly-off comprising day and night firings against autonomously-designated and ground-designated targets resulted in Martin-Marietta achieving a three-hits-from-three-firings record and winning a $45.6 million contract for a further 26-month development programme. Phase 2 concluded with a three-month Operational Test programme, from June to August 1980, during which three aircraft flew representative combat missions against simulated enemy armour, ADA and opposing aircraft. Sadly, 1980 ended on a tragic note. On 20 November 1980 AV-04 departed on a routine tail incidence/drag test, accompanied by a T-28D photo chase plane. Flying in close formation, the two collided, and only the pilot of the T-28 survived.

US Army test phase

In May 1981 AV-02/-03/-06 were handed over to the US Army, in preparation for the AH-64's final Operational Test II (OTII) evaluation at Ft Hunter-Liggett. This marked the first time the AH-64 had flown in service hands since the original 1976 fly-off. Under the eye of Army AAH Project Manager Major General Edward M. Browne (one of the strongest supporters of the AAH since before its inception), 2,500 hours were accumulated in advance of a major exercise with the 7th Infantry Division, in August. The AH-64 was deployed for 400 flying hours in difficult desert conditions where temperatures reached 110°F

(43°C). One of the most impressive performances of OPII was turned in by the Martin-Marietta PNVS, which had always been superior to its rival. The same was not true of its associated TADS. Design changes incorporated after Martin-Marietta had won the system fly-off forced a delay of six months in its development, and so defects remained to be corrected. Production go-ahead for the first batch of 13 TADS/PNVS systems was not obtained until 30 April 1982.

AH-64 for the Corps

In September 1981 the US Marine Corps conducted a limited (two-week) assessment of the AH-64's suitability for Marine operations, including shipboard compatibility tests. The Corps had a requirement for 120 AH-64s, for delivery in 1985, and so joined a list of other customers beginning to express an interest in the aircraft. These included Saudi Arabia and West Germany, which had then launched its PAH-2 attack helicopter requirement. Also in September 1981, the first photographs of Soviet Mi-24 'Hinds' operating in Afghanistan were released. Soviet armed helicopter philosophy was quite different to the West's, particularly the doctrine being developed for the AAH, and so the Mi-24 was a very different beast to the AH-64. Nevertheless, the 'Hind' menace became yet another worry for NATO generals already horrified (in public at least) by Soviet armoured superiority in Europe. It also remained the most obvious 'Red' parallel to the AH-64. It was then, during the final stages of AAH Phase 2 testing, late in 1981, that the name Apache was first applied to the AH-64.

The deadline for an AH-64 production decision, known as DSARC III (Defense Systems Acquisition Review Council), was fixed for 10 December 1981. Funding for the first 14 aircraft (Lot 1) had already been included in the 1982 budget, which would, hopefully, see deliveries begin in November 1983 and IOC in October 1984. However, delays in assimilating the results of OPII delayed this decision until March 1982. It was not until 15 April 1982 that full-scale go-ahead for Apache production was finally given. There then followed a complicated delay in funding, not helped by the rising costs of the programme which had been steadily increasing since the oil crisis and recession of the mid-1970s. The $365 million that had been requested for FY82 was increased to $444.4 million, but now this would buy only 11 helicopters. As a result the next (Lot 2) batch of 48 AH-64s was put on hold until a new deal could be hammered out between the DoD and its contractors.

Another element of fall-out from OPII was the decision to move to an uprated version of the T700 engine, the T700-GE-701, rated at 1,690 shp (1259 kW). The -701 engine had already been run on the SH-60B Seahawk (as the T700-401) and the improved performance it promised would greatly benefit the Apache in 'hot-and-high' conditions. On 15 January 1982 AV-05 made its maiden flight with the new turboshaft which would become the definitive production engine for the Apache. Testing was completed by August.

Price wars

While the Apache embarked on a European sales tour in 1982 and completed advanced environmental testing in the US, disputes over its affordability continued. Hughes submitted its production proposals for Lot 2 while AV-02 was amazing the crowds at the Army Air 82 show, held at Middle Wallop – the home of British army flying – and the subsequent Farnborough air show. The US Army had increased its Apache requirement to 536 aircraft, but was then forced to cut this back to 446. On this basis Hughes estimated the total programme cost would be $5,994 million. The US Army had always accepted that the unit cost would creep up from $1.6 million (in 1972 dollars) but was now faced with a price per aircraft of over $13 million (rising to $16.2 million later that year). The AAH was faced with serious political opposition from proponents of a lower-cost Cobra-based aircraft, one which might be far more attractive to other customers such as Germany. (Germany conducted an evaluation of the AH-64 from 25 June to 16 July.) However, the Apache had powerful friends. A letter dated 22 July 1982, from General Bernard C. Rogers NATO C-in-C Europe to the Apache's chief detractors in the Senate, spelled out the threat to Europe posed by the Warsaw Pact, and the urgent need for a counter. It ended with the words "we need the AH-64 in Europe now and cannot afford the luxury of another trip to the drawing board."

A reassessment on all sides led to the conclusion of the Lot 2 production agreement in November 1982. Hughes agreed to supply 48 aircraft under the terms of three phased contracts, each worth $105.6 million. The US Army, in turn, increased its intended buy of Apaches to 515. Work continued apace at Hughes's huge newly-developed Mesa, Arizona facility, which had 240,000 sq ft (22300 m²) of floor space. Hughes had committed to build the facility in July 1981, as the November 1983 delivery date for the first Apache had remained constant throughout all the wrangling and uncertainty. Mesa acted as the assembly point for components sourced from 36 states, including the major airframe assembly supplied by Teledyne Ryan Aeronautical in San Diego. It was here that the first production Apache, PV-01, began to take shape in spring 1982. The first production TADS/PNVS set was delivered in July 1983. As the first three production aircraft progressed down the line at Mesa a welcome FY84 purchase of 112 aircraft was approved, bringing the total to 171 to date.

Apache handover

The first Apache for the United States Army was rolled out in a ceremony held at Mesa, ahead of schedule, on 30 September 1983 – eight years to the day of the first flight and just 18 months after ground had been broken at Mesa. The aircraft was accompanied by an Apache warrior, brandishing a rifle and riding a white horse, beneath a massive Stars and Stripes. The stated price of the aircraft, its 'over the fence' cost according to the then-Project Manager Brigadier Charles Drenz, was $7.8 million in 1984 terms or $9 million in real-year terms. This equated to a unit cost of approximately $14 million when development costs were included. Hughes planned to accelerate production to a peak of 12 per month by 1986, with purchases of 144 AH-64s in FY85 followed by 144 (FY86) and 56 in (FY 87) in prospect.

PV-01 made its 30-minute maiden flight on 9 January 1984, flown by chief test pilot Steve Hanvey and Ron Mosely. By then the prototype fleet had logged over 4,500 hours in the air. This noteworthy event was obscured in

the headlines by the announcement on 6 January 1984 that Hughes Helicopters was about to become a subsidiary of McDonnell Douglas. Under an agreement signed by Jack G. Real, President of Hughes Helicopters, Sanford N. McDonnell, Chairman of McDonnell Douglas, and William R. Lummis, administrator of the estate of Howard Hughes, McDonnell Douglas agreed to purchase 100 per cent of Hughes Helicopters' stock for $470 million (and to pay off debts owed to the estate) – a very reasonable price. The reasons for the sale of Hughes Helicopters for such a seemingly bargain basement price were not readily apparent. Certainly, after the death of Howard Hughes in 1976, the huge and complex industrial monster he left behind was labyrinthine and inefficient. Hughes Helicopters should have been in a healthy position, with a secure future and large order book, but Summa Corporation had incurred major debts to the estate of the late Howard Hughes and Hughes Helicopters itself, apparently, had not made a profit in 30 years. Although Hughes initially was allowed to operate under its original identity, its new ownership spelled immediate change. Aircraft production ceased at Culver City and the workforce there dropped from 5,000 to 1,800. It was Hughes Helicopters' 50th anniversary year.

Buy-out negotiations with McDonnell Douglas had been finalised on 16 December 1983, but prior to that Hughes attracted attention from 15 other interested buyers. A possible influencing factor in Summa Corporation's decision to dispose of Hughes Helicopters was revealed in 1985 when the US Army launched an investigation into McDonnell Douglas's accounting methods. Payments were suspended while Army Under-Secretary James R. Ambrose was ordered to investigate "serious charges of accounting irregularity." Major errors dating back to 1983, and beyond, were discovered. McDonnell Douglas defended itself, claiming that these problems predated its total assimilation of Hughes, but the Army disputed these claims, too. In the midst of these negotiations Hughes Helicopters finally disappeared, on 27 August 1985, to become the McDonnell Douglas Helicopter Company. The dispute between the Army and McDonnell Douglas did not directly involve the cost of the Apache, the price of which fell slightly as production continued. In FY86 terms the unit cost of an AH-64 was down to $7.03 million, or $13.9 million if procurement, acquisition (type R&D and development expenses) and Hellfire development costs were included.

The first handover of an Apache to the US Army took place on 26 January 1984, although this was only a formality since the heavily-instrumented aircraft concerned, PV-01, would remain with Hughes/McDonnell Douglas along with PV-02. PV-03, handed over in May, was the

first aircraft to be truly built to production standards, but initially it, too, remained in use with the manufacturer. PV-04 and PV-05 were the first examples to be handed over to the Army, in July 1984, and, along with four of their successors, operated from Mesa and the Yuma Proving Ground as part of the Initial Key Personnel Training (IKPT) programme. PV-08 and PV-10 were tasked with operational trials alongside the subject of the Army's Advanced Helicopter Improvement Program (AHIP) – the OH-58D Kiowa Warrior. These trials were conducted at Hunter-Liggett. It was not until the delivery of PV-13 that an Army crew could fly an Apache away and call it their own.

Air-to-air Apache

In 1984 the prospect of sales to the USMC was resurrected by the display of an aircraft at the annual Marine Corps League convention in Washington, DC. This was remarkable for the fact that the Apache was fitted with two AIM-9H Sidewinders, bolted on to the end of the stub wings. McDonnell Douglas also offered an air-to-air Stinger and anti-radiation Sidearm missile fit, for delivery to the Marines in 1988. The USMC has always wanted to acquire

Above: The AH-64's rotor blades feature a high (21-in/55-cm) constant camber and an additional fixed trailing-edge tab. This upturned tab positions the blades' centre of pressure for best aerodynamic performance (to 27° rather than the usual 25°), cancelling the nose-down pitching associated with a cambered airfoil. The airfoil section was named HH-02 and is based on the NASA 6400 airfoil. Each blade has five stainless steel spars to reduce the effect of a direct hit, coupled with separate skin plates to prevent cracks propagating. Approximately 60 per cent of each blade is load-bearing (stainless steel) structure. The rest of the blade comprises composite Nomex honeycomb and a fibre-glass skin. Each blade has a leading edge of 040-gauge AM355 stainless steel and a submerged de-icing blanket to provide resistance to abrasion. The US Army requirement for resistance to sand erosion specified 450 hours of hovering over sand before replacement.

Above left: This 1989 view of the Mesa plant shows AH-64A production in full swing. The Mesa facility was purpose-built by Hughes Helicopters, which was bought out by McDonnell Douglas in 1984 and became the McDonnell Douglas Helicopter Company in 1985. The plant was expanded in 1986, from 570,000 sq ft (52950 m²) to an immense 1,904,500 sq ft (176930 m²).

AH-64 Apache and Longbow Apache

Above: The AIM-9 Sidewinder missile was first introduced to the AH-64A as a result of USMC interest in the aircraft. Tests were also undertaken, in 1988, with the Sidewinder-based AGM-122A Sidearm anti-radiation missile.

Right and below: Both Apache crew can use the Honeywell IHADSS helmet-mounted display as their primary flight information display and weapons controller. The helmet's monocle sight can be slaved to the Chain Gun® cannon to follow the crew member's line of sight (below).

Apaches (and has also placed a stronger emphasis on helicopter air-to-air operations that the US Army) but the Apache's price tag has kept it off the Corps' shopping list to this day.

First deliveries, first problems

Initial deliveries were made to US Army Training and Doctrine Command (TRADOC) bases at Ft Eustis, Virginia (home of the Army logistics school), and Ft Rucker, Alabama (the Army's centre of flying training). Qualified pilots transferred from Ft Rucker to Ft Hood, Texas, where units were trained at a battalion level. By the mid-1980s the free-spending Reagan years were in full swing, and in autumn 1984 Defense Secretary Casper Weinberger authorised the acquisition of an additional 160 Apaches (at an FY85 cost of $1.6 billion), bringing the total on order for the Army to 675. This was subsequently increased yet again to 807 aircraft, a number which surprised even the Army. With an eye on the ever-rising costs of the Apache the Army suggested that 48 AH-64s of the FY85 acquisition be delayed, but this was rejected by Congress on the grounds that it would actually add $1.2 million to the unit cost by lengthening the production schedule. Apache acquisition was ultimately amended as follows: 138 (FY85), 116 (FY86), 101 (FY87), 77 (FY88), 54 (FY89), 154 (FY90) and a follow-on batch of 10 (FY95), for a grand total of 827 AH-64A Apaches. The unevenness in these numbers is a reflection of the troubles that hindered Apache production throughout those years. The acceleration to the 12 aircraft per month target did not go smoothly, and neither did Hellfire or TADS/PNVS development/production. Then the investigation by the Defense Contract Auditing Agency (as mentioned above)

intervened and by June 1985 the US government was withholding funds amounting to $3,500 million from McDonnell Douglas.

By January 1986, 68 aircraft had been handed over when suddenly a new and more serious problem reared its head. On 15 January routine maintenance discovered a crack in a rotor blade, a component that had a 4,500-hour service life but had in fact only accumulated 330 hours. Another 12 cracks were found across the inventory. On 27 January 1986 the Apache was grounded, and the US Army refused to accept any more deliveries. Hughes/McDonnell Douglas had been proud of the survivability tests the rotor system had passed, and photographs of the blades intact after hits from 23-mm shells were the centrepiece of every company presentation. The outcome of a rapid and intensive investigation was an immense relief to all concerned: the fault lay not with the design or materials or manufacturing process but with a defective tool that creased the trailing edge of the blade. Later that year a second fault arose when a flight critical bolt failed in the flight control system. The hardened bolt, supposedly proof against a 12.7-mm round strike, had suffered hydrogen embrittlement and sheered off. Although these bolts were replaced with a revised material, the example that broke was found to be the only one so affected.

Into the field

The first unit to convert to the Apache was the 7th Battalion, 17th Cavalry Brigade at Ft Hood, which began its 90-day battalion-level conversion in April 1986. The 7-17th was followed by the 1st and 2nd Battalions, 6th Cavalry Regiment, 6th Cavalry Brigade. These two units departed the United States in September 1987 for the Apache's first deployment to Europe. Their 38 AH-64s

were part of Reforger '87 (REturn of FOrces to GERmany), flying 725 hours in large-scale exercises in night and bad weather to achieve a mission-capable rate of 90 per cent. Upon completion, the aircraft of the 1-6th remained at Illesheim to became the first Apache unit to be based in Europe, while its sister battalion returned to Ft Hood. By 1990 Germany had became home to eight AH-64 battalions, with over 160 aircraft. As early as 1987 Apaches were replacing Cobras in Army National Guard units. The first was D Company, 28th Aviation Regiment, North Carolina ANG. By 1991 nine regular Army units were active in the USA and, by 1994, 33 of 35 battalions (including seven Army National Guard and two Army Reserve battalions) were combat ready. By 1 September 1989 McDonnell Douglas had handed over 500 Apaches. The 700th delivery was made in December 1992 and the 800th AH-64 was delivered in July 1993. ARI (Army Restructure Initiative) 'downsizing' cut back the number of intended/deployed Apache units and changed their composition. However, although units were withdrawn from Germany, the first Apaches arrived in Korea in March 1994 with the 17th Aviation Brigade (5-501st AVN). The last of 821 AH-64As destined for the US Army (excluding prototypes) was delivered on 30 April 1996. This was the 915th production Apache.

Over 200 AH-64s have been ordered by export customers. The first of these was Israel, in 1990, followed by Saudi Arabia, United Arab Emirates, Egypt, Greece, the Netherlands and the United Kingdom. Details of these users and other prospective Apache customers can be found in the AH-64 operators section that follows. Confirmed Apache production, in early 1997, stood at 1,040 aircraft for delivery by the year 2000.

HARS (heading and attitude reference system) is the Apache's inertial navigation system which uses a Doppler radar altimeter and stabilised gyros to provide the pilot with attitude signals for pitch, roll, yaw and heading, along with velocities and acceleration. On engine start-up the HARS requires six to nine minutes to spin up and align itself, although a hasty and less accurate start can be made within four to six minutes. Of course, if the helicopter has not moved since the HARS was last shut down, realignment can be accomplished in 90 to 120 seconds. The Apache's reliance on Doppler is one of its greatest shortcomings. Doppler errors are easily induced, particularly over water, so a strap-on GPS kit is essential mission equipment (though it is not approved as a primary flight instrument). This situation will change with the arrival of the AH-64D and its embedded GPS.

for fighting in the dark. For Apache crews, night-time operations are perhaps even more crucial, as the AH-64's vulnerability to infantry SAMs and gun fire is immeasurably increased on the daytime battlefield. The AH-64 crew can conduct NoE operations at night, locate, identify and destroy targets and then find their way home again – thanks to the Apache's TADS/PNVS.

TADS/PNVS and IHADSS

Design of the TADS/PNVS system and the AAH went hand-in-glove. The system chosen for the AH-64 was built by Martin-Marietta (now Lockheed Martin Orlando) and approved for production in February 1982. As its awkward acronym implies, the system is divided into two parts – the AAQ-11 Mk III PNVS and AN/ASQ-170 TADS – which are independent of each other. The system comprises a dual FLIR for pilot and gunner with additional optical sensors and a Litton Laser Range-Finder/Designator (LRF/D). The steerable PNVS (Pilot's Night Vision System) is mounted above the Apache's nose and provides wide-angle (40° horizontal x 30° vertical field of view/FoV) FLIR imagery for the pilot. The PNVS can be slewed up to 90° off the aircraft's centreline and +20°/-45° in elevation. When not in use the sensor housing can be rotated through 180° to protect its optics. FLIR imagery can be displayed on the pilot's console 5.5-in x 5.5-in (14-cm x 14-cm) CRT Video Display Unit (VDU). The VDU is used typically as a back-up system, because the Apache is flown, and fought, using the Honeywell IHADSS (Integrated Helmet and Display Sight System).

The huge IHADSS helmet, which incorporates standard visors (including laser protective visors) and radio, has a helmet-mounted sight for the right eye, which uses a bulky side arm to mount a small combiner glass in front of the eye. This is the HDU (Helmet Display Unit), or 'hudu'. The pilot's PNVS imagery can be displayed on the HDU, with flight information overlaid, in the same fashion as a conventional aircraft HUD. The PNVS FLIR produces a one-for-one image – it has no magnification – so the (two-dimensional) image the pilot sees in the HDU should correspond with the view outside the cockpit. The PNVS and IHADSS can be slaved so that the FLIR follows the pilot's head and looks where he is looking. An IR head tracking system mounted behind each Apache crew member's head will slew the PNVS at a maximum rate of 120°/sec in azimuth and 93°/sec in elevation, and it can be used to cue the gunner's TADS FLIR.

The TADS (Target Acquisition and Designation System) is more complex, and boasts slightly better FLIR imagery. The TADS system is housed below the PNVS using two roughly hemispherical turrets mounted side-by-side yet capable of independent movement. The complete TADS system can be slewed through 120° and from +30°/-60° in elevation, and is divided into 'day' and 'night' sides. To starboard is the massive 23-cm (9-in) aperture FLIR which is equivalent to the PNVS FLIR. The CPG's (Co-Pilot/

Above: TADS that have been upgraded to OI (optically improved) configuration – that is, most in service – have been modified with a series of optical filters to protect the CPG from laser energy. They will also protect the FLIR from video 'bloom' caused by lasers. Four filter setting are available: normal (clear, no protection), S (Short, provides protection against short-wavelength lasers), L (Long, protects against long-wavelength lasers) and MAX (combined L and S filters). The DVO system has filters applied to fixed optics which are thus always in place.

Right: The Apache's fixed rotor mast allows the transmission and gear box to be removed without interfering with the main rotors. The rotor mast is fixed to the fuselage at eight points and, as the rotor drive shaft runs through it, no flight loads are imposed upon the drive shaft itself. This greatly aids the Apache's agility.

After a long and somewhat troubled development, the Apache began to establish itself as the world's premier battlefield helicopter. The Apache's sophistication brought with it the ability to conduct regimental-sized operations, at night, in the European theatre. The key to its success was its TADS/PNVS sensor system, which for many years had no rival, and the Hellfire missile which has always solidly maintained its claim to be able to destroy any target on the battlefield. Allied with this was the US Army's comprehensive training and exercise system which has evolved to such a degree that the full-scale air/land manoeuvre battles now fought at the US Army's National Training Center are accomplished as a matter of routine. The US Army trains to fight at night. It has poured money into giving all its combat forces – air and land – the ability to manoeuvre and fight around the clock. Desert Storm experience underlined how effective this capability is against an enemy unprepared

Gunner) FLIR differs from the pilot's in having selectable fields of vision: 50°, 10°, 3.1° and 1.6°. Target tracking can be achieved manually, with the image auto-tracker or the laser spot tracker. The spot tracker facilitates target handover from another laser designator. The image auto-tracker has the capability to offset-track one target while automatically tracking another. Automatic linear motion compensation aids in the tracking of moving targets. All TADS imagery can be relayed to the CPG's 'hudu', or the 'ort'. The ORT (Optical Relay Tube) is a small monochrome display in the front cockpit, positioned in the middle of the 'T-bar' of weapons/laser controls that dominates the CPG's station. From here the co-pilot can control all the Apache's weapons and sensors.

Finding and marking targets is the job of the TADS, and on the port side of the nose are the rest of the systems required to do this. Here the TADS has three windows, arranged like traffic lights, behind a vertical, two-facet optical screen. The uppermost of these sensors is the DVO (Direct View Optics) – an optical telescope with a x4 magnification capability at an 18° FoV or x16 magnification at 4° FoV. Beneath this is a near-IR TV system which offers up to x127 magnification with a much-reduced FoV (as little as 0.45°). The third station houses the Apache's laser rangefinder and target marker. All the TADS/PNVS have filters to protect the crew from the potentially devastating effects of battlefield lasers. The Apache's own neodymium laser is definitely not eye-safe and has an effective range of up to 20 km (12 miles). All Apache training ranges must have a large (21 km/13 miles wide) laser backstop.

FLIR pros and cons

The TADS/PNVS system was once without equal and there is still nothing better in service. However, it was over 10 years in development and it has been over 10 years since it was fielded, so, needless to say, technology has moved on significantly. Perhaps the biggest flaw in the TADS/PNVS system was incurred at the very beginning of the AAH design. Mounting the sensors on the nose of the aircraft, just about the lowest point on the Apache apart from the gun and the wheels, forces the AH-64 to unmask completely from terrain to find/designate targets. Keeping the optics stabilised and remote from airframe vibration was a major concern, so a mast-mounted solution was rejected from the start. At the time it was seen as too great a technical challenge. A roof-mounted sight was not included on any AAH design, either, so the Apache was built around a nose-mounted sensor fit. The TADS/PNVS uses two sets of gimbals – a 'coarse' outer set and a 'fine' inner set – coupled with rate-integrated gyros to keep the sensor turrets aligned and stable. Apache maintainers know that the system is not

perfect and will admit that the bulk of the aircraft's regular down-time is caused by vibration-induced malfunctions – as one said, "90 per cent of my problems are in that nose." Apache crews know that the one rule for TADS/PNVS operations is to "boresight, boresight and boresight", to ensure that the system is always up and running correctly.

Ironically for a helicopter designed to fly and fight on the Central European Front, typical central European cold wet weather causes the biggest problems for the AH-64 FLIR. All FLIRs are subject to IR crossover, a phenomenon encountered when humidity and ambient temperature conspire to turn target and terrain the same cold, flat temperature, and the AH-64A FLIR offers no discrimination between either. In situations where target discrimination is not completely clear the CPG can change the polarity on the targeting FLIR, switching from 'white hot' to 'black hot'. The system also has selectable, infinite gain (contrast). Acknowledged limitations in FLIR performance are an important reason why the Apache has a combined FLIR/TV system.

The Apache has a video-recording system linked to the TADS/PNVS. Although now outdated and bulky (and incompatible with any other outside video system), the tactical benefits of such an onboard system are immense. Having reached its battle position under cover, the Apache will pop up, quickly view the target, record the scene and then remask to watch the tape. This allows the crew the luxury of assessing the enemy at length without endangering themselves. Over the tactical radio net, the Apache teams will then make the final engagement decisions, allocate targets, fine-tune the shooter/designator pairs, and wait for the word to go. A new 'Hi-8'-based video system is currently in flight-test for the AH-64A. Developed by TEAC and Merlin, the new recorder uses an industry-

The Apache is fitted with the AN/APR-39(V)1 or APR-39A(V)1 radar warning receivers. The RWR cockpit display produces a radial strobe showing a line of bearing to the detected radar. An audio signal is emitted from the RW control panel and in the crews' headphones. The alarm's frequency represents the strength of the threat signal. A missile alert lamp is also illuminated. The RWR can be set to alert the crew to specific signals or all emissions in the area. AN/APR-39A(V)1 is more advanced and uses an onboard threat library to identify radars and display appropriate symbology. APR-39A(V)1 also has a more sophisticated aural warning. If a threat is detected a synthetic voice will announce, "SA, SA-8 12 o'clock tracking." A second mode provides a more terse warning: "missile, missile 12 o'clock tracking." Twin RWR antennas are located on the rear of the fin cap and forward on cheek fairings. A single antenna is found under the tailboom.

standard format that offers sharply increased horizontal line resolution, with output at 525-line standard (the existing Apache system uses a non-standard 875-line resolution).

M230E1 Chain Gun® cannon

The Apache's weapons are divided into two (tactical) categories: area weapons and point weapons. Starting at the front of the aircraft, the M230 Chain Gun® cannon is the Apache's secondary area weapon (due to its relatively short range). The Chain Gun® was a unique invention, pioneered by Hughes as an integral part of the AH-64's development. The concept behind the Chain Gun® is straightforward. The name derives from its ammunition feed mechanism, which uses a one-piece metal chain to feed linkless shells from a central magazine. Hughes had already done substantial research on 7.62-mm and 20-mm chain gun concepts and scaled up their designs to produce the 30-mm M230. Using aluminium-cased ammunition (half the weight of brass), the Apache can carry approximately 1,200 rounds (the AAH requirement was for 320) – 1,100 in the magazine and 90 in place on the chain feed to the gun. The gun's feed mechanism is a continuous, flat rectangular 'loop' driven by a 6.5-hp (4.84-kW) motor. The chain loads ammunition (along the starboard side of the aircraft) into the breech and seals it until the gun is fired – a simple system resistant to dirt and wear. The M230 fires a 'loosely NATO-standard' round, compatible with the UK's ADEN and French DEFA 30-mm shells. The gun fitted to production Apaches is the M230E1, which can trace its lineage back to the XM230A, first test fired in April 1973. It has a maximum rate of fire of 600-650 rounds per minute (60 per second) and 'spools up' to this rate in just 0.2 seconds. Time of

flight to 1,000 m (3,280 ft) is two seconds, and 12.2 seconds to 3000 m (39,843 ft). The Chain Gun® is accurate, but is used primarily as an area weapon for suppressive fire 'to keep heads down'.

One extra item of equipment that crews would have liked during Desert Storm was a laser tracker to follow rounds 'down range'. The Apache does not carry tracer rounds, so, if firing at night, the gunner can only see his fall of shot if rounds are actually impacting on the target at which he is looking. If the gunner is 'head-down' using the TADS and the gun is not correctly aligned, the gunner may have to zoom back out from the target to redirect his fire, possibly losing the target in the process.

Conventional M230E1 ammunition is the M789 HE dual-purpose (HEDP) round. Each shell has a 0.76-oz (21.5-g) explosive charge and a shaped charge liner that collapses, upon impact, into an armour-piercing molten metal jet. The projectile body also fragments up to a range of 4 m (13 ft). In tests, Chain Gun®-fired rounds penetrated more than 2 in (5 cm) of rolled homogenous armour at 2500 m (8,202 ft), but, during Desert Storm, Apaches destroyed T-55 tanks with the Gun alone. For fire training purposes inert M788 rounds are used, while dummy M848 rounds are used for function checks of the gun mechanism.

Rockets – the area weapons system

The Apache's primary area weapons system is its 2.75-in rockets. The rockets in use today are known as the Hydra 70 family, a name which applies to any warhead fitted to the Mk 66 rocket motor. The Mk 66 has replaced the earlier Mk 40 motor and has a longer tube, improved double-base solid propellant and a different nozzle/fin assembly. Increased velocity and spin improve trajectory stability for better accuracy, though its smoke trail and launch signature remain the same as the Mk 40's. Mk 40 rockets were developed by the Army's Redstone Arsenal and are carried in a 19-round pod, although a seven-round pod is also available. The pods are inexpensive enough to be disposable, but are sturdy enough to be reused. Rocket warheads come in several forms. The most basic of these is the M151 HE warhead, traditionally referred to as the '10-pounder'. The M151 is an anti-personnel, anti-material warhead with a burst radius of 10 m (33 ft). Fragments are lethal up to 50 m (164 ft). The M274 Smoke Signature (training) round is a ballistic match for the M151. It carries a potassium perchlorate/aluminium powder charge to provide 'flash, bang and smoke' for training.

The M229 HE warhead is referred to as the '17-pounder' and uses 4.8 lb (2.17 kg) of B4 high-explosive, the same as in the M151. The M247 HE warhead is no longer in production but is held in reserve stocks. It uses a small shaped-charge warhead of composition B explosive.

The 13.6-lb (6.16-kg) M261 HE multi-purpose submunition (MPSM) warhead can be used against light armour and vehicles. It adds an M439 fuse, programmable to detonate between 550 m (1,640 ft) and 7000 m (22,966 ft), along with nine M73 submunitions. The M73s are dispensed approximately 150 m (492 ft) above the target. Each

bomblet has a steel body and a 3.2-oz (91-g) shaped charge to penetrate armour. The submunition then explodes into approximately 195 fragments, each travelling at 5000 m/sec (16,404 ft/sec). At 1000 m (3,280 ft) a single M261 warhead will cover an oval area of 56 x 17 m (184 x 56 ft), decreasing to 22 x 13 m (72 x 43 ft) at 5000 m (16,404 ft). Each M73 can penetrate up to 4 in (10.16 cm) of armour. The M267 Smoke Signature (training) round uses three M75 practice submunitions with small pyrotechnic charges. The M267 fulfils the same training role as the M274.

The M255E1 flechette warhead contains 1,180 60-grain hardened steel flechettes and is primarily an anti-personnel/soft target weapon, although it does have a limited air-to-air application. M156 White Phosphorous (smoke) rounds are used for target marking and incendiary purposes. The M156 has a 2.2-lb (1-kg) WP filler with a small HE bursting charge. The M257 Illumination warhead provides one million candlepower over an area of 1 km² (10,764 sq ft) for at least 100 seconds (descending on a parachute at 4.5 m/sec; 15 ft/sec).

Close-in tactics

Rocket and gun attacks can be made from the hover, as running fire or as diving fire. Before any attack, it is crucial to remember to check the 'four Ts' – Target (verify azimuth, and that target is correct), Torque (select the correct torque required to maintain altitude and do not change it), Trim (horizontal and vertical) and Target (check it again). When firing in the hover the AH-64 pilot may not be able to see directly over the aircraft's nose and will have to use other reference points to maintain position. When engaging a target with running fire the Apache crew will select an IP 8 to 10 km (5 to 6.2 miles) from the target, then depart the IP flying NoE to mask the helicopter's approach. At 6 km (3.7 miles) the Apache will pop up just enough to reacquire the target visually, then level out. Rocket engagements can begin at 5000 m, cannon at 1500 m, and the aircraft will enter a shallow (3° to 5°) 100-kt (184-km/h, 115-mph) dive before opening fire. The pilot should disengage at 3000 m (using rockets) or 1000 m (using guns) to break for terrain cover. The helicopter should never overfly the target.

Diving attacks are used only in circumstances where there is minimal ADA (air defence artillery) and LoS to the target is obstructed, or a high concentration of firepower is needed at a precise point, or weight/temperature restrictions prevent hover fire. From approximately 3000 ft AGL the Apache will dive at 10° to 15° (30° for a steep dive) and engage the target before breaking away above 1000 ft AGL. Dive recovery has to be planned in time to avoid the controls 'mushing' from an abrupt recovery at high airspeed.

Of course the key to the Apache's success as a tank-killer is its point target weapons system – the Rockwell AGM-114 Hellfire missile. Each Hellfire is just 7 in (17.8 cm) in diameter, 64 in (162.5 cm) in length and weighs 99.5 lb (45 kg), except for the AGM-114F which is slightly longer and heavier. The basic weapon, the AGM-114A, is no longer in production and stocks are being used in live-fire training. The AGM-114B is a version for naval use with HERO (Hazard of Electronic Radiation to Ordnance) safeguards. The AGM-114C is the baseline model in current Army

The altitude from which rockets are fired, and the range to target, determine the angle of impact and fragmentation pattern. Rockets fired with a high angle of impact produce fragmentation patterns that are close together. A rocket fired at NoE altitudes produces an elongated pattern.

The Apache training system

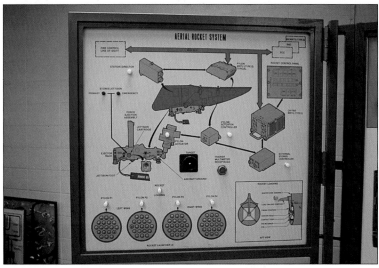

All aviators who come to *Ft Rucker* for Apache training begin their studies in the classrooms of the *Goodhand Simulator* complex, learning about the basic systems of the AH-64. This elementary, but essential, phase involves a series of animated 'billboards' and a lot of 'book learning'.

More sophisticated systems training is undertaken on the *TSDT – TADS Selective Task Trainer*. Ft Rucker has eight *TSDTs* (including two on the flight line at Hanchey AAF), which use *Silicon Graphics* computers to generate *FLIR* imagery and symbology, and teach basic cockpit 'switchology'

Left: The third stage in Apache training sees students progressing onto the CWEPT (Cockpit, Weapons and Engine Procedure Trainer). Students start in the back (pilot's) seat to learn engine start/shut-down procedures. This is often their first encounter with twin-engined helicopter operations. In 1996 Ft Rucker trained 275 Apache fliers, 75 of whom were for the US Army.

Below: This is the control desk for the unique Apache Crew Trainer, from where missions are monitored and controlled.

Above: A single Apache Crew Trainer (ACT) has been built from a modified CWEPT, to which has been added wrap-round screens plus an Evans and Sutherland 3-D graphics system. The ACT allows crews to fly realistic missions (using a complete graphical terrain database of Ft Rucker), while integrating FLIR and HDU flying. A developed version of this system, for the AH-64D, will allow missions to be 'flown' and linked to other participants, via satellite – a revolutionary mission planning aid.

Right: Ft Rucker's AH-64A full-motion simulator was developed at a time when computer graphics technology did not have the capability to accommodate two crew in one station, so pilot and CPG sit separately while 'flying' the same aircraft.

*Left: The front (CPG's) cockpit of the AH-64A is dominated by the **ORT** and its 'T-bar' handgrip. On the front console the CPG has a fire control panel (left) and a set of basic flight instruments (right). On the port side-console (from front to back) can be seen the Hellfire missile control panel, data entry keyboard, anti-icing controls, power lever quadrant, fuel control panel, interior lighting controls and circuit breakers. The starboard side-panel contains the communications system control panel, AN/ARC-186 radio controls, Doppler control panel and a blank area (with provision for KY-58 secure voice control) used for map storage. The pilot and CPG have identical collective controls, but slightly different cyclic grips. The CPG cyclic (centre stick) is folded to the floor in this photograph.*

*Above: The **ORT** (Optical Relay Tube) is the primary station where the **CPG** can monitor TADS/PNVS imagery, then select, designate and shoot targets. Its bulky construction is also the greatest threat to the CPG's well-being in the event of a crash. The hooded monocle display at the top can be used head-down, while the screen below allows the CPG to remain 'head-up'. Beneath the open screen are video-source (TADS or PNVS) and filter selection switches. Flanking the open screen are gain, brightness, grey-scale and FoV adjustment switches. On the left-hand grip can be found the sensor select switch (FLIR, DVO, DTV), weapons action switch (gun, rocket, missile), weapons trigger, primary FoV (wide, medium, narrow, zoom) controls and image autotracking controls. On the right side of the 'T-bar' grip can be found the laser spot tracker controls, manual turret slew controls, FLIR polarity switch (black/white), video recording switch, main laser trigger and boresighting controls.*

AH-64D Longbow Apache

1 Pilot's Night Vision Sensor (PNVS)
2 Rotating PNVS turret
3 Target Designation Sight unit (TADS)
4 Night vision sensor (FLIR)
5 Direct Vision Optics (DVO)
6 EW antenna
7 Chain Gun® cannon muzzle
8 Environmental Control System (ECS) evaporator and fan
9 Co-pilot/gunner's rudder pedals and cyclic pitch controls
10 Signal data converter
11 Armament control panel
12 Sight viewer
13 Gunner's windscreen panel
14 Starboard side cockpit entry hatch
15 Pilot's windscreen panel
16 IR head position sensors for IHADSS system
17 Co-pilot/gunner's armoured seat
18 Collective pitch and engine condition controls

19 Side console panel
20 Avionics equipment bay, port and starboard
21 Link return chute, ammunition
22 Mainwheel shock absorber mount
23 Pilot's instrument console
24 Blast screen between cockpits
25 Cockpit hatch balance strut
26 Starboard stub wing weapons carriage
27 Cable cutter
28 Pilot's armoured seat
29 Collective pitch lever
30 Engine condition levers
31 ECS compressor
32 Boarding steps

33 Stowage bay
34 Avionics equipment
35 Forward fuel cell
36 Flight control system mechanical linkages
37 Rotor head hydraulic actuators (three)
38 Cooling air intake
39 EW antenna
40 Temperature sensor
41 Rotor blade root attachment points
42 Composite main rotor blades with stainless steel spars
43 Mast-mounted Longbow MMW radar radome
44 Longbow radar avionics
45 Articulated radar scanner
46 Omnidirectional airspeed sensor

47 Rotor blade lead-lag friction dampers
48 AN/ALQ-144 'disco light' infra-red jammer
49 Rotor head swash plate mechanism
50 Laser warning receiver
51 Gearbox mounting frame
52 Main gearbox
53 Generator
54 Ammunition bay and feed drive

55 Stub wing attachment joints
56 Port engine intake
57 Engine transmission right-angle gearbox
58 Gearbox input shaft
59 Tail rotor output shaft
60 Engine accessory equipment gearbox
61 Intake particle separator air duct
62 General Electric T700-GE-701C turboshaft
63 Environmental control system

64 Auxiliary Power Unit (APU)
65 APU exhaust
66 'Black Hole' infra-red suppression exhaust ducts
67 Hydraulic reservoir
68 Central maintainance walkway
69 Electro-luminescent lighting strip
70 Tail rotor transmission shaft
71 Shaft bearings
72 Tail rotor control rod
73 Intermediate gearbox
74 Tail rotor final drive shaft
75 Swept main rotor blade tip

Self-protection fit

Behind the Apache's rotor mast is the AN/ALQ-144(V) IR countermeasures set – the 'disco light' jammer. ALQ-14[ ] transmits modulated radiation at high and low frequencies using an electrically heated source, to confuse IR-guided SAMs. The Apache also has an onboard radar jammer, the AN/ALQ-136, to defend it from ground-based fire control radars. The ALQ-136's signals induce range and angle errors in the hostile tracking radar. The transmit antenna for the ALQ-136 is located on the TADS housing, between the FLIR and DVO turrets. The receive antenna is situated above the fuselage, behind the pilot's canopy.

McDonnell Douglas AH-64D Longbow Apache
US Army Material Command/OPTEC/TEXCOM

The first 'AH-64D' to fly was an AH-64A with a dummy radome. The six pre-production aircraft that followed were full-standard AH-64D conversions – though the last two of these were not equipped with the Longbow MMW radar. This aircraft is the fourth AH-64D development aircraft (90-0423), which first flew on 4 October 1993. The Longbow flight test programme is currently split between Mesa, Arizona, and Ft Hood, Texas – in the charge of the US Army Material Command's Apache Attack Helicopter Project Manager's Office.

Crew protection and crashworthiness

The Army specified that the Apache crew must survive a vertical descent of 42 ft/sec (12.8 m/sec) applied to the landing gear. Such an impact translates to a 37-*g* load on the crew. The Apache's sliding seats attenuate that load to a highly unpleasant, but survivable, 13-*g* load. During early flight tests after a catastrophic engine failure one of the Apache prototypes dropped 300 ft (91.4 m) straight down. The crew walked away. All Apache crews have unshakeable faith in their aircraft, provided it does not come down sideways. The crew's seats provide ballistic armour protection through blast/fragmentation shields, around and between the two seats. In October 1995 Phoenix-based Simula Inc. was awarded a contract to install and test a system of airbags for the AH-64A. Head and torso injuries account for more than half of the crew injuries sustained during otherwise survivable crashes, and the Army has determined that such injuries could be cut by 50 per cent using airbags. A series of 30 drop tests conducted during 1993 confirmed the suitability of air bags for an attack helicopter. The Apache air bag modification kits are due to be fielded in 1997. Air bags will be located to the side and in front of each crew member. In a series of simulator tests held at Ft Rucker, crews were subjected to three 'inadvertent' air bag deployments which reportedly did not interrupt the mission or compromise the aircraft. The Apache's air bags are designed not to obscure critical flight instruments.

Hellfire launch

In a LOAL (Lock-On After Launch) engagement the AGM-114K Hellfire II can be fired in three pre-launch programmed trajectories. Two launch modes are available – normal (sometimes referred to as 'rapid') and ripple. In normal mode only missiles coded on the priority (autonomous guidance) channel can be fired. In ripple engagements priority and alternate (remotely designated) channel missiles are fired, alternately.

Longbow Hellfire

Martin-Marietta (now Lockheed Martin Orlando) and Westinghouse won a two-year $30.5 million US Army contract for initial production of the AGM-114L Longbow Hellfire II in January 1995. Up to that point Rockwell had been the Army's sole supplier of Hellfires. Allied with the initial $31 million production funding contract for the fire control contract, the contract provided a major boost for the two firms at a time when the RAH-66 had been officially shelved. In June 1995 Lockheed Martin and Rockwell formed a joint company to manufacture the AGM-114L. This ended fierce competition between the two for production batches of the AGM-114L. Belfast-based Shorts Missile Systems is the prime contractor for the UK's acquisition of Hellfire II and Longbow Hellfire missiles.

76 Final drive right-angle gearbox
77 Tail rotor pitch control servo actuator
78 VHF/FM antenna
79 Electro-luminescent formation lighting strip
80 GPS antenna
81 Rear radar warning antennas
82 Tail navigation light
83 Dual twin-bladed teetering tail rotor

84 All-moving tailplane
85 Tailplane hydraulic actuator
86 Castoring tailwheel
87 Cable deflector
88 Chaff/flare launcher
89 ADF antenna
90 Rolls Royce/Turboméca RTM 322 alternative engine for British army aircraft
91 IFF antenna
92 ADF loop antenna

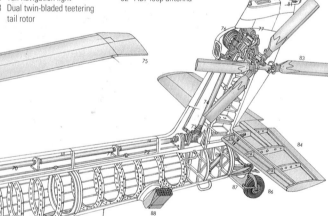

Badrocke/97

93 Doppler antenna fairing
94 Survival packs, port and starboard
95 Anti-collision strobe light
96 Port navigation light
97 Ground equipment stowage bay, battery bay to starboard
98 VHF antenna
99 Rear fuel cell
100 ECS condenser
101 Port stub wing
102 Electro-luminescent formation lighting strip
103 Weapons pylons with articulated carrier/launchers
104 Articulated carrier hydraulic actuator
105 Four-round missile launcher
106 Hellfire anti-armour missiles, maximum load 16

107 19-round 70-mm rocket launcher
108 2.75-in Hydra 70 rocket
109 Dual ATAS Stinger launcher, for wingtip mounting
110 (FIM-92) Stinger air-to-air self-defence missile
111 Chain Gun® ammunition magazine,1,200 rounds
112 Port mainwheel
113 Boarding step
114 Cable cutter
115 Swivelling ventral gun turret mounting
116 Ammunition feed and link return chutes
117 Gun elevation hydraulic actuator
118 Articulated gun mounting frame
119 Cable deflector framework
120 M230 Chain Gun® 30-mm cannon

Above left: The rear (pilot's) cockpit on the AH-64A has an instantly more spacious feel to it than the CPG's. The screen in the console centre is the video display unit (VDU) and beneath it are the horizontal situation indicator (HSI) and smaller, hydraulic systems gauges. To the left are the airspeed indicator (ASI) and standby ASI. Further left are the strip indicators for the Apache's engine torque, turbine gas temperature, engine gas generator, oil and fuel levels. Below and beside them, on an 'L-shaped' panel, are the fire control switches. The black and yellow canopy jettison handle is clearly marked. On the right side of the console are the radar altimeter, radio-call placard, encoding barometric altimeter, RWR display, vertical speed indicator (VSI), clock, HARS controls and accelerometer. To the far right can be seen the (red and yellow) icing severity meter, radar/IR countermeasures panel, chaff dispenser control and RWR control panel. Below them is a bank of caution/warning lights. The circular lens above the coaming on each Apache cockpit is the boresight reticle unit. The rear cockpit side-consoles are dominated by a bank of radio (and some weapons) controls.

Above and below: Both cockpits in the AH-64D have been transformed by the addition of twin Bendix King MFDs, while still retaining some of their 'old-style' feel. The 6 x 6-in (15 x 15-cm) screens were monochrome on development AH-64Ds, but will be full-colour in production aircraft. The first colour displays were delivered to McDonnell Douglas in late 1996. Note how instruments have been raised above the coaming in the pilot's cockpit.

Left and above: The M230E1 30-mm Chain Gun® has a void space above it, to fold into in the event of a crash, protecting the crew. The Chain Gun's 'chain' can be seen above, at the point where it interfaces with the ammunition flatpack. The chain carries rounds to the right to feed the gun

Above: 30-mm rounds are loaded using the motorised uploader/downloader which propels shells up a flex chute, along the port side of the fuselage and into the flatpack or 'ammo can'.

Above and left: All AGM-114 Hellfires are painted black, with olive drab markings. Yellow (3 x 3-in) square markings on the front of the missile denote an HE warhead. Brown squares to the rear signify a solid propellant motor. Inert handling training rounds are designated M34; training rounds with functional seeker heads (above) are M36s.

Above and left: US Apaches use 2.75-in Hydra 70 rockets, typically fired from 19-round M261 pods. Rockets are packed with their fins taped up, prior to loading. Blue warheads denote training rounds. Live rockets are olive drab with yellow warheads.

Right: The Shorts Starstreak/ Helstreak air-to-air missile will most likely be carried by the UK's WAH-64Ds in a two-round wingtip canister, as seen here. The three darts of the missile's warhead are plainly visible on this model.

Right: The MATRA Mistral has been carried for 'form and fit' tests on the AH-64, but no test firings have ever been made. Air-to-air Mistral is already operational on French army Gazelles.

Left: The 30-round M130 chaff launcher is located on the tailboom. Apaches do not routinely use flares – they are ineffective at low-level, tend to hit the tail rotor and can set surrounding vegetation on fire.

Tail section and rotor

The Apache features a semi-rigid, teetering, twin-bladed tail rotor mounted at offset degrees of 60° and 120° rather than 90°. Each pair of blades has one stainless steel spar and two aluminium spars and is fastened to its own delta-hinged hub. The airfoil is a NASA 63-414 section. This unusual design has provoked some disagreement, not least within the Apache community, as to why it was implemented. The accepted answer has always been for reasons of noise reduction. Certainly, the tail rotor's low rotation speed of 634 ft/sec (193 m/sec) cuts back on aircraft noise, but the offset position was also definitely a function of the T-tail and the need to accommodate the Apache in a C-141B. The teetering twin-blade approach is unique, to date, and did away with the need for conventional centrifugally-loaded oscillating bearings. However, the resultant Coriolis loads (whirling blades deforming into a cone shape rather than a flat disc) during operation called for a high-strength titanium rotor fork. The original AAH mock-up had featured a folding tail, a design feature that was retained by AV-01 and AV-02. However, field tests proved that by careful positioning two AH-64s could be accommodated in the hold of a C-141B (the dimensions of which had been the constant limiting factor for AAH designers) without removing the tails. This allowed Hughes to dispense with the heavy and fatigue-sensitive structure.

Tailplane design

The Apache was originally designed with a horizontal stabiliser mounted on the fuselage, at the base of the vertical tail. The design was first trialled on a modified OH-6A, which led to concerns about the effect of rotor downwash on aircraft handling. The stabiliser was repositioned to the top of the tail, resulting in a T-tail and a problem. The stabiliser had been designed as a work platform for field maintenance and so was a heavy, load-bearing structure. Time did not allow the production of new, lighter units for the T-tail, so AV-01/-02 initially flew with this weight penalty. The design of the stabiliser for Phase 2 flight tests was reversed: a straight leading edge replaced a swept one and the trailing edge was swept where previously it had been straight. This new lightweight T-tail, fitted to AV-02/-03 only, was part of the Mod 1 package. However, the position of this fixed T-tail ultimately resulted in an unsatisfactory nose-up attitude, hindering NoE flight and sensor suite operations. The T-tail was finally replaced by a low-set all-moving tailplane, lengthened (by 2½ ft /0.76 m) and linked to the flight control system. The new stabilator design was first flown on AV-04. The unit was fitted with an electric folding motor to facilitate air transportation.

Air transportability and self-deployment

The basic requirement for the AH-64A was for two aircraft to be carried in the C-141B and six in the C-5A. Fitting two Apaches into the StarLifter was a complicated task, requiring the removal of the entire rotor head, folding the vertical tail and stub wings, plus kneeling the landing gear to allow the aircraft to 'scrape' in. On a Galaxy the rotors and wings simply had to be folded back, but the tail and rotorhead remained untouched. The Apache was granted its air transportation certificate in November 1981 when Hughes loaded two aircraft onto a C-141B in 80 per cent of the allotted time. With rotors, stub wings and other components removed (transport configuration), three AH-64As can be carried by the C-17, along with two cargo pallets and 50 personnel. If the Apaches remain in tactical configuration (wings and major components in place) two aircraft can be accommodated by C-17, along with four cargo pallets and 38 personnel. AH-64D loads are similar, with the added need to remove the mast-mounted radar. The AAH requirement also called for self-deployment ability of an 800-nm (1481-km, 920-miles) ferry range with a 20-kt (37-km/h, 23-mph) headwind and a 45-minute reserve. This permitted a wartime Reforger deployment from the US to Germany via Goose Bay (Canada), Frobisher Bay – now known as Iqaluit – on Baffin Island (Canada), Sondrestrom (Greenland), Reykjavik (Iceland) and Prestwick (Scotland).

Longbow directional infra-red countermeasures

Increasing attention is being paid to improving the protection of low- and slow-flying aircraft – chiefly large transports and helicopters – from the universal threat of IR-guided SAMs. As missile seeker technology becomes more advanced and the missiles themselves become faster, conventional (passive) chaff/flare technology is lagging behind the missile's ability to discriminate and destroy its target. As a result, much current research has been devoted to active IR countermeasures, so-called Directional Infra-Red Countermeasures (DIRCM), which can detect, track and disable an incoming missile using an intense beam of modulated energy. The high-value Apache is seen as one of the prime applications of this new technology and the UK MoD has already selected one system for integration on AAC AH-64Ds. This is the ARI 18246 NEMESIS DIRCM, developed by Northrop Grumman, GEC-Marconi Radar and Defence Systems, British Aerospace Systems & Equipment (BASE), Rockwell International and Westinghouse. The Westinghouse AN/AAR-54 Passive Missile Approach Warning System (PMAWS) detects the IR signature of a missile plume and classifies it as a threat. Up to six sensors located around the airframe can give 360° coverage and the PMAWS's fine angle-of-attack sensor allows the missile track to be handed over to the IRCM tracking sub-system at long range and in all weathers. Rockwell provides the NEMESIS Fine Track Sensor (FTS) which optically tracks the missile using a high-resolution, large-area focal plane array. FTS can continue to track a missile even after its motor has burned out. The missile seeker head is then jammed and disabled by NEMESIS's high-powered, modulated arc lamp transmitter, developed by Northrop Grumman. GEC-Marconi supplies the system's transmitter unit – an agile, four-axis turret (similar to that used in the TIALD system) housing the complete FTS and jamming system. BASE is involved in NEMESIS component assembly, integration and development to meet future threats. When the technology becomes available, NEMESIS can integrate a laser powerful enough to burn out missile seeker heads. A similar system is under development by Lockheed Sanders. Lockheed's ATIRCM (Advanced Threat IR CounterMeasures) system combines a laser and xenon lamp optical jammer plus advanced chaff/flare combined with the existing AN/AAR-47 missile warning system. Cued by the AAR-47, the ATIRCM transmitter focuses on the missile seeker head to jam it with a deceptive IR waveform.

Main rotor head

When it came to designing the Apache rotor system, Hughes did not forget its Vietnam experience. Even though the OH-6 was worlds apart from the YAH-64, it had a profound effect on the latter's design. This was most obvious in the YAH-64's fully-articulated rotor head, which was essentially a scaled-up version of that of the OH-6A. A series of 22 redundant laminated straps are used to fix the blades to the fully-articulated rotor head. These straps are flexible enough to permit blade flapping and feathering, and fatigue tests have shown that up to 10 can fail and the Apache will still remain flyable. The blade retaining bolts are expandable, a design feature first incorporated on the OH-6, to permit easy blade folding for transportation. The main rotor mast is a static, non-rotating design. It houses an inertia-welded Nitralloy drive shaft which, like all elements of the main rotor system, has a fatigue life of +4,500 hours. Even if the drive shaft were to fail, the mast carries much of the rotor loads and controls would not be affected for an autorotation. The mast is bolted directly to the fuselage and will sustain an impact of 20g before collapsing. Like the OH-6 before it, there has never been a recorded case of the AH-64 suffering a mast failure in flight or in a survivable crash.

Swept blade tips

Results from the flight test portion of Phase 2 testing forced a revision in the blade tip design of the AH-64. The original straight tips were cambered, and a constant-thickness and constant-chord section were added. Coupled with a 20° sweep applied to the final 20 in (51 cm) of the blade, and tip weights inside the blade, this new design delayed the onset of drag divergence as tip speeds approached Mach 1, the so-called 'Mach truck' effect (the build-up of a large shock wave in front of the blades was likened to the 'bow wave' of America's giant Mac trucks). The new tips also provide a useful dynamic twist by using the upload on the retreating tip to decrease the angle of attack. The blade tips are designed to be replaced every 1,000 to 2,000 flying hours but are susceptible to abrasion faster than the rest of the blade.

Apache powerplant

The basic AH-64A was powered by the General Electric 1,696-shp (1265-kW) T700-GE-701 turboshaft, which was downrated to provide reserve power in 'red-line' combat/emergency situations. From the 604th production aircraft these engines were uprated to 1,890-shp (1409-kW) T700-GE-701C standard. All AH-64Ds will be fitted with the more powerful -701C engine. The UK's Longbow Apaches will be re-engined with the Rolls-Royce Turboméca International (RRTI) RTM322 turboshaft, an engine designed from the outset to compete with the T700 while offering greater power. The RTM322 is rated at 2,100 shp (1566 kW) and has already been flown on the Sikorsky S-70C/UH-60, EH101 and NH90. The RTM322-powered Longbow Apaches will have a newly-developed FADEC (Full-Authority Digital Engine Control), modified from that fitted to the EH101. Although this existing FADEC system will have to be altered to cope with the Apache's dynamic characteristics, it should have the hidden advantage of being immune to electronic interference during shipborne operations – a potentially important future UK Apache role.

Longbow radar jammer

The AH-64D will be the first US Army helicopter to receive the Advanced Threat Radar Jammer (ATRJ), under development by ITT Avionics for the US Army's Communications and Electronics Command (CECOM). ATRJ is being developed under a $54.7 million contract for various US military aircraft including the OH-58D, RAH-66, UH-60/MH-60, MH-47, MH-53 and V-22. ATRJ will counter continuous wave and coherent/non-coherent pulse radars, with a multiple threat handling capability. It will also have a Precision Direction Finding (PDF) capability linked into the Longbow's sensor- and weapons-cueing systems. A production decision for the system is expected in September 1998, with the first of up to 1,000 units in service by 2000. ATRJ is one of several systems currently under development by the Joint Integrated Avionics Working Group (JIAWG) and its MIL-STD 1553 architecture will make it compatible with the Apache's AN/AVR-2A laser detection/warning system and the ATIRCM/Nemesis active IR-countermeasures systems now under development.

Starstreak/Helstreak

Shorts Missile Systems and Lockheed Martin have combined (with McDonnell Douglas) to market the high-velocity Starstreak anti-aircraft missile for the AH-64A/D. If the missile is adopted by the US Army, Shorts would manufacture the components in Belfast, while Lockheed Martin would assemble the missiles in Troy, Alabama. An air-launched version of Starstreak (dubbed Helstreak) is the 'preferred choice' of the UK's Army Air Corps to arm its AH-64Ds. Starstreak is a laser-beam-riding anti-aircraft missile, capable of Mach 3/4, with an effective range of 300 m (984 ft) to 7000 m (22,966 ft). Starstreak has a reported single-shot Pk of 96 per cent. Each individual missile is 1.4 m (4.6 ft) in length, 13 cm (5.1 in) in diameter and has a launch weight of 16 kg (35.27 lb). After launch the missile body deploys four fins which spin-stabilise the missile. The nosecone is discarded to expose three metal darts. The darts disperse after motor burn-out and are guided to the target using a laser matrix. Each dart has a small explosive charge but causes most of its damage to the target through kinetic energy. Shoulder-launched Starstreaks require the operator to track the target with the laser until impact. As a result, Starstreak is largely immune to ECM and IRCM, but can be hampered by electro-optical countermeasures, terrain or poor weather.

Laser-guided rockets

Although a Hellfire missile is the Apache's most accurate weapon, it is also the most expensive (the unit cost of a basic Hellfire is in excess of $35,000). In an attempt to provide the AH-64, and other helicopters, with a precision weapon that does not cost more than some of its targets, Texas Instruments has unveiled a laser guidance package for 2.75-in rockets such as the Hydra 70 or CRV7. The system uses an adapted Paveway seeker head with small thruster ports arranged around the forward section of the projectile for manoeuvre control. Thus modified, the cost of individual rockets is estimated at between $10,000 and $12,000.

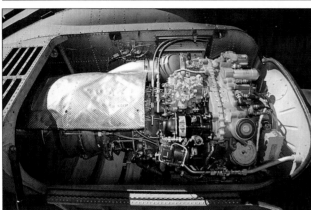

Above: At regular intervals (approximately every 45 days) Apaches are thoroughly washed down. Accumulated dust and dirt can affect the Apache's overall weight by as much as 100 lb (45 kg) if not kept under control. Note how the tailplane can be used as a maintenance platform. The same is true of the engine cowlings.

Left: A T700-GE-701 turboshaft fitted to an AH-64A. The engines are built in Lynn, Massachusetts.

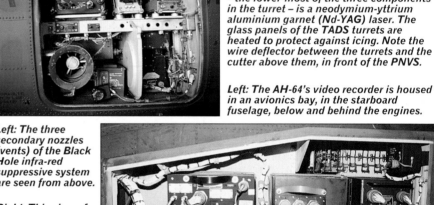

Above: Visible above the TADS optical and laser turret (right) is the LRU-28 transmitting antenna for the Apache's ALQ-136 radar jammer. The Apache's laser – the lower-most of the three components in the turret – is a neodymium-yttrium aluminium garnet (Nd-YAG) laser. The glass panels of the TADS turrets are heated to protect against icing. Note the wire deflector between the turrets and the cutter above them, in front of the PNVS.

Left: The AH-64's video recorder is housed in an avionics bay, in the starboard fuselage, below and behind the engines.

Left: The three secondary nozzles (vents) of the Black Hole infra-red suppressive system are seen from above.

Right: This view of the port cheek fairing shows LRUs (line replaceable units) for the TADS and laser systems (top row), dimmer controller, IHADSS symbol generator and fire control computer (bottom row).

Above: The Apache's rotor head is fully articulated, allowing the blades to 'hunt' (lead or lag) individually. The flexible elastomeric bearings, which regulate this effect, are the large rectangular blocks seen at the end of each blade.

Left: The Sperry-built air data sensor, positioned above the rotor head, is referred to as the 'Pacer System'. It monitors air velocity, temperature and pressure, and is vital for the flight instruments and weapons fire control system.

Right: The AH-64D's Longbow MMW radar.

Above: The Apache's rotor blades are each attached to a delta-hinged hub. The whip FM/AM antenna above the fin is not found on all AH-64As. Two AN/APR-39 RWR antennas are located to the rear of the fin cap.

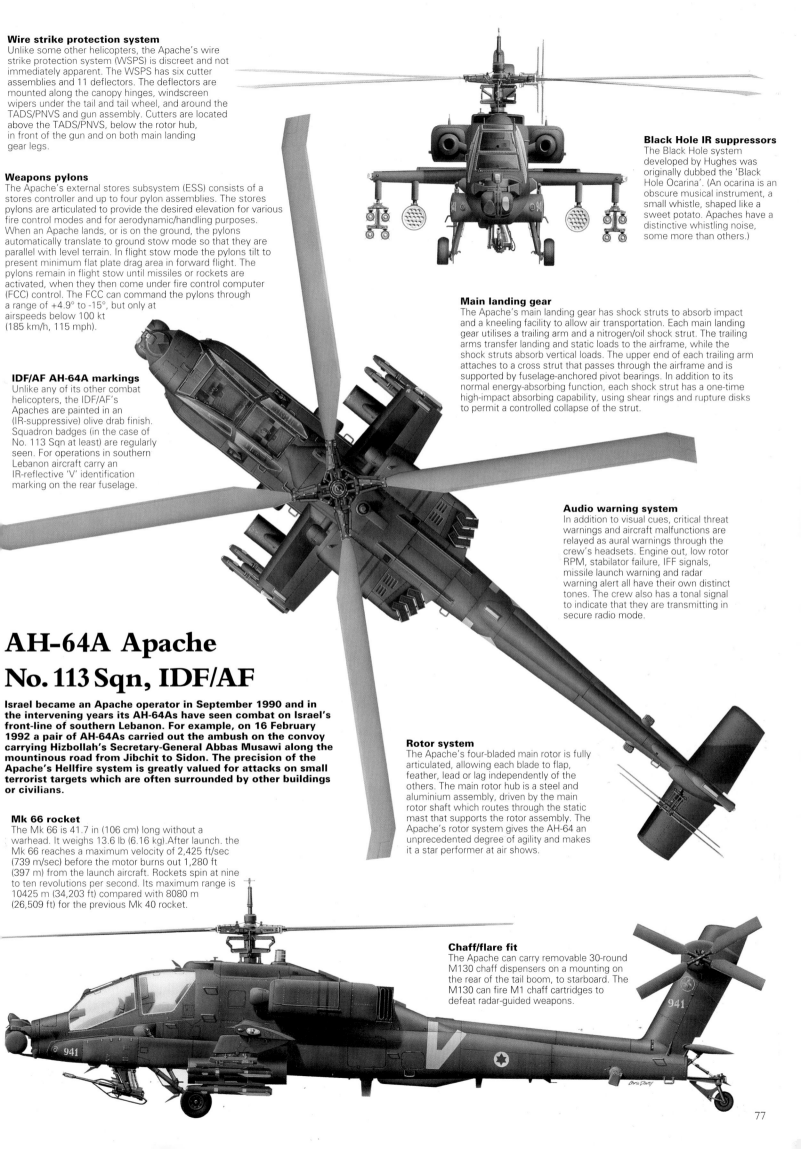

Wire strike protection system
Unlike some other helicopters, the Apache's wire strike protection system (WSPS) is discreet and not immediately apparent. The WSPS has six cutter assemblies and 11 deflectors. The deflectors are mounted along the canopy hinges, windscreen wipers under the tail and tail wheel, and around the TADS/PNVS and gun assembly. Cutters are located above the TADS/PNVS, below the rotor hub, in front of the gun and on both main landing gear legs.

Weapons pylons
The Apache's external stores subsystem (ESS) consists of a stores controller and up to four pylon assemblies. The stores pylons are articulated to provide the desired elevation for various fire control modes and for aerodynamic/handling purposes. When an Apache lands, or is on the ground, the pylons automatically translate to ground stow mode so that they are parallel with level terrain. In flight stow mode the pylons tilt to present minimum flat plate drag area in forward flight. The pylons remain in flight stow until missiles or rockets are activated, when they then come under fire control computer (FCC) control. The FCC can command the pylons through a range of +4.9° to -15°, but only at airspeeds below 100 kt (185 km/h, 115 mph).

IDF/AF AH-64A markings
Unlike any of its other combat helicopters, the IDF/AF's Apaches are painted in an (IR-suppressive) olive drab finish. Squadron badges (in the case of No. 113 Sqn at least) are regularly seen. For operations in southern Lebanon aircraft carry an IR-reflective 'V' identification marking on the rear fuselage.

Black Hole IR suppressors
The Black Hole system developed by Hughes was originally dubbed the 'Black Hole Ocarina'. (An ocarina is an obscure musical instrument, a small whistle, shaped like a sweet potato. Apaches have a distinctive whistling noise, some more than others.)

Main landing gear
The Apache's main landing gear has shock struts to absorb impact and a kneeling facility to allow air transportation. Each main landing gear utilises a trailing arm and a nitrogen/oil shock strut. The trailing arms transfer landing and static loads to the airframe, while the shock struts absorb vertical loads. The upper end of each trailing arm attaches to a cross strut that passes through the airframe and is supported by fuselage-anchored pivot bearings. In addition to its normal energy-absorbing function, each shock strut has a one-time high-impact absorbing capability, using shear rings and rupture disks to permit a controlled collapse of the strut.

Audio warning system
In addition to visual cues, critical threat warnings and aircraft malfunctions are relayed as aural warnings through the crew's headsets. Engine out, low rotor RPM, stabilator failure, IFF signals, missile launch warning and radar warning alert all have their own distinct tones. The crew also has a tonal signal to indicate that they are transmitting in secure radio mode.

AH-64A Apache
No. 113 Sqn, IDF/AF

Israel became an Apache operator in September 1990 and in the intervening years its AH-64As have seen combat on Israel's front-line of southern Lebanon. For example, on 16 February 1992 a pair of AH-64As carried out the ambush on the convoy carrying Hizbollah's Secretary-General Abbas Musawi along the mountinous road from Jibchit to Sidon. The precision of the Apache's Hellfire system is greatly valued for attacks on small terrorist targets which are often surrounded by other buildings or civilians.

Rotor system
The Apache's four-bladed main rotor is fully articulated, allowing each blade to flap, feather, lead or lag independently of the others. The main rotor hub is a steel and aluminium assembly, driven by the main rotor shaft which routes through the static mast that supports the rotor assembly. The Apache's rotor system gives the AH-64 an unprecedented degree of agility and makes it a star performer at air shows.

Mk 66 rocket
The Mk 66 is 41.7 in (106 cm) long without a warhead. It weighs 13.6 lb (6.16 kg). After launch. the Mk 66 reaches a maximum velocity of 2,425 ft/sec (739 m/sec) before the motor burns out 1,280 ft (397 m) from the launch aircraft. Rockets spin at nine to ten revolutions per second. Its maximum range is 10425 m (34,203 ft) compared with 8080 m (26,509 ft) for the previous Mk 40 rocket.

Chaff/flare fit
The Apache can carry removable 30-round M130 chaff dispensers on a mounting on the rear of the tail boom, to starboard. The M130 can fire M1 chaff cartridges to defeat radar-guided weapons.

AH-64 Apache and Longbow Apache

Above: An AH-64A manoeuvres hard with a load of Hellfire training rounds and Hydra 70 rocket pods. Note how the TADS sensors have been rotated inwards to protect their optics in flight, while the PNVS is exposed.

Right: The Apache's Hydra 70 rockets can be fitted with M433 multi-option fuses. Impact fusing allows surface and subsurface warhead bursts. Targets in open terrain will be engaged with superquick fuses that detonate upon contact. Targets with overhead protection, such as heavy tree cover or in fortified emplacements, will be engaged with a delay/forest penetration setting. Timed fuses produce airbursts and are most effective against targets with no overhead protection. Flechette, smoke and illumination warheads incorporate timed fuses, which are controlled by motor burnout. MPSM warheads can use M439 fuses, remotely set from the aircraft with range (time) to target information. Once fired, the forward motion of the rocket initiates fuse countdown. At a point slightly above and before the target, the submunitions are ejected and their ram air decelerators inflate. This arms the submunitions and places them in a near-vertical descent over the target.

service. It has a semi-active laser seeker and an improved low-visibility detection capability, compared to the A model. The AGM-114C also flies a flatter trajectory to the target with a low-smoke motor. The AGM-114F (sometimes referred to as interim Hellfire) has a tandem warhead for use against reactive armour.

The next version was developed as a result of Gulf War experience and began life as the Hellfire Optimised Missiles System (HOMS), now referred to as the AGM-114K Hellfire II. The AGM-114K has been totally redesigned and features improved tandem warheads, electro-optical countermeasures hardening, a semi-active seeker head and a programmable autopilot for trajectory shaping. This new autopilot works by regulating launch speed from 300 kt to Mach 1.1, allowing a steeper terminal dive. The AGM-114K's seeker has been improved to overcome backscatter interference (as discussed later). All previous models of Hellfire used an 8-kg (17.6-lb) conical shaped charge warhead with a copper liner cone. The HE charge shapes the liner into a supersonic jet of molten metal that is effective against every armour technology known today. In the Hellfire II the copper liner has been replaced by molybdenum steel with a larger precursor charge. Hellfire II is believed to have a maximum range in excess of the 8000-m (26,247-ft) range quoted for earlier versions. Hellfire has been extensively tested on US ranges against Soviet (and modern US) armour and on the battlefield during Operation Desert Storm. When used against the Iraqi army the striking power of Hellfire was absolute – a single Hellfire strike

would destroy any target, except perhaps at the edges of the engagement envelope. Prior to the war US intelligence reported that Iraqi T-72s were being fitted with armoured fences set 18 ft (5.5 m) away from the tanks to defeat tandem, shaped-charge warheads. A T-72 was set up in this configuration in the US and shot, and destroyed, with a single Hellfire. Longbow Apache will use a version of the Hellfire based on AGM-114K, the AGM-114L. This version will be laser- or MMW radar-guided.

Hellfire employment

When a Hellfire leaves the rail it accelerates at 10g and reaches Mach 1.3 within six seconds in a g-bias climb (i.e., the missile climbs sharply on a defined parabola to a predetermined altitude, to begin searching for the laser spot). Depending on the type of missile, range to target, launch altitude and designation mode, the missile climbs to between 500 ft (152 m) and 1,500 ft (457 m) for a terminal dive on the target. The minimum range for a Hellfire engagement is 500 m (1,640 ft) and textbook maximum range is 8000 m (26,248 ft). Because the missile needs to climb to engage a target, a low cloud ceiling will hamper Hellfire operations as the missile can lose lock-on. This is one realm where the radar-guided AGM-114K will transform Apache operations.

Hellfire can be launched in two designation modes: Lock-On Before Launch (LOBL) in which the AH-64 self-designates, and Lock-On After Launch (LOAL) in which the target is designated by another laser, on the ground or in the air. The Apache can designate its own targets up to ±10° off-boresight. If another Apache is designating for the 'shooter' (indirect designating) the maximum angle between the laser LoS (Line of Sight) and shooter LoS must be ±60° for the designator to remain visible. The Hellfire's trajectory shaping and seeker scan-pattern force minimum engagement ranges to increase, in LOAL mode, if launch altitude increases above target altitude. As launch altitude increases the missile's ability to see the target at shorter ranges decreases. With an AGM-114F, minimum LOAL range is 2000 m (6,561 ft) if the launch aircraft is 50 ft (15.24 m) above the target (800 m/2,625 ft for AGM-114C). In LOBL mode, minimum range decreases to 1400 m (4,593 ft) for an AGM-114F and 800 m (2,625 ft) for an AGM-114C. During the early stages of Desert Shield Apache crews were afflicted with 'dirt diver' Hellfires that came off the rails and plunged straight into the desert. The problem was one of laser backscatter, wherein the beam was diffracted by dust and sand in the air and reflected back at the designator. This problem is not unique to a desert and can be caused by fog, snow or haze. If the missile seeker is tracking backscatter the seeker head LoS and designator LoS should differ (by more than 2°) and this should alert the CPG that he needs to re-acquire the target. In the desert the backscatter was caused by the Apache's own dust cloud so the solution was to launch a missile and wait several seconds before firing the laser to allow the missile to get clear.

Laser technique

A target must remain illuminated by the laser 'sparkle' once the Hellfire is in terminal phase; once the seeker is tracking, the laser cannot be turned off. To achieve 90 per cent Pk (probability of kill) the target must be illuminated for eight to 10 seconds. The CPG has to be conscious of illumination faults such as boresight error, spot jitter (caused through motion of the designator), beam divergence (the further the laser is from the target, the wider the spot will be on the target), attenuation (the beam will be scattered by obscurants or bad weather), overspill (placing the spot too high on the target so it 'slips' over onto the terrain behind) and underspill (placing the spot too low on the target so that false targets are created in the foreground).

'Servicing' the target

To fire a Hellfire the CPG must consider four elements – mode, code, quantity and type. The mode will be LOBL or LOAL (with LOAL-LO and LOAL-HI options depending on the desired trajectory of the missile). The code is a NATO-standard four-digit code that matches the missile seeker head to the pulsed frequency of the laser. Missile codes are issued in blocks, at a unit level, and then allocated at a company level. Each Apache will have its own code, but can also store up to eight codes (A to H) to designate for other aircraft if required. Codes are entered via the Apache's data entry keyboard. Since laser codes are allocated to individual aircraft, knowing which 'chalk' has been allocated which codes is an essential element of the mission brief. The CPG selects the number of missiles he wishes to allocate to a code, then selects 'type', which will always be laser-guided in the AH-64A. A maximum of two codes can be used at the same time, referred to as upper and lower channels. Normal procedure is to allocate the upper channel to the Apache's own code and the lower channel to a remote designator. It is possible to allocate both channels to remote designators, so that the shooter can remain hidden while firing missiles at two separately designated targets.

The laser rangefinder provides distance to target and LoS provides azimuth. For an LOBL engagement the missiles seeking the first selected code will lock-on if they are within the laser spot LoS. A solid box appears on the HDU target display, indicating that the laser return is valid. The CPG verifies that the range to the target is within limits and that the laser has a firm hold on the target. Missiles can be fired with the laser on or off, but the laser must be engaged

The accuracy and effectiveness of any weapons launch from a helicopter is dictated by the aircraft's flight conditions. Hellfires, for example, are not always silver bullets. Rotor downwash acts on any projectile, causing its trajectory to change. A noticeable change in trajectory will occur when the Apache is operating below effective transitional lift. This distortion is most pronounced with rockets, but will also trouble guided missiles, especially if they are fired at short range. If the Apache is hovering in ground effect, air flowing down through the rotor system causes the missile to pitch up as it leaves the rail. When the missile passes beyond the rotor disc, air flowing upwards (bouncing off the ground) causes the missile to wobble and can induce lateral (azimuth) and linear (range) errors. When the Apache is hovering out of ground effect, the downwash strikes the missile only once. However, the increase in velocity of this downwash (increased because of the additional power needed to maintain the hover out of ground effect) may further worsen linear dispersion.

Above: This sequence of photos shows the first launch of a production-standard Hellfire, at the Yuma Proving Ground, in 1984. In January 1985 the Hellfire officially entered the inventory.

Above right: Positive threat ID with the FLIR system is acknowledged to be difficult. While the crew can easily detect the heat signature of a potential target, determining whether the 'blob' is friend or foe is less straightforward. The phenomenon of IR crossover – caused at night when targets have cooled to the same temperature as the surrounding terrain – can make even acquisition impossible. IR crossover occurs most often when the environment is wet, as moisture in the air creates a buffer in the emissivity of objects. The PNVS FLIR lacks the magnification of the TADS and so cannot reliably detect wires or other small objects.

for terminal guidance. It takes an eight-second (approximate) 'sparkle' to ensure the missile will find the target. For an engagement at maximum range an AH-64A may have to remain exposed for 45 seconds (including acquisition time and 37 seconds of flight). For a remote LOAL engagement the shooter's wingman will lase the target and provide the range and azimuth information. The shooter points at the target and can fire with, or without, a solid lock. Upon firing, the shooter calls the time of flight for the missile and calls for 'laser on' from the designating aircraft. In a LOAL engagement the shooter can remain permanently masked, and out of harm's way.

If the engagement is autonomous (self-designating) or remote (designated from another source), with all missiles on the same code, a proficient crew could reasonably expect to have two or possibly three Hellfires in flight simultaneously. Crews generally train to fire (depending on range) with an eight-second separation to allow adequate time to transition from one target to another. If the LOAL engagement is a 'ripple' (missiles on two separate codes), a good crew could have four missiles (two autonomously- and two remotely-guided) in the air at once. Launch separation times between an autonomous missile and a remote missile can be as little as two seconds.

JAAT – co-operative tactics

In 1986 a new form of combined Army/Air Force operations was pioneered by 7-17 Cavalry, 6th Cavalry Brigade, almost by accident. A phone call from the AFRes's A-10-equipped 917th TFG, requesting the use of the AH-64's weapons range at Ft Hood, led to a deal. The 'Hogs' could

come and drop their bombs if the 7-17 Cav could try out their laser designator with the A-10's Pave Penny marked target seeker. When the A-10s hit the target first time using the Apache's laser, both teams realised that a small revolution was in prospect. This early exercise lead to formal AJAAT (Advanced Joint Air Attack Teams) trials at Nellis AFB. The Ft Hood Apaches (which had become the 3-6 Cavalry) joined with the USAF's 422nd TES in 1987 to conduct operations in high- and low-threat environments on the Nellis ranges. Phase II saw the team moving to Ft Hood in December for night-time/bad-weather operations, and in Phase III the AJAAT trials moved to Ft Still, to work out against an unfamiliar target array. The success of the 300 missions flown paved the way for today's JAAT tactics. To the Army, JAAT becomes AJAAT when an 'Advanced' helicopter, such as the Apache, is designating rather than troops on the ground (for example).

The AH-64's optics allow it to find and identify targets at ranges unavailable to A-10s. This in turn translates to safer stand-off ranges for the A-10s, whose Pave Penny trackers can see the Apache's lasers at ranges in excess of 8000 m (26,246 ft). A-10 pilots could, for example, make blind firing passes at targets hidden in tree lines that they never saw, simply by following the HUD cues. Although the A-10's GAU-8 cannon has a well-deserved reputation for destruction, the 'Hog' has to close to a range of 2,000 ft (610 m) for it to be guaranteed effective. The longer-ranged IR Maverick is the A-10's preferred weapon, but its seeker head has a magnification capability of just x6 compared to the Apache's x127 system. This alone underlines the value of the Apache to the JAAT mission.

Apache FACs and scouts

JAAT also brought about the birth of two-ship Apache scout teams. During the early trials traditional scout helicopters were too slow to keep up with the JAAT teams, so the 3-6 Cav started to use three two-ship Apache sections in favour of traditional scout/gun combinations. The role of the Apache scout is crucial. The scout conducts the target brief and relays it to the Air Force aircraft, if there is no FAC. This is the 'nine-line' FAC-to-fighter brief, which specifies IP, heading to target, target elevation, target description, target co-ordinates, target marks (laser code), friendly forces, egress direction plus any necessary remarks (hazards, restrictions, threats or abort code).

If no FAC is available the scout will also hand over the incoming aircraft to the designating AH-64s. The scout maintains communications to higher headquarters and acts as 'traffic cop' to marshall the next troop of AH-64s entering the area. The Apaches should not be fighting an engagement alone but should be calling up artillery support to drive the enemy into the kill zone, break off comms antennas and button up the tanks. The squadron Fire Support Officer (FSO) is the link between the aviators and the gunners, and it is he who must have pre-planned the artillery engagement to the flanks or the rear of the kill zone. The artillery unit's Forward Observer (FO) should be airborne with the scouts, to best integrate his battery's fire.

The A-10s fly in four-ship formations which permit pairs of aircraft to make independent attacks. If both pairs are needed for a single attack, they will be controlled by two Apaches simultaneously. When conducting this type of four-ship attack, each A-10 section is given its own laser code. A single AH-64 works a four-ship section by putting all the A-10s on a single code for a sequential attack.

The Apaches do not remain passive on the battlefield. While designating for an A-10 an AH-64 can also be shooting a target that has been coded and designated by its wingman. It can also cover the A-10 coming off its attack.

The A-10's Pave Penny seeker has a laser-to-target offset of 60° (similar to the Apache's own limit), and although attacks can be made outside that range they are undependable. Ingressing to the target, the A-10s may make a recce 'bump' at their IP to find the Apache's laser then remask to maintain terrain cover en route. The laser is detectable at ranges up to 20 km (12.4 miles). At the IP the A-10s will expect the initial brief from the scout commander on the common UHF frequency (which is a Have Quick secure radio). FM radios are used to talk to the ground forces, while the Apaches use an internal VHF net.

Running the attack

Once handed over to the designating AH-64, the A-10s receive the specific target brief. This comprises target location (a six/eight-digit map UTM), target description (e.g., 'northernmost tanks'), elevation (derived from the AH-64's fire-control system and input to the A-10's sight), laser code (chosen to deconflict with the Hellfire codes in use and entered to the Pave Penny through cockpit switches – a typical training code would be 1668), laser-to-target line (ensures that the A-10 is within the parameters to see the laser and also allows the A-10 pilot to calculate the AH-64's position by drawing a back azimuth from the target),

The Apache/Kiowa 'gun' and 'scout' team has fallen into disuse. This is largely due to the US Army's massive ARI restructuring which has forced aviation units to do more with less. Though the number of Apaches deployed by each attack helicopter battalion has increased, so too have the demands made of them, and Apaches must now undertake their own scout and security missions. It is also true that the AH-64 outclasses the available scout helicopter, the OH-58C Kiowa. With the advent of the OH-58D, the scout/cavalry community now has a far more capable mount, arguably more capable than the AH-64 in some respects.

AH-64 Apache and Longbow Apache

This Apache is loaded with a varied air-to-air missle armament. On the port pylon is an AIM-9M Sidewinder AAM, with a FIM-92 Stinger to starboard. The Air-To-Air Stinger (ATAS) is the weapon with which the US Army has conducted the most extensive trials (note the cameras on the wingtips to film separation tests). Its small size allowed two missiles to be carried on each station – at the expense of fuel, rockets or Hellfires. A wingtip-mounted twin-launcher has been developed as a result. Opponents of an air-to-air role for the Apache believed that adding AAMs might distract crews from their primary mission. However, the arrival of the AH-64D Longbow Apache will undoubtedly bring with it an expanded air-to-air role for the Apache.

restrictions (an optional call, perhaps to keep the A-10s from overflying impacting artillery) and remarks (requesting the A-10s to call when departing the IP so the designator is ready). Every Apache within the AJAAT team must be capable of making this brief and designating targets. This vital task is notionally the responsibility of the aviation commander, but he will frequently have to delegate.

Co-ordination between A-10s and Apaches of the 2-22nd AVN during the 101st Airborne Division's assault on Objective Toad, in Iraq, on 20 February 1991 was cited as a perfect example of JAAT in action. Two teams of A-10s working with the Apache's Air Liaison Officer and Air Battle Captain attacked Iraqi bunkers with Mk 82 bombs and CBUs. Only the lack of any Iraqi armour prevented the use of the A-10's Mavericks. With the A-10 no longer dominant in the close-air support role, the AH-64 is capable of working equally well with the LANTIRN-equipped F-16. The F-16 brings with it the added dimension of being able to operate at night, which was never the A-10's forte.

Air-to-air weapons

The US Army does not yet anticipate a major air-to-air combat role for the Apache or the Longbow Apache, which is more suited to the task. US Army units do not train for this mission, unlike US Marine Corps attack helicopter pilots. As a result, a dedicated air-to-air weapon for the Apache has been frequently discussed but never deployed. Initial US trials were conducted with AIM-9 Sidewinders, at the White Sands Missile Range in November 1987. Although further Sidewinder trials were undertaken, serious attention moved to a modified version of the FIM-92A, the AIM-28 Air-to-Air Stinger (ATAS). ATAS trials also began in 1987 and by 1989 test firings had been undertaken at the Yuma Proving Ground. The Stinger could be carried in a two-missile box housing on the ends of the AH-64's stub wings. Only a single (larger) Sidewinder could be carried on a specially-developed rail. Trials were also undertaken with the anti-radar Sidearm, a modified RF-homing AIM-9 developed as a small and affordable anti-radiation missile. Successful Sidearm trials were conducted at China Lake Naval Weapons Center in

April 1988. Captive carry trials of the Shorts-developed Helstreak/Starstreak anti-aircraft missile began in 1990, followed by six live firings at the Yuma Proving ground in 1991. The Helstreak is the main contender for the UK's air-to-air weapon and is also being regarded with some seriousness by the US Army. The first of the US Army Starstreak trials resulted in access panels on the AH-64 being jarred open by the missile's shockwave. This problem was quickly solved and the firing programme encountered no debris damage from the missile plume – one of the major concerns regarding the high-velocity Starstreak.

In early 1997 the US Army drafted a Mission Need Statement calling for an improved air-to-air armament for the AH-64. Limitations of the Stinger were acknowledged, including its lengthy engagement 'time-lines' – during which the Apache is exposed to enemy fire. The US DoD now anticipates a further two-year trial of what it dubs the Air-to-Air Starstreak (ATASK) under the supervision of Army Aviation's Applied Technology Directorate, Ft Eustis. A series of 20 firings will be made against drone targets during this phase. As a result, the UK decision to acquire Starstreak/Helstreak, once expected in 1997, will be delayed perhaps until 1999. The BAe/MATRA Mistral AAM is also an outside contender for the UK requirement.

Standard Apache weapons have a limited air-to-air application. In fixed gun mode the M230E1 has a round impact set at 1575 m (5,157 ft) with a time of flight of 3.9 seconds. Hydra 70 rockets with M255E1 flechette warheads are perhaps the AH-64's best anti-helicopter weapon. Upon detonation the flechettes are deployed at a 12° angle, and the flechette cloud becomes cylindrical in shape after 150 m (492 ft) of travel, over 15.7 m (49.7 ft) in diameter. Test firings indicate that at ranges of 2000-2500 m (6,562-8,202 ft) three pairs of rockets will have a 75 to 82 per cent chance of scoring a hit. Hellfire can be used to engage

Above: The first launch of a Sidewinder (AIM-9M) was made by an Apache at the White Sands missile range, New Mexico, in November 1987. Several factors led to the adoption of the Stinger missile in favour of the Sidewinder, but one of the most significant of these was the Sidewinder's dramatic launch signature.

Above: The first launch of a Sidewinder (AIM-9M) was made by an Apache at the White Sands missile range, New Mexico, in November 1987. Several factors led to the adoption of the Stinger missile in favour of the Sidewinder, but one of the most significant of these was the Sidewinder's dramatic launch signature.

Left: This photograph shows the first launch of an Air-To-Air Stinger (ATAS) at the Yuma Proving Ground in 1989. Like the aircraft above, this Apache is fitted with cameras above the stub wings and on the rear fuselage to record the launch. ATAS capability was one of the primary elements planned for the AH-64A+/AH-64B upgrades, using a newly-developed two-round box launcher, but this never progressed beyond the trials stage. There is now a good possibility that the US Army might adopt the Shorts Starstreak/ Helstreak AAM, which is undergoing joint US/UK trials for Britain's Army Air Corps.

targets at up 8000 m (26,247 ft). The preferred employment method is to designate the target indirectly, allowing the Apache to fire from cover.

Ft Rucker – where it all begins

Before any Apache pilot can come to grips with the AH-64's technical sophistication and tactical employment he, or she, must be fully conversant with the aircraft's basic qualities. All flying training for the US Army begins in the pleasant surroundings of Ft Rucker, Alabama, home to the network of airfields, training areas and 500 helicopters of the US Army Aviation Center. The 1st Aviation Training Brigade handles the huge amount of flying conducted at Ft Rucker. Basic flying training for helicopter pilots is increas-ingly undertaken on the Bell TH-67A Creeks of the 1-212 AVN (Training). Once students have become IFR qualified with the TH-67As of 1-223 AVN, those destined for the Apache move to the 1-14 AVN at Hanchey AAF. 1-14 AVN conducts all Apache flying at Ft Rucker (with 48 AH-64As at its disposal) and AH-64D training will begin in 1997.

New students, arriving with 'bars and wings', are faced with three stages of AH-64 training. The complete AH-64 qualification course takes 62 training days. Five days of introductory academics are followed by the Contact Phase (Day 6-15). This is literally the students' first contact with the aircraft, comprising seven days in the CWEPT (Cockpit, Weapons, Engine Procedure Trainer). For many

All US Army, and a great deal of non-national, Apache training is conducted at Ft Rucker. The full conversion course lasts for 12 weeks and two days. Apache flying at Ft Rucker is based at Hanchey AAF, home to the 1-14 AVN ATB. 'D' Company is 1-14's active AH-64 unit. It has seven flight platoons, which in order (first to seventh) are – Apache, Loco, Cochise, Geronimo, Natchez, Mescalero and Apache (again). The names derive, in the most part, after famous Apache warriors or Apache tribes.

Right: This is the 'bag' – the screened-off rear cockpit of an Apache from where the student pilot must fly the aircraft using the FLIR alone. 'Bag' training is conducted by day and by night and is the most strenuous element of the Apache flying training course. Note the grey outline around the canopy. This is detonating chord to blow off the canopy in the event of an emergency rescue.

Right: This student is attempting one of the most demanding elements of flying training at Ech (pronounced 'Ek') Field, one of Hanchey's busy satellite airfields. Ech is the scene of slope training, where students learn to land the aircraft safely on an incline. This Apache is positioning for a slope landing in the 'bag'. The pilot cannot see the ground behind and around him and forward vision is provided by the FLIR alone.

students this will be their introduction to twin-engined helicopter operations and they will learn basic operational procedures (start-up, shut-down, emergency routines) from both seats. This portion of the training also involves a sizeable amount of classroom learning 'by rote', aided by a large animated schematics of onboard systems such as the hydraulic, fuel, electric systems. Flying training follows, alternating with returns to the classroom for half-day periods. One Instructor Pilot (IP) will be allocated to two students for their first 12.4 hours of contact flying in the AH-64. They will undertake basic take-off and landing training, emergency procedures (engine failures at altitude or in the hover) and flying in mission configurations (using rolling take-offs to simulate a full weapons load, for example).

The second phase (days 16-36) of training is the most demanding, and perhaps the most demanding flying training requirement anywhere. The student must master flight using only the PNVS, at day and night, flying in the 'bag'. The 'bag' is a shrouded Apache rear cockpit, where all light is blocked out to simulate night-time operations. Students fly with only the PNVS and Helmet-Mounted Display (HMD). Basic flight information is superimposed over the FLIR imagery in the HMD monocle, so with just one eye, in the dark, the student pilot must learn to handle the Apache as if it were the most routine of afternoon trips. PNVS day training (all in the 'bag') comprises 18 flight hours followed by 7.2 hours of actual night operations. Throughout this demanding stage the IPs of 1-14 AVN are not trying to fail pilots, and those students who experience difficulty will be allowed a recheck. However, for some the stress of flying with just a 1 x 1-in black-and-white TV 'window' is just too much.

The third phase, the Gunnery Phase (days 37-55), is the students' introduction to the Apache's weapons system and its tactical employment. It involves a substantial amount of simulator training and live-fire experience. After 10.5 hours of simulator training the Apaches go to the ranges for four live firing days, which still have to interleave with training in the classroom. The student will fire all Apache weapons, spending one day in the front seat, then one day in back, then repeating that sequence at night, culminating with a check ride. Having learned how to fly the aircraft, by day or night, and used all of its systems, the student then returns to the simulator complex for Combat Skills training and the final evaluation (days 56-62). This is where the attack mission is taught – deep attack tactics, mass engagements, zone/route reconnaissance tactics, BDA, gunnery fire correction. In the words of one senior IP, "(we teach) everything, which seems to be our mission of late."

Apache and the US Army today

The Apache force, and the US Army with it, is currently in some doctrinal confusion about the exact role of the AH-64 on the battlefield. Not so long ago, the situation was clear: the US Army had two combat helicopter missions – Attack and Scout/Cavalry. Attack units flew Apaches to destroy enemy (armoured) forces or leveraged targets. The Scout/Cavalry mission was more diverse. While it included scouting for the attack force, the OH-58s and AH-1s of the 'Cav' undertook guard and screening missions for their own armoured units, route and logistics site reconnaissance, and still maintained the capability to engage in (limited) shooting matches of their own.

Once the Apache was operational in Europe the division between these two roles disintegrated, not least because the AH-64 had better sensor systems than its scouts, which in any case were not fast enough to keep up with the Apaches. While the OH-58C/AH-1F team in Cavalry units continued to work well (and just how well has long been a cause of friction between Apache and Cobra

communities), both of these ageing types are about to disappear from the inventory in favour of the OH-58D Kiowa Warrior (see *World Air Power Journal*, Volume 15). This will transform the scout role in the US Army and should pave the way for the reintroduction of workable Scout/Attack teams once more.

The Army's ARI (Army Restructure Initiative) has reinvented many aspects of Army aviation by virtue of the inventory cuts and budget restrictions inherent in it. Under ARI, surviving Apache battalions were boosted from 18 to 24 aircraft, because the Apache must now act as its own scout. (Previously, battalions had operated with a mix of 18 AH-64As and 13 OH-58Cs.) The Hellfire-capable and Mast Mounted Sight-equipped OH-58Ds will not routinely scout for Apaches because, as one Apache pilot put it, "they'll be too busy with their own things to do"; what's more, there will not be enough to go around. Today, the Apache is firmly its own scout. ARI diluted the Apache's role from 'classic, pure attack' to one of security. Now the Apache, expressly designed to kill tanks in the Fulda Gap, and its crews, must undertake the screen, guard and other missions that were never its forte. Obviously, the Apache has many strengths that lend themselves to this mission, but attack crews have their misgivings. Some question the wisdom of placing the Army's most capable and expensive asset so consistently in harm's way – in a role, after all, that the OH-58 once fulfilled. However, it is inevitable that as Army doctrine increasingly coalesces around 'Stability and Support Operations' (the emerging tenet replacing the cumbersome Operations Other Than War/OOTW concept) the Apache will find itself on unfamiliar ground, and one need look no further than Bosnia to see the truth in that.

Attack helicopter units

Each divisional commander will employ his attack helicopters as he sees fit. Under ARI two (Apache) attack helicopter battalions (ATKHBs) are attached to heavy divisions and one to light divisions. The few AH-1Fs that survived into 1997 with these units are being replaced by OH-58Ds. Each Apache ATKHB has 24 aircraft divided into three companies (ATKHC), plus a headquarters/headquarters company (HHC) and aviation unit maintenance (AVUM). The AVUM provides unit-level maintenance for the battalion. The three ATKHCs provide an offensive capability against armour, personnel and infrastructure/

logistics targets. Each company has its own headquarters section, a scout platoon (three AH-64s) and an attack platoon (five AH-64s). The expected fully mission-capable (FMC) rate is 75 per cent – six aircraft. A two-ship 'lead/wingman' team (platoon) is the basic operational grouping, as its offers a high degree of flexibility and mutual support between teams. Each team will have a platoon leader, while the company commander will fly as a member

Apaches at Hanchey: the uppermost aircraft is exiting a tiny forest clearing after let-down and departure practice, while the aircraft above is engaged in the long sequence of slope training.

During normal peacetime operations US Army Apache crews fly, approximately, 70 hours every six months. This annual figure of 140 flying hours might seem very low – and is one reason why there is a certain amount of resistance from other US Army aviation helicopter crews to joining the AH-64 community. It is not, however, an unusual total in the military helicopter community as a whole. System reliability for the Apache itself (originally specified as 2.8 hours MTBF) has improved from 3.83 hours to 4.15 as the aircraft became mature.

The OH-58C Kiowa scout was a successful partner to the AH-1 Cobra, but far less so for the AH-64. The Kiowa has none of the sensors and equipment of the Apache, nor the performance to keep up with the larger helicopter in the field. Kiowa crews rely on their aircraft's small size and NoE flying to survive, but can be forced to operate within lethal range of enemy ADA to carry out their missions. As the OH-58D Kiowa Warrior enters wider service, remaining OH-58C units are preparing to trade in their Kiowas for Warriors. (To US Army crews a 'D' is never an AH-64D but always an OH-58D. The AH-64D is always the 'Longbow'.)

A masked Apache presents a small target but its nose-mounted sensors are also hidden from the target. This is where the crew must make maximum use of their aircraft's agility to pop up, acquire the target and remask. The AH-64 autopilot even has a 'bob-up' mode to facilitate this. The Apache's noise signature is negligble beyond 1 km (3,270 ft) – 75 per cent of that noise is caused by the tail rotor.

of the third team, positioning himself as required. An Air Assault Division, such as the 101st, follows the same aviation battalion organisation, while an Airborne Division (such as the 82nd) will have a single OH-58D ATKHB.

Attack helicopter tactics

The ATKHB is an instrument of precise firepower, with the manoeuvrability to mass combat power at a decisive time, yet one which should always work as part of a combined arms team. The Apache is tasked with nine primary missions: to attack massed armour or light forma-

tions, to attack in depth to extend the influence of its own land forces, to dominate avenues of approach, to reinforce ground forces by fire, to defeat enemy penetrations, to protect the flanks of a friendly force – be it on the move or static, to provide security for the movement and passage of lines by ground forces, to conduct reconnaissance and, finally, to conduct search and attack missions.

The Apache's role in offensive missions is categorised in several ways. The first of these is a 'movement to contact' – to gain or re-establish contact with the enemy, though not necessarily to engage it. Engagements from a manoeuvre to contact should be against targets of opportunity, or through chance rather than design. The primary function of a movement to contact is to place the Apache battalion in a secure position to conduct its pre-planned attack.

Attacks are sub-divided into two categories, 'hasty' and 'deliberate'. A hasty attack takes advantage of an enemy's weakness or sustains the momentum of the main attacking force. A deliberate attack is conducted against an enemy that is well-organised and cannot be turned or bypassed. It will be pre-planned and briefed using all the intelligence, and time, available. After a successful attack comes 'exploitation', to prevent the enemy from regrouping or withdrawing. The ATKHB will still be operating as part of a larger force and will attempt to strike the flank and rear of the enemy force. Then comes the 'pursuit', in which the Apache ATKHB will leave flank and contact engagement to the ground forces and instead reach deep to cut off the retreating enemy force and block any relieving forces. This calls for precise and well-planned C^2 co-ordination between friendly forces.

There are two forms of defensive operations which concern the ATKHB, 'area' and 'mobile'. ATKHBs conduct area defence in terrain where the enemy has a mobility advantage and must be denied avenues of approach or specific areas. A mobile defence allows the enemy to advance to a point where it is vulnerable to attack

AH-64A anti-armour deep attack

This series of diagrams describes a typical AH-64 deep attack mission – an attack directed against enemy forces not currently engaged but which could influence division or corps operations within the next 24 to 72 hours. This particular mission could also be termed an interdiction against a moving force. Deep attacks are made against high-risk/high-payoff targets, but the attack helicopter battalion (ATKHB) itself is a high-value target and this must always be born in mind before committing it. Deep attacks by corps ATKHBs help the corps commander to shape the battlefield and set the terms for close operations.

❶ Right: *The arrow indicates the direction of movement of an enemy armoured column. The engagement area (EA), a valley, will have been scouted by other aircraft from the aviation unit, or determined from map terrain analysis or overhead imagery. A 15-km (9.3-mile) bracket has been choosen, though this will vary in relation to the size of the unit, terrain and avenues of approach. The red cross marks the 'trigger point' where the armoured column will be directly in the centre of the engagement area and where maximum firepower can be brought to bear. Attack helicopters use terrain for masking and concealment. They may be behind terrain fetaures, but also among terrain features concealed by intervening folds in the hill 'mass' or by vegetation.*

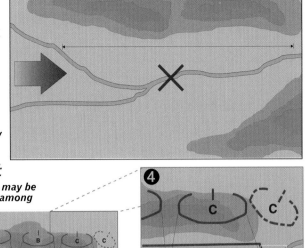

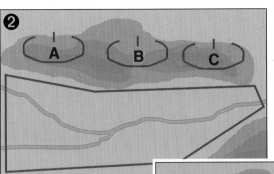

❷ Above: *Company-sized battle positions (BPs) are established – A, B and C. BPs are selected to provide good fields of fire, cover, conceelaed routes of entry and exit, range and relationship to targets. BPs must allow the attacking units to cover their own rear and flanks.*

❸ Left: *The EA must have recognisable boundaries, 'channelisation' of moving enemy elements and limited escape routes. Fields of fire are established, taking into account the need to prevent overkill while covering all the targets.*

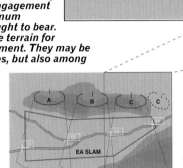

❹ Above: *Target reference points (TRPs) for supporting artillery fire are set up by the fire support officer.*

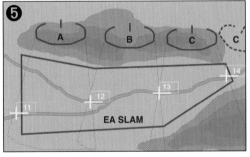

❺ Above: *The engagement area is always given a name ('slam' is a generic title). TRPs (yellow crosses) are used as aiming points or references for quickly shifting fire (left, right, add, drop). The placement of these RPs at the intersections of sector boundries would allow them to be used for smoke markers to define those boundries during the battle. Alternative BPs are set up, for use if the primary BPs become unusable, threatened or if the engagement has to be repositioned to continue the attack.*

❻ Right: *Each battle position (A, B, C) will be occupied by three two-ship Apache teams. Phase lines (PLs) are used to mark and control areas, and trigger actions. Like EAs, they are always named. The vertical PL 'Trigger' serves as a 'trip wire' to initiate the engagement. PL 'Red' is a 'no-penetration' line. If enemy forces reach this point the Apaches will have to shift to alternate BPs. Range markers are set up to define the theoretical maximum range of the Hellfire (8 km) and enemy ADA fire (6 km). Red crosses serve as range markers for individual battle positions.*

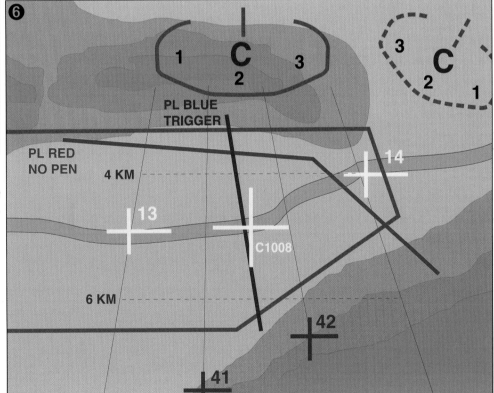

by two sub-divided units, one to contain the advancing force and one to destroy it.

Task Force Normandy was a classic example of an ATKHB 'deep' operation, an attack mission directed against forces not currently engaged but one which will shape the outcome of future events. Deep operations are high-risk, high-payoff missions.

Traditional scout missions are now part of the Apache crew's repertoire. Such missions fall into two broad categories, reconnaissance and security. Reconnaissance missions may be conducted for a zone (covering all routes, obstacle and terrain in a defined area), an area (gaining

detailed information on a specific area such as a ridge line or woods), a route (alone which ground units may be preparing to travel) or as a reconnaissance in force to provoke the enemy into revealing itself. Security missions can be categorised as screen (to provide early warning), cover (operating independently of the main force to distract the enemy), guard (keeping the enemy out of range of the main force), area (securing a specific area such as a convoy route) and air assault security (protecting an LZ).

The defined capabilities of the Apache ATKHB include mobility, speed, range and versatility. Mobility: the ability to rapidly move the force to the decisive place at the

Hughes Danbury Optical Systems produces the AH-64's AN/AVR-2A(V) laser detecting set (LDS). The AVR-2A is both an essential operational item and a useful training aid. It detects, identifies and characterises laser-aided weapons directed against the Apache from a 360° hemisphere around the aircraft, and in ±45° of elevation. The AVR-2A will also detect laser training devices during MILES/AGES (Multiple Integrated Laser Engagement System/Air-to-Ground Engagement System) field training exercises, such as those conducted at NTC. The AVR-2A(V) operates in conjunction with the Apache's AN/APR-39(V) radar warning receiver. The two combined systems provide the AH-64 crew with visual and aural warning of gun/missile threats on a cockpit display. Exterior sensors come in the form of four SU-130A(V) antennas – two facing forward, two facing aft.

optimum time. The area of operations for the ATKHB will be the entire corps or divisional sector. Speed: attack helicopters move across the battlefield at speeds in excess of 3 km (1.86 miles) per minute. Planning airspeeds are 100-120 kt during daytime and 80-100 kt at night. Range: targets can be attacked up 150 km/93 miles across the FLOT, without additional fuel. Versatility: no longer are there specific airframe-based mission responsibilities. The AH-64 can carry 16 Hellfires, which allow the battalion to engage 384 enemy targets at ranges up to (and beyond) 8 km (5 miles).

The specific limitations imposed on the Apache ATKHB include the weather and Combat Service Support/CSS. With a 500-ft (152-m) cloud ceiling the Hellfire's engagement profile forces the Apache to get too close to the target and exposes it to enemy ADA. The same is true if visibility is reduced to >3 km (1.86 miles). For CSS, an ATKHB will normally require two established FARPs, one for a specific mission and one for future operations, stocked with fuel, ammunition and spares. Each FARP will typically have four rearm/refuel points, allowing the entire battalion to be turned around in two hours, or less.

AH-64 at NTC

Since 1982 the US Army has been training with battalion-sized exercises at the National Training Center (NTC), located in the desert at Ft Irwin, California. These exercises entail an entire battalion deploying to the NTC for a period of several weeks to train in air and ground manoeuvres against the Army's OPFOR (OPposing FORces) units, which use Soviet equipment and tactics. Sessions at the NTC are conducted semi-annually, perhaps

every 18 months, and involve up to six weeks in the field. Before deploying, units form hard crews who will fly together consistently. Apache units do not fly uniformly during peacetime with hard crews, in order to spread experience around the unit and avoid crews becoming complacent with each other. In time of war, this practice would cease and hard crews would be flown constantly. Pre-NTC training will be undertaken for several months without distraction, before the battalion deploys.

Train the way you fight

The first week at NTC is given over to outfitting every aircraft with the Loral MILES (Multiple Integrated Laser Engagement System) laser simulation system and transponders essential for accurate scoring on the ranges, followed by a work-up flying period. The second and third weeks are spent in the 'box' (the NTC manoeuvre area) deployed in the field, living with aircraft and following the OPFOR engagement syllabus. Conditions in the NTC are demanding. The Santa Ana winds can blow at up to 30 kt (55 km/h; 34 mph) and the high ambient temperatures make it easier to over-torque rotors. All operations are conducted under the supervision of the central 'Star Wars building' centre which runs the exercise, backed up by Operational Controllers deployed in the field. Missions begin on day one of the war against the 'Krasnovian' forces who have invaded Mojave from the east. Blue forces start west and work east. The Apaches fly screening missions looking for forward security elements of the invading forces. Operating in pairs for the scouting mission, the Apaches fly 'at the same altitude as the tanks' in front of the advance Bradley IFVs of their own ground forces, operating

The Apache's AN/ARC-201 secure radio is an airborne VHF/FM transceiver for use in the SINCGARS system. SINCGARS provides a jam-resistant radio capability by using a frequency-hopping transmission system that changes frequency many times a second, in an apparently random manner. For successful communications the radios in use must be synchronised and on a common net. Each AN/ARC-201 has an internal clock; one radio set will be designated as the 'master', and any time differences will be adjusted on the others.

on a common radio net. Apaches operating in the traditional deep attack role will go deep to attack Krasnovian installations and armour, through weak points in the defences.

The mission planning imperative

All Apache missions begin with an in-depth mission brief, no matter what the objective or the urgency of the mission. A typical mission analysis begins when the unit commander, operations officer (S3), intelligence officer (S2) and fire support officer (FSO) receive the tasking from higher command. The mission analysis team assembled as a result will include the above personnel and their assistants, plus the unit adjutant (S1), supply officer (S4), liaison officer (LNO), individual company planners (as many as are attached to the regiment), EWO, safety officer and senior IP. This team will spend as much time as it can (up to 90 minutes) on its mission analysis, even under the most extreme circumstances. The S2 will update the IPB (intelligence preparation of the battlefield) and conduct the terrain analysis. This utilises the OCOKA procedure (Observation and fields of fire, Cover and concealment, Obstacles and movement, Key terrain and Avenue of approach). The S2 also conducts weather analysis and threat evaluation to produce the 'illustration of the enemy', which is a situational map and enemy course of action (COA) sketch. The assistant S3 integrates the brigade's mission with other operations in the area. He ensures that the practical details for the mission – battlefield calculus, battle position/engagement area graphics, communications cards – are ready. The FSO will co-ordinate required field artillery support, determining what units are available, where they are deployed, types of ammunition and available stocks, and target priorities. If NBC operations (including smoke) are anticipated, then substantial additional planning is required. An assessment of the enemy ADA capabilities is essential – their available weapons, their employment parameters and how they are integrated with the primary target. The battalion S4 identifies the logistics required for the missions and the constraints on them and comes up with the battalion combat power assessment. The S1 determines medevac and casevac procedures. The XO (executive officer) has the

ultimate responsibility of analysing the level of risk inherent in the mission and whether or not it is acceptable. Finally, the battalion commander reviews the mission intent, adds his own guidance, and approves the course of action.

The results of this mission analysis will include draft route and communication cards, mission graphics, an assessment of friendly forces in the operational area, the mission statement, the commander's intent, the enemy assessment and course of action sketch. A battlefield matrix will have been developed that combines seven defined elements: artillery, C^2, intelligence, manoeuvre forces (infantry, armour and aviation assets), mobility/counter-mobility (engineering support), combat service support and deployed AAA/ADA.

Above and top: Apache units deploy to the National Training Center every 18 months or so and are well-versed in desert operations as a result. Conditions in the Mojave are demanding and can stretch the capabilities of men and machines. However, the frequent complaint of many flyers – lack of power, particularly in hot-and-high conditions – is not one heard from Apache crews.

AH-64 Battle Drills

US Army Aviation battle drills are essential, basic 'collective actions' used by aviation units that have suddenly encountered a threat. They are learned by every crew through exhaustive, repetitive training, so that they become second nature in combat situations. They should require little or no orders to execute and are generally applied to platoon-sized or smaller units. Battle drills are initiated by the first element of the platoon in response to a specific threat from a given direction. The primary objective is to warn the other crews, then initiate a reaction. Battle drills for air threats or ground threats can be categorised in four ways – break, dig, split or static drills.

A break drill allows aircraft to respond to a threat from the flank. In a break the AH-64s will turn to orientate on the threat while manoeuvring to avoid, threaten or engage it.

A dig drill is designed for an air threat approaching from ±15° to the Apache formation's direction of flight. The objective is to separate friendly elements to avoid the threat or distract the threat while other AH-64s manoeuvre against it.

A split drill is carried out in response to a threat from the rear and (almost by definition) the aircraft will be responding from a disadvantageous position.

A static drill is designed for friendly aircraft operating from a static position, such as a BP (Battle Position) or during slow forward flight (such as a screening operation).

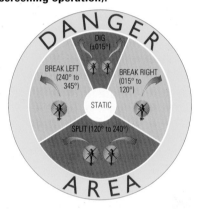

The FORM OF AN ALERT CALL is tightly defined, and will follow the pattern of : "Gun 2, target tanks, 300 metres, break right, engage" or "Gun 1 targets, 360, 5000 metres, dig."

Battle Drill Templates

Battle drills are run on the assumption that a two-ship element (of the platoon) is the basic and most efficient manoeuvring element. This battle drill template (left) shows the appropriate response to a threat (dig, break or split) depending on how it is encountered. If a threat encroaches upon the Danger Area there will hopefully be enough time for one aircraft to make the essential alert call and initiate the appropriate drill.

ALERT CALLS *are the most critical element of the battle drill. The call consists of key words and phrases and initiates a specific response. The first crew to observe the threat must **ACT** to manoeuvre on the target and maintain visual contact. Secondly it must **DETERMINE THREAT STATUS** – known or unknown, 'bandit', 'bogey' or 'target'. Then this crew must **TELL** the rest of the formation – stating its own callsign, threat status, distance to threat, required drill and any other essential information. The rest of the formation must act immediately to perform the drill or mask, or to continue, as required. If there are **FOLLOW-ON ELEMENTS** behind this formation they will support the engaged platoon if required, bypass the engagement or mask to avoid the threat.*

Gun 2 of the lead platoon sees attacking targets at bearing 030° to the formation.

He acts (orientates on the threat) and determine's its intentions.

As Gun 2 manoeuvres to cover the tanks he alerts the rest of his platoon and the follow-on Apache platoon.

Gun 1 acts (manoeuvres to a vantage position and engages the threat to cover Gun 2).

Gun 2 tells Gun 1, and the remainder of the company, that he sees the threat and is engaging.

The second platoon leader hears Gun 2's alert call. He executes a hook right to place his platoon in a position to support the first platoon.

From this position the engagement is extensively wargamed in an attempt to predict every possible enemy action and the Apaches' counter to it. It is a major task, but an essential one for every AH-64 mission. Each wargame is run with a strict timeline. The S2 plays the enemy, the S3 plays friendly forces. The FSO supports the S3, and any NBC operations are also included. The S4 organises support measures, such as FARPs, while the S1 runs medevac. The company commanders manoeuvre their units on the imaginary battlefield and the 'games' are run and rerun until time expires; there are no real answers, only potential ones. The US Army has a mission planning system called Terrabase, which is similar to the USAF's Elvira system. Terrabase uses US military mapping information to generate a three-dimensional, computer-based model of the engagement area. This is of crucial importance when it comes to working out the battle positions of each Apache team. A 3-D model allows the wargames to see the actual fields of fire and identify the 'dead space' where Apaches cannot be seen or cannot see the target.

The final 'production of order' will reunite the planning team to produce all the mission-relevant information for the entire battalion. This will include area of operations maps and sketches, holding area maps, engagement area maps, order of battle, ADA threat, communications frequencies, en route/navigational information, fire support graphics, FARP plan, medevac locations and a mass of other details, which must be digested by every crew.

The entire planning process can take up to six hours with an experienced team, or up to eight hours with new staff. During an NTC deployment, for example, this is exactly what each unit will strive to achieve for maximum training benefit. In time of emergency, such as when planning for a hasty attack, the planners will have to go straight to the wargame phase, leaving the S2 to catch up as best he and his team can. Before the mission (approximately 90 minutes prior to launch), the battalion will ideally conduct a rehearsal, but the most important element remains the mission analysis procedure. This intense planning requirement obviously affects the operational tempo of the unit. Although 'sortie' levels depend on the mission, an attack battalion will, hopefully, be allocated just one deep attack mission per night as a function of planning.

Mission launch

Once inside the aircraft, the crew run through the pre-start checklist: batteries on, APU on-line, cool the TADS/PNVS, boresight, HARS (Heading and Attitude Reference System) position input, then engine start. Once the engines are running the rest of the onboard systems come on line. The AH-64 handles well, but nothing is 'hands off' in the Apache and the pilot has to maintain control input for every second the aircraft is in the air. The pilot flies with the PNVS if required, but can also use the TADS FLIR in an emergency. The pilot may also be allocated control of the rockets while the gunners uses the 30-mm cannon. Once in the air the CPG runs through his SWRM ('swarm') procedure: Sight (select HDU or TADS, day or night), Weapons (activate, select appropriate type and fusing), Range (manual – set at 3 km/1.8 miles as an *en route* 'battlesight' – or automatic, using the laser rangefinder) and Messages (who has control of which weapons, and when). There is a third ranging system, dubbed 'automatic', that uses a flat-earth, line-of-sight/slope-to-target calculation combined with the Apache's radar altimeter. It is little used but, like the manual setting, has the advantage of not requiring the laser – making the Apache that much more undetectable.

The lead/wingman team offers maximum operational flexibility, since it enables proper look-out techniques, aggressive manoeuvring, rapid weapons employment and good mutual support. There are two basic tactical formations: combat cruise and combat spread. In a combat cruise

Left: Night operations are generally undertaken using the onboard *FLIR* systems, and not *NVGs* (though it is noteworthy that *TF* Normandy used both systems). The *PNVS* is superior to *NVGs* as it combines *FLIR* imagery with overlaid flight symbology on the *HDU* or cockpit displays, allowing the pilot to fly 'head-up and eyes-out'.

Below: The AH-64A has g limits of +3g/-2g. The Apache has operational pitch limts of ±30° and roll limits of ±60°. The Apache has been rolled, but finding someone who will admit to doing so is another matter.

spread the wingman positions himself to best cover the lead, offset to the lead's right side by 10° to 45°. This is also the basic night-flying formation. The combat cruise keeps aircraft staggered, passing through hostile areas with the minimum footprint. Aircraft should avoid flying in trail; if the enemy is alerted by the first aircraft, it is a simple task to shoot at those following in a straight line behind. However, combat trail formations are used when speed is required, or when transiting through defiles or close terrain. The combat spread formation allows both aircraft to cover each other as the two Apaches fly roughly parallel by ±10°. The team must be scanning the terrain, ready to spot incoming fire, and at no time should both crews be looking in the same direction.

Attacks can be made from a variety of attack patterns, dictated by the number of Apaches involved and the type of target, weapons capabilities (enemy and AH-64), disposition of friendly forces and the need to reattack. The clover-leaf pattern allows a team in combat cruise to attack a small target from several differing directions, firing on the inbound leg of each 'leaf'. The 'L' pattern uses a four-ship to attack from two different directions (at 90° to each other) and places maximum firepower on a point for a short duration. In an 'L', the fire of one team should cross the line of the other, forcing the enemy to attempt to engage in two directions at once. The 'inverted V' is a disengagement pattern from combat cruise if the team suddenly takes fire. Lead engages with cannon and breaks away covered by his wingman, firing rockets. Continuous fire can be directed from 'racetrack' or 'wagon-wheel' patterns, particularly used to cover air assault landings and pick-ups.

Panamanian debut

In 1989, eager to flex the Apache's muscles in combat, 11 aircraft from 'B' Company, 1st Battalion, 82nd Airborne Division were deployed by C-5A to Fort Armador, Panama, in advance of Operation Just Cause (the US military ousting of Panama's President Manuel Noriega). The

Apache's first taste of combat was brief and indecisive. Operating as Task Force Wolf, the Apaches undertook combat missions in conjunction with AH-1Es and OH-58Cs, from the early hours of 20 December 1989 until the ceasefire was declared on 9 January. This was the first combat use of NVGs by US Army aviation units, and also the combat debut of the Hellfire. During the assault on General Noriega's headquarters, two Hellfires were fired through selected windows in the building from a distance of 4 km (2.5 miles). Apaches chalked up 247 combat hours during Operation Just Cause, and several aircraft were hit by ground fire, including one aircraft which was hit 23 times and survived. In all, the Apaches of TF Wolf achieved an 81 per cent mission-capable rate.

It was in Iraq that the Apache finally won its true battle honours, during Operation Desert Storm. Army aviation units did not have the experience of the 39-day air war, before troops moved into Kuwait and Iraq, but the AH-64 had an essential part to play in the success of the air campaign. Three Iraqi radar sites close to the Saudi border had to be destroyed to allow the first wave of coalition

Below left and below: As the armoured build-up in Saudi Arabia accelerated in Operation Desert Shield, the AH-64 became even more in demand. Despite the hectic pace of training during the months leading up to G-Day, only a single AH-64A was lost (on 20 January 1991), and its crew survived.

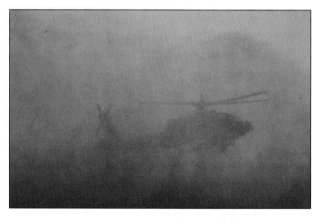

Above: Much has been made of the Apache's supposedly poor serviceability during Operation Desert Storm, but criticisms of the aircraft's record do not bear up to the facts. One 1st Cav veteran of the war in Iraq remembers that of the 18 AH-64s attached to his battalion only one ever needed an engine change. In contrast, each of the OH-58Cs attached to his unit needed to have engines changed and one UH-60 lost three in succession.

Above right: FARPs (Forward Air Refuelling Points) were established by UH-60s and CH-47s that carried fuel and supplies into Iraq, ahead of armoured units. This allowed the Apaches to jump far into Iraq, scouting for and engaging enemy units.

Opposite top: Apaches came to Saudi Arabia by sea. For example, the aircraft of the 4th Brigade, 1st Armoured Division self-deployed from their base at Katterbach, Germany, to Valkenburg AFB, Holland, on 29 November 1990. From there they were loaded onto ships at Rotterdam. It took seven days to get from Katterbach to Rotterdam, but a further three weeks before all 124 helicopters were on board and underway to the Kuwaiti theatre of operations. They arrived in Saudi Arabia on 2 January 1991.

Opposite centre: These aircraft are seen deployed at a forward airstrip, 50 km (31 miles) south of the Kuwaiti border, just prior to Desert Storm.

Opposite bottom: It is almost impossible to discern the Apache in this photograph, which dramatically illustrates the 'brown-out' dust-storms that so hamper desert operations. The key to surviving this sudden loss of visibility is to expect it and keep the aircraft level while climbing away or executing a rolling landing.

attack aircraft safely into western Iraq to attack the Iraqi 'Scud' sites that threatened the political fabric of the coalition forces.

Task Force Normandy

CENTCOM planners decided that the mission could be accomplished in one of three ways: inserting SOF troops to destroy the sites, inserting SOF troops to laser designate for AH-64s, or allowing Air Force aircraft to attacks the sites. Using SOF personnel always entailed an element of risk if the troops were compromised before reaching their target. USAF aircraft could attack the radar sites but could not guarantee that they had been 100 per cent destroyed – the crucial requirement which General Schwarzkopf repeated again and again. Only the AH-64s could bring enough fire-power to bear on the targets and undertake the BDA required to confirm that they had been destroyed. The obvious choice for the mission was the AH-64As of the 1st Battalion, 101st Aviation Brigade, which was one of the US Army aviation units most experienced in night operations. The 1-101st teamed up with the USAF's 1st SOW, whose GPS/INS-equipped MH-53Js would lead the attack force into Iraq. The operation was codenamed Eager Anvil, but Lieutenant Colonel Richard A. Cody named the task force Normandy, in honour of the troops of the 101st who parachuted behind enemy lines into Normandy in advance of H-Hour on D-Day.

Training for the mission began on 26 September 1990 when Lieutenant Colonel Cody's Apaches began to train at night with MH-53Js of the 20th SOS in the FOB Bastogne area. (FOB Bastogne was a Forward Operations Base established to defend the 101st's massive Area of Operations, AO Normandy, 85 km/53 miles south of the Kuwaiti border. It was named after the Belgian town of Bastogne where the 101st Airborne famously held out against besieging German forces during the Battle of the Bulge in 1944.)

The team's helicopters flew the same mission profile that would be required of them on the night – 50 ft (15.24 m) AHO (above highest obstacle) at 120 kt (110 mph; 177 km/h) – and engaged their target with Hellfires and rockets. The route was never flown for real, to ensure their mission was never revealed. Three teams had been organised for the three targets – Red, White and Blue – each with three Apaches plus Pave Low IIIs. It was later determined that the northwestern-most radar site was not linked to the others, so it was dropped from the target list. As a result, the Blue Team was integrated with the others and the mission was flown by four AH-64s, with one spare. On 14 January 1991 the two teams made their way from the 101st's tent-city home of Camp Eagle II (CEII) over 220 nm

(407 km, 253 miles) to King Khalid Military City. The helicopters arrived radio-silent, refuelled, and departed for Al Jouf, doing their best to look like just another training flight. Al Jouf was a small single-runway staging strip, northeast of Tabuk, that was the closest Saudi airfield to the Iraqi border. Only on 15 January did Cody and his S2 (intelligence officer) reveal details of the mission and its target to the rest of the task force. At around 14.00 the following day, word arrived that H-Hour would be 03.00, 17 January 1991.

The first mission of the war

At 00.56 on 17 January 1991 Lieutenant Colonel Cody lead the White team of two MH-53Js and four AH-64As out of Al Jouf. The Red team, led by Captain Newman Shufflebarger, departed 12 minutes later. In all there was a total of nine AH-64As, two MH-53Js and one UH-60 in the air. One Apache acted as a back-up and the Blackhawk was a SAR aircraft, which waited at the border. The Apache crews flew with their FLIRs and ANVIS-6 NVGs. Formation was kept tight, with just three rotor spans between aircraft, and no external lighting. The Pave Lows dropped chemical lights at specific GPS reference points which the AH-64s used to update their onboard Doppler navigation systems. The flight to the target area would take 90 minutes and the round trip back to CEII would be 900 nm (1667 km, 1,036 miles). Even though Al Jouf was

'close' to the border, it was still far enough away to require the Apaches to refuel en route. Ordinarily a FARP would have been established in northern Saudi Arabia, but the danger this would cause in exposing the task force called for a another solution. Lieutenant Tim DeVito came up with the 'single tank option', fitting just one 230-US gal (870-litre) fuel tank to the right inboard pylon and giving the aircraft a 440-nm (815-km, 506-mile) range while still carrying eight Hellfires, 19 Hydra 70 rockets and 1,100 rounds of 30-mm ammunition.

TF Normandy was fired at twice over Iraq, by ground forces alerted by the sound of their passing, but no-one was hit. At 20 km (32 miles) south of the target the MH-53Js delivered their last position update and then peeled off to orbit at their RV. The Apaches approached the radar sites at 60 kt (111 km/h, 69 mph), then each team split into two two-ship groups positioned 500 m (1,640 ft) apart. The two radar sites were close to the Iraqi/Saudi border – the furthest of the pair was only 7 miles (11 km) behind the border – but approximately 69 miles (111 km) lay between them. Each radar site had a combination of Spoon Rest, Squateye and Flatface dish radar antennas, a tropo-scatter radar, generators, EW vans, barracks and ZPU-4 AAA. At 02.37 both teams were in position and marked their targets with the laser spot tracker from 12 km (19 miles) out. At 02.37.50 came Tom Drew's "party in 10" call, followed 10 seconds later by "get some." At a distance of 6 km (3.7 miles) each Apache fired two Hellfires at its primary target, an element of the radar system. The ZPU-4 guns did not come under fire until the radar sites were seen to be destroyed. Some aircraft got as close as 800 m (2,624 ft) to attack targets with their Chain Gun® cannons. The raid was over in 4½ minutes. The Pave Lows were waiting for confirmation of the mission, to relay it to Riyadh. Codeword 'Charlie' meant minimal destruction, 'Bravo' partial and 'Alpha' total. 'Alpha, Alpha' meant no friendly casualties. The Red team had been allocated objective 'Nebraska' and White team objective 'Oklahoma'. From his Apache, named *Rigor Mortis*, Lieutenant Colonel Cody transmitted the phrase, "White Six, Oklahoma, Alpha, Alpha."

A 20-mile (32-km) wide strip had been opened in the Iraqi radar network and SF troops were inserted by MH-47 to place 11 radar reflectors marking the safe corridor for coalition aircraft. As the Apaches turned south to regroup they flew at 100 ft (30.5 m) and 140 kt (259 km/h, 161 mph). Minutes after the firing had begun, the first wave of F-15Es and EF-111s swept overhead at 400 ft (122 m) to knock out fixed 'Scud' sites near H2/H3 airfields. The

Apache crews could see them coming through their NVGs until the jets extinguished their external lights 20 miles (32 km) from the border. At 02:51 F-117s knocked out the air defence control centre for the region, completing the job. TF Normandy returned to Al Jouf at 04.30 to debrief. Early the next morning they flew back to KKMC, rearmed with Hellfires and returned to CEII – only 15 hours after the attack – ready to face any potential Iraqi counter-attack against the 101st.

Apache in Operation Desert Storm

The three-day, 100-hour ground war that commenced at 04.00 (local) on 24 February 1991, G-Day, was accomplished with lightning speed thanks to the mobility of the coalition armoured divisions. US Army aviation's chief contribution to the victory came through its airlift and airmobility assets. The Army deployed 1,193 helicopters in support of Desert Shield/Storm, and only 277 of these were Apaches. On G-Day, an entire brigade of the 101st Airborne Division was moved into Iraq, by air, to Forward Operating Base Cobra, 35 km (22 miles) southeast of As Salman. Apaches were always in the air running screen and security missions for their own ground forces. Their importance to the ground forces was summed up by the words of Major General Griffith, commander of the 1st Armored Division, who said, "I don't want another minute to go by without Apaches out in front of this division."

Apart from TF Normandy the first Apaches into Iraq were 18 aircraft from 2-6th Cav, based at Illesheim, ('Fighting Sixth'), which crossed the border to attack Iraqi communications and surveillance facilities on 16 February 1991. Ten days later 2-6th led the 3rd Armored Division into Iraq and the unit claimed 211 Iraqi armoured vehicles

The AH-64 was one of the success stories of Operation Desert Storm. Yet, despite the amount of literature generated by that brief war, the Apache's achievements go largely unrecorded. One senior commander from a Europe-based attack battalion remembered events thus: "As an aviator who had fought Cobras in Vietnam, (in) my mind's eye (I) expected to see a period of rapid improvement from the initial combat missions. This did not happen. From the first mission on, each aircrew and unit functioned in full synchronization. I attribute this to peacetime training and the great stand-off range of the Apache. The Apache crews very quickly and methodically killed enemy formations in order of priority – tanks with Hellfires, BMPs with rockets and 30-mm, and wheeled vehicles with 30-mm...a great measure of our success (in Desert Storm) can be attributed to the Aviation Branch."

*Right: Throughout
Desert Storm and
subsequent regional
operations Apaches
retained their dark-green
(IR-suppressant) finish.*

*Below: The Operation
Provide Comfort
deployment to Turkey
was frustrating for all
those invoved, as
political restrictions
prevented them from
defending the Kurdish
refugees they were
supposed to be
protecting.*

*The Apache is fitted with
the RT-1296/APX-100(V)1
and RT-1557/APX-100(V)
IFF system. APX-100
operates on Modes 1, 2,
3/A, 3/C and 4,
transmitting specially
coded identification of
position or emergency
signals as required. Each
mode offers progressively
more code combinations
and ease of use. Mode 4
is the classified
operational mode for
security identification.
IFF antennas are
installed on top of the
fuselage aft of the
canopy, and under the
fuselage as an integral
part of the UHF-AM
antenna. Some Apaches
have an IFF antenna
located on the work
platform forward of the
main rotor mast and aft
of the tailboom jack pad.
IFF transmission from
the upper antenna can
cause the PNVS to
malfunction and slew to
the centreline before
returning to the pilot's
LoS. If this occurs, the
transponder must be
disengaged or rerouted
to the lower antenna.*

Al Busayyay, destroyed two Iraqi divisions and over 200 tanks/APCs, and captured 248 Iraqi troops. Apaches from the Ft Rucker-based 2-229th Attack Helicopter Regiment ('Flying Tigers') flew 5,900 incident-free hours to the end of Desert Storm. The unit was involved in the destruction of Iraqi forces along the A-Hammar causeway bridge and the Basrah highway. Apaches from 2-1st Aviation Regiment ('Strike Eagles') flew 235 combat hours and all of its missions were 'cross-FLOT' (Forward Line Of Troops), in day and night. The 2-1st engaged targets of opportunity up to 60 km (37 miles) behind enemy lines, destroyed 35 tanks and took the surrender of over 400 prisioners. The Ft Hood-based 1-3rd Aviation Regiment, (now the 2-101st 'Death Angels' based at Ft Campbell) flew 750 combat hours, including the destruction of Iraqi fire trenches. The 1-3rd was credited with one of the highest direct-fire tank kill totals of the war. Weisbaden-based 5-6th Cavalry Regiment ('Knight Raiders') conducted operations across its corps' sector, including deep attacks and armed reconnaissance. At the time of the ceasefire it was preparing to attack elements of the Republican Guard.

A significant contribution

Singled out for special mention among all the Desert Storm Apache units was the 4-229th Attack Helicopter Regiment ('Flying Tigers'). Deploying from Illesheim, and logging 1,478 hours from January to April 1991, the 4-227th destroyed 100 armoured vehicles in the US Army's first night 'cross-FLOT' and deep attack mission of the war. The 4-229th then made an unprecedented reattack of Iraqi armoured targets, through intense enemy fire, to destroy a brigade-sized element and block reinforcement of the Iraqi frontline. For this achievement the 4-229th was awarded the Army's Valoros Unit Award.

destroyed in the space of just 45 minutes. Elements of the 3-227th Aviation Brigade ('Spearhead Attack') are credited with pushing further into Iraqi territory than any other US unit. The 3-227th deployed from Hanau in September 1990 and, during one deep attack mission, it advanced 400 km (249 miles) to attack tanks in the Euphrates valley. The 2-227th Aviation Regiment, also based at Hanau, deployed in December 1990 and by the end of the war had flown over 3,200 hours. The unit is credited with destroying 200 Republican Guard vehicles and maintaining a 100 per cent mission-availablity rate during combat. The 1-82nd Aviation Brigade ('Wolfpack') deployed from Ft Bragg in August 1990 and flew 1,893 hours until April 1991. The 3-1st Aviation Regiment ('Night Eagles') deployed from Katterbach and over a three-day period flew 280 combat hours. Its Apaches flew deep attacks against

AH-64s flew around the clock, ahead of the advance, engaging Iraqi units as they found them, until it almost became routine. Of all the gun camera/FLIR imagery seen during the war, a team of AH-64s brought back one of the most chilling sequences. Through the TADS of one aircraft a column of Iraqi AFVs could been seen, stationary on a road where their crews believed themselves to be hidden by the smoke from Kuwait's burning oil fields and immune from attack. From a distance of 5 km (3.1 miles) the Apaches could see clearly through the smoke and engaged the column with Hellfires. The silent TADS video showed the lead and trail vehicles destroyed first, to cut off any escape route, and then, methodically but in less than a minute, the dozen or so remaining APCs were wiped out. The Iraqi crews who had been standing in groups, smoking, had no warning and no way out.

Apache ascendant

Any targets that were found were destroyed – over 800 tanks and tracked vehicles, 500 other military vehicles, 60 bunkers/radar sites, 14 helicopters, 10 combat aircraft plus innumerable artillery and AAA positions were claimed by Apaches. A total of 2,876 Hellfires was fired by AH-64s. One Apache was shot-down, by an RPG round fired point-blank from a surrendering Iraqi position. The Apache was hit in the rotor system and crashed, but both crew walked away. All aircraft damaged during fighting returned to base. The overall mission-capable rate for the AH-64 in the desert was over 85 per cent. One unit flew its 36 aircraft constantly for four days, with limited maintenance support, and all remained fully mission-capable. One AH-64 killed two tanks with the same Hellfire. During the appalling weather of 25/26 February, Apaches were the only Army aviation asset to remain operational. During Desert Storm, Apaches did not fly definable 'sorties', for they were active and moving almost constantly. In seven days of operations one AH-64 pilot logged 70 combat

hours, which was by no means unusual. The bulk of missions flown were movement to contact and hasty attacks. The war in Iraq was the ultimate 'fluid environment'. Typically, two-ship teams operated, with the lead Apache carrying rockets for area security and the wingman in 'heavy Hellfire' (16 missiles) configuration. Many pilots in action in Iraq had never fired a live Hellfire before and many remember the (standard) two-second delay after trigger-pull, encountered for the first time, with a mixture of terror and amusement. When the Iraqi surrender was accepted at Safwan it was six Apaches (from 4-229th AVN and 2-6th Cav) that escorted the C-in-C's Blackhawk to the meeting. Even then the Apache's mission in Iraq was not quite over.

The last action of a brief war

On 2 March 1991, after the ceasefire of 28 February, AH-64As from 1-24th Attack Battalion (24th ID) were patrolling the Euphrates valley when the 'battle of the Rumaylah oil fields' broke out. Elements of the Republican Guard's Hammurabi Division were attempting to escape further north, but began shooting at US troops. The US responded with withering MLRS and tank fire, backed up by three companies of AH-64As from the 1-24th. The Apaches fired 107 Hellfires (for 102 hits), 100 70-mm rockets and 2,000 rounds of 30-mm ammunition to destroy 32 tanks and 100 vehicles over the course of an hour. Successful Hellfire engagements began at 6700 m (21,982 ft) – a remarkable distance – and the shooting continued until 15.00. A single US soldier was wounded. One M1A1 tank was damaged and another desroyed, both by secondary explosions from Iraqi vehicles.

After the ceasefire came Operation Provide Comfort and Operation Haven, a hastily prepared humanitarian mission to protect the Kurds in northern Iraq. Iraq's Kurdish population immediately came under attack from the Iraqi army after their uprising against Saddam Hussein failed when the

The ocean-going Apaches

Hughes and McDonnell Douglas made several attempts to adapt the AH-64A for a dedicated naval role. The first of these 'marinised' versions came in 1984. An Apache equipped with Harpoon or Penguin anti-ship missiles, Sidewinders for self-defence, TOW missiles and a mast-mounted radar was proposed for both USMC and USN use. In USMC service the proposed 'sea Apache' could operate in support of amphibious operations from LHAs or LHDs to protect the assault force at sea and on the beach-head. USN aircraft could be based on frigates to provide distant protection for battle groups from surface threats. The 'sea Apache' would have had a combat radius of 142 miles (228 km) and a mission endurance of 2.8 hours

These ideas matured into a more developed 'Naval Apache' concept which was unveiled in 1987. This aircraft was radically modified through the addition of a completely redefined forward fuselage (plus IFR probe) with the avionics shifted to a ventral housing, increasing the fuel load. TADS/PNVS sensors and cannon were replaced by a Hughes AN/APG-65 radar. Redesigned stub wing/undercarriage sponsons could mount Sidewinder missiles and the 'Naval Apache' retained its Harpoon anti-ship missile capability. Hopes for over 100 sales proved to be premature.

Below right: The US Army maintains a large fleet of Apaches for test and trials duties. This is one of the aircraft attached to the Airworthiness Qualification Test Directorate, now based at Ft Rucker. Until 1996 AQTD was based at Edwards AFB as the Aviation Engineering Test Activity (AETA).

Right: Seen here is AV-05, in use with McDonnell Douglas Helicopters as a technology demonstrator for the US Army's LHX programme. McDonnell Douglas and Bell Helicopter Textron joined forces as the 'Superteam' to bid for LHX. The competition was eventually won by the 'First Team' combination of Boeing/Sikorsky with the RAH-66A Comanche. The YAH-64 was dubbed the ACE (Advanced Cockpit Evaluator) and (over the course of several incarnations) was fitted with fly-by-wire controls, a sidestick controller and advanced cockpit avionics. It joined a dedicated trials group of helicopters which included a Bell 222 with the high-agility 680 tail rotor system and a NOTAR MD500.

US refused to actively back them. In April/May 1991, Apaches were deployed to Turkey and provided 24-hour armed support for the fleet of transport helicopters supplying the Kurdish refugee camps in the mountains. The aircraft involved were from the 6th Squadron, 6th Cavalry Regiment and self-deployed from Illesheim on 24 April 1991 for the 23-flight hour, 3,000-mile (4828-km) journey to Turkey – a unique achievement. The Apaches of the 'Sixshooters' operated with four Hellfires, 38 rockets and a full load of Chain Gun® cannon ammunition in temperatures of over 100°F (37.7°C). Their night-fighting capability was particularly useful against Iraqi units operating under cover of darkness.

Lessons of Desert Storm

During Operation Desert Storm some operational problems were encountered, of varying degrees of seriousness. Sand ingestion led to beter filtration. Ingestion problems in the air turbine starters and fuel boost pump were caused chiefly by the dust clouds spun up by aircraft landing and taking off alongside each other, and not by routine flight. Abrasion of the Hellfire seeker heads was encountered, and the 'dirt diver' missile problem was another minor irritant. For the

pilot, the greatest hazard (true of any desert operations) was 'brownout' – losing contact with the ground in the dust cloud created by the rotor. When taking off the pilot simply had to anticipate the problem and ensure that the aircraft remained straight and level until out of the 'dust storm'. When landing, the technique was to roll ahead of the cloud until safely on the ground – an option not available to a helicopter with skids. The Apache's dust cloud can also betray its position to the enemy. NTC experience has shown that the AH-64's dust signature can be seen up to 10 km (6.2 miles) away, so the pilots must choose their operating conditions with care.

The most important lesson of Operation Desert Storm, learned with tragic effect, was that the Apache can kill at distances that far exceed its ability to identify the target. At night, FLIR contrast was negligible and aircraft needed to get within 2 km (3.2 miles) of a target before making a positive ID, which placed the Apache well within any ADA envelope. This also opened up the possibility of blue-on-blue kills, or 'friendly fire', which, as it turned out, was the greatest threat to coalition forces. On 17 February 1991 the lead pilot in a formation of three Apaches, in error of his actual position and inaccurate in his vehicle ID, fired on a US Army Bradley and M113, destroying both with Hellfires. Before deploying to Iraq some units had undergone a hasty exercise at Ft Riley where every type of Iraqi combat vehicle likely to be encountered in the desert was paraded for the crews to give them some additional recognition practice. The Apache crews found they could not positively ID the targets as hostile beyond 3 km (4.8 miles). Since then, major R&D effort has been expended on developing an effective battlefield IFF system for the US Army. A visual 'threat library' of IR imagery is under development for the Apache and other aircraft, but remains a long-term project. What is needed is an improved battlefield sensor system, one that retains the benefits of the AH-64A's optics with an added level of sophistication and discrimination. That solution, along with many others, will be found in the AH-64D Longbow Apache.

Apache improvements

Since the earliest days of AH-64A operations there have been attempts to upgrade the aircraft. In the mid-1980s McDonnell Douglas began studies of the Advanced Apache/Apache Plus, which was later referred to, unofficially, as the 'AH-64B'. The AH-64B would have had a revised, updated cockpit with a new fire control system, Stinger air-to-air missiles, a redesigned Chain Gun® and a fin-mounted video camera. AH-64B was aimed at the US Army, but a similar AH-64G was proposed for the German anti-tank helicopter requirement, now filled by the Euro-copter Tiger. In 1988 funding was released for an AH-64 Multi-Stage Improvement Program (MSIP) to improve the Apache's sensor and weapons suites while integrating new digital databus and communications systems. The MSIP was abandoned before it reached the hardware stage. The

reason was that new technologies, which had always been 'earmarked' for application to the Apache, were finally becoming real – and with them came the possibility for transforming the already formidable Apache into something even better. A series of upgrades was proposed after Operation Desert Storm, the so-called AH-64A+/Desert Storm fixes. These included VHF/FM NoE communications improvements (a long-recognised Apache problem), a desert filtration kit, ground-proximity warning system, TADS/PNVS and Chain Gun® accuracy improvements, GPS, new HF radio, SINCGARS secure radio, improved IFF and flight control computer upgrade. Like the proposed MSIP these changes were abandoned in favour of a far-reaching and highly integrated transformation of the AH-64A, through the addition of a revolutionary new radar system and completely revised onboard systems.

Millimetre-wave (MMW) radar guidance had always been an option for Hellfire guidance, but was rejected for the AH-64A as the technology was not mature enough. In the Airborne Adverse Weather Weapon System (AAWWS), Westinghouse, in collaboration with Martin-Marietta (now Lockheed Martin Orlando), developed the Longbow MMW radar. Longbow is now being integrated into the US Army's Apache fleet, transforming existing aircraft into AH-64D Longbow Apaches. MMW technology overcomes the existing limitations in the Apache's targeting optics/laser combination. At present, the AH-64A can simultaneously engage two targets using its own designator, at a range of up to 8000 m (26,247 ft), day or night. However, the laser and FLIR are constrained by atmospheric conditions and the Hellfire's range is limited if the cloud ceiling is less than 400 ft (122 m) AGL. To make a self-designated kill at maximum range, the AH-64A must unmask for 37 seconds.

Longbow – the next generation

The Longbow radar is largely impervious to atmospheric interference, allows the Apache to fire-and-forget all 16 AGM-114Ls in rapid succession, and gives the aircraft a new lethal SEAD capability. The Longbow system comprises the mast-mounted fire control radar (FCR), a programmable signal processor and the Longbow Hellfire missile. The Longbow radar can scan a 50-km² (19.3 sq-mile) swathe of territory and detect up to 1,024 potential targets. Of these, 128 can be classified and displayed simultaneously, and software improvements will increase this to 156. The system will prioritise 16 targets depending on the desired engagement criteria and the target characteristics (wheeled,

tracked, airborne, moving, static etc.). Longbow programme officials are keen to point out that while the radar can 'classify' a target, it does not 'identify' it. It can, however, determine if a contact is a wheeled vehicle or a tank or an air-defence system. The FCR has a detection range of 8000 m (26,247 ft) against moving targets and 6000 m (19,685 ft) against static ones. The Longbow's SEAD capability is provided by its radar frequency interferometer (RFI), a sophisticated RWR that can identify and target any emitting (ADU/air defence unit) system on the battlefield. The RFI has 360° coverage – 'fine' in its 180° forward hemisphere, and 'coarse' in the rear 180°. The system will provide an azimuth to target, although not a range. The Longbow radar also gives the AH-64D an effective air-to-air targeting capability. Longbow's MIL-STD 1760 databus will accept ATAS on its wingtip stations, but Stinger integration is not a priority purely on cost terms.

Digital warrior

The AH-64D has a totally new digital databus/systems fit, which is at the heart of the Longbow. Although the AH-64D is based on the AH-64A, the modification process involves reducing each Apache to a shell before the new equipment is added. The first item to be stripped out is the AH-64A's old wiring, to be replaced by four dual-channel MIL-STD 1553B data buses and lightweight wiring. The

Above: Greece was the first European customer for the Apache and was subsequently followed by the Netherlands and the UK – who both opted for the AH-64D. There are still several small batches of Apaches to be sold in Europe, but Boeing/McDonnell Douglas is now looking further east for the next round of substantial sales.

Top: In 1990 Israel became the first export customer for the AH-64A. In Israeli service the Apache is known as the Peten (Cobra) and the Israel Defence Force/Air Force is believed to operate three squadrons of the AH-64As. Israel is an obvious potential customer for the AH-64D Longbow Apache.

Apache over Bosnia

United States Army ground forces were committed to NATO's peacekeeping effort in Bosnia-Herzegovina in December 1995 after the Dayton peace accords brought the country's three-year civil war to an end. Spearheading the US Implementation Force (IFOR) contingent was the 1st Armoured Division under the command of Major General William Nash. The deployment of the division from its bases in Germany was a major logistical task, and its AH-64A Apache attack helicopters played a key role in ensuring that US forces were able to successfully deploy into Bosnia.

At the start of the deployment the division's aviation component, its 4th Brigade, was based at Hanau, near Frankfurt. It contained two Apache-equipped units – the 2-227th and 3-227th Attack Helicopter Battalions. The 7th Combat Aviation Battalion provided logistic support with Sikorsky UH-60 Blackhawks, and the 1st Squadron, 1st Cavalry had OH-58Ds for scout and target-marking work. Getting the brigade to Bosnia was difficult due to snow storms in central Europe that delayed its self-deployment to US staging areas around Taszar air base in southern Hungary. By the end of December 1995 advanced elements of the brigade had leapfrogged from Taszar to a forward operating base in Croatia, near Zupanje, to provide close air support for US Army engineers building a huge pontoon bridge over the River Sava for the main tank units of the division. Boeing CH-47 Chinooks were used to airlift the pontoon sections and the Apaches flew security patrols around the site to prevent interference with the bridging operation.

It took another month for all of the US division to be established in its bases around IFOR's North East Sector, and for the 4th Brigade to set up its main operating base at Tuzla air base alongside the USAF's 4100th Air Base Group. The old Yugoslav air force base proved an ideal location because of its runways and old hardened aircraft shelters. As US troops – along with Russian, Nordic, Polish and Turkish troops – began to separate the

warring factions in the northeast of Bosnia, the Apaches were regularly tasked to fly patrols along the Zone of Separation to deter infringements. Helicopters had to fly in pairs due to US concerns about hostile attacks on their forces, and when VIPs were airborne in helicopters two Apaches were always tasked to 'fly shotgun'. Twenty four AH-64As have been deployed to Bosnia, some with improved systems fit to enhance their operational capabilities. Six aircraft have a real-time datalink to allow them to send FLIR/DVO video imagery to local command units. Three of these have an additional SATCOM capability to allow direct transmission to national command authorities in the USA.

The Apaches were called upon during February and March 1996 to support IFOR operations in Sarajevo. They flew security missions around the city on 3 September when US Secretary of State Warren Christopher came to visit.

By the summer of 1996, the IFOR mission was all but complete, with the warring factions so impressed by its firepower – particularly the heavily armed Apache – that they had been all but confined to barracks. The two US Apache battalions continued their patrols but also began to carry out live firing training on the large British run ranges at Glamoc, firing their cannon, rockets and Hellfire missiles in a series of very impressive firepower demonstrations. They also participated in joint firing exercises with allied air and ground forces. In December 1996 IFOR began to withdraw and the 4th Brigade started to deploy back to Germany, handing over its duties to aviation elements of the 1st Infantry Division, the US ground component in NATO's new Stabilisation Force (SFOR) for peacekeeping into 1997. The Apache's deadly reputation played a major part in ensuring Bosnia's warring factions were not tempted to take on IFOR. Peace through superior firepower.
Tim Ripley

An IFOR Apache lands in typical winter weather at Taszar, in Hungary.

new databus is allied with totally integrated 6-32 bit processors and coupled with an uprated onboard electrical system which can cope with peak loads of 90 kVA (the Improved Electrical Power Management System/IEPMS). This digital architecture empowers the Longbow's 'manprint' (manpower integration) cockpit layout. Gone are the dials and 1,200 switches of the AH-64A, to be replaced by a Litton Canada upfront display, two AlliedSignal Aerospace 15-cm x 15-cm (6-in x 6-in) colour (initially monochrome) CRT displays and just 200 switches. The CRT displays and helmet-mounted displays use improved Honeywell raster-generated symbology to combine the DVO, FLIR and radar sensor data. The display processors (which 'drive' the screens) are capable of handling a digital colour moving-map, when such a system becomes available. An improved Plessey AN/ASN-157 Doppler navigation system and Honeywell AN/APN-209 radar altimeter have also been incorporated. AH-64D will have a dual embedded GPS and inertial navigation (EGI) fit plus AN/ARC-201D VHF/FM radios. EGI is being developed as a tri-service project. The improved navigation fit for the AH-64D gives it near all-weather capability compared to the adverse weather-capable AH-64A. Hamilton Standard has also developed an advanced lightweight FCS computer to take advantage of the 32-bit processor system. The larger volume of avionics in the AH-64D has forced the expansion of the Apache's cheek fairings, to become EFABs (Enhanced Forward Avionics Bays)

Communications revolution

Mission planning will be greatly eased by the AH-64D's data transfer module (DTM). The DTM allows key mission data such as flight routings (waypoints/hazards, FARP location, FLOT location), enemy/friendly forces dispositions, unit sectors, battle positions, priority fire zones and communications (callsigns, frequencies, secure codes) to be input directly to the AH-64D's mission computer on a single cartridge. The DTM will ease the battalion mission planning load, but the AH-64D's Improved Data Modem (IDM) will revolutionise the way the AH-64D flies and fights. The high-speed (16 KB/sec) IDM uses the newly developed variable message format (VMF) based on the 18820 protocol, which allows an AH-64D not only to talk to other AH-64Ds, OH-58Ds and RAH-66s but also to Rivet Joint (RC-135), J/STARS (E-8), airborne A^2C^2S (UH-60C 'C+CHawk'), the battalion TOC (Tactical Operations Center) and armoured manoeuvre units. IDM uses a communications standard that is tri-service (and still expanding in scope), digital, multi-channel, secure (using Have Quick and SINCGARS systems) and applicable to virtually any radio. The MMW/RFI system provides the Longbow commander with a digital picture of the battle-field where all targets are classified and prioritised using clear symbology. Targets can be classified as tracked,

wheeled, air defence, helicopter or fixed-wing aircraft. Once the radar has scanned the engagement area, automatic target handover to the fire control system takes place "faster than it takes to read this sentence", according to one Longbow programme official. The Longbow TADS/PNVS can be slaved to the MMW radar for visual ID, but in most cases the radar exceeds the FLIR's target recognition capability. In the words of a Longbow project officer, "The AH-64A finds the target and asks you what it is; the AH-64D finds it, then tells you." Target sort and handover can be accomplished with a few keystrokes.

More importantly, the engagement parameters can be changed with as little effort. Longbow Apache divides the battlefield using information transmitted in real-time to all the other members of the attack team. The prioritisation system allows targets to be clearly marked as 'shoot first', 'shoot second' or 'already shot at'. This minimises overkill and allows the battalion/company to make maximum use of its missiles. The Longbow can also minimise fratricide by setting up a 'no-fire zone' where it is impossible to engage targets, without man-in-the-loop override. The AH-64A is terrain-dependent, which limits the engagement areas and battle positions available to the attack force. AH-64As have to operate in relatively close formation to maintain LoS communications and station-keeping. The Longbow's C³ capability allows it to conduct on-the-spot target handovers, without any of the intensive pre-briefing of the AH-64A mission – then find and kill virtually any targets regardless of conditions. The AH-64D has greater stand-off range and its digital communications fit enables aircraft to disperse widely. The rapid-fire, fire-and-forget AGM-114L can bring massive firepower to bear in a short time, during which the AH-64D is not exposed to enemy ADA fire.

Power for the AH-64D

The Apache's existing General Electric GE T700-GE-701 turboshafts are to be completely replaced by uprated 1,723-shp (1,285-kW) T700-GE-701C engines. The -701C has already been fitted to existing AH-64As from the 604th production aircraft (delivered in 1990). When the Longbow programme was initiated, the US Army planned to field a dual standard of upgrade. The full-upgrade AH-64Ds would be complemented by AH-64Cs which would not have the MMW radar or -701C engines. This designation was abandoned in 1993 with the decision to rebuild all aircraft to AH-64D standard, even though not all would be equipped with the Longbow radar. The AH-64C designation was an unnecessary complication (not least for the US Army's logistics system) and no longer exists. Apaches without the MMW radar will now be known simply as AH-64D Apaches while radar-equipped aircraft will be AH-64D Longbow Apaches.

The advent of the AH-64D will transform the composition of Army aviation battlefield units. However, the

Longbow is not being fielded in isolation and is ultimately expected to work with the RAH-66A Comanche stealthy advanced scout. After intense uncertainty about the future of the Comanche, including its virtual cancellation, the RAH-66A now has a proposed first unit equipped (FUE) date of 2005. Current Army attack helicopter battalions comprise 24 AH-64s, divided among three companies, each with three AH-64A scouts and six attack-dedicated AH-64As. With the introduction of the AH-64D, battalions will graduate to nine Longbow aircraft and 15 baseline (AH-64D) aircraft. The objective for future battalions is to again have 24 aircraft, but divided between 15 Longbow AH-64Ds and nine Longbow-equipped RAH-66As.

The US Defense Acquisition Board authorised a 51-month AH-64D developmental programme in August 1990. In December this was extended to 70 months to incorporate AGM-114L missile development. On 11 March 1991 an AH-64A (82-23356) made its maiden flight as an aerodynamic testbed with a mast-mounted radar housing. The first of six actual AH-64D prototypes (89-0192) flew on 15 April 1992. A total of 232 full-standard Longbow Apaches will be fielded from a total of 758 examples in the current inventory. In June 1994 the Army demonstrated that is was capable of converting an AH-64D to Longbow AH-64D standard in four hours, as required. This involved the transfer of -701C engines, the Longbow radar and associated equipment from the first prototype AH-64D to the sixth, which was then flown for 30 minutes.

Full-scale production authorised by US Under-Secretary of Defense Paul Kaminsky on 13 October 1995 for 232

Opposite page above: The US Army has abandoned plans to field a dual-standard AH-64C/D, which originally called for the conversion of 308 AH-64Cs and 227 AH-64Ds. Now all 758 Apaches will be rebuilt to the full AH-64D standard. However, not all will be routinely equipped with the Longbow radar.

Above: Initial MMW-guided Hellfire tests have been completed and proved to be largely successful. As in the original tests, some problems emerged, but they were far less serious.

Top: The first US Army unit to transition to the Longbow Apache will be 1-227 AVN, based at Ft Hood, Texas. Instructor pilots from 1-227 will begin their training in July 1997 and the AH-64D will be active with the unit by December of that year.

aircraft. The complete US Army AH-64D contract also calls for 13,311 AGM-114L missiles, 227 fire control radars and 3,296 launchers. AH-64D remanufacture began at Mesa in November 1995, in advance of the December 1995 contract for the remanufacture of the first batch of 24 aircraft. Deliveries of the first AH-64Ds are due in March 1997. From start to finish it takes 15 months to convert an AH-64A into an AH-64D. The maximum remanufacture rate of eight per month will be reached in the last quarter of 2001. The first operational unit will be equipped by July 1998 and deliveries will continue until 2008.

The Longbow received spectacular validation in a series of field tests. Between 30 January and 9 February 1995, at China Lake, a team of AH-64As and AH-64Ds conducted preliminary gunnery trials against moving and static T-72s and static ZSU 23-4s. Eight gunnery 'events' were flown, half by day and half by night, and targets were protected by smoke (including IR obscurant smoke), decoys and camouflage netting. These Phase 1 trials paved the way for the 'all-out' force-on-force IOT&E (Initial Operational Test & Evaluation) trials, held at Ft Hunter-Liggett, California, between 6 and 31 March 1995. Two units ('A' Company and 'B' Company, 2-229th AVN) from Ft Rucker conducted a series of paired trials, AH-64A ('B' Co./eight aircraft) versus AH-64D ('A' Co./six aircraft). Twelve missions were flown at night – seven close attack and five deep attack – along with three daytime close attack missions. The Apaches were hunting an integrated threat force of US/Russian armour and mostly Russian ADA systems comprising 20 M1A1 MBTs, 10 M2/3 Bradley IFVs, six 2S6 Tunguskas, two SA-8B 'Geckos' (9K33 Osa), one SA-11 'Gadfly' (9M38 Buk), three SA-13 'Gophers' (9M37 Strela-10), one SA-15 'Gauntlet' (9M330 Tor), 10 SA-18s (9K38 Igla) and a Swedish-built Ericsson Giraffe radar. This 'red' force used smoke, RF/IR blankets, conformal RAM camouflage netting, decoys, corner reflectors and active jammers to further defend itself. No external SEAD, artillery support, or area weapons (rockets) were available to the Apaches. The tanks involved were advanced US Army M1A1 Abrams, with sophisticated reactive armour, active countermeasures and an anti-helicopter capability of their own. The parameters of the test were designed to isolate the attack helicopters and confront them with a 21st century threat. The AH-64Ds flew in a 'heavy Hellfire' configuration, with 12 AGM-114Ls and four

The AH-64A Apache – A Swedish perspective

Since 1988 the Swedish army has operated two companies of what it refers to as 'anti-tank' helicopters – 20 MBB BO 105CBs (local designation Hkp 9A) equipped with the Emerson Heli-TOW system. In March 1995 the Chief of the Army requested the Director of Army Aviation to undertake a technical demonstration programme of a dedicated attack helicopter. In 1996 Sweden was facing a major defence review and the army felt the time was at hand to evaluate its requirement for, and the benefits of, a modern multi-role attack helicopter.

A list of potential types was drawn up for evaluation, including the MDH AH-64A Apache, Bell AH-1W Super Cobra, Agusta A 129 Mangusta, Eurocopter Tiger, Atlas/Denel CSH-2 Rooivalk, Mil Mi-28 'Havoc' and Kamov Ka-50 'Hokum'. The primary purpose of the evaluation was to determine how aircraft would perform in a Swedish environment, so the army insisted that its pilots be trained to fly each type under evaluation, and act as systems operators/gunners. Aircraft had to be available for evaluation in mid-1995, undertake live weapons firings and require a minimum of operating/support costs. The choice was narrowed to the AH-64A and Mi-28. The Swedes recognised that one was a mature system and the other still in the early stages of development, but were interested in examining the two completely different design philosophies and doctrines behind the Apache and the 'Havoc'.

Planning for the four-week evaluation began in April/May 1995. Upon arrival in Sweden the aircraft would self-deploy to the Northern Military District to undertake tactical missions and live-firing exercises. This would be followed by air-to-air target firing and tactical missions in the Central and Southern Military Districts. As a result, each aircraft would be exposed to the full range of Swedish geography and climate.

The Swedish Defence Material Administration (FMV) and the United States Army Security Command, with the support of the Swedish Army Aviation Centre and McDonnell Douglas Helicopters, agreed to supply two USAREUR AH-64As, then stationed in Hanau. A Swedish crew was trained by MDH at Mesa to fly the Apache and operate its systems. A team of Swedish tactical advisors travelled to Ft Rucker to undertake detailed mission planning. The two Apaches (86-9029/86-9033) were flown from Germany by a mixed US/Swedish crew, arriving at the 2nd Army Aviation Battalion in Linköping on 12 August 1995.

The Apaches were scheduled to undertake a range of tactical scenarios, including operational redeployment between military districts, avoiding enemy fighter aircraft, engagement of enveloping forces, deep strike operations, operations in the Swedish archipelago, engagement of enemy air assault forces, delaying operations against mechanised forces, and supporting attacking armoured forces.

Swedish terrain, tactics and military posture mean that standard US operational procedures, such as artillery and air support, were impossible. The Swedes learned that the Apache had the flexibility to operate throughout the country and could be redeployed over substantial distances while still carrying an effective weapons load. Even without the use of EW systems, the Apaches avoided the JA 37 Viggens of F21 Wing, which were hunting them

during their redeployments. In the event, missions were not flown at night, although the Swedes recognise that night operations are preferable, indeed essential, in their Arctic environments (in northern Sweden six months of the year are spent in almost permanent darkness). The autonomous nature of AH-64A operations stretched Sweden's (substantial) C³ network and highlighted the need for an improved communications fit on the aircraft. The Apache's radios are not compatible with Swedish radio systems. Two days of maritime operations with navy and marine units in the archipelago proved that the Apache was very vulnerable on the outer coastline and needed the shelter of the inner archipelago to protect it from hostile fire. However, the Marines were impressed by the AH-64A and thought that the Apache could play an important role in supporting (or repelling) amphibious attacks. Furthermore, the Hellfire missile (Rb 17) is already in service as a coastal defence weapon in Sweden and is compatible with the Apache's own weapons.

During a simulated air drop by an air force Hercules, the Apaches 'shot down' the aircraft using Hellfire. During anti-armour missions the Apache proved to be far superior to Sweden's existing Hkp 9As. Air-to-air trials were conducted against towed targets at the Swedish Anti-Aircraft School, Väddö. The targets were 'cold' (with no IR signature, perhaps not the most realistic simulation) and the FLIR and DVO were unable to acquire them within the prevailing safety limits. When the gun did lock-up a target the autotracking system failed and no direct hits were ever made on any target. Live-firing trials were limited to the Apache's rocket system, as Sweden already has the Hellfire in service (as a coastal defence missile) and is familiar with its performance. There were also cost and safety factors in this decision. A manual rocket firing was made and the rockets missed the target area by several hundred meters.

A total of 99 hours was flown by the two aircraft during the four-week evaluation. During that time, there were periods when one or both AH-64As were unserviceable. The Apaches suffered from software problems in the FCC and badly maintained rocket pods; an APU clutch had to be changed, a TV camera had to be replaced, a laser unit had to be replaced, several bulbs had to be changed, one gun suffered a hardware failure and rotors needed repairing. As a result, five of the planned 20 missions were cancelled due to technical problems. Additional missions were also cancelled to allow ground crews more time to prepare for weapons tests. The Apache's

navigation and fire control systems suffered several problems. Co-ordinates in latitudes higher than 65°N could not be entered and, as a result, planned night attack missions were not flown.

A single Mi-28 was supplied by Rosvoorouzhenie to the FMV under a contract signed in August 1995. The evaluation helicopter (Mi-28 prototype 042) was airlifted by Il-76 to Luleå on 7 October 1995. Using Mi-24s and Mi-28s in Moscow, the Swedes had trained one test pilot and two service pilots to fly the Mi-28. Swedish personnel ultimately flew as weapons systems operators during the evaluation, and not as command pilots (the Mi-28 does not have dual controls). Since the Russian pilot was not a fluent English speaker, all operational missions were tightly pre-briefed and flown with a translator airborne in another aircraft. The Mi-28 flew a number of tactical missions that mirrored the Apache programme. The Swedish evaluation found that the sighting system worked well and was easy to use, even in the hands of an inexperienced crew. The Mi-28 was rated as highly survivable, with good ballistic protection for the crew and with an extensive onboard RWR and ECM system. The MMI (Man Machine Interface/ergonomics) of the Mi-28 was generally good and will be improved. The aircraft handled well, although crews had some reservations about their early production standard aircraft in this area. Current production Mi-28s are completely lacking in any night-fighting capability. Mil is working to remedy this problem with the much improved Mi-28N, which has been compared (perhaps over-optimistically) to the AH-64D.

The official Swedish Army Aviation Centre report on the evaluation stated that the Mi-28's weapons accuracy was "good and astonishingly repeatable," particularly taking into account the range of firing parameters and poor weather conditions. Both 9M1154 Shturm and 9M120 Ataka guided missiles were fired against stationary targets (to a maximum range of 4680 m/15,354 ft, with the Mi-28 flying at 200 km/h, 124 mph IAS), with 1-m (3.3-ft) accuracy. Rockets were found to be accurate up to a range of 4000 m (13,123 ft), with 35 hits registered from 40 firings. Four unexploded rockets were later found and questions were raised about the production quality and safety standards of Russian ammunition. Gun firings were unsuccessful due to bad boresighting.

The Mi-28 was flown for a total of 30 hours, never failed to undertake a mission, and experienced the minimum of technical snags. On one occasion an engine automatically throttled back

The AH-64A maintained its reputation as an complex and effective aircraft during the Swedish army aviation evaluation.

after plume ingestion from a rocket firing. This was a safety measure which performed as expected, and the aircraft was ready for flight within an hour, to resume firing tests. The aircraft also experienced a failure of the flare dispenser. The Swedish opinion of the Mi-28 was that it was a robust and reliable helicopter well-suited to field conditions. Reservations were expressed about the classification and standards of its electrical system and some design features. Integration of the required modern avionics would require additional electronic shielding and filtering. Availability of the necessary specifications, airworthiness certification, technical manuals and maintenance documentation was an unknown.

The evaluation of the AH-64A concluded that it was a highly-complex aircraft, requiring a well-trained and co-ordinated crew. Successful missions demanded an intensive level of mission planning. Its onboard systems allowed detection of targets, by day and night, at ranges meeting all Swedish requirements. A large proportion of Swedish wartime personnel are drawn from a (trained) conscript force, who were deemed to be capable of supporting Apache operations. The attack helicopter demonstration programme to date has provided much first-hand experience and broadened the Swedish understanding of modern attack helicopter operations. The programme will continue through to 1999/2000, with a view to presenting a final proposal, prior to the next major Parliamentary defence review in 2001. An AH-64D Longbow Apache evaluation will take place during that timeframe. A Eurocopter Tiger evaluation was scheduled for February 1997.
Robert Hewson

The Mi-28 'Havoc' prototype deployed to Sweden surprised many with its good performance.

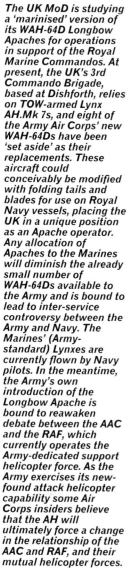

The UK MoD is studying a 'marinised' version of its WAH-64D Longbow Apaches for operations in support of the Royal Marine Commandos. At present, the UK's 3rd Commando Brigade, based at Dishforth, relies on TOW-armed Lynx AH.Mk 7s, and eight of the Army Air Corps' new WAH-64Ds have been 'set aside' as their replacements. These aircraft could conceivably be modified with folding tails and blades for use on Royal Navy vessels, placing the UK in a unique position as an Apache operator. Any allocation of Apaches to the Marines will diminish the already small number of WAH-64Ds available to the Army and is bound to lead to inter-service controversy between the Army and Navy. The Marines' (Army-standard) Lynxes are currently flown by Navy pilots. In the meantime, the Army's own introduction of the Longbow Apache is bound to reawaken debate between the AAC and the RAF, which currently operates the Army-dedicated support helicopter force. As the Army exercises its new-found attack helicopter capability some Air Corps insiders believe that the AH will ultimately force a change in the relationship of the AAC and RAF, and their mutual helicopter forces.

AGM-114Ks, plus 330 30-mm rounds. The AH-64As flew with an all-AGM-114K loadout.

The results of the test were staggering. The AH-64Ds achieved 300 confirmed kills, the AH-64As notched up just 75. Four AH-64Ds were shot down while the AH-64A force lost 28 aircraft. Most importantly, in the eyes of many, the Longbows failed to make a single blue-on-blue kill; the AH-64As made 34. One test official stated, "In all my years of testing, I have never seen a tested system so dominate the system it is intended to replace." An opposing 'red' force member paid a more succinct tribute when he said, "We always knew when it was the Longbow Apache attacking. Everybody died with no warning." In fact, so successful were the tests that the Pentagon's OT&E office cancelled the final two elements in the programme. According to the AAH Program Manager Colonel Robert Atwell, "In a very, very short time frame we figured out that the A model would be incapable of operating on what we consider the modern battlefield. It's time to move on to the next generation."

Before that happens, some problems remain to be corrected. The AH-64D's communications fit is not perfect and the existing TADS/PNVS is now starting to show its age, particularly when used alongside the Longbow radar. Longbow itself has some difficulty in acquiring stationary targets, and AGM-114K's ability to deal with multiple countermeasures has not been 100 per cent proven. A US General Accounting Office report stated that after evaluation it became clear that there were instances where the radar failed to detect and identify targets. Some missile engagements failed against multiple countermeasures such as smoke/jammers. The pilot's greatest wish is for a radio system that is truly independent of terrain. The AH-64D's digital communications suite is far better than that of the AH-64A, but can still be improved.

To date, the six Longbow Apaches have amassed over 5,000 flying hours. This handful of aircraft has achieved a 92 per cent availability figure and a 96 per cent successful launch rate with the Longbow Hellfire. Operational testing of the Longbow is complete and the AH-64D test fleet has begun to look forward to the next century and Task Force XXI. In early March 1997 the US Army initiated its Task Force XXI exercise at the NTC, Ft Irwin, California. Two Longbow Apaches are integrated into this advanced warfighting skills/technology exercise. Task Force XXI will be the first operational fielding of the AH-64D's IDM in conjunction with the US Army's entire combat force. It also marks the US Army's continued advance into the digital battlefield.

The Korean theatre

The armoured threat in Europe, the Apache's *raison d'être*, has all but disappeared. However, with the end of Cold War Superpower tension, attention has returned to the Korean peninsula where hostilities have simmered for nearly 50 years. The Democratic People's Republic of Korea (North Korea) is an isolated, heavily-militarised Communist dictatorship that claims the territory of its southern neighbour and is gripped by a worsening domestic situation fuelled by floods, famine and the indifference of its former political allies. Crews based in Korea during Desert

Storm remember standing armed alerts while the world's attention was focused on Iraq. As one put it, "we reckoned the North Koreans just had to do something, our forces there were so depleted. They missed their best chance."

During rising tension in 1996, the Apache force stationed in Korea was quietly boosted. The North Korean army has some T-72-class MBTs, but most of its armoured forces are far less sophisticated and well-protected, including Soviet-supplied T-54/55s and Chinese copies. Nevertheless, as one experienced observer pointed out, "Kim Chong Il's generals have 2,600 tanks; that's substantially more than Hitler needed to overrun Poland or France – and it's only 37 miles from the DMZ to Seoul." Any armoured thrust towards Seoul, the Republic of Korea's capital, is a 'straight shot' down what is called the Uijonbu corridor, and the conventional wisdom today is that friendly forces would not have time to regroup if the city were lost, as they did in 1950. The central avenue of approach is the central Chorwon Valley (Korea's Fulda Gap). It is here that the Apache battalions based in South Korea train to bottle-up advancing North Korean armour. Any heavy attack is anticipated in the winter, when the paddy fields are frozen. Summer brings with it the monsoon and much unpredictable weather. Korea offers a good flying environment for the Apache pilot. Operating temperatures and air density allow an aircraft with weapons and auxiliary fuel to hold five hours on station. Far more than West Germany ever was, Korea is 'Apache country'.

Universal Apache

The end of Desert Storm brought with it a clamour for the Apache from customers worldwide, but particularly in the Middle East. Countries that had been toying with the idea of acquiring the Apache began to sign on the dotted line, and many others, like the UK and Holland, at last drew up serious requirements for an attack helicopter. A flood of new orders was answered with deliveries to Saudi Arabia and a batch to the UAE in 1993. In 1994 Egypt took delivery of its first batch of AH-64As, and in the following year so did Greece. The second batch for the UAE was handed over in 1996 and Egypt's second batch will be delivered in 1997. Dutch and British aircraft will follow.

While McDonnell Douglas's salesmen were busy with the Apache, its crews were back in action again. In December 1995 USAREUR AH-64As were deployed to Bosnia as part of NATO's determined IFOR (Implementation FORce) contingent monitoring the Dayton peace agreement. It is a testament to the Apache's reputation that the AH-64 force was never fired upon.

The Apache and its crews have shown that they are more than capable of dealing with any existing armoured threat. Intensive training, absolute dominance in combat and complete faith in their aircraft mean that US Army aviation Apache crews are still the masters of the modern battlefield. Future threats belong to the realm of the AH-64D, and people involved in the Longbow programme admit they have only begun to scratch the surface of the Longbow Apache's capabilities. One senior British officer, transitioning to the AH-64 at Ft Rucker in 1996, reflected that "the step up from AH-64A to AH-64D is even more profound than the gap between Lynx and AH-64A. There is just no comparison."

As this article was being compiled, the news emerged that McDonnell Douglas had been acquired by the Boeing Company in a $13.3 billion deal ($63 per share). As a result, Boeing will inherit and expand McDonnell Douglas's mantle as the world's leading producer of combat aircraft. Boeing-Vertol has substantial helicopter experience of its own, and the company has a 50 per cent stake in the Bell/Boeing V-22 Osprey and Boeing/Sikorsky RAH-66A Comanche programmes. With the acquisition of the Apache, only the AH-1W and UH-60 helicopters lie outside Boeing's sphere of influence in the United States.

During 1997 all of McDonnell Douglas's divisions, including McDonnell Douglas Helicopters, will operate under the name of the Boeing Company. The Apache will undergo its third major change of title, and the emergence of the 'Boeing AH-64' is not far away. Boeing enjoys a respectable order book for the Apache, with more in prospect, coupled with the major AH-64D remanufacturing effort for the US Army. To the aircraft's crews the change-over will not be so obvious. One senior IP spoke for many when asked what the most important things were for him when it came to flying the Apache. He replied, "to serve my country, and kill tanks."

Robert Hewson

Above and below: The advent of the AH-64D Longbow Apache heralds the rejuvenation of the Apache and should bring about a burgeoning order book in the near future. The most recent customers for the aircraft have all opted for the AH-64D and, apart from the Eurocopter Tiger, there is no obvious rival for the Longbow on the battlefield or the market.

AH-64 Apache Production

US Army		Export Customers		
Fiscal Year funding	**Production total**	**Country**	**Total ordered**	**First delivery date**
FY73	3	Israel	18	September 1990
FY79	3	Saudi Arabia	12	April 1993
FY82	11	UAE	20	October 1993
FY83	48	Egypt	24	February 1994
FY84	112	Greece	20	February 1995
FY85	138	UAE	10	1996
FY86	116	Egypt	12	1997
FY87	101	Netherlands	30	1998
FY88	77	United Kingdom	67	1999
FY89	54			
FY90	154	*Total deliveries to US Army*		**827**
FY95	10	*Total export orders/deliveries*		**213**

United States of America US Army Aviation

Forces Command (FORSCOM) HQ Ft McPhearson, Atlanta, GA

The US Army Forces Command (FORSCOM) is the major Army command responsible for the combat readiness, sustainment and training of active component (AC) and reserve component (RC) Apache units based in the Continental US (ConUS).

I Corps (ICORPS), HQ Ft Lewis, WA

The corps, known as 'Eye Corps', is based at Ft Lewis, WA and is composed primarily of light infantry combat units, the vast majority of them RC units, dispersed to over 20 states including Alaska and Hawaii. Several light infantry AC divisions were assigned to I Corps in the 1980s, none with AH-64As assigned, but they were inactivated or reassigned by the early 1990s.

The corps aviation brigade is the 66th Aviation Brigade at Camp Murray, WA, a Washington Army National Guard (WA ArNG) command that will complete transition of its assigned units by FY98. It had two AC Apache units, 4-501 AVN (ATK) and 5-501 AVN (ATK), that were forward-deployed from 1993 with the Eighth US Army (EUSA/8ARMY) in the Republic of Korea, but these units were reflagged and reassigned in 1996. The UT ArNG-assigned 211th Aviation Group, or regiment, has been assigned two ArNG Apache battalions, and with recent realignments a third has

been added, 1-285 AVN of the Arizona ArNG. AVIM (aviation intermediate maintenance) and combat support capability for the AH-64A fleet is provided by elements of the 103rd Corps Support Command (103 COSCOM), a USARC-assigned unit based in Des Moines, IA.

66th Aviation Brigade, Camp Murray, WA; 66 AVN BDE
WA ArNG-assigned

211th Aviation Group (Regiment), West Jordan, UT; 211 AVNGRP
UT ArNG-assigned unit commands the following units:

1-183 AVN (ATK) (ID ArNG)	AH-64A	Boise Air Terminal, ID
1-211 AVN (ATK) (UT ArNG)	AH-64A	West Jordan AP, UT
1-285 AVN (ATK) (AZ ArNG)	AH-64A	Pinal AP, Marana, AZ

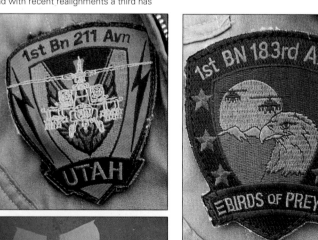

Above: The insignia of Idaho ArNG Apache unit 1-183 AVN (ATK).

Above left: The badge of Utah ArNG AH-64A unit 1-211 AVN (ATK).

Left: 'C' Company, 1-227 AVN ('Vampires') has applied this bat marking to its AH-64As.

III Corps (IIICORPS), HQ Ft Hood, Texas

Tracing its combat history to 1918, when it was first activated in France, III Corps gained the nickname 'Phantom Corps' during the Battle of the Bulge in 1944. Since 1954 it has been based at Ft Hood, TX and is composed primarily of heavy armour units with a sustainment mission for the European theatre. The corps achieved peak strength in the late 1980s with five AC armour and mechanised infantry divisions, and numerous brigades, commands and groups. Several RC divisions are aligned with III Corps for training and readiness. In the late 1980s the corps was responsible for eight combat Apache battalions and squadrons. By 1997, III Corps was down to five AH-64 battalions and squadrons, a force level that is expected to be maintained through the turn of the century. AVIM and corps sustainment is provided by units of the 13th Corps Support Command (13 COSCOM), also based at Ft Hood.

6th Cavalry Brigade

The 6th Cavalry Brigade (Air Combat) is III Corps' aviation brigade with heraldry and lineage that dates back to the Civil War. The brigade has pioneered many of the tactics and organisational advancements in Army aviation since its most recent activation in 1975. It was the first aviation brigade to become operational and combat-ready with the Apache. The first three Apache battalions were fielded to the brigade from April 1986 to 1988. In early 1988, one of the units, 2-6 CAV, was deployed to Germany for the Reforger '88 exercises and remained in-country, being assigned to the 11th Aviation Brigade; this marked the first overseas deployment of the type. The brigade has also deployed Apaches since 1991 to support Joint Task Force SIX in the war on drugs, operating from remote locations along the southwest US border. 6th CAV operated one RC and three

1st Cavalry Division

The 1st Cavalry Division Aviation Brigade is based at Ft Hood, TX and is assigned a single AC Apache battalion, 1-227 AVN. This unit transitioned from AH-1 Cobras in 1988-89 and was deployed with the division to Saudi Arabia in 1990 for Operation Desert Shield/Storm. The unit has recently transitioned to the ARI force structure and it is in line to become one of the first operators of the Longbow Apache in 1997.

1st Infantry Division

The 1st Infantry Division (Mechanized) was assigned to III Corps after its return from the Vietnam War in the early 1970s. The division, known as 'The Big Red One', gained the Apache in the late 1980s, operating it with 1-1 AVN from Marshall AAF at Ft Riley, KS until the battalion was inactivated in 1995. The division flag was reassigned to reflag the 3rd Infantry Division assigned to V Corps in Germany in 1996.

The extensive facilities and live-fire ranges at Ft Hood led the Army to decide to field the first Apache units here in 1984, forming a task force to plan the introduction of the AH-64 into the force structure. The Apache Training Brigade (ATB) was activated in 1985 to develop the Single Station Unit Fielding and Training Program (SSUFTP), later shortened to UTP, and the brigade was responsible for fielding all AC and RC Apache units, 31 in all. In 1992 the brigade was redesignated as the Combat Aviation Training Brigade (CATB), reflecting the addition of the OH-58D(I) Kiowa Warrior fielding responsibility. In 1996 it was redesignated as the 21st Cavalry Brigade (21 CAV BDE) to reflect preparations for the fielding of AH-64D Longbow Apache units from 1997.

21st Cavalry Brigade (Aviation), Hood AAF, Ft Hood, TX

21 CAV BDE	AH-64A	(AH-64D to be gained 1997)

AC Apache units until 1996, when it was reduced to one AC and one RC unit of the type. In the summer of 1996, the 6th ACCB headquarters and its remaining AC Apache unit were forward-deployed to Korea, reporting to the 8th Army. The brigade gained a second AC Apache squadron, redesignated from an attack battalion previously deployed there. While 6 ACCB is on deployment, the 385th Aviation Group of the Arizona ArNG commands the single USARC squadron.

6th Cavalry Brigade (6 CAV BDE/6 ACCB), Hood AAF, Ft Hood, TX
Command forward-deployed to Korea, 1996

385th Aviation Group (Regiment) (385 AVN GRP), Pinal Airpark, Marana, AZ
AZ ArNG-assigned unit commands the following unit:

7-6 CAV (AC)	AH-64A	Montgomery County AP, Conroe, TX

The 7-6 CAV, a USARC unit, has trained to augment the 1st Cavalry Division for contingency operations but is attached to 6 CAV BDE in peacetime. AVIM support for the 'First Team' Apaches is by C Co./227th Aviation Regiment.

1st Cavalry Division Aviation Brigade (4th Brigade) (1CD AVN BDE), Ft Hood, TX

1-227 AVN (ATK)	AH-64A (AH-64D in 1997)	Robert Gray AAF, W. Ft Hood, TX

2nd Armored Division

The 2nd Armored Division, 'Hell on Wheels', was based at Ft Hood from 1946 until it was reflagged as the 4th Infantry Division (M) in 1996. The command's aviation brigade operated 1-3 AVN from 1988 to 1991 when the battalion was inactivated. The 5th Infantry Division (M) was reflagged as the 2nd AD in 1993, with the 1-502 AVN from the 5th's aviation brigade becoming the division's attack battalion, based at Hood AAF. The battalion was reflagged as 1-4AVN in 1996, assigned to the 4th Infantry Division.

4th Infantry Division

The III Corps-assigned 4th Infantry Division has been located at Ft Carson, CO since its return from Vietnam in the early 1970s. Its 1-4 AVN began to field its Apaches in 1990 and operated them until the battalion was inactivated at Butts AAF, Ft Carson, CO in late 1995. The 'Ivy Division' flag was relocated to Ft Hood, TX by early 1996 to reflag the assets of the 2nd Armored Division, and 1-4 AVN reflagged the 1-502 AVN at Hood AAF in early 1996. The unit remains there today and is an important element in the Force XXI experiments that will shape the force structure and future of Army warfighting systems. The 404th ASB provides AVIM capability to the division.

49th Armored Division

The 49th Armored Division, the 'Lone Star Division', is the only ArNG division equipped with AH-64A Apaches. The battalion began to transition from AH-1S Cobras at its base at Ellington Field, Houston, TX in late 1991, becoming combat-certified in 1994. The Texas ArNG division remains an element of the strategic reserve force but its proximity to III Corps at Ft Hood gives it a

reinforcement mission to that corps. The battalion remains in the AOE structure, and is not expected to transition to ARI until FY98.

49th Armored Division Aviation Brigade (49 AVN BDE), Mueller AP, Austin, TX
TX ArNG-assigned

1-149 AVN (ATK)	AH-64A	
		Ellington Field, Houston, TX

4th Infantry Division (Mechanized) Aviation Brigade (4ID AVNBDE), Ft Hood, TX

1-4 AVN (ATK)	AH-64A/D	Hood AAF, Ft Hood, TX

5th Infantry Division

The 5th Infantry Division was located at Ft Polk, LA from 1975 to 1993, assigned to III Corps. The 1-5 AVN transitioned to AH-64As in 1991 and by 1993 the battalion was reflagged as 1-502 AVN. The 'Red Diamond Division' was relocated to Ft Hood, TX and was reflagged as the 2nd Armored Division in 1993 with the 1-502 AVN.

Above: This AH-64A carries the markings of 5-6 CAV, one of the former spearhead Apache units in Germany.

Below: The uniquely sharkmouthed Apaches of 1-229 and 3-229 AVN highlight the fact that the 229th Regiment is the (only) official inheritor of the 'Flying Tigers' heritage.

XVIII Airborne Corps (XVIIIABNCORPS)
HQ Ft Bragg, North Carolina

The XVIII Airborne Corps has been headquartered at Ft Bragg, NC since 1951 and the 'Dragon Corps' has been the Army's contingency corps for strategic, rapid-reaction land warfare since 1958. The corps routinely trains its force to deploy worldwide. Since the 1980s it has been assigned from four to five AC divisions, along with numerous brigades, commands and groups from all the combat branches. In the early 1990s the 18th Airborne Corps operated as many as 12 Apache battalions with 216 combat-coded aircraft, and by 1997 it was down to a force level of 10 AC and RC units with an increased aircraft strength of 240 AH-64As. Major support and AVIM is provided by the 1st Corps Support Command (1 COSCOM).

The aviation brigade for the corps is the 18th Aviation Brigade (Corps) (Airborne). The first Apaches had been assigned by 1988 when the North Carolina ArNG had begun to train with the aircraft. The brigade was one of the first Army commands deployed to Saudi Arabia in 1990. No

Apache units were directly assigned to the brigade, and units with the Florida, North Carolina and South Carolina ArNGs continued to train, but never deployed. 18th AVN BDE gained its first organic Apache units after returning from duty in Operation Desert Storm in 1991 when the 229th Attack Regiment (Group) was activated with two AH-64A units. The FL and SC ArNG units train with and are supported by the group, and at least one of these units has a European reinforcement mission.

229th Aviation Group (Regiment) (229 AVNGRP), Simmons AAF, Ft Bragg, NC
Group commands the following units:

1-229 AVN (ATK)	AH-64A	Simmons AAF, Ft Bragg, NC
3-229 AVN (ATK)	AH-64A	Simmons AAF, Ft Bragg, NC
1-130 AVN (ATK) (NC ArNG)	AH-64A	Raleigh-Durham AP, NC
1-151 AVN (ATK) (SC ArNG)	AH-64A	McEntire ANGB, SC

3rd Infantry Division

The 3rd Infantry Division (Mechanized) flag was relocated from Germany to reflag the 24th Infantry Division (M) at Ft Stewart, GA in 1996. The 'Marne Division' is the primary armour force assigned to XVIIIABNCORPS and is the only division in the corps equipped with two Apache battalions. The 1-111 AVN, belonging to the Florida ArNG, relocated from Craig Field to NAS Cecil

Field, FL in early 1997. The 603rd ASB provides AVIM support to the AH-64As.

3rd Infantry Division (Mechanized) Aviation Bde (3ID AVNBDE), Hunter AAF, GA

1-3 AVN (ATK)	AH-64A	Hunter AAF, Savannah, GA
1-111 AVN (ATK)	AH-64A	NAS Cecil Field, FL

24th Infantry Division

The 24th Infantry Division (Mechanized) was located at Ft Stewart, GA from 1975 until 1996 when it was reflagged as the 3rd ID(M). The division's attack battalion, 1-24 AVN, transitioned from AH-1s in 1989. The battalion was reflagged as 1-3 AVN in 1996.

82nd Airborne Division

The 'All Americans' of the 82nd Airborne Division are a light infantry division that is completely airmobile and parachute-deployable, based at Ft Bragg, NC. The division's attack battalion, 1-82 AVN, received its first Apache in 1987, becoming operational with the type at Simmons AAF in 1988. They deployed with the division to participate in Operation Desert Shield/Storm and the battalion operated the AH-64A until 1994, when it transitioned to the OH-58D(I) Kiowa Warrior. The unit was augmented from 1991 by 'E' Company, a USARC company that was assigned to enhance the battalion during combat operations.

101st Airborne Division

The 101st Airborne Division (Air Assault) is the Army's only air assault division based at Ft Campbell, KY. The aviation brigade gained its first Apache battalion in 1988, a second in 1989 and the third converted from HueyCobras in 1991. The unit was deployed with XVIIIABNCORPS, seeing extensive combat in Operation Desert Storm. The 2-229 AVN, based at Guthrie AAF, Ft Rucker, AL was assigned to the 101st during Desert Storm. It is the only Army division with three AH-64A attack units. The assigned AC unit 3-101 AVN was inactivated in 1995 and replaced by the RC battalion 8-229 AVN, the first unit to complete the transition to the ARI structure.

101st Airborne Division (Air Assault), Aviation Bde, 101 AD(AASLT), Ft Campbell, KY

1-101 AVN (ATK)	AH-64A	Campbell AAF
2-101 AVN (ATK)	AH-64A	Campbell AAF
8-229 AVN (ATK) (USARC)	AH-64A	Goodman AAF, Ft Knox, KY

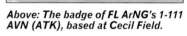

Above: The badge of FL ArNG's 1-111 AVN (ATK), based at Cecil Field.

Above left: The insignia of 3-229 AVN, the famous 'Flying Tigers'.

Left: This 'death's head' badge is worn by Apaches of 'B' Company, 1-227 AVN ('Reapers'), at Ft Hood.

3rd US Army (THREEUSA/3rd Army), Ft McPherson, GA

The 3rd US Army is the theatre Army assigned to the US Central Command (USCENTCOM). During peacetime no Apache units are assigned but units would be drawn from other commands, including the contingency corps, XVIII Airborne Corps. During Operation Desert Shield/Storm, approximately 300 Apaches were deployed to the theatre.

US Army Europe/7th Army (USAREUR/7A)
HQ Campbell Barracks, Heidelberg, Germany

The US Army Europe/7th Army is the command that provides the land warfare force for the US European Command (USEUCOM) and represents just a fraction of the combat power available to NATO's Supreme Allied Commander, Europe/Supreme Headquarters Allied Powers (SACEUR/ SHAPE). The command has been based in Germany since 1950 and during the Cold War it was sustained by several corps of US Army soldiers; through most of the 1980s and into the early 1990s it was sustained by V Corps at Frankfurt, Germany and VII Corps at Stuttgart. Three divisions were to equip with the Apache in-theatre and were assigned two battalions each of the type. A total of five Apache units was assigned directly to V Corps and VII Corps by 1991. The 11th Aviation Brigade was assigned 2-6 and 6-6 CAV along with 4-229 and 5-229 AVN (the latter battalion being redesignated as 2-3 AVN in

1991), while the 12th Aviation Bde gained the 5-6 CAV in 1990. The theatre army would have been reinforced by III Corps and XVIII Airborne Corps in a contingency, and at its peak in 1991 it had a paper force of over 500 AH-64As that could be expected to be deployed to Europe within 60 days of an emergency.

Force reductions have been dramatic and VII Corps was inactivated in March 1992. VII Corps' aviation brigade, the 11th Aviation Brigade, was reassigned to V Corps at that time, replacing the 12th Aviation Brigade, which became a group assigned to the 11th. By 1995, 2-3 ATK, 3-4 ATK and 4-229 were inactivated. In 1997 V Corps continued to be equipped with 11th AVN BDE, 1 ID(M) and 1AD, operating a total cadre of 96 Apaches. The 3rd Corps Support Command (3 COSCOM) provides AVIM services.

AH-64 Apache Operators

The substantial number of Apaches allocated to the Ft Rucker-based 1-14 AVN (Training) are all based at Hanchey AAF.

V Corps, HQ, Heidelberg, Germany; VCORPS

12th Aviation Brigade (12 AVN BDE), Illesheim AAF, Ansbach, Germany;

11th Aviation (Group) Regiment, Illesheim AAF, Ansbach, Germany; 11 AVN GRP
Group commands the following battalions:

2-6 CAV (AC)	AH-64A	Illesheim AAF, Ansbach
6-6 CAV (AC)	AH-64A	Illesheim AAF, Ansbach

1st Armored Division

The 1st Armored Division, traditionally known as 'Old Ironsides', is based at Bad Krueznach, Germany having reflagged the assets of the former 8th Infantry Division (M) and relocated its headquarters from Ansbach, Germany. Its aviation brigade was originally equipped with 2-1 AVN and 3-1 AVN, which transitioned from AH-1Fs in 1989-90. These units were replaced by 2-227 and 3-227 in late 1991, undergoing conversion to the ARI structure in 1994.

1st Infantry Division

The 1st Infantry Division (Mechanized) flag was moved from Ft Riley, KS in early 1996 to reflag the assets of the former 3rd Infantry Division. The attack battalion of the 'Big Red One' was redesignated as 1-1 AVN from 3-1 AVN at that time. The Wurzburg, Germany-based division is a heavy unit.

3rd Armored Division

The 'Spearhead Division' was based in Germany from the 1950s until 1992. Its aviation brigade fielded AH-64As with two battalions in 1989, 2-227 and 3-227 AVN. 3AD deployed with VII Corps to fight in Operation Desert Storm (3-227 AVN deployed with the 12th Aviation Brigade). Within a year after its return, the aviation brigade of the division was reassigned to the 1st Armored Division, with the two Apache battalions and the other division assets inactivated.

3rd Infantry Division

The 3rd Infantry Division (Mechanized) was headquartered at Wurzburg, Germany, and was subordinate to VII Corps. The two

In late 1995 Apaches of 2-227 AVN were deployed to Bosnia to support the 1st AD Task Force Eagle and NATO forces of the Implementation Force (IFOR), while involved in Operation Joint Endeavor. 3-227 AVN has been inactivated. The 127th ASB provides AVIM support to the division's Apaches.

1st Armored Division Aviation Brigade/ 4th Brigade (1AD AVN BDE), Hanau, Germany

2-227 AVN (ATK)	AH-64A	Fliegerhorst AAF, Hanau

A reinforced brigade-sized task force was to replace the 1st AD in Bosnia in late 1996-97, augmented by Apaches from 2-6 CAV. The 603rd ASB is the brigade's AVIM component.

Aviation Brigade/4th Brigade (1ID AVNBDE), Katterbach AHP, Ansbach, Germany

1-1 AVN (ATK)	AH-64A	Katterbach AHP, Ansbach

assigned attack battalions transitioned to the Apache in 1990. 2-3 AVN was deployed to Saudi Arabia and was assigned to support VII Corps in the Gulf War. 3-3 AVN did not deploy, remaining in Europe with most division assets until called to deploy a task force in support of Operation Provide Comfort in Turkey and Iraq from April 1991. In early 1992 the 3rd Infantry Division flag was relocated to Ansbach, Germany to reflag the assets of the 1st Armored Division. Its aviation brigade was inactivated but its structure stayed intact, becoming the 159th Aviation Group at Ft Bragg, NC. 2-3 AVN and 3-3 AVN were inactivated in 1992, its aircraft and aircrews reassigned to the ConUS. The 3rd Infantry Division was itself reflagged as the 1st Infantry Division in 1996 and its flag was reassigned to Ft Stewart, GA to reflag the former 24th Infantry Division.

Eighth US Army (EUSA/8th Army) HQ, Yongsan, Seoul, Republic of Korea

The Eighth Army is the theatre US Army responsible for the land defence of the Korean peninsula, allied with the forces of the Republic of Korea (RoK). The four-star commander of EUSA is also the commander of the UN Command (UNC), US Forces Korea (USFK), and the RoK-US Combined Forces Command (RoK/US CFC, or just CFC). American and Korean forces operate together in the CFC Ground Component Command (CFC-GCC). Only a few major US units are assigned to 8th Army and in any contingency they would be heavily reinforced by ConUS units.

The theatre aviation brigade is the 17th Aviation Brigade. It operated two attack battalions forward-deployed from I Corps,

4-501 and 5-501 AVN, which transitioned from AH-1Fs in 1993-94. From May 1996 the 6th Cavalry Brigade (Air Combat) was deployed to Korea from Ft Hood, TX with 3-6 CAV. The 5-501 AVN battalion was redesignated as the 1-6CAV and was reassigned to the 6 ACCB. The other battalion, 4-501 AVN, was reflagged as 1-2 AVN.

6th Cavalry Brigade (Air Combat), 6 ACCB/6 AVN BDE, Desiderio AAF, Camp Humphreys, RoK
Brigade forward-deployed from Ft Hood, TX, 1996

1-6 CAV (Air Combat)	AH-64A	Camp Eagle, Hoengsong
3-6 CAV (Air Combat)	AH-64A	Camp Humphreys, Pyongteak

2nd Infantry Division

The 2nd Infantry Division (Mechanized) is the largest US combat formation based in Korea. The 'Indianhead Division' is based at Camp Casey, Tongduchon, Korea and has recently deployed one of its manoeuvre brigades to Ft Lewis, WA. The division's

attack battalion operated AH-1 HueyCobras until the summer of 1996, when 4-501 AVN was reflagged as 1-2 AVN.

2nd Infantry Division Aviation Brigade (2ID AVN BDE), Camp Stanley, Uijongbu, RoK

1-2 AVN (ATK)	AH-64A	Camp Page, Chunchon

Training and Doctrine Command (TRADOC) HQ Ft Monroe, VA

The US Army Training and Doctrine Command manages weapon system training and doctrinal implementation, including basic, combat, technical and warfighting skills for all aviators. The principal aviation training centre for the Aviation Branch is the US Army Aviation Center, headquartered at Ft Rucker, Alabama. After an aviator completes initial entry rotary-wing (IERW) training, he advances to 1-14 AVN (Training), assigned to the Aviation Training Brigade (ATB) for type qualification and combat skills training on the Apache. The battalion was formerly designated as the 7th Aviation Training Battalion (7 ATB). Upon completion of training with ATB, aviators are assigned to the 21st Cavalry Brigade, assigned to III Corps/FORSCOM at Ft Hood, TX where they enter unit training or a sustainment programme and will report to a combat Apache battalion for additional training. The assigned 1st Aviation Brigade conducts advanced combat skills and leadership training for US Army and international officers, with the FORSCOM-assigned 2-229 AVN assigned to the brigade in peacetime, performing as a combat laboratory and development support unit.

US Army Aviation Center (USAAVNC) HQ Ft Rucker, AL

Aviation Training Brigade, AL; ATB

1-14 AVN (Training)	AH-64A (AH-64D in 1997) Hanchey AAF, Ft Rucker	

1st Aviation Brigade (Air Assault), AL; 1 AVN BDE

2-229 AVN (Attack)	AH-64A	Guthrie AAF, Ft Rucker

US Army Aviation Logistics School

A major component of the USAAVNC is the Army Aviation Logistics School (USAALS) at Ft Eustis, VA, which trains most maintenance personnel for Army aviation platforms. The school is assigned grounded airframes for the maintenance instruction role, and it should receive its first GAH-64Ds in 1997. USAALS has acquired a number of Apache systems trainers, modified from AH-64A airframes that were written off due to accidents.

US Army Aviation Logistics School (USAALS) Ft Eustis, VA

Department of Aviation Trades Training	GAH-64A (GAH-64D in 1997)

Army Material Command (AMC), HQ Alexandria, VA

The Army Material Command (USAMC/AMC) is the major command responsible for acquisition, depot-level maintenance, research and development, and systems test of Army aviation assets. The AH-64D programme and Apache modernisation efforts are a critical AMC task. The aircraft listed here are contractor-operated are maintained at company facilities at Falcon Field, Mesa, AZ.

Program Executive Office, Aviation (PEO-AVN) St Louis, MO

Apache Attack Helicopter Project Manager's Office (AAH PMO)
(Y)AH-64D
Apache Modernization Project Manager's Office (AM PMO)
AH-64A

Several AMC major subordinate commands are focused on aviation activity, including the **Aviation & Missile Command** (AMCOM) activated in late 1996 and consolidating throughout 1997. The Redstone Arsenal, Huntsville, AL, will become the headquarters for AMCOM.

The command's **Aviation, Research, Development & Engineering Center** (AVRDEC) is focused on aviation technology and systems. One of its principal activities is the **Aviation Applied Technology Directorate** (AATD) at Ft Eustis, VA, which is involved in several Apache product improvement programmes including the joint cockpit air bag system (JCABS). Several AH-64A Apaches are involved in the programme.

Communications-Electronics Command (CECOM), headquartered at Ft Monmouth, NJ, is the major subordinate command that develops and acquires Army systems for command, control, communications, computer and intelligence/electronic warfare (C^4IEW). CECOM is responsible for those systems mounted in airframes, tying them into the service's data and voice networks. The

This AH-64A is one of those detached from the 1-14 AVN to the Aviation Technical Test Center, based at Cairns AAF, Ft Rucker.

Command's **Research, Development and Engineering Center** (RDEC) manages new systems integration through its **Command/Control & Systems Integration Directorate** (CCSID), at Ft Monmouth. Aviation-related projects are tested by the **Electronic Systems Division's Airborne Engineering Evaluation Support Branch** (AEESB) at the Naval Air Warfare Center Aircraft Division (NAWC/AD) at Lakehurst, NJ. That test unit was formerly known as the Aviation R&D Activity (AVRADA). It utilises a number of AH-64A/JAH-64A Apaches.

Depot maintenance is the responsibility of the **Industrial Operations Command** (IOC), HQ Rock Island Arsenal, IL. The **Corpus Christi Army Depot** (CCAD), NAS Corpus Christi, TX, is the only one of more than a dozen depots that conducts helicopter repair. Apaches from around the world are flown to CCAD when they require overhaul and updating.

The **Test and Evaluation Command** (TECOM) is the major subordinate command responsible for material testing. From its headquarters at Aberdeen Proving Ground, MD it operates a number of diverse test facilities and ranges to support its objectives.

The **Aviation Technical Test Center** (ATTC), located at Ft Rucker, AL, is the organisation responsible for testing aviation systems. It was formerly known as the Aviation Development Test Activity (ADTA) and supports numerous customer requirements including those of AMCOM and PEO Aviation. ATTC's **Airworthiness Qualification Test Directorate** (AQTD), previously known as the Aviation Engineering Test Activity (AETA) and assigned to the former AVSCOM, operated at Edwards AFB, CA until 1996 when the unit relocated to Ft Rucker, AL. ATTC provides a wide variety of testing including lead-the-fleet, flight and performance data, and weapons testing and trials, utilising about half a dozen Apaches.

Test and Evaluation Command (TECOM) HQ Aberdeen Proving Grounds, MD

Aviation Technical Test Center (ATTC) Cairns AAF, Ft Rucker, AL
AH-64A/JAH-64A

Israel
Tsvah Haganah Le Israel/Heyl Ha'Avir (Israeli Defence Force/Air Force)

Israel's Apaches are allocated to 113 Sqn and 127 Sqn, based at Ramon (Canaf 25), and 190 Sqn based at Ramat David (Canaf 1). An initial order for 19 was placed in 1990, and delivered by 1991, and at least 40 (in total) have been delivered since.

No. 113 Sqn was formed in October 1955, as the IDF/AF's first Dassault Ouragan fighter-bomber unit. Its squadron badge bears a remarkable similarity to that of the AA's 2e Escadrille, EC1/12 – from whom some of the Israeli aircraft were delivered. No. 113 Sqn later transitioned to the Mystère IVA, IAI Nesher and became the first IDF/AF Kfir squadron in 1976. As the Kfir was phased out of service No. 113 Sqn was disbanded in 1987, only to be reformed on 12 September 1990 after the delivery of the first AH-64As.

In August/September 1993 Israel took delivery of 24 AH-64As (plus two UH-60A) from surplus US Army Europe stocks, as a 'thank you' for support during Operation Desert Storm. The first batch of 18 Apaches was drawn from units at Giebelstadt, Hanau and Illesheim, and comprised 84-24235, 84-24252, 84-24258, 84-24263, 84-24288, 84-24291, 84-24292, 84-24294, 84-24298, 84-24302, 85-25351, 85-25422, 85-25444, 85-25447, 85-25451, 84-25452 and 85-25462. All were delivered by C-5A from Ramstein AFB. The arrival of these aircraft in September led to the establishment of the IDF/AF's second AH-64 squadron. The additional six aircraft are believed to have been delivered in September 1993.

The Apache is known as the Peten (cobra) in IDF/AF service. Israel became the first, and so far only, foreign operatror to use its aircraft in combat during November 1991. Following a Hizbollah ambush on an Israeli patrol in southern Lebanon, Apaches undertook a night attack with Hellfires against a 'Hizbollah base'. This attack was part of a much larger offensive in the area involving TOW-armed Bell AH-1S Cobras,

Even in Israeli terms the IDF/AF's Apache fleet is publicity shy. Despite the substantial number of aircraft that have been delivered over the years only one squadron has been publically acknowledged, though not officially identified. This is No. 113 'Wasp' Squadron, whose badge is seen opposite.

Hughes 500MD Defenders and RPVs.

Apaches were active during Operation Grapes of Wrath – Israel's 1996 retaliatory incursion into Lebanon following Hizbollah rocket attacks on Israeli border settlements. Apaches initiated the operation, attacking a Hizbollah HQ in southern Beirut, on 11 April 1996. A total of 550 combat missions was flown by all types involved in the two weeks of attack and counter-attack.

Late in 1996 Israel became the first export customer for the improved AGM-114K Hellfire II missile, which is now in IDF/AF service.

United Arab Emirates
United Arab Emirates Air Force

On 23 January 1992 MDH announced that confirmation had been reached in December 1991 with the UAE for the purchase of 20 AH-64As. The first of these aircraft was handed over in a ceremony in Abu Dhabi on 3 October 1993, and deliveries continued into the following year. The AH-64As are assigned to the Apache Squadron, part of Western Air Command headquartered in Abu Dhabi. The Apaches are based at Al Dhafra. An additional 10 aircraft are currently on order. The UAE has submitted an application to the US DoD to acquire 30 Advanced Threat Radar Jammers for its AH-64 fleet, worth $82 million.

The United Arab Emirates became the second export customer for the AH-64A when it ordered an initial batch of 20 aircraft in 1991.

Saudi Arabia
Royal Saudi Land Forces

Twelve AH-64As were delivered in 1993 to Army Aviation Command, based at King Khalid Military City. Saudi Arabia is not known to have taken delivery of AGM-114, but they are certain to have been included in the deal. The AH-64s operate in conjunction with Bell 406CS Combat Scouts.

Saudi Arabia was refused delivery of full-spec OH-58D Kiowa Warriors, and instead was given TOW-armed Bell Combat Scouts. The Saudi AAC now has 12 Hellfire-capable AH-64As.

Egypt
Al Quwwat Al Jawwiya Il Misriya (Arab Republic of Egypt Air Force)

Egypt first ordered a batch of 24 AH-64As for delivery from 1995. In December 1994 the Pentagon offered Egypt an additional batch of 12 AH-64As, four spare Hellfire launchers, 34 rocket pods, six additional T700 engines and one spare TADS/PNVS system in a $318 million package. This order was confirmed during the Dubai IDEX show of March 1995, and a Letter of Intent for another 12 AH-64As was also signed. All aircraft in question would be of the latest US Army standard with imbedded GPS, but with a localised radio fit.

This deal was an important one for McDonnell Douglas as it bridged the six-month gap from July 1996 between the last AH-64A delivery and the first AH-64D. The aircraft in service are believed to be allocated to the air force's single attack helicopter regiment.

Greece
Elliniki Aeroporia Stratou (Hellenic Army Aviation)

Greece was the first European export customer for the AH-64. The Hellenic Ministry of Defence signed a Letter of Offer and Acceptance with the US Army on 24 December 1991 finalising the purchase of 12 AH-64As, with a option for eight (which could be increased by another four), and deliveries began by sea in June 1995. Twenty Apaches are now in service with 1 Lokos (company), 1 Tagma Epidolkon Elikopteron (attack helicopter battalion), based at Stefanovikion. In April 1995 US sources announced that a follow-on contract for 24 aircraft was expected to be signed that year. The status of this contract is unknown.

The Greek army's acquisition of 12 AH-64As in 1995 will no doubt influence neighbouring Turkey's plans to expand and improve its own attack helicopter fleet.

The Netherlands
Royal Netherlands Air Force

The Dutch requirement for an attack helicopter was officially a search for a multi-role armed helicopter that could undertake escort, reconnaissance, protection and fire-support missions. In that respect they did not clearly target the Apache, even though Apache was what the Dutch military was seeking. The performance criteria for the new helicopter were clearly influenced by the AH-64. It had to be night/adverse-weather capable, have a maximum speed of 150 kt (277 km/h, 172 mph), an unrefuelled range of at least 285 miles (489 km) and a mission endurance of 2.5 hours, plus missile rocket and gun armament.

The helicopter programme was governed by Holland's unique democracy-driven Defence Material Procurement Process (DMP). DMP involves rigorous Parliamentary checks on virtually every military acquisition effort, no matter how small. The Dutch evaluated the Bell AH-1W and Agusta A 129 before opting for a choice between the Eurocopter Tiger and the AH-64D Apache. The AH-1W was deemed by the Dutch authorities to be the only Cobra variant actually available, and no (proposed) improved versions were evaluated. Even though the allocated budget would buy 40 AH-1Ws, the type was considered to be lacking in performance and operational capability. Agusta offered 36 upgraded A 129 Internationals, but the developmental status of this helicopter counted against it.

McDonnell Douglas offered 30 AH-64Ds for a nominal $962 million, while Eurocopter offered 34 Tigers for $1.09 billion. The US offered AH-64As for initial training, while Germany offered BO 105s. The DMP led to disagreement between the RNLAF, which publicly advocated the Apache, and the Ministry of Economic Affairs (MEZ), which preferred the Tiger. Dutch industry also supported the Eurocopter bid on the grounds of future Dutch participation in the Tiger/Tigre project. This tension between the RNLAF and MEZ led to the postponement of the cabinet decision from December 1994 to January 1995 to an indeterminate date in the future. Industrial offsets were crucial to the Netherland's 1993 selection of the Eurocopter Cougar in preference to the Sikorsky Blackhawk, and so the pressure was obviously on MDH if it was to win the (adjusted) DFL1.553 billion ($890 million contract). Both the German Chancellor Helmut Kohl and the French Minister for Foreign Affairs Alain Juppé visited the Dutch Prime Minister Wim Kok to lobby on behalf of Eurocopter.

In April a 21-page Apache Decision Memorandum was submitted by the government to Parliament, in favour of acquisition of the AH-64D. It reiterated the fact that at the time the Apache had an operational record of over 700,000 flying hours while Tiger had 720. The slide in the value of the dollar was also a persuasive factor, for the deal would now cost only DFL1.1 billion ($710 million) – although this weakness would also affect industrial offsets. The US bid was $12 million less than Eurocopter's bid for 34 Tigers, although Dutch officials said that was not a significant factor.

At the time Eurocopter stated that it "accepted" the Dutch decision. By early May 1995, however, a special hearing had been arranged for Eurocopter Chairman Jean-François Bigay before the Dutch Defence Committee to restate the case for Tiger. Intense political pressure was brought to bear from France and Germany to change the decision and there were many who agreed that the immediate military requirement was less important than the long-term implications for European industry and security co-operation. Eurocopter strongly disputed the results of the AH-64D/Tiger performance evaluation and MDH's estimates of life-cycle costs. Dutch military officials declined to stage a head-to-head fly-off between the two helicopters.

On 24 May 1995 the Netherlands became the third NATO nation to select the AH-64 and the first export customer for the AH-64D. Prime Minister Kok stated that the Apache was chosen because of its "proven high quality and timely availability" coupled with the "lateness and technical risk of the Tiger." A Letter of Offer and Acceptance signed on that day specified 30 AH-64D-standard aircraft for delivery in early 1998. For an order of 30 helicopters the Dutch received a 100 per cent off-set deal plus a long-term industrial co-operation deal, to include AH-64A/D remanufacturing, AH-64D component manufacture, F-15, F/A-18, C-17 and other engine component work, Phillips CD-I technology, and Akzo Nobel Twaron fibre (body armour) technology.

The RNLAF AH-64Ds will not be delivered with the Longbow's MMW radar, but do have the facility to add the radar in the future (six sets may initially be acquired). Likewise, they are compatible with the radar-guided Longbow Hellfire, even though only laser-guided weapons have been ordered. They retain all the fully-digital mission fit of the AH-64D allied with the glass cockpit, Improved Data Modem and embedded GPS/INS. The 30 AH-64Ds will be built at Mesa as part of Apache Production Lot P13 and will be delivered over a five-year period.

The new helicopters will form the centrepiece of the newly-evolving Dutch

In November 1996 12 US Army AH-64As were leased to the Dutch air force to allow crews to begin initial type training before the delivery of their AH-64Ds in 1997/98.

The Dutch Apaches will be AH-64Ds, but without the Longbow radar. This is one of the AH-64D prototypes, wearing a Dutch roundel.

rapid-deployment Air Mobile Brigade which will become operational in 1998. The Dutch 11th Air Mobile Brigade will have three infantry battalions and an aviation battalion, comprising two transport squadrons (one with 13 CH-47D Chinooks, one with 17 AS 532 Cougars) and two Apache attack squadrons. The Apaches will form a tactical helicopter group at Gilze-Rijen AFB with armed BO 105s. The transport helicopters will be based at Soesterberg AFB. The 11th AMB is attached to NATO's ACE Rapid Reaction Corps and its mission will be to deploy within 15 days for combat operations to any location, worldwide. The RNLAF has adopted US attack helicopter training and undertaken the bulk of its pilot and maintenance training in the USA.

The first Apache squadron is 301 Sqn 'Redskins' (motto: 'Per Sapientiam Efficens et Immortalis'). On 17 December 1996 the '301st Tactical Helicopter Squadron' completed its training with the Ft Hood-based 21st Cavalry Aviation Brigade, becoming the first allied unit to graduate from the US Army's helicopter collective training programme. The second Dutch Apache unit, 302 Squadron, will follow in 1997. In advance of its own aircraft the RNLAF agreed to accept 12 US Army AH-64As for initial training, in a nominal FMS loan of $1 each.

On 13 November 1996 12 AH-64As were handed over to the RNLAF at a ceremony held at Gilze-Rijen AFB. The aircraft, which had flown from Hanau, were 85-25430, 85-25465, 85-25471, 85-25472, 85-25474, 85-25480, 85-25482, 85-25485, 86-8970, 86-8983, 86-9029 and 86-9033. The lease did not become active until 17 January 1997 and any flying conducted before then was undertaken by US Army pilots.

United Kingdom
Army Air Corps

Since 1980 the spearhead of the British Army Air Corps had been its TOW-armed Westland Lynx AH.Mk 1/7s. The addition of TOW missiles to the Lynx made it an excellent 'armed helicopter', but it was obviously no match for a dedicated battlefield attack helicopter (AH). Acquisition of an AH had been a long-standing UK requirement but one which was not pursued until after the Gulf War. As early as 1988 a senior British Army Air Corps officer, Lieutenant General Sir David Ramsbottom, had expressed his preference for the AH-64.

The Apache sales effort in Europe had begun in 1982 but it was only in the late 1980s that the more experienced stewardship of McDonnell Douglas, coupled with several years of practical operational experience, allowed serious marketing efforts to began. European NATO members had long been debating the acquisition of a new anti-armour helicopter and MDH squarely targeted the UK/Italian/Spanish/Dutch Tonal Light Attack Helicopter (LAH) programme. Germany and France were perceived as by then being too deeply involved in their joint PAH-2/HAC-3G/HAP project, which was further advanced than that the LAH group. LAH studies were centred around a growth version of Italy's Agusta A 129 Mangusta, which was ultimately considered to be too small, and the partnership fell into abeyance.

The UK's search for an AH was renewed in the mid-1980s, with approximately 127 aircraft being sought. From this point a formal UK requirement, Staff Target (Air) Cardinal Point Specification 428 (previously GSR 3971), was finally endorsed in June 1991. A competitive tendering/assessment phase was initiated by MOD(PE) for an 'off-the-shelf' helicopter, followed by an invitation to tender (ITT) for the supply of aircraft, munitions and support systems. The ITT was issued in February 1993 and by the following November had attracted five bids: the Agusta A 129, the Boeing/Sikorsky RAH-66A Comanche, the BAe/Eurocopter Tiger, the GEC-Marconi Avionics Cobra Venom and the Westland/McDonnell Douglas WAH-64D Longbow Apache. A final sixth bid came late, in September 1994, from the Marshall/Denel Kestrel (Rooivalk). The Kamov Ka-50 was also touted as an outside, and unlikely, competitor. The A 129 and the RAH-66A soon dropped out of the race, leaving the others chasing a potential order of over 90 helicopters. The definitive bids were made by 20 February 1995. Each set of tender documentation comprised 10 or more copies and typically weighed two to three tons.

The AH Target Operational Characteristics (AHTOC) document specified the essential AH performance points. The new helicopter must have night/adverse-weather capability, be highly survivable, boast a substantial payload/range combination and high weapons Pk factor. In total, 678 individual AHTOCs were included in ST(A) CPS 428. From the outset, the

This retouched photograph shows an AH-64D Longbow Apache with notional Helstreak missiles, the UK's 'preferred' weapons choice.

Apache's bid was a strong one. Not only was it the Army's preferred choice (if not in official terms), but McDonnell Douglas's

In addition to being the first exported full-standard Longbow AH-64Ds, AAC WAH-64Ds will be uniquely powered by RTM322 engines – in common with the RAF's and RN's EH101 Merlins.

teaming with Yeovil-based GKN Westland would secure jobs at the UK's only helicopter manufacturing firm while providing invaluable technical experience and future co-production possibilities. Important technology transfer issues, such as the MMW radar, RF seekers and laser guidance systems, would also be involved.

The AH-64D on offer to the Army Air Corps, always referred to as the Westland Attack Helicopter (WAH-64D) Apache, was a full-standard Longbow aircraft with MMW radar and digital systems. The WAH-64D was offered with baseline T700 engines, or more powerful Rolls-Royce/Turboméca RTM322 turboshafts. The latter would provide commonality with the RAF/RN EH101 helicopter and, it was maintained, could be fitted at little additional cost. Primary armament for the WAH-64D would be the RF-homing AGM-114L Longbow Hellfire, although standard AGM-114K Hellfire IIs were also on offer. Rocket armament would be provided by the Bristol Aerospace CRV 7 70-mm system, already in UK service. An air-to-air armament was specified for the British Apaches from the outset and the weapons of choice included the air-to-air Stinger and a version of the Shorts Starstreak high-speed anti-aircraft missile, the Helstreak. An 18-month Helstreak development programme, in conjunction with the US Army, was underway by mid-1995.

In a competition that became increasingly politicised and fractious, the Eurocopter Tiger (Tigre) team played the 'European' card heavily, particularly in the light of the UK's C-130J and CH-47 acquisitions. Eurocopter firmly believed it offered a risk-free option to the UK (as development costs were already underwritten by the French and German governments), with the promise of a 20 per cent stake in the project if the Eurocopter bid was successful. Eurocopter teamed with British Aerospace's Defence Dynamics division, considering it a full partner and offering a 100 per cent offset deal. The UK was already involved in the development of the Trigat missile (intended as the primary armament for anti-tank UHU/HAC Tiger/Tigre versions), and as Trigat's future was closely linked to that of the Tiger a closer British involvement in either project would be welcome. A UK Tiger buy would also be a pointer to closer European defence ties between the UK, France and Germany.

GEC-Marconi mounted a vigorous campaign in support of its Cobra Venom proposal, based on the Bell AH-1W SuperCobra. The Cobra Venom would be TOW/Hellfire compatible (with a newly designed four-station pylon wing), but its primary armament was the GEC-Marconi Brimstone, an RF-homing anti-tank missile based on the chassis and motor of the Hellfire with a UK-designed and -built seeker head. Cobra Venom featured an advanced, purpose-designed avionics suite that GEC-Marconi was also offering for the US Marine Corps' proposed AH-1W Integrated Weapons System (IWS) upgrade. The cockpit boasted impressive colour MFDs and a colour moving map display – and was the only avionics/software fit in the competition to be developed in the UK. Its T700 engines would also be built in the UK by EGT. In June 1995, GEC-Marconi also added the Marines' proposed four-bladed rotor system for the AH-1W (4BW) to its Cobra Venom specification.

The dark horse in the competition was the Denel (Atlas) Rooivalk which, like the Tiger, was still in development. Favourable pilots' opinions coupled with the 'x-factor' of a *quid pro quo* deal with the SAAF involving a purchase of BAe Hawk trainers meant the Rooivalk was a stronger competitor than some believed. The Rooivalk's good standing may not have been unconnected with the US blocking GEC from offering the full Brimstone armament, which uses the chassis and motor of Hellfire, on the Rooivalk. In 1994 Rockwell was prohibited from supplying any missile components due to allegations that Armscor had broken UN arms embargoes. This left Atlas able to offer only the South African-developed Kentron ZT35 Swift as the Rooivalk's primary armament, with perhaps a Brimstone MMW seeker or even an all new Somchem motor from the SAHV SAM. The US opposition was seen to be wholly political in nature and was smoothed over soon after the competition ended.

The Army Air Corps did not undertake an evaluation of the AH types on offer, although several AAC pilots did fly in the various aircraft. Their experiences were unconnected with the formal evaluation that was conducted by the MoD AH Project Office, using Boscombe Down's test pilots.

Firm prices were submitted on 30 September 1994 and final bids for the £2 billion ($3.2 billion) contract were submitted on 20 February 1995. A huge emphasis was placed on the amount of technology transfer and industrial offsets on offer to British industry. The Dutch selection of the AH-64D in May 1995 only increased the standing of the Westland/MDH team, but the impending UK decision was still seen by most manufacturers as the one that would set the seal on all future markets. In April 1995 the UK MoD selected the Northrop/Grumman Nemesis DIRCM system for its future attack helicopter in a deal worth £193 million ($271 million). The Dutch decision to buy the Apache prompted discussions between MDH and Westland to explore the possibility of setting up a European support centre in the UK for all Europe-based AH-64s. The Dutch have also proposed the possibility of establishing a pan-European AH training centre.

On 13 July 1995, in an announcement rushed through before the summer Parliamentary recess, the Westland WAH-64D was announced as the winner of the UK's attack helicopter competition. UK Defence Secretary Michael Portillo, who had to overcome intense Treasury opposition to the early announcement, approved a £2.5 billion project for 67 WAH-64Ds, saying it was "the equipment that best does the job." The actual WAH-64D contract award was made to Westland in March 1996. The aircraft will (presumably) be known as the Apache AH.Mk 1. Although the total involved was lower than the Army had hoped, each aircraft would be equipped with the Longbow MMW radar. The initial UK order comprises 68 Longbow radars, 980 AGM-114L missiles and 204 missile launchers. Westland estimated that its workshare would be £800 million ($352 million). A Eurocopter statement read, "Eurocopter can only deeply regret this sovereign decision and deplore this (lost) opportunity to set up a new co-operation with Great Britain." BAe said that the decision would cost the jobs of 200 people involved in the LR Trigat project. By August 1995 the US Army had awarded a $3.2 million contract to Shorts, in association with McDonnell Douglas and Lockheed Martin, for Starstreak/Helstreak trials. The primary benefit, not appreciated by many, of an all-Longbow fleet for the UK derives from the heavy emphasis that will be placed on the Apache's air-to-air mission in British service. Helstreak is an essential element of this emerging doctrine.

The British army's 300 helicopters are currently organised into two divisional regiments (supporting the UK's armoured divisions), two regiments attached to the 24 Airmobile Brigade, a regiment stationed in Northern Ireland and a Territorial Army (reserve) regiment. The Apache will replace the armed Lynx in the combat role, and the 'de-TOWed' Lynxes will become Light Utility Helicopters (LUH), joining the Lynx AH.Mk 9 Light Battlefield Helicopter (LBH) in restructured AAC regiments. Once the transition to WAH-64D is complete, no armed Lynxes will remain in AAC service, although the TOW thermal sight will be retained. Under current plans (not yet finalised), Nos 3 and 4 Regiments AAC, based at Wattisham, will comprise two squadrons each of eight WAH-64Ds and four LUHs, plus a single squadron of 11 LBHs. No. 9 Regiment, AAC (currently based at Dishforth) will have two squadrons of eight WAH-64Ds with an amphibious assault tasking, plus a single squadron of 10 LUHs. The Army anticipates having a total of 48 Longbow Apaches active in the field. This new fleet of combat helicopters will require a new fleet of support vehicles (fuel tankers, ammunition carriers, mobile command/mission planning stations), all rugged and air-transportable.

Initial crew training ('conversion to type') will be undertaken on AH-64As with the US Army at Ft Rucker. These early crews will make their AH-64D conversion at Mesa. The AAC has not yet made a decision on where its unit-level 'conversion to role' training – as undertaken by the US Army's 21st Cavalry Aviation Brigade (formerly CAT-B) at Ft Hood – will take place. A variety of training options and training sites is still under evaluation. The target in-service date (ISD) has slipped from December 1998 to December 2000. The ISD relates to the formation of the WAH-64D OCU, which will be No. 671 Sqn at Middle Wallop. The OCU will establish with an initial complement of eight aircraft. The first WAH-64D will arrive in the UK in April 2000. This aircraft will be dedicated to type Military Aircraft Release (MAR) certification procedures at Boscombe Down. Two aircraft for the Project Office will follow in April, with an additional pair arriving in May. Deliveries will then continue at the (approximate) rate of one per month until January 2004.

Potential Apache Customers

Kuwait

The Kuwaiti requirement for a new attack helicopter to replace its TOW-armed Gazelles was generated immediately after Operation Desert Storm. An imminent order for the Apache was then expected but never materialised. By early 1995 the AH-64A was believed to have been selected once more and a $700 million order for 16 aircraft was announced but never formalised.

This deal would be crucial in helping MDH bridge the gap between the last AH-64A deliveries and the first AH-64Ds. Press reports suggested that Kuwait was pushing to acquire AH-64D Apaches, though the Longbow radar is not yet cleared for export. The sale of AH-64s to Kuwat has stalled, however, reportedly becuase McDonnell Douglas was having difficulties in disposing of the Kuwait Air Force's withdrawn fleet of A-4KU Skyhawks. McDonnell Douglas had agreed to handle the sale of the Skyhawks, before the Iraqi invasion, as part of the Kuwaiti F/A-18 deal. The intervening conflict left the aircraft, and their spares stock, in a less than desirable condition, and despite strenuous efforts McDD has failed to interest a buyer.

Chances of an Apache sale may be dashed by Kuwait's 1996 decision to acquire 16 Hellfire-capable Sikorsky UH-60L Blackhawks (with 500 Hellfires and 38 launchers). The UH-60Qs are believed to have been offered instead of AH-64Ds and are fitted with a FLIR system downgraded from that in use with similar US Army special operations MH-60 DAP (Defensive Armed Penetration) helicopters. Confirmation of this deal has yet to be announced, however.

Bahrain

In 1991, after the cessation of hostilities in the Gulf, it was announced that Bahrain had ordered six AH-64As. This deal was never completed.

Republic of Korea

MDH chose the Farnborough air show to announce on 9 September 1992 an FMS deal with the Republic of Korea for 37 AH-64As, which was then the largest export order for the Apache. This deal subsequently fell through but in October 1996 Korean interest in a new attack helicopter was revived.

An initial Army requirement for 18 helicopters has been proposed, to enter service after 2000, and the Army hopes to acquire between 38 and 48 aircraft to replace its AH-1S fleet. The Apache is the front-runner, though the Eurocopter Tiger is also a potential candidate. If Korea does opt for an Apache acquistion, it may also consider re-engining them with RTM322 turboshafts, as fitted to the WAH-64D. A procurement decision is anticipated in 1997.

Other near- and mid-term future customers for the Apache may include **Malaysia**, **Singapore**, **Qatar** and **Japan**.

US Army operator details supplied by **Thomas M. Ring**

All export AH-64 Apache details by **Robert Hewson**

The Air Force of Zimbabwe

Today's Air Force of Zimbabwe is a relatively young force – albeit one with a long pedigree. Since it was established, in its current form, in 1980 the AFZ has developed into a small but highly professional force. It has built on resources inherited from pre-independence days and also added entirely new capabilities, such as its F-7 fighter force. The AFZ can now justifiably claim to be one of the most capable forces in the region.

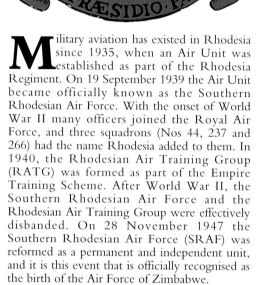

Military aviation has existed in Rhodesia since 1935, when an Air Unit was established as part of the Rhodesia Regiment. On 19 September 1939 the Air Unit became officially known as the Southern Rhodesian Air Force. With the onset of World War II many officers joined the Royal Air Force, and three squadrons (Nos 44, 237 and 266) had the name Rhodesia added to them. In 1940, the Rhodesian Air Training Group (RATG) was formed as part of the Empire Training Scheme. After World War II, the Southern Rhodesian Air Force and the Rhodesian Air Training Group were effectively disbanded. On 28 November 1947 the Southern Rhodesian Air Force (SRAF) was reformed as a permanent and independent unit, and it is this event that is officially recognised as the birth of the Air Force of Zimbabwe.

Due to the political changes taking place in southern Africa in early 1950s, Southern Rhodesia, Northern Rhodesia and Nyasaland formed the Federation of Rhodesia and

Above left: A trio of F-7s, including a single Guizhou FT-7BZ, prepares to depart from Thornhill. The AFZ operates two versions of the single-seat Chengdu F-7II. These examples are both F-7IINs, with the twin-pylon wing.

Left: The AFZ maintains a substantial helicopter element. Its primary heavy-lift capability is provided by the AB 412 Griffon, which entered service in 1986. Today, active aircraft are pooled between No. 7 and No. 8 Squadron.

Above: Nowhere else in the world could this formation of Hunter FGA.Mk 9, F-7IIN and Hawk Mk 60A be seen, except in Zimbabwe. It is an effective illustration of the AFZ's combat power and relative sophistication.

Nyasaland in September 1953. The Southern Rhodesian Air Force had no counterpart in the north and remained unchanged except in name, becoming the Rhodesian Air Force. On 15 October 1954 Queen Elizabeth II bestowed the title 'Royal' on the air force and it officially became the Royal Rhodesian Air Force (RRAF). The Federation of Rhodesia and Nyasaland was dissolved on 31 December 1963, with Southern Rhodesia becoming Rhodesia, Northern Rhodesia becoming Zambia and Nyasaland becoming Malawi. The majority of aviation assets remained with the RRAF, with a token transport element allocated to Zambia.

On 11 November 1965 Rhodesia made a Unilateral Declaration of Independence (UDI) and became an independent sovereign state. Britain immediately declared this act illegal and sanctions were imposed, a move which was supported by the United Nations. Sanctions proved effective and many elaborate schemes were devised to circumvent them. During the sanctions period the RRAF managed to acquire several new types, namely the Aermacchi AL 60B Trojan, Reims-Cessna FTB-337G Lynx, SIAI-Marchetti SF-260M and SF-260W Genet, BN-2A Islander and the AB 205. Existing types (Alouette III, Vampire, Provost and Dakota) were supplemented from various sources.

Between 1964 and 1979 a liberation war was waged between the Rhodesian government and an alliance of the Zimbabwe African National Union (ZANU) and the Zimbabwe African Peoples Union (ZAPU). During this conflict the RRAF was stretched to its limit to provide air support to the Rhodesian army in its fight

Left: No. 1 Squadron operates the AFZ's venerable Hawker Hunters from its base at Thornhill. Like other AFZ units, this squadron has a number of reserve pilots who are primarily personnel from the former Rhodesian Air Force.

Above: No. 6 Squadron operates three different versions of the SIAI-Marchetti SF-260 (SF-260M/ W/TP), all of which can be seen here. The sleek SF-260 is known locally as the Genet – a type of large African mongoose.

Below: All AFZ Chengdu F-7s wear the white (Chinese-style) gloss finish in which they were delivered. Most carry the Zimbabwe national flag on the starboard side of the fin and the 'Great Zimbabwe Bird' emblem to port.

Above: The AFZ's F-7 force provides the Air Force with a potent air-to-air interceptor force that is almost unmatched in the region. Acquisition of such a capability was a priority for the Air Force and the first aircraft were acquired from China, as a result, in 1986. They are flown by the reformed No. 5 Squadron which was previously a Canberra operator.

Left: The F-7II is powered by the Wopen WP-7B engine – just one of the many improvements made over the preceding, F-7A (J-7I). When No. 5 Sqn began to operate the type, the unit had new purpose-built facilities constructed at Thornhill.

Below: Until they were retired in 1991, two Chengdu FT-5s (Chinese-developed two-seat MiG-17s) were used by No. 5 Squadron for fast jet conversion training. They were replaced by a pair of more suitable FT-7BZs. Both FT-5s were placed into storage but it is hoped to restore one to flying condition for display purposes.

against the liberation armies. In March 1970 the 'Royal' prefix was dropped and the name reverted to the Rhodesian Air Force. Hostilities intensified in the mid-1970s, leading to the Lancaster House peace talks of 1979. With the prospect of peace and independence, the liberation movements started to send potential pilots and technicians for training to North Korea, Romania, Yugoslavia, Egypt, Nigeria and the USSR. In 1979 Rhodesia's name was changed to Zimbabwe-Rhodesia, although the title of the air force remained unchanged. On 18 April 1980 Zimbabwe gained its independence and the Rhodesian Air Force officially became known as the Air Force of Zimbabwe (AFZ).

After independence

The period from independence to 1987 proved to be a very difficult time for the AFZ. Soon after independence there was an exodus of experienced white pilots and technicians, which created a major manpower problem. To enable the AFZ to overcome these difficulties an agreement was reached with the Pakistani air force, which provided flying instructors, pilots and technicians from 1983 to conduct training programmes. Most of these officers had returned to Pakistan by 1990 and now only two

The FT-7BZ gives the AFZ a supersonic training capability. The omission of the F-7's two internal cannons frees up more space for fuel in the FT-7BZ and compensates for the space lost through the addition of the second cockpit.

The Hunter remains a valued asset in the AFZ, one with established ground-attack credentials and a long operational history. Six aircraft remain in service with No. 6 Squadron, and are still the AFZ's primary attack aircraft. After 34 years of service no replacement is in sight.

Pakistani air force flying instructors are attached to the AFZ, both on a normal exchange programme. In 1980 the initial batch of pilots and technicians who were trained outside the country prior to independence started to return home to join the AFZ. The varying degrees of proficiency and training of these pilots meant that several were found to be unsuitable for integration into the AFZ. China and Libya were to provide initial training facilities for potential pilots and technicians to the AFZ after independence. In 1983 the first batch of locally selected trainee pilots was sent to China, returning in 1986, and most of them continue to serve the AFZ today. All training of pilots and technicians is now conducted locally by the AFZ, which is also starting to train pilots for other Southern African Development Community air forces. Presently, the AFZ sends its officers for specialised training to China, Britain and the United States.

In addition to the manpower shortage, many aircraft were becoming obsolete and the years of sanctions meant that they had not been replaced by new types. Although sanctions were dropped in 1980 the budget for buying new aircraft was not large, and careful planning was needed to replace ageing types. The C-47s were replaced by CASA C.212s, the Vampires by Hawks and the AB 205s by AB 412s. Although No. 5 Squadron received two Canberras – a B.Mk 2 and a T.Mk 4 – from ex-RAF stocks in 1981, the end was in sight for this type. The Canberras were withdrawn from use in 1983 and, as the budget did not stretch to a replacement, No. 5 Squadron was deactivated.

There was much speculation at the time that the AFZ had obtained F-6s and F-7s from China, and also that there was the possibility of MiG-29s from the Soviet Union. The truth of the matter is that, besides two FT-5 trainers, the only fighters delivered to the AFZ were Chengdu F-7s, which were later joined by two

Above right: In 1981 this two-seat Hunter T.Mk 81 was obtained from the Kenyan Air Force (Kenya retired its Hunters in 1979 and five aircraft were eventually passed on to Zimbabwe). This aircraft is the only Hunter trainer in AFZ service.

Right: This aircraft is one of the original batch of 12 Hunter FGA.Mk 9s delivered to the then-Royal Rhodesian Air Force in 1963. During this sortie it was flown by the commanding officer of No. 1 Squadron.

Guizhou FT-7s. No. 5 Squadron was selected to operate the Chengdu F-7 and was reactivated at Thornhill in 1986 when the first F-7 arrived.

The AFZ suffered a major setback on the night of 25 July 1982 when saboteurs gained access to Thornhill Air Base and planted explosive devices on a number of aircraft. The four newly-arrived Hawks, nine Hunters and a single Reims-Cessna FTB-337G were all damaged to varying degrees. One Hawk was written off, two were so badly damaged they had to be returned to British Aerospace for rebuild, and the fourth aircraft was repaired on site. Of the nine Hunters, eight were damaged beyond repair and the ninth was repaired to ground instruction status. The FTB-337G was destroyed.

In the early 1980s access to the Mozambique port of Beira was threatened by the ongoing war between FRELIMO and RENAMO. At the request of the Mozambique government, an operation was conducted against RENAMO by Zimbabwean Armed Forces to ensure access to the port via the Beira Corridor. From 1983 the AFZ provided operational support for its army in the shape of Alouette IIIs, AB 412s and CASA C.212s, with the Hunters, Hawks and

FTB-337Gs fulfilling the ground attack role. This operation was concluded in April 1993 when the peace process in Mozambique was implemented.

Current operations

The AFZ and the Zimbabwean Army are independent forces falling under the Commander Defence Forces, who reports to the Minister of Defence and then to the C-in-C (President of Zimbabwe). The AFZ has two active bases, Manyame and Thornhill, and in addition it utilises a number of forward airfields. Manyame (formerly New Sarum) is located on the south side of Harare International Airport. Situated 25 km (16 miles) to the south of Zimbabwe's capital, Harare, Manyame is the home of the AFZ's transport and helicopter squadrons. Transport duties are undertaken by No. 3 Squadron operating Aviocars, Islanders and a single SF-260TP, on loan from No. 6 Squadron. Operational helicopter duties are the responsibility of No. 7 Squadron using the Alouette III, AB 412 and AS 532. Helicopter training falls under the aegis of No. 8 Squadron, which operates the Alouette III and the AB 412.

Above: A No. 1 Squadron Hunter FGA.Mk 9 turns on to the 'piano keys' at Thornhill. Thornhill has been a jet base since the first de Havilland Vampires arrived there with the (reformed) No. 2 Squadron in 1958. No. 1 Squadron itself briefly operated as a combined Hunter/Vampire unit.

The BAe Hawk Mk 60 (left) is now the AFZ's primary jet trainer and replaced the Vampire upon delivery in 1982. At that time the AFZ had just two Vampires (an FB.Mk 9 and T.Mk 11) still in service. The row of Hawks seen here (below left) are all ADEN Mk 4-armed Hawk Mk 60s lined up on No. 2 Squadron's dispersal, at Thornhill.

Manyame and Thornhill each have an Air Servicing Flight (ASF) and a unit of the Air Force Regiment attached to them. The ASF's function is to provide all servicing for based aircraft except for first-level maintenance, which is carried out by each squadron. The Air Force Regiment is tasked with the security of all AFZ installations and aircraft in addition to operating the low-level air defence systems. Manyame is home to the School of Technical Training (STT) which is tasked with the training of all technicians prior to their operational postings. The School of Flying Training (SOFT) is based at Thornhill and is responsible for the ground training of all future pilots for the AFZ.

Training

The AFZ has a very stringent selection process for prospective pilots. After attaining the necessary academic qualifications upon leaving school, approximately 80 candidates spend two weeks at the Officer Selection Board. After this selection process there will be approximately 25 candidates left. They become Officer Cadets within the AFZ and move on to the SOFT. Phase one of this course comprises basic military training and lasts 31 weeks. The successful candidates then move on to phase two, which comprises ground training and academic subjects; this phase lasts 19 weeks. At the end of the initial training period about 20 Officer Cadets will qualify for basic flying training on the SF-260M/Ws of No. 6 Squadron. The SF-260 is considered a good basic trainer by the AFZ, for although it is hard to handle it is a forgiving type. The serviceability and safety record of the SF-260 is superb, with only one (SF-260M) being lost in a crash since 1989.

The Officer Cadets will fly 140 hours over the next eight to nine months on the Genet before they can qualify as pilots. After successfully

Thornhill is located 10 km (6 miles) east of the central town of Gweru and is home to the AFZ's fighter and training squadrons. No. 1 Squadron, operating Hunter FGA.Mk 9s and a single Hunter T.Mk 81, still reigns supreme in the ground attack role. Fast jet training and light ground attack duties are the domain of the Hawk Mk 60s and Mk 60As of No. 2 Squadron. Operating Chengdu F-7IIs, F-7IINs and Guizhou FT-7BZs, No. 5 Squadron fulfils the air defence role. In addition to the fighter squadrons, Thornhill also houses No. 4 Squadron operating Reims-Cessna FTB-337Gs in the light ground attack role and two Cessna O-2As used for anti-poaching patrols. The last squadron based at Thornhill is No. 6 Squadron, which operates the SIAI Marchetti SF-260M, the SF-260W and the SF-260TP in the training role. Each squadron within the AFZ is split into two flights: 'A' Flight is responsible for all air operations within the squadron and 'B' Fight is responsible for all training duties.

Right: The shark-like profile of Stelio Frati's classic SF-260 design is distorted through the addition of an Allison C250B turboprop – the result of the SF-260TP modification. Eight turboprop conversions were carried out on existing SF-260Ws, in Zimbabwe. This No. 6 Squadron aircraft is seen in flight near the Great Zimbabwe ruins.

Below: The SF-260s now in service with the AFZ were acquired in the late 1970s in a circuitous fashion. This aircraft is a weapons-capable SF-260W 'Warrior', today operated purely in the training role.

qualifying, the Officer Cadets are commissioned into the AFZ as Air Sub-Lieutenants. Of the 80 original candidates, between 12 and 15 normally qualify as pilots. There are four possibilities open to an Officer after graduating, but due to operational requirements he may not always be posted to the squadron of his choice. Some go straight to No. 2 Squadron flying Hawk Mk 60/60As for further training as fast jet pilots. Another possibility is to be posted to No. 3 Squadron, to be trained as a transport pilot flying the CASA C.212 or the BN-2A Islander. The last fixed-wing option available is to join No. 4 Squadron, flying the FTB-337G Lynx. The final alternative is to become a helicopter pilot by joining No. 8 Squadron. Like many air forces around the world, the AFZ has decided to allow women to qualify as operational pilots. Officer Cadet Matimba became the first woman to qualify as a pilot in the AFZ when she graduated on 25 October 1996 at Thornhill. She has since been posted to No. 4 Squadron.

The other function of No. 6 Squadron – besides basic pilot training – is to train flying instructors. To qualify for selection for Flying Instructor School (FIS) a pilot must have a minimum of 500 flying hours and have a high average flying assessment. After being selected as a possible instructor the pilot will be attached to No. 6 Squadron, where he will fly 78 hours on the SF-260M/W/TP over a six-month period. If the pilot is successful and he graduates as an instructor, he will remain at No. 6 Squadron for a full basic training course. In addition to using the SF-260TP for training and standardisation, they are also used for courier/liaison duties.

The SF-260M has long been used as a basic trainer, a fact underlined by the red-and-white scheme worn by aircraft in service with No. 6 Squadron. The SF-260s replaced Hunting Provosts in the training and COIN roles.

Despite UN sanctions, the Rhodesian Air Force clandestinely obtained 17 SIAI-Marchetti SF-260Ms and 14 SF-260Ws in 1977. Known locally as the Genet, the SF-260Ms were used as trainers and the SF-260Ws, fitted with under-wing hardpoints, were used as light ground attack aircraft. However, since independence the SF-260M/Ws have been used as trainers. In 1984 the AFZ started to convert some of the SF-260Ws to turboprop SF-260TPs using the Allison C250B engine. By 1992, when the project was completed, eight SF-260Ws had become SF-260TPs, leaving five unconverted (one SF-260W was lost in 1979). At present, No. 6 Squadron has approximately 12 SF-260Ms, five SF-260Ws and eight SF-260TPs on strength.

Fighters

Before a pilot moves to either No. 1 Squadron to fly Hunters or No. 5 Squadron to fly the F-7, he must undergo fast jet training on the Hawk Mk 60s and Mk 60As of No. 2 Squadron. Like Nos 1 and 5 Squadrons, No. 2 Squadron is based at Thornhill, enabling all potential fast jet pilots to be closely monitored. An order for eight Hawk Mk 60s was placed in January 1981, with the first four aircraft being delivered in July 1982. The second batch followed in October 1982. The two Hawks that had to be rebuilt after the attack at Thornhill were redelivered in October 1984. In 1990 a follow-on order was placed for five Mk 60As, built to the later export standard, and these aircraft were delivered in September 1992.

The primary role of No. 2 Squadron's Hawks is fast jet training, but it also provides a very important ground attack and reconnaissance capability. As a secondary task the Hawk can be used for point defence and interception of subsonic aircraft. To become an operational jet pilot in the AFZ the hopeful candidate first joins the Jet Flying Training School (JFTS) at No. 2 Squadron. Here he learns about basic jet flying, in a course lasting 80 flying hours over a six-month period. From there he moves to the Operational Conversion Unit (OCU) at No. 2 Squadron to learn advanced jet flying and weapons training (ground attack, interception and ACM). This part of the course lasts 86 hours over a six-month period, after which, if he is successful, he will become an operational jet pilot. At this stage he will be posted to either No. 1 or No. 5 Squadron. As mentioned earlier, No. 2 Squadron's Hawks have a very important role as a ground attack aircraft, and they also provide the AFZ with its only true reconnaissance capability. The Hawk can carry the full range of standard NATO ground-attack weapons in addition to the Vinten 18/300 reconnaissance pod, while the Mk 60A is also wired for the AIM-9L. The Hawk has enjoyed an excellent safety record, with only one example lost, after a

Left: With the SF-260 now relegated to training duties, the AFZ relies on the proven FTB-337G Lynx for light attack duties. This aircraft is seen at low level over the Matobo National Park.

Below: Two Cessna O-2s were donated to Zimbabwe by the US government in 1993. Though maintained and operated by No. 4 Squadron, these aircraft are owned by the National Parks Board.

Above: No. 4 Squadron's O-2s can be equipped with an underwing FLIR turret for use on night-time surveillance missions against rhino and elephant poachers in Zimbabwe's protected national parks.

low-level bird strike – both student and instructor ejected safely.

Hunter survivors

The Royal Rhodesian Air Force ordered 12 Hawker Hunter FGA.Mk 9s which were all delivered between late 1962 and early 1963. Assigned to No. 1 Squadron at Thornhill, the Hunter FGA.Mk 9s were used extensively during the war prior to independence. Armed with four 30-mm ADEN cannons, bombs and rockets, the Hunter proved to be extremely effective in the ground attack role. After independence and the lifting of sanctions the AFZ was able to obtain additional Hunters to supplement those aircraft still in service. The first delivery took place in 1981, when four Hunter Mk 80s (export version of the FGA.Mk 9) and a single Hunter Mk 81 trainer were delivered from the Kenyan air force. During 1983 five Hunter FGA.Mk 9s were delivered from surplus RAF stocks. The final delivery took place in 1987 when a further four Hunter FGA.Mk 9s, also from ex-RAF stocks, arrived at Thornhill. Currently, No. 1 Squadron has approximately

six Hunters FGA.Mk 9s and a single Hunter Mk 81 on strength, with an additional five FGA.Mk 9s in storage. The Hunter provides the AFZ with its primary ground attack aircraft but it also has a limited air-defence role. Maintenance and serviceability are good, considering that the aircraft is over 30 years old, but the squadron does suffer from a shortage of spares . The Hunter also has a very good safety record and only one aircraft has been lost in the last 10 years. On average, a No. 1 Squadron pilot flies approximately 18 hours per month, and in addition to full-time pilots the squadron has a small number of reserve pilots on strength. After the recent withdrawal of the Hunter from service in Chile, Oman, Singapore and Switzerland, the only other country still operating the type is India. After 34 years of service, the AFZ is considering how to replace the Hunter.

F-7 arrival

In 1986 approximately 12 Chengdu F-7s were delivered to No. 5 Squadron at Thornhill, along with two Chengdu FT-5s. These aircraft were delivered by sea from China and assembled

at Thornhill by AFZ personnel with the assistance of technicians from the People's Republic of China. The F-7s were of two types – F-7II and the F-7IIN – and provided the AFZ with its first supersonic interceptor. The major external difference between the two types is that the F-7II has only one hardpoint under each wing, while the F-7IIN has two. Both versions of the F-7 have a centreline station under the fuselage. The initial batch of F-7 pilots was trained in China, but, as with all other squadrons, all new pilots joining No. 5 Squadron are now trained in Zimbabwe. Like most versions of the MiG-21, the F-7 is very fast and it handles well at high speed, although it is hampered by its lack of range. This is not considered a major problem by the AFZ, as the type's primary role is point defence and interception. The F-7 does have a secondary ground attack role, although this is normally left to the more suitable Hunter. The F-7IIN is armed with twin 30-mm cannon and has provision for short-range infra-red missiles, possibly the Chinese-built PL-7 and the AIM-9L, in addition to other air-to-ground weapons. Pilots belonging to No. 5 Squadron fly an average of 25 hours per month, which is quite high by AFZ standards. Since being delivered in 1986, two F-7s (exact type unknown) have been lost in accidents. The aircraft are well liked by the pilots of No. 5 Squadron and are affectionately called 'Arrows' (the callsign of the squadron) after the shape of the aircraft.

Two Chengdu FT-5s were operated by No. 5 Squadron as fast jet trainers between 1986 and 1991, providing the F-7 pilots with a suitable trainer. They were withdrawn from use and placed in storage in 1991 when No. 5 Squadron received two Guizhou FT-7BZs, giving the

The CASA C.212 Aviocar is a versatile light transport now in service with No. 3 Squadron, alongside BN-2A Islanders, at Manyame. A batch of six aircraft was delivered by 1984. They were followed by a second order in 1986, doubling the size of the AFZ's Aviocar force.

AFZ a supersonic trainer. At present, it is hoped to return one of the FT-5s to flying condition as a museum aircraft, using the other one as a spares source. Like the F-7s and FT-5s before them, the FT-7BZs were delivered by sea from China and assembled at Thornhill. Besides acting as fast jet trainers the FT-7BZ has a limited ground attack role, although it does lack the twin 30-mm cannons of the F-7IIN.

Light ground attack

Although the AFZ utilises the Hawk and the Hunter in the ground attack role, there has always been a requirement for a slower aircraft to be used for COIN operations. In the war before independence this role fell to the SF-260Ws of No. 6 Squadron and the FTB-337Gs of No. 4 Squadron. Since 1981 the SF-260Ws have been utilised solely for training purposes, leaving the light ground attack duties to No. 4 Squadron's Reims-Cessna FTB-337Gs. In January 1976 the Rhodesian Air Force received 18 Reims-Cessna FTB-337Gs, which were followed by three further examples in 1977. Due to the sanctions that were in force at the time, these aircraft were purchased under the same cloak of secrecy as the SF-260, the Trojan and the AB 205. Known locally as the Lynx, the Reims-Cessna FTB-337G replaced the Aermacchi AL60B Trojan with No. 4 Squadron at Thornhill. The Lynx can be armed with twin Browning 0.303-in machine-guns which are mounted on top of the wings. In addition to these guns, it can also carry 37-mm rockets and an array of different types of bombs. Although the primary role of the Lynx is light ground attack, it also fulfils the secondary roles of casevac, search and rescue and courier duties. At present, No. 4 Squadron has approximately 12 FTB-337Gs on strength, although some are kept in storage. Serviceability of the aircraft is good despite an occasional

Above: A single Aviocar is in use with No. 3 Squadron as a VIP transport. It was delivered in 1984 and serves alongside the rest of the AFZ's regular transport and VIP fleet at Manyame.

Right: This Aviocar is seen overhead the spectacular Sanyati Gorge at Lake Kariba, which straddles Zimbabwe's northwestern border with Zambia. The Aviocar was introduced into AFZ service as a Douglas C-47 replacement.

spares shortage, with no aircraft being lost in accidents recently.

In 1993 the United States government donated two ex-US Navy Cessna O-2As to the Zimbabwe government for the bio-diversity programme (anti-poaching patrols). Although these aircraft are officially owned by the National Parks Board they are operated by No. 4 Squadron, which provides the pilots and maintains the aircraft. These aircraft are used solely for anti-poaching patrols and do not perform any other duties for the AFZ. Equipped with an infra-red video system mounted in a pod under the port wing, the O-2A's role is to locate and identify poachers. Once the poachers have been located their position is relayed to ground troops from the army and Parks Board who are tasked with apprehending them. The majority of these operations are conducted against rhino and elephant poachers along the Zambezi Valley and in Hwange and Gonarezhou National Parks/wildlife reserves.

Prior to independence the AFZ transport duties were performed by 10 elderly C-47 Dakotas and six BN-2A Islanders of No. 3 Squadron. A replacement was needed for the C-47 and in 1983 five CASA C.212 Aviocars were delivered to No. 3 Squadron at Manyame. The following year another C.212 was delivered, this one configured as a VIP example. An order for six more Aviocars was placed and these aircraft were delivered in December 1986. The AFZ has lost two Aviocars in accidents, one in 1985 and one in 1987. Those two have been replaced with two new examples delivered in August 1989 and June 1990, bringing the total order to 14 aircraft. The C-47s continued to serve with No. 3 Squadron until they were withdrawn from use in 1991, and are now stored at Manyame awaiting a decision on their future. Currently, the AFZ is looking at the

This AB 412 Griffon of No. 8 Squadron is seen outbound to the training area at Chimanimani, in Zimbabwe's eastern highlands.

Left: The ubiquitous Alouette III, 'the Huey of Africa', is as highly appreciated in AFZ service as it is elsewhere around the world. Alouette IIIs serve with Nos 7 and 8 Squadrons.

Below left: This AB 412 is one of two operated as dedicated VIP transports by No. 7 Sqn at Manyame.

Below: This view across the ramp at Manyame shows three different types, including two of No. 3 Squadron's five BN-2A Islanders.

possibility of either replacing their engines with turboprops and returning them to service, or selling them. The C.212 now forms the backbone of the AFZ's transpor fleet, with its main role comprising general transport duties, support of the army and paratrooping. In addition, the Aviocar is also used for communication flights, search and rescue operations, medevac and VIP transport duties.

Despite sanctions, a total of six BN-2A Islanders was obtained between 1976 and 1977, five from Mozambique and one from South Africa. They are used mainly for communication flights, casevac and VIP transport duties, and are ideal for operations in and out of small bush landing strips. The Islanders suffer from a lack of spares and there is a possibility that they may be replaced by another type in the near future. Like most types in the AFZ, the Islander has a good safety record, with only one aircraft being lost in a crash in 20 years of service. No. 3 Squadron also operates a single SF-260TP (on loan from No. 6 Squadron) which is used for courier duties; being more economical than the C.212 or the BN-2. The pilots of No. 3 Squadron fly an average of 25 hours per month

and they are made up of both full-time and reserve officers. No. 3 Squadron also maintains the immaculately restored Provost T.Mk 52 which is still flown by Air Vice Marshall Harvey at air shows and other events.

Helicopters

Operated by Nos 7 and 8 Squadrons based at Manyame, the AFZ's helicopter fleet comprises approximately 25 Alouette IIIs, two VIP AB 412s, six AB 412 Griffons and two Eurocopter AS 532 Cougars. No. 7 Squadron is the AFZ's operational squadron, and No. 8 Squadron performs the role of helicopter training. No. 8 Squadron is also secondarily tasked with supporting No. 7 Squadron as an operational squadron, especially in times of conflict.

No. 7 Squadron operates approximately 14 Alouette IIIs as well as two VIP AB-412s and two AS 532 Cougars. Although the AB 412 Griffons are officially on No. 8 Squadron's strength, they are used on a pool basis with No. 7 Squadron. The main task of No. 7 Squadron is to provide tactical support for army units but it also has many varied secondary tasks. These include anti-poaching patrols, police

support, casevac, SAR and civilian emergency support services. The Alouette IIIs were first delivered in 1962 and over the years many aircraft have been acquired from various sources. During the war for independence the Alouette III probably saw more action than any other type of aircraft, and became known as the 'Huey of Africa'. The Alouette IIIs are used for both troop transport (G-car) and gunship (K-car) roles. When operating in the 'Fire Force' role, troop insertion is performed by either three Alouette IIIs (G-car) or two AB 412s, with a single Alouette III (K-car) armed with a 20-mm cannon as a gunship.

No. 7 Squadron is also tasked to provide VIP helicopter transport for senior officers and dignitaries. Two AB 412s configured for VIP operations were delivered in August 1983; they wear a smart blue-and-white colour scheme and have a secondary air ambulance role. The most recent acquisition by the AFZ is two Eurocopter AS 532 Cougars, operated by No. 7 Squadron. The first of these helicopters was delivered in April 1995, followed by the second in September 1996. Painted in the same blue-and-white scheme as the VIP AB 412, the Cougars are fitted out for the VVIP role.

No. 8 Squadron was formed in 1978 as a front-line squadron to operate the AB 205, known locally as the Cheetah. Eleven of these helicopters were delivered in October 1978, under great secrecy since sanctions were still in full force. They provided the Rhodesian Air Force with a medium-lift capability and saw extensive service in the latter part of the independence war. All but three of the Cheetahs were grounded in 1983 and placed in storage, at which time No. 8 Squadron was deactivated. The three remaining Cheetahs were assigned to No. 7 Squadron, where they continued to operate until 1986 when the type was finally withdrawn from use.

Within No. 7 Squadron, 'C' Flight was established in 1983 as a helicopter training unit. Operating the Alouette III, 'C' Flight was

Left: This ex-South African Vampire T.Mk 55, one of many Vampires acquired during the 1970s, survives (just) as a well-used fire trainer at Thornhill's fire station.

Above: Like many users the AFZ found its C-47s almost irreplaceable and several aircraft are still in open storage at Manyame, awaiting a final decision on their fate. This particular example was one of two VIP aircraft in use with the AFZ.

Above: The RAF ancestry of this English Electric Canberra T.Mk 4 is obvious for all to see. It is one of three aircraft (two B.Mk 2s and a T.Mk 4) delivered in 1981 but soon withdrawn from use in 1983. All are stored at Manyame.

Above: This well-preserved Vampire FB.Mk 9 guards the gate at Manyame. A T.Mk 55 performs the same function at Thornhill.

Right: Perhaps the most visible sign of the AFZ's regard for its heritage is the Air Force's airworthy Provost T.Mk 1/52 (the aircraft is something of a hybrid). Flown by Air Vice Marshall Ian Harvey (an 11,500-hour military pilot, 7,500 hours of which were logged on the Alouette III), the Provost is often seen at public displays.

responsible for training helicopter pilots until 1985 when No. 8 Squadron was reformed and took over this role. No. 8 Squadron has on strength seven Alouette IIIs for training purposes and six AB 412 Griffons. When a newly qualified pilot arrives at No. 8 Squadron he will fly 120 hours on the Alouette III over an eight-month period, before qualifying as a helicopter pilot and moving on to No. 7 Squadron. Only experienced Alouette III pilots are allowed to convert to the AB 412; this course lasts for 40 hours over a one-month period. In 1986 10 AB 412 Griffons were delivered. They are the military version of the basic AB 412 and are used in the assault, transport and battlefield support roles. The AB 412 provides the AFZ with a good medium-lift helicopter which can carry 13 passengers or eight fully equipped troops, as opposed to four in the Alouette III. The AFZ has lost three AB 412 Griffons since they were delivered although none of these crashes has occurred in the last six years. Another example is undergoing a major rebuild after it was involved in an attempted jail break, receiving many bullet holes around the engine in the process. Although Nos 7 and 8 Squadrons are considered to be separate entities, they share many of the same facilities and operate very closely together.

The future

The AFZ has come a long way in the 16 years since independence and it has a very good safety record, especially over the last 10 years. One area of concern at the moment is the shortage of spare parts for certain types of ageing aircraft but, despite this, serviceability remains very good. The level of training, not only of the pilots but also for technicians, is of a very high standard and has resulted in a very professional air force that has great pride in itself. The primary role of the AFZ is the defence of Zimbabwe and it has a policy of non-aggression towards other African countries. Its main tasks are to defend the airspace of Zimbabwe, provide a counter strike against any aggressors and provide close air support for the army. It also has many secondary tasks such as supporting the civil powers (police), providing emergency relief support and anti-poaching patrols. It is committed to supporting the peace-keeping duties of the United Nations within Africa and is currently involved in these duties in Angola and Somalia. The AFZ is eval-

uating an offer made by United States in 1995 to supply two ex-USAF C-130Bs, although no decision has been made yet. Despite having to work within a budget – which, like many other air forces in the world today, is not always sufficient to meet it needs – the future of the Air Force of Zimbabwe looks promising. As with all air forces, the AFZ would like to purchase new aircraft but only if the budget allows, for there are many other pressing needs in the country.

Ian Malcolm and Dave West

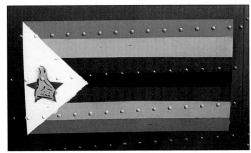

Air Force of Zimbabwe

Order of Battle 1980

Unit	Base	Type
No. 1 Sqn	Thornhill	Hunter FGA.Mk 9
No. 2 Sqn	Thornhill	Vampire FB.Mk 52/T.Mk 11/T.Mk 55
No. 3 Sqn	Manyame	C-47 Dakota, BN-2A Islander
No. 4 Sqn	Thornhill	Reims-Cessna FTB-337G
No. 5 Sqn	Manyame	Canberra B.Mk 2/T.Mk 4
No. 6 Sqn	Thornhill	SF-260M/W
No. 7 Sqn	Manyame	Alouette III
No. 8 Sqn	Manyame	AB 205

Order of Battle 1996

Unit	Callsign	Base	Type
No. 1 Sqn	PANZER	Thornhill	Hunter FGA.Mk 9/T.Mk 81
No. 2 Sqn	COBRA	Thornhill	Hawk Mk 60/60A
No. 3 Sqn	FALCON	Manyame	C.212 Aviocar, BN-2A Islander
No. 4 Sqn	HORNET	Thornhill	Reims-Cessna FTB-337G, Cessna O-2A
No. 5 Sqn	ARROW	Thornhill	Chengdu F-7II/N, Guizhou FT-7BZ
No. 6 Sqn	TIGER	Thornhill	SF-260M/W/TP
No. 7 Sqn	SCORPION	Manyame	Alouette III, AB 412, AS 532
No. 8 Sqn	SPIDER	Manyame	Alouette III, AB 412

This combination of Hunter and F-7 reflects the many facets of AFZ operations today. The Air Force of Zimbabwe has avoided stagnation by following a wise path of careful modernisation yet maintains its links with the past.

Sukhoi 'Flanker' Variants: Part 2

Su-27K prototypes and pre-production batch (T10K)

Russian fixed-wing naval aviation began with the deployment of the VTOL/STOVL Yakovlev Yak-38, which eventually served aboard four dedicated ships known as 'heavy aircraft carrying cruisers'. These vessels were relatively small and were cheaper to operate than the full-size carriers used by the US Navy. Unfortunately, it rapidly became apparent that the Yak-38's limited payload/range capability made the small carriers an extremely inefficient way of providing naval air power. It was realised that larger carriers, carrying more efficient, conventional fixed-wing aircraft types, would actually provide a more cost effective way of providing air power at sea.

The decision was taken to build a new class of aircraft-carriers, and to adapt the Su-27 and MiG-29 to serve aboard them. The project to produce a navalised, shipborne version of the Su-27 was launched at the same time as the Soviet carrier programme, with an initial four full-scale aircraft-carriers ordered sometime before 1979. The *Tbilisi* was laid down in 1983, and was launched on 5 December 1985. The aircraft was seen as a single-role fleet air defence aircraft, which would form one element in a mixed air wing alongside An-71 or Yak-44 AWACS platforms and MiG-29K multi-role strike fighters. As such, the Su-27K was developed from the basic air force Su-27, and not from the enhanced multi-role Su-27M then also under development.

The sheer size of the Su-27 presented one of the biggest obstacles to using the aircraft on a cramped carrier deck, and to stowing it below decks. Folding wings would clearly be required, but the Sukhoi OKB took the bolder step of providing tailplane folding as well. A mock-up (coded '20' and based on the early T10S configuration with square-cropped fins and the early canopy) was built with these features, although it lacked many of the other features now associated with the Su-27K, including canard foreplanes and twin nosewheels.

A number of Su-27s were used to test different aspects of the intended Su-27K production configuration. They included the canard-equipped T10-24, which was used for approach handling tests, and the 'hooked' T10-25. Both of these aircraft had late-type canopies, but the T10-25 had early square-topped fins. The two aircraft (along with an early Su-27UB and even the third basic T10) were also used for the crucial early take-off trials from a dummy carrier deck. The first 'deck' take-off was made from the dummy deck at Saki on 28 August 1982, by Nikolai Sadovnikov flying the T10-3. The dummy deck was subsequently rebuilt to incorporate a ski-ramp identical to that fitted to the *Tbilisi*, which was intended to reduce the take-off run. The T10-25 made the first ski-jump take-off from this ramp on 25 September 1984. The ski-ramp trials were particularly important, since it had already been decided that the development of a powerful steam catapult would not be possible within the timescale set for the first of the new carriers and that the Su-27K

Above: The first T10K prototype is seen in flight. It had a standard Su-27 wing, with neither folding nor double-slotted trailing-edge flaps, though it did have an inflight-refuelling probe, a strengthened undercarriage and an arrester hook.

Right: The cockpit of one of the Su-27K prototypes shows only the most minor differences from a land-based 'Flanker-B'.

would have to make unassisted take-offs, using a combination of restrainers and take-off ramps. The T10-25 made the first arrested landing (again at Saki) on 1 September 1984, flown by Victor Pugachev. The T10-3, T10-24 and T10-25 were followed by a batch of T10K (Su-27K) prototypes, each of which differed slightly from the others. They were ordered in 1984, along with a pair of MiG-29K prototypes. The definitive T10K was designed under the direction of Konstantin Marbashev.

The first Su-27K prototype (T10K-1, coded '37') followed the T10-24 and featured canards (which can be deflected only symmetrically, from +7° to -70°), a retractable inflight-refuelling probe and an offset location for the IRST, which was not fitted. The aircraft was fitted with a distinctive square-section arrester hook below a shortened tail sting, but lacked the twin nosewheels and folding wings of the definitive Su-27K configuration. The new tail sting was similar to that fitted to the T10-25 and T10U-02, with a high, upward-pointing centreline, but also considerably shortened. Since it retained standard Su-27 wings, it lacked the definitive T10K double-slotted flaps and outboard ailerons. It is believed that this aircraft was not cleared to operate from carrier decks. The T10-37 made its maiden flight on 17 August 1987, with Pugachev as pilot, and was destroyed in a non-fatal accident during 1988. The canard-equipped aircraft (and perhaps the T10-24 and the later T10Ks) may have been referred to as 'Flanker-B2s' even though

they had not entered service (the usual criterion for allocation of an ASCC reporting name).

Between five and eight subsequent prototypes were built to a standard which approximated more closely to the intended production configuration. Because this featured new canard foreplanes, outboard ailerons and double-slotted flaps, it was felt necessary to produce a relatively large prototype batch. This batch of aircraft included aircraft coded '39' (T10K-2), '59' (T10K-4), '69' (T10K-5), '79' (T10K-6), and '109' (T10K-9). At least two of the Su-27K prototypes flew without code numbers. All had twin nosewheels, wing and tailplane folding, and double-slotted trailing-edge flaps. The new flaps took up virtually the full span of the trailing edge and were built in two sections. The inboard flap sections operated symmetrically as flaps, while the outboard sections operated differentially as drooping ailerons at low speeds.

The Su-27K prototypes were also all fitted with square-section arrester hooks below their abbreviated tail stings, and none had brake chutes. The tail sting was shortened to prevent it from striking the deck during a high-Alpha touchdown, and this forced the designers to find a new location for the chaff/flare dispensers

'Blue 109' was the last T10K prototype, and was closest to the production configuration. As such it was deployed to sea on the first operational cruise of the Kuznetsov.

previously housed in the tail sting and the adjacent box fairings. Sukhoi was forced to reduce the number of chaff/flare dispensers and relocate them further forward, eight triple launchers per side, with the foremost launcher adjacent to the fin leading edge. Later prototypes also had an extra pair of inboard underwing weapons pylons, raising the total number to 12, including the wingtip stations. The Su-27K is also reported to have a modified IRST, with a wider field of view.

Carrier landing trials began at 13:46 (local) on 1 November 1989, when Victor Pugachev landed the second Su-27K aboard the carrier *Tbilisi*. After a touch-and-go with a 50-m (165-ft) deck roll, Pugachev landed and took the No. 2 arrester wire, becoming the first Russian pilot to land a conventional aircraft aboard the carrier. The second prototype (T10-39) was the first full-standard Su-27K, featuring folding wings and the full array of double-slotted trailing-edge flaps and outboard ailerons. Takhtar Aubakirov (in the MiG-29K) made the first ski-jump take-off from the *Tbilisi* and was followed by Pugachev in the Su-27K.

The fourth prototype (T10K-4) is seen here carrying wingtip Sorbtsiya ECM pods, which are seldom seen on the navalised 'Flanker'.

Initial trials demonstrated approach speeds of between 220 and 240 km/h (137 and 150 mph) and take-off runs of 100 m (328 ft) (unladen) and 180 m (590 ft) (loaded). The first public display of the T10K occurred at Zhukhovskii on 18 August 1991, when Pugachev used an Su-27K to perform a display of aerobatics and slow fly-pasts with hook, undercarriage and flaps lowered.

Russian naval pilots began carrier operations on 26 September 1991 when Colonel Timur Apakidze landed aboard the *Tbilisi*. Service trials were highly successful and led to State Acceptance Trials (beginning in the autumn of 1992), which were successfully passed in October 1994. This was probably just as well, since the first batch of 18 aircraft was built between 1992 and 1993. Mikoyan was understandably disappointed, since its

contender was effectively sidelined even before it was officially terminated in late 1993.

The larger number of Su-27K prototypes performed the bulk of the take-off and landing trials aboard the *Kuznetsov*, testing the carrier's own systems and procedures

as well as those systems aboard the aircraft. The Su-27K quickly built up a wealth of carrier experience. Only two MiG-29K prototypes had been built (due to the type's aerodynamic similarity to the tried and tested MiG-29M) and so this type played a smaller part in general carrier trials.

Su-27K production series (T10K, OKB Su-33) 'Flanker-D'

Had the Soviet Union's ambitious plan to build four aircraft-carriers reached fruition, perhaps as many as 72 production Su-27Ks would have been required simply for their air wings, plus attrition replacements and aircraft equipping disembarked squadrons and training units. A similar number of MiG-29Ks would also have been required, along with a significant number of shipborne AEW aircraft. Unfortunately for aircraft manufacturers, the end of the Cold War led to a massive down-scaling of the USSR's carrier programme. The fourth vessel was cancelled before work could begin, while the third (*Ulyanovsk*) was scrapped on the slipway. The second, *Varyag* (formerly *Riga*), may now also have been scrapped. With the *Admiral Kuznetsov* (formerly *Tbilisi*, and before that *Brezhnev*) the only carrier left for service with the Russian navy, it became increasingly difficult to justify the continued development of three separate dedicated aircraft types.

The AEW aircraft was abandoned first, replaced by a more simple derivative of the Ka-29. If only one fixed-wing type was to be procured for the new carrier, logic would have dictated that it should be the MiG-29K. The MiG's formidable multi-role capability made it the most versatile of the aircraft available, while its relatively small size and compact dimensions meant that more aircraft could be accommodated aboard the carrier. The aircraft was more modern, with more advanced avionics and weapons, and had also reached a more advanced stage of

development. Finally, it offered considerable commonality with the MiG-29M. (In many respects, the MiG-29K could be compared to the night-attack F/A-18C (or even the F/A-18E), while the Su-27K is more comparable to the pre-'Bombcat' modded F-14A. It is instructive to note that the US Navy is increasing the number of F/A-18s aboard its carriers, while reducing the number of F-14s, and many powerful voices have suggested that all-F/A-18 air wings should be deployed.) In the end, though, the Sukhoi aircraft was selected for production and service, with the Russian navy being forced to accept the aircraft's (and thus the carrier's) more limited role.

The Su-27K does enjoy some significant advantages over the MiG-29K. The aircraft has the same internal fuel tankage as the land-based Su-27 and thus has an extremely long range, although it cannot take off from a carrier deck at anything approaching maximum all-up weight. Furthermore, there has never been much suggestion that the Su-27K was selected for production for other than political reasons. In the liberalised USSR, the Sukhoi OKB rose to a position of pre-eminence, with its head, the charismatic Mikhail Simonov, serving on the Supreme Soviet committee overseeing the military industrial complex. Here he used his influence to ensure that whenever one aircraft type only would be ordered, it would be a Sukhoi aircraft. Before entering service, the production Su-27K was redesignated Su-33 by the OKB, but the aircraft remains a

navalised version of the basic IA-PVO interceptor, with the same basic 'Slot Back' radar and with only the most rudimentary ground attack capability. It is uncertain whether the AV-MF use the Su-33 designation.

The *Kuznetsov*'s first truly operational deployment took place in early 1996. The ship's complement included the Su-27K-

equipped 1st Squadron of the Severomorsk Regiment. At least eight of the unit's aircraft (including 'red 65', 'red 77', 'red 83', 'red 84', 'red 86') were deployed to Kubinka during early 1995 for the final phase of the unit's work-up. Although a production batch of 18 Su-27Ks has reportedly been built (20 according to some sources, 16 according to others), the *Kuznetsov*'s complement

Above: Production Su-27Ks are shore-based at Severomorsk. This one has had its tarpaulin covers peeled back for work on the radar.

Below: On board the Kuznetsov, Su-27Ks take off without a catapult, using deck restraints, jet blast deflectors and a ski ramp instead.

Sukhoi 'Flanker' Variants

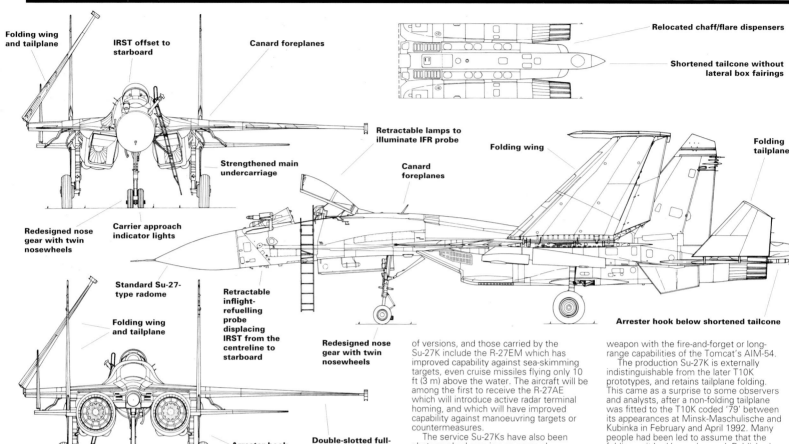

Folding wing and tailplane

IRST offset to starboard

Canard foreplanes

Relocated chaff/flare dispensers

Shortened tailcone without lateral box fairings

Redesigned nose gear with twin nosewheels

Carrier approach indicator lights

Retractable lamps to illuminate IFR probe

Canard foreplanes

Folding wing

Folding tailplane

Strengthened main undercarriage

Standard Su-27-type radome

Folding wing and tailplane

Retractable inflight-refuelling probe displacing IRST from the centreline to starboard

Redesigned nose gear with twin nosewheels

Arrester hook below shortened tailcone

Arrester hook below tailplane

Double-slotted full-span trailing-edge flaps and outboard drooping ailerons

included the last Su-27K prototype (coded 'blue 109') in addition to at least 10 production Su-27Ks (including 'red 64', 'red 65', 'red 76', 'red 84', 'red 85', 'red 87'). The *Kuznetsov* left its port on 24 December 1995, accompanied by the 'Sovremenni'-class guided missile destroyer *Brestrashny*, the 'Krivak'-class frigate *Pylkly*, the 'Boris Chilikin'-class replenishment ship *Dnestr*, the 'Olemka'-class replenishment ship *Olemka*, and the 'Sliva'-class tug *SB406*. Commanded by Captain Alexander Chelpanov, the ship spent two months in the Mediterranean, during which it made port visits in Syria, Malta and Italy. Service

Having already auto-folded its wings and tailplane, an Su-27K taxis in. The Su-27K is the Russians' first carrierborne non-VTOL fast jet.

introduction of the Su-27K made it eligible for a separate NATO reporting name suffix, and the aircraft is now understood to be known by the ASCC reporting name 'Flanker-D'. The reporting name is unlikely to be used, however, since its correct designation (and the OKB's Su-33 designation) are widely known and used. The 'Flanker-D' reporting name had previously been erroneously ascribed to the Su-27K prototypes and pre-production aircraft, but was not applied until the variant entered service.

Service Su-27Ks have been seen carrying the usual IA-PVO load-out of R-27 (AA-10 'Alamo') and R-73 (AA-11 'Archer') AAMs under the wings, engine nacelles and on the centreline, although the extra pair of underwing hardpoints actually allows the carriage of two additional R-27s, bringing the BVR armament to eight missiles. The R-27 is available in a number

of versions, and those carried by the Su-27K include the R-27EM which has improved capability against sea-skimming targets, even cruise missiles flying only 10 ft (3 m) above the water. The aircraft will be among the first to receive the R-27AE which will introduce active radar terminal homing, and which will have improved capability against manoeuvring targets or countermeasures.

The service Su-27Ks have also been photographed carrying an unusual centreline pod, which some experts have provisionally identified as a reconnaissance pod, while others suggest that it is an equipment pod associated with some kind of carrier landing system. The box-like central part of the pod has a single square port in the underside and has conical dielectric fairings fore and aft. There have been suggestions that the aircraft can alternatively carry a fuel tank on the centreline, or a UPAZ buddy inflight-refuelling store. Wingtip missile launch rails can presumably be replaced by Sorbtsiya ECM pods, while a range of bombs and unguided rockets (podded and large-calibre single rounds) and the Kh-31 (AS-17 'Krypton') ASM can be carried underwing. None of these alternative stores have been photographed under production Su-27Ks, which seem to fulfil a pure fleet air defence role. By comparison with the F-14, the Su-27K offers greater potential mission radius and endurance, and considerably better combat persistence, with up to eight BVR missiles and four short-range IR-homing missiles, although it lacks a

weapon with the fire-and-forget or long-range capabilities of the Tomcat's AIM-54.

The production Su-27K is externally indistinguishable from the later T10K prototypes, and retains tailplane folding. This came as a surprise to some observers and analysts, after a non-folding tailplane was fitted to the T10K coded '79' between its appearances at Minsk-Maschulische and Kubinka in February and April 1992. Many people had been led to assume that the folding unit had been dropped. Published figures indicate that the Su-27K has a slightly shorter span tailplane, but this cannot be confirmed. The Su-27K is said to be slightly faster (20 km/h; 12 mph) than the land-based fighter at altitude, but has a lower service ceiling (700 m/2300 ft lower, at 17000 m/55,775 ft). Figures also indicate that the aircraft has a slightly shorter wheelbase and a slightly wider track, perhaps indicating different oleo rake and splay angles, or perhaps indicating inaccurate published dimensions.

One weapon frequently ascribed to the Su-27K is the gigantic Kh-41, an air-launched version of the 3M80 'Moskit' anti-ship missile, sometimes known under the codename ASM-MSS. This has a passive/active radar terminal seeker capable of picking out its target from among a group of ships. A 320-kg (705-lb) warhead represents more than double the lethality of the Exocet's warhead, and 50 per cent greater lethality than the Harpoon's. The missile has a sea-skimming range of 150 km (93 miles) or 50 km (31 miles) after a 250-km (155-mile) 'cruise', and a maximum speed in excess of Mach 3. This weapon is, in fact, not yet compatible with the aircraft at all since development of the air-launched version of the SS-N-22 'Sunburn' was suspended in 1993. If development is completed, a single Kh-41 would be carried below the centreline.

Despite the apparent abandonment of the MiG-29K, highly placed sources suggest that production of the aircraft is still under consideration. If it does enter service, the Russian navy will have obtained its originally favoured aircraft mix, and the carrier will be a more versatile weapon. The *Kuznetsov* could accommodate 52 aircraft of all types, and with 16 Su-27Ks embarked, and with other types totalling up to 20 aircraft (Ka-27PSs for SAR, Ka-252PLs or Ka-27Ks for ASW, Ka-29/252TBs for transport and assault, Ka-31s for airborne early warning and Su-25UTGs for training), funding a production batch of MiG-29Ks to provide a squadron of 16 MiG-29Ks aboard the carrier would be a sensible step.

Specification
Dimensions: fuselage length including probe 21.185 m (69 ft 6 in); folded span 7.4 m (24 ft 3 in); tailplane span 9.80 m (32 ft 2 in); overall height 5.85 m (19 ft 2 in); wheel track 4.40 m (14 ft 5 in); wheelbase 5.872 m (19 ft 3 in)

Sukhoi Su-27K 1st Squadron, Severomorsk Regiment AVMF

This Su-27K was one of those deployed aboard the *Kuznetsov* during its first operational cruise, gaining the St Andrew's flag insignia after its return. The production Su-27K serves with a single naval fighter regiment, based at Severomorsk. The unit applies red code letters, thinly outlined in white, and some aircraft carry the squadron badge of a diving sea eagle on their fins. Some aircraft also carry the post-Soviet St Andrew's flag insignia of the Russian navy. There are persistent suggestions that MiG-29Ks may still be acquired to augment the Su-27Ks, which have no real ground attack capability. The aircraft has often been compared to the pre-'Bombcat' A-model F-14 Tomcat, a superb interceptor, but one lacking multi-role capabilities.

Designation
The Sukhoi OKB's use of an Su-30 series designation (Su-33) hides the fact that the Su-27K is closely based on the standard air force and PVO interceptor, with the same radar, avionics and weapons. It does not feature any of the advanced avionics systems or multi-role capabilities associated with the Su-35. The designation was almost certainly applied in order to win 'new project' funding for the aircraft. Plans exist for a more advanced carrierborne 'Flanker', the Su-27KM, but funding is unlikely to be found.

Folding tailplanes
The Su-27K is a very large aircraft, and to ease deck handling and hangar deck stowage, the tailplanes and wings are foldable.

Radar
The 'Slot Back' radar used by the MiG-29 and Su-27 has plenty of power and range performance, but processing capacity is inadequate for autonomous operations, with poor mass raid discrimination, threat prioritisation and multi-target tracking. This makes the aircraft dependent on GCI or AWACS control. Fortunately, the pilot's situational awareness is improved by the use of datalinked data, and by using suitable tactics, which take account of the aircraft's weaknesses.

Cockpit
The Su-27K's analog cockpit is very similar to that of the baseline Su-27, with a handful of new controls for actuating the tailhook and wing folding, and with a refined ILS indicator. Conversion to the carrierborne variant is thus extremely straightforward, and there is no dedicated two-seat version.

FCS
Despite the presence of canard foreplanes, the Su-27K retains the analog FBW FCS of the baseline Su-27, and does not have the Su-27M's digital unit.

Warload
With its three-station wing, the Su-27K can carry a maximum load of eight R-27 (AA-10 'Alamo') missiles for BVR combat, with four shorter-range R-73 (AA-11 'Archer') AAMs for close-in combat. This gives a remarkable degree of combat persistence, even without the internal 30-mm cannon, which is carried in the starboard LERX, with 150 rounds of ammunition.

Tailcone
The Su-27K has a shortened tailcone provided to allow higher angles of attack on touchdown without risking a tailscrape. This in turn permits slower landing speeds and a shorter landing run. The smaller tailcone has less space for chaff and flare expendables, which are relocated in the upper fuselage, further forward. The carrier arrester hook is mounted below the tailcone.

Alternative stores
The Su-27K may be able to carry a UPAZ inflight-refuelling 'buddy' pod on the centreline, or a fuel tank. More usually the aircraft carries a small box-like pod, believed to be associated with the carrier landing system.

IFR probe
In order to extend endurance or mission endurance, the Su-27K can make use of inflight-refuelling, using a retractable probe on the forward fuselage.

Powerplant: two Saturn Lyul'ka AL-31F afterburning turbofans each rated at 74.53 kN (16,755 lb st) dry and 122.59 kN (27,558 lb st) with afterburning
Weights: maximum take-off weight 29940 kg (66,000 lb) – this may represent the maximum carrier launch weight; maximum inflight (post inflight-refuelling) weight 33000 kg (72,752 lb) – this may also represent the maximum land-based take-off weight
Fuel and load: up to 6500 kg (14,330 lb)
***g* limits:** maximum design gross weight +8 *g*
Performance: maximum level speed 'clean' 4,240 kt (2300 km/h; 2,645 mph); service ceiling 17000 m (55,775 ft); range clean 1,620 nm (3000 km; 1,864 miles); approach speed 130 kt (240 km/h; 149 mph) or 287 kt (250 km/h;330 mph) according to some sources

Two Su-27Ks are seen on the deck of Kuznetsov. The right-hand aircraft is lined up to use the ski-jump as soon as the left-hand aircraft clears the ramp.

Su-27KM (T10KM)

There were once said to have been plans to produce a more advanced carrierborne Su-27 based on the Su-27M, with the same digital FBW control system and multi-mode Zhuk radar, and perhaps with vectoring engine nozzles (which Simonov always said would be a feature of the definitive carrierborne 'Flanker', "in its final form"). Such an aircraft could have superseded the Su-27K on the production line, perhaps after the first air wing or two had gained experience using the basic Su-27K.

No advanced version of the Su-27K has materialised, and the prospects for such an aircraft are poor, now that the Russian navy

has only a single carrier. The advanced carrierborne aircraft would reportedly have been designated Su-27KM, or T10KM, but it was abandoned before the OKB started issuing new designations on a near-weekly basis. Although a fully navalised new-build version of the Su-27M can probably now be discounted, it is quite possible that the existing Su-27Ks could be usefully upgraded to improve their capabilities.

Incorporating the modifications of the Su-27SM mid-life upgrade would add a Zhuk radar and would give compatibility with the RVV-AE 'AMRAAMski' missile and the widest possible range of advanced air-to-

surface precision-guided weapons. AL-31FM or AL-35 engines could be fitted to increase thrust. Much the same level of capability could be attained by emulating the Su-27SMK upgrade and fitting a developed version of the original radar for compatibility with RVV-AE and with air-to-surface weapons like the Kh-25, Kh-29, Kh-31 and KAB-500. A similar level of capability could be achieved more cheaply by adding the modified radar and TV display of the Su-30M.

It can be seen that a relatively high level of air-to-ground capability could be incorporated into existing Su-27Ks by retrofit, perhaps as part of a mid-life upgrade, making these aircraft significantly

more useful and reducing the attractiveness of a MiG-29K purchase.

Unlike McDonnell Douglas with its F/A-18, and (less successfully) Grumman with its F-14, Sukhoi has failed to market an advanced variant of the Su-27K as a potential carrier- or land-based aircraft, producing a common aircraft which might appeal to the AV-MF, the Russian air forces and export customers. The aircraft's compact dimensions when 'folded' are a useful feature, while the type's slower approach speed, strengthened undercarriage and powerful arrester hook could make sense to a number of land-based operators.

Su-27P

Despite the Su-27's enormous internal fuel tankage, Sukhoi continued to look at ways to extend the endurance and range of the aircraft. One of the earliest attempts was to fit a retractable inflight-refuelling probe to two Su-27s, one a single-seater, which became the Su-27P, and one a two-seater, which became the first Su-27PU. The two aircraft were used for a variety of trials, including a 15-hour 42-minute endurance flight, and a flight from Moscow to Russia's

Pacific coast and back, a distance of 13440 km (8,700 miles). The aircraft were refuelled in flight four times by Su-24 and Il-78 tankers.

No photos have been published of the Su-27P, as far as is known, but the Su-27P is understood to have had most of the same modifications as were applied to the aerodynamic prototype for the Su-27PU, with inflight-refuelling probe, offset IRST and recontoured tail sting. Systems were proven for extended endurance flights, but the practicality of using a single-pilot aircraft on very long flights was always open to

question. Despite this, Mikhail Simonov was once widely reported as claiming that a single-seat version of the Su-30M was actually in service.

Notwithstanding this report, it is widely assumed that the advantages offered by the Su-27P were therefore not sufficient to attract an order from the IA-PVO and it is generally believed that the sole prototype was stripped of its armament and weapons systems and allocated to the 'Test Pilots' display team. This team is based at Zhukhovskii and is manned by pilots from the LII Gromov Flight Research Institute and

sponsored by the commercial Jupiter Insurance Company. The Su-27P's inflight-refuelling probe, and especially its long-range navigation systems, would have made it a natural choice for extended-range operations overseas, which were demonstrated when it made a non-stop flight to the International Air Tattoo at Boscombe Down. When it arrived, it was found to have had the probe removed (if indeed one had ever been fitted), and there was no evidence of a new long-range navigation system or the recontoured tail sting.

Su-27PD

The abandonment of the extended-endurance single-seat Su-27P left the prototype surplus to requirements. Stripped of its radar and weapons systems (including the IRSTS), and with no visible retractable inflight-refuelling probe, the prototype became an Su-27PD. It was used by Anatoly Kvotchur of the 'Test Pilots' display team, which also operates a number of similarly modified Su-27PUs.

The Su-27PD is now painted in the same red, white and blue colours as the Su-27PUs used by the 'Test Pilots' team, and is coded '595'. The aircraft does not appear to have a retractable inflight-refuelling probe below the port side of the cockpit, and the mounting for the IRST (which has been removed) is entirely absent, so it is not possible to tell if it ever had an IRST offset to starboard. Some experts suggest that the Su-27PD is actually converted from a standard Su-27, and not from the Su-27P prototype.

The Su-27P was converted to serve as an Su-27PD display aircraft. Another single-seat Su-27PD has an inflight-refuelling probe, and was newly built for the display role under the same Su-27PD designation.

Su-27PU (T10P or PU, OKB Su-30)

The Su-27PU resulted from a PVO requirement for an interceptor capable of operating at extended ranges and having very long endurance. Its roles would be to secure Russia's remotest borders and to provide air cover for naval forces. The target endurance for the new fighter was 10 hours, and assumed the use of inflight-refuelling. Two quite different aircraft were apparently designed to meet the requirement, one a single-seater (the Su-27P) and the other a two-seater which became the Su-27PU. The project was undertaken under the supervision of Alexei Knyshev; Igor Emelianov was responsible for the original long-range, high-endurance interceptor and took overall charge of the multi-role Su-30M. The weapons system was designed by Victor Galushko. There may once have been plans to produce a navalised and carrier-capable version of the Su-27PU, but, in the event, the single-seat Su-27K was selected to serve aboard the *Kuznetsov* (at that time the *Tbilisi*) and its (unbuilt) sisters.

It should have been obvious from the start that only a two-pilot aircraft could operate successfully for up to 10 hours at a time, since a single pilot would inevitably become too fatigued over such a period. The same considerations ruled out a two-seat aircraft with a dedicated pilot and weapons systems operator. The long-endurance interceptor would have to have two pilots, sitting in identical cockpits, either of whom could assume command, fly the aircraft or operate the radar and weapons systems at any point of the mission. Engine starting, weapons selection, navigation data inputs and updates and command ejection could thus be initiated from either cockpit.

Instead of simply providing a fixed probe, or a bolt-on retractable probe fairing, Sukhoi designed an extremely neat and compact fully retractable probe which would lie flush with the fuselage skin below the port side of the windscreen, and be partially covered by a faired 'door' when retracted. Installation of this probe forced a relocation of some of the systems and equipment normally installed directly behind the instrument panel, most notably the electro-optical IRST sensor, which was moved from the centreline to the starboard side of the windscreen. This probe design proved so successful that it was soon adapted for the carrierborne Su-27K, the Su-27IB fighter-bomber and the modernised and updated Su-27M.

As well as a new cockpit and the inflight-refuelling probe, the extended-range interceptor would clearly need to have systems and avionics proved for operation for extended periods, inferring a much higher level of reliability. Operating at extended ranges, and over some of the most featureless terrain at the fringes of the Soviet Union, the aircraft would necessarily need a new navigation system. The designers modelled the new navigation suite on that used by Aeroflot's international airliners, with GPS, LORAN, Omega and Mars, but miniaturised to allow it to be carried in a fighter, and simplified for what could in effect be single-pilot operation (if the front- or backseater was 'resting').

In some ways it might have been sensible to base the Su-27PU on the

Right: The 02-10 was a two-seat prototype which tested many of the features subsequently added to the Su-27PU, including the inflight-refuelling probe. It also had a raised, upward-pointing tailcone and an arrester hook for dummy deck trials.

Below: The true Su-27PU prototype was 'blue 05', which made its maiden flight on 31 December 1989. The aircraft subsequently flew with ground attack weapons in support of the Su-30M programme, though it may never have been fully converted to Su-30M standards.

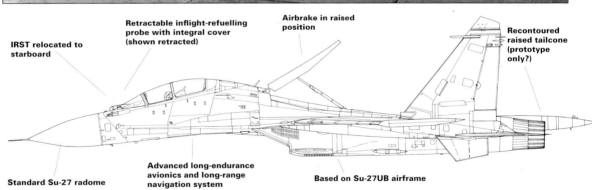

IRST relocated to starboard

Retractable inflight-refuelling probe with integral cover (shown retracted)

Airbrake in raised position

Recontoured raised tailcone (prototype only?)

Standard Su-27 radome

Advanced long-endurance avionics and long-range navigation system

Based on Su-27UB airframe

Su-27IB, with its spacious side-by-side cockpit. The two pilots could have sat together, enjoying excellent communications, perhaps with radar displays and weapons selection controls between them. In the event, it was decided to base the new fighter on the standard

tandem-seat Su-27UB airframe, which was already flight-cleared and easily available.

Flight trials of some of the features of the Su-27PU began in the early 1980s, using the Komsomolsk-built second prototype Su-27UB, an aircraft coded 'blue 02' and sometimes referred to as 02-10 or (wrongly)

The 'Test Pilots' team uses a pair of stripped Su-27PUs alongside its Su-27PDs. They may be designated Su-27PUDs, or perhaps Su-30Ds. One is seen here beside an inverted Su-27PD.

The 'Test Pilots' Su-27PUs were probably the only production Su-27PUs, and were specifically built for use in the aerobatic display role, with long-range navigation systems for overseas flying.

as the T10PU. This aircraft was fitted with the new inflight-refuelling probe and had its constant-section cylindrical tail sting replaced by a more streamlined fairing, fatter further forward and curving in to more of a point. This may have housed increased fuel tankage, but was primarily redesigned to sit and point higher, to reduce the risk of tail scrapes during high-Alpha landings. This was probably a legacy of its use in ski-jump and arrested landing trials. The aircraft was one of those used for the famous 15-hour 42-minute, 13440-km (8,700-mile) endurance flight from Moscow to Russia's Pacific coast and back on 23 June 1987. It also made a 12-hour proving flight to the North Pole on 6 June, with three inflight-refuellings.

The first of two Su-27PU prototypes (T10PU-5, 'blue 05', probably the fifth two-seater built and T10PU-6) made its maiden flight at Irkutsk on 31 December 1989, piloted by Yevgeni Revunov. This aircraft had the inflight-refuelling probe and offset IRST, but had a standard Su-27 tail sting, with the larger box-like chaff/flare

dispenser fairings. It was probably converted from an existing Su-27UB, and was not a new-build airframe. The new type was designated T10-4PU by the Irkutsk plant. The internal fuel tankage was unchanged from that of the Su-27UB, and the unrefuelled range was quoted as 1,620 nm (3000 km; 1,864 miles). With inflight-refuelling, a range of 2,808 nm (5200 km; 3,231 miles) was possible. The prototype is believed to have been fitted with the new navigation suite, and probably had a full-standard Su-27PU rear cockpit when it first flew. The avionics and systems were proved for continuous use for periods in excess of 10 hours, and an aircrew toilet/relief system was incorporated, as well as a new oxygen system.

It was soon revealed that the Su-27PU was fitted with a new modification of the basic 'Slot Back' radar, broadly equivalent to the modifications which produced the MiG-29SM. The new radar offered a limited degree of air-to-ground capability (later to be exploited in the Su-30M), and, more significantly, simultaneous dual target

engagement capability. In an attempt to enhance the Su-27PU's combat capability, the aircraft was offered with an optional equipment fit which would allow it to operate as a command post or mini-AWACS, using its radar and datalink equipment to control up to four other fighters, which in turn could operate in 'radar silence'. In this configuration, the Su-27PU would carry a dedicated fighter controller in the rear cockpit, which would be reconfigured with new radar displays and equipment. Sukhoi suggested that the aircraft would operate with long-range/long-endurance single-seat Su-27Ps, or with other Su-30s or ordinary PVO Su-27s.

In the absence of a PVO order for the Su-27PU, the basic interceptor was redesignated Su-30 by the Sukhoi OKB, which began seeking export orders for what it referred to as the Su-30K, stressing its ability to carry simple air-to-ground weapons such as unguided bombs and rockets. It was soon apparent that the basic Su-30 was not flexible or versatile enough, and Sukhoi began developing the aircraft into a multi-

role long-range fighter/fighter-bomber under the designation Su-30M. Only two production Su-27PUs are believed to have been built (with inflight-refuelling probes and long-range navigation systems, but without weapons systems, and perhaps without radar). These aircraft were ordered by and delivered to the 'Test Pilots' aerobatic team based at the LII Gromov Flight Research Institute airfield at Zhukhovskii. They are painted red, white and blue, and are sponsored by a commercial insurance company, operating with a single-seat Su-27PD. The two aircraft are coded '596' and '597'.

In early 1996 *Flight International* suggested that 30 Su-30s had been assembled at Irkutsk, and that the type was entering service with the IA-PVO at Savotsleyka. This cannot be confirmed and seems very unlikely. The picture accompanying the *Flight* report clearly showed a standard Su-27UB, with no inflight-refuelling probe and still with the centreline IRST ball. The aircraft had previously been claimed to be 'entering service' in early 1993, but it seems that the original single-role Su-30 (Su-27PU) is effectively dead, replaced by the multi-role Su-30M and its export derivative, the Su-30MK.

Su-30M (T10PM)

With its modernised radar, the Su-30 enjoyed a degree of latent ground attack capability (using bombs and rockets). The addition of guidance/datalink pods gave the aircraft some compatibility with Kh-31P (AS-17 'Krypton') ARMs (the SPO-32 Pastel RWR pod, which also contained an SPS-161 ECM jammer and which was carried on the forward centreline hardpoint), and the type was initially offered as a replacement for the MiG-25BM in the SEAD (Wild Weasel) role. The air-to-ground capabilities of the type were enhanced by Victor Galushko, who redesigned the aircraft's weapons system. A TV display was added, bringing compatibility with the KAB-500KR guided bomb, and with Kh-29T missiles, together with provision for the ARK-9 datalink pod on the rear centreline pylon. This latter pod allowed the aircraft to carry the Kh-59M (AS-18 'Kazoo') TV-guided missile. The laser-guided Kh-29L (AS-14 'Kedge') used the laser channel of the upgraded OLS-27 for target designation.

As well as the normal range of air-to-air weapons associated with the basic Su-27, the Su-30 can also carry up to eight RVV-AEs, with two on the centreline, two under the nacelles, and two under each wing. In the ground attack role, weapons options were much the same as for the Su-34, although sometimes fewer examples of each weapons type are carried by the Su-30. The Su-30MK, for instance, carries only two Kh-59M 'Kingbolts' or four Kh-25Ms (on twin carriers on the central underwing pylons). Four rocket pods can be carried on the same twin carriers. The Su-34 carries three Kh-59s (the extra one carried on the centreline), or six KH-25s or rocket pods (the extra ones carried on the inboard

underwing pylons). Similarly, the Su-30MK carried two fewer Kh-31s than the Su-34 (on the inboard and central underwing pylons, but not below the engine nacelles). The two variants each carried six Kh-29T ASMs or KAB-500 laser-guided bombs.

When carrying dumb iron bombs, the aircraft can carry eight 500-kg bombs (a twin carrier outboard, single bombs on the other underwing pylons and under the nacelles) or seven KMGU-2 CBUs. The Su-34 can carry 12 500-kg bombs (with extra twin carriers in tandem on the centreline) or the same number of

KMGU-2s. Alternatively, the Su-34 could carry 16 500-kg bombs on quad carriers underwing and in tandem on the centreline.

One weapon offered with the Su-30MK only was the SPPU gun pod, two of which could be carried on the central underwing hardpoints, facing forward or aft.

The original Su-27PU prototype ('blue 05') was photographed carrying a variety of unguided air-to-surface weapons, but it is unclear whether it was actually fitted with the upgraded radar or the TV display, and it may not ever have become a true Su-30M. The first Su-30M made its maiden flight on

The prototype Su-30M was displayed at Dubai in 1993, but has otherwise kept a low profile. A number of Su-27UBs have masqueraded as Su-30Ms at other international air shows, but lack the variant's TV display.

14 April 1992 in the hands of G. Bulanov and V. Maximenov and was probably 'blue 56', which was demonstrated at Dubai in 1993, albeit with very little fanfare. This aircraft was fitted with an inflight-refuelling probe and offset IRST, and was displayed carrying a range of weaponry.

'Blue 321' (actually a UB) was painted in camouflage and laden with air-to-ground weapons for static displays at a variety of international air shows and exhibitions. The multi-role Su-30M was offered to the Russian air forces as a low-cost alternative to the Su-27IB to replace the Su-24, but was never seriously considered. The aircraft was then described as having a coherent pulse-Doppler radar, a helmet-mounted target designator and the ability to carry up to six PGMs. After the 1993 Dubai air show, Mikhail Simonov acknowledged that the two-seat Su-30M had not been procured, but that the Su-27IB would be bought in small numbers to act as pathfinders for a single-seat version of the Su-30M.

The front and rear cockpits of the Su-30 are similar to those of the Su-27UB. The rear cockpit retains full dual controls, and appears to have a combined HUD repeater, radar and TV display. This raises the possibility that no Su-30 is yet fully equipped for the ground attack role.

Su-30MK (T10PMK)

The Su-30MK designation is reserved for export versions of the Su-30M. The Su-30M prototypes and demonstrators effectively became demonstrators and prototypes for the Su-30MK when the chance of a Russian air forces order finally vanished. It could be argued that the Su-30MK displayed at the Chilean FIDAE air show in 1994 ('blue 603') was the first true Su-30MK, in that it was configured specifically as a demonstrator for potential overseas customers, with a sanitised but fully operational rear cockpit and a spectacular disruptive camouflage colour scheme.

The familiar Su-27UB demonstrator seen at numerous Western air shows was repainted in camouflage (and recoded '321') to serve as an Su-30MK demonstrator. Although it has frequently been laden with the type of sophisticated air-to-ground weaponry which you might expect to see on an Su-30MK, the aircraft's transformation is literally only skin deep. The aircraft has no inflight-refuelling probe, and remains to all intents and purposes a standard Su-27UB. At the 1993 Paris Air Salon, Sukhoi nevertheless maintained that the aircraft was the 'prototype Su-30MK', but were careful not to allow access to the rear cockpit, which might have given the game away.

If Sukhoi's claims are correct (and they are not always), India has now formally placed an order for the Su-30MK, and these aircraft will be the first production examples of the variant. At the 1996 Farnborough air show, it became apparent that the aircraft ordered by India would not be a straightforward Su-30MK, but would instead probably incorporate features from the Su-30I and from the Su-37. (The Indian

It is uncertain as to whether '603' is actually an Su-30MK, or merely a specially modified Su-27UB, lacking the capability to use the laser- and TV-guided PGMs it is often seen carrying. The Su-30MK was designed for export and combines long endurance avionics and advanced PGM compatibility. Its capabilities remain unproved.

Su-30MK is described below under the Su-30II heading.) The Sukhoi OKB cast its net widely for customers, and projected a 'can-do' image. The Su-30 project chief, Igor V. Emelianov, joked at the 1993 Paris Air Salon that, "If the RAF wants to buy the Su-30MK, we can deliver them next year."

Any production Su-30MK will bear a close resemblance to the late production Su-27UB, on whose airframe it is based. MTOW is 500 kg (1,100 lb) higher than even the latest Su-27UBs, and performance has been restored to single-seat standards in most respects (the Su-30MK is only 20 km/h; 12 mph slower at sea level, only 155 km/h; 96 mph slower at altitude, and has a service ceiling only 200 m/655 ft lower). One puzzle is that Sukhoi figures indicate that the Su-30MK has the same empty weight as the single-seat Su-27, and not the

higher weight of an Su-27UB.

The most recent Sukhoi and Rosvoorouzhenie sales literature describes the multi-role version of the Su-30 simply as the Su-30K, and not as the Su-30MK. Confusingly, the Su-30K designation has also been applied to the canard-equipped Su-30I.

Specification
Sukhoi Su-30MK
Dimensions: as for Su-27UB
Powerplant: two Lyul'ka Saturn AL-31F turbofans each rated at 122.59 kN (27,557 lb st) with afterburning
Weights: empty operating 16380 kg (36,112 lb); normal take-off 25000 kg (55,115 lb); maximum take-off weight

34000 kg (74,957 lb) (the latest sales literature gives slightly lower normal and maximum take-off weights, of 24800 kg/54,675 lb and 30450 kg/67,130 lb respectively)
Fuel and load: internal fuel as Su-27UB, maximum weapon load 8000 kg (17,636 lb)
g limits: +8 at basic design gross weight;
Performance: maximum level speed 'clean' at sea level 729 kt (1350 km/h; 839 mph); maximum level speed 'clean' at altitude 1,147 kt (2125 km/h; 1,320 mph); limiting Mach No. 2.0; service ceiling 17500 m (57,400 ft); unrefuelled range 1,620 nm (3000 km; 1,864 miles); range with one inflight-refuelling 2,808 nm (5200 km; 3,231 miles); range with two inflight-refuellings 3,774 nm (6990 km; 4,343 miles); take-off run 550 m (1,805 ft); landing roll 670 m (2,200 ft)

Above: '321' wore a convincing operational colour scheme, and was often displayed carrying air-to-surface weapons, but was actually a repainted Su-27UB demonstrator which had been seen many times at Farnborough and Paris air shows.

Above right: The Su-30's long endurance and heavy payload capability gave it good potential for adaptation to the ground attack and long-range strike roles. There is some question as to whether a real air-to-ground weapons system has been integrated into the aircraft yet, however.

Right: This highly unrepresentative loadout nevertheless manages to convey an idea of the range of weapons which can be carried by the Su-30MK. These include TV-, laser- and radar-guided bombs and missiles, as well as the full spectrum of air-to-air weapons.

Su-30I

In 1996 a single canard-equipped Su-30 was reported to be undergoing final assembly at Irkutsk. This aircraft will reportedly be

designated Su-30I (with the I suffix standing for Istrebeitel, or fighter), although it has also been referred to as the Su-30K in ITAR-TASS's *Russia's Aerospace News*. The canard will improve take-off and landing performance, and will also enhance agility.

It is uncertain whether the new aircraft will be fitted with the new flight control system of the Su-27M, although this seems unlikely. The aircraft will apparently retain the basic N-001 radar of the standard 'Flanker'. The canard-equipped Su-30 would,

of course, be an excellent operational aircraft in its own right, or may be intended as a trainer for the carrier-based Su-27K or even for the Su-27M, for which no two-seat version is available.

Su-30MKI

In late 1996 it was announced that India had signed a $1.5 billion contract for the supply of 40 Su-30MK fighter-bombers. The same contract was part of a $3.5 billion arms deal which also covered India's MiG-21 upgrade, the supply of additional precision-guided weapons and a licence-production agreement for an eventual total of 100 Su-30 aircraft. India's Su-30s will be designated Su-30MKI (Su-30 II according to some reports) and will eventually all be fitted with thrust-vectoring AL-37FU engines, canard foreplanes and an advanced phased-array radar.

Initial deliveries were due, at the time of writing, to begin in May 1997, consisting of a batch of eight aircraft of which the first four will be basic Su-30s with virtually no ground attack capability. The first group of Indian pilots was training in Russia. Initial operating unit was scheduled to be No. 24 Squadron, currently flying the MiG-21bis. The first Su-30s were expected to be based at Pune, operating as part of the South

This model of a canard- and vectoring nozzle-equipped Su-30 represents the intended final configuration of the aircraft ordered by India.

Western Air Command. Further aircraft deliveries will be made in a four-phase programme, with the final aircraft to be delivered in 1999-2000. At present only the final batch of 22 aircraft will be delivered in the full Su-30MKI configuration, with canard foreplanes and thrust vectoring, but the remainder are scheduled to be modified eventually. The second batch of aircraft are slated to feature some Western avionics, with France's Sextant Avionique the most likely supplier.

Initial batch aircraft will probably be fitted with the Su-27's standard N-001 radar, but a more advanced radar is sought, although not yet determined. Both Western and Russian sources are being studied. Most Su-30MKIs are expected to have fully missionised rear cockpits, without flight controls, although a handful may have rudimentary rear-seat controls for training purposes.

A requirement exists for 100 Su-30MKIs to equip five squadrons. Licence-production will be undertaken by a HAL assembly line at Ozhar near Nasik. In Indian service the Su-30MKI will augment strike aircraft such as the Jaguar and MiG-27. Weapon options are likely to include the Kh-59M and Kh-31 ASMs and R-77 AAMs.

Su-27IB prototype (T10V)

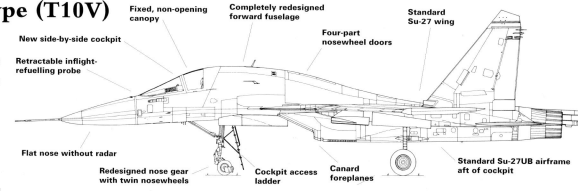

Fixed, non-opening canopy

Completely redesigned forward fuselage

Standard Su-27 wing

New side-by-side cockpit

Four-part nosewheel doors

Retractable inflight-refuelling probe

Flat nose without radar

Redesigned nose gear with twin nosewheels

Cockpit access ladder

Canard foreplanes

Standard Su-27UB airframe aft of cockpit

For most of its early career the T10V-1 ('Bort 42') was referred to by the bureau as the Su-27KU, with the clear inference that it was the aerodynamic prototype of a carrier training variant. It existence was revealed in a TASS photograph, which showed the aircraft making an approach to the carrier *Tbilisi*, in a series of pictures showing trials aboard the vessel. The Su-27IB designation was specifically denied until the 1993 Paris Air Salon at Le Bourget, and when the aircraft was displayed to Russian and CIS leaders in the big display at Minsk-Maschulische in 1992 the sign-board was covered before TASS photographers could shoot it. The canvas cover 'slipped', however, revealing the suffix IB. The Sukhoi OKB continued to deny the IB designation for more than a year, and Simonov himself claimed that the aircraft was "better for instruction in carrier landing and air-to-surface weapons delivery than as a dedicated operational strike aircraft in its own right."

This statement was accurate in a limited sense, in that 'Bort 42' lacked any radar or air-to-ground weapons systems, but was perhaps a little disingenuous: the aircraft was designed by Rollan Martirosov as the aerodynamic prototype for his definitive Su-27IB (Su-34), which was intended as a dedicated operational strike aircraft. Certainly the 'Su-27KU' would have been of little use as a carrier trainer, since it lacked an arrester hook, folding wings or a carrier landing system, although there may once have been plans to produce a similar version with these features and with the Su-27K's double-slotted flaps.

'Bort 42' was converted from a standard Su-27UB trainer, with the new side-by-side cockpit section (including the new nose gear) simply grafted on ahead of fuselage frame 18, and with a strengthened Su-27K main gear fitted. The nose undercarriage unit was entirely redesigned, with twin wheels, and retracted rearwards to lie in an enlarged bay covered by four separate doors, with tandem pairs laterally flanking the bay. The new side-by-side cockpit was designed to provide better forward visibility for both crew members, and to facilitate better inter-crew communications while also offering more space for avionics and fuel. The cockpit aft of the seats was extremely tall, allowing the crew to conduct 'relaxing exercises' during long flights. The Su-27IB may be the world's only combat aircraft whose cockpit is optimised for Tai Chi. Ahead of the cockpit the new nose was given a broad, flat profile which reduced frontal radar cross-section and improved visibility forward over the nose, while posing some challenges to the designers of the aircraft's proposed radar antenna. Simonov claimed that the new nose shape could accommodate a version of the Phazatron Zhuk radar if required, although "clearly, some redesign would be necessary." To maximise resistance to ground fire, the new cockpit was designed

in the same manner as that of the Su-25, constructed in the form of a solid bathtub from 17-mm titanium alloy sheets. The weight of armour and fuel tank protection amounted to 1480 kg (3,263 lb). Additional titanium armour was scabbed on to the cabin sides.

Some sources suggest that the Su-27IB had the actuators of its variable intake ramps disabled or removed, effectively

Right: The aerodynamic prototype for the Su-27IB retained the main landing gear and rear end of a standard Su-27UB, mated to a new forward fuselage and nose gear.

Below: Though the Su-27KU designation was sometimes used to describe 'Bort 42', the aircraft was never a carrier trainer.

leaving the aircraft with fixed-geometry intakes. They prevented high supersonic speed, but this was not felt to be important for the low-level ground attack role. It is not known whether the definitive production Su-27IB (Su-34) will have variable-geometry intakes. The ability to cruise at very high supersonic speeds was not considered to be vital for the low-level strike role, but radius of action was crucial, and the Su-27IB was provided with a retractable inflight-

The Su-27IB's new forward fuselage provides a superb, roomy and comfortable environment for its crew, but the visibility from the new low-drag cockpit is poor by comparison with the view from the cockpit of the Su-27 or Su-27UB.

refuelling probe to allow buddy refuelling.

Access to the new cockpit was through a hatch in the front edge of the nosewheel bay, but no integral ladder was provided, necessitating a reliance on ground support equipment. In emergency, the transparent cockpit panels could be explosively jettisoned, using pyrotechnic charges along the central frame which separated them. The pilots sat on a pair of K-36DM ejection seats, sequenced to give the fastest possible escape while minimising the risk of the seats colliding.

In its new guise as the T10V-1, the aircraft made its first flight on 13 April 1990 (it may have already flown as an Su-27UB, or may have been converted from an Su-27 taken from the production line). Anatoly Ivanov was the pilot for the first flight, which was made from Zhukhovskii.

Su-27IB pre-series and production (T10V, OKB Su-34)

The Su-34 designation is applied by the OKB to the production version of the T10V (Su-27IB), although the air force continues to refer to the aircraft as the Su-27IB. The variant was designed as a replacement for the Su-24, and so used the same side-by-side cockpit arrangement. This cockpit was first flown on the Su-27IB testbed, which was also fitted with canard foreplanes to enhance take-off and landing performance. The canards were originally developed to enhance the take-off and landing characteristics of the carrierborne Su-27K, and were always going to be useful for a heavyweight ground attack version of the 'Flanker'. It should have come as no surprise to see them on the Su-27IB (Su-34). They are believed to be linked to a new fly-by-wire control system, related to that of the Su-27M, which allows the canards to be used for gust alleviation in low-level flight.

The Su-27IB also has a 'second-generation' glass cockpit (similar to that of the Su-27M/Su-35) with a single wide-angle HUD for the pilot and four CRT multi-function display screens dominating the centre of the panel. There are smaller, secondary CRT radar and RHAWS displays (a total of seven CRT displays is fitted). The aircraft has full dual controls, but the left-hand seat would not normally be occupied by a fully rated pilot. The cabin of the Su-27IB (Su-34) is armoured and fully pressurised, allowing a 'shirt-sleeve' operating environment at altitudes up to 10000 m (32,810 ft). The cockpit is equipped with a food heater and a toilet, and access is via a hatch in the nosewheel bay. The basic armoured cockpit bathtub is believed to be further protected by flush-fitting composite armour skin panels on the forward fuselage sides.

The first full-standard Su-27IB (Su-34) was 'Bort 43' (T10V-2), which first flew on 18 December 1993 in the hands of Igor Votintsev and Yevgeni Revunov. The aircraft was then flown to Zhukhovskii from

Novosibirsk by Revunov and I. E. Soloviev. The T10V-2 represents the definitive Su-27IB (Su-34) configuration, and as such is fitted with 12 hardpoints, having an extra pair under each wing.

The second production standard aircraft, 'Bort 45' (T10V-5), first flew on 28 December 1994 and subsequently became the Su-32FN prototype (described separately). As far as can be determined, the T10V-4 was a static test aircraft. There may be a T10V-3 coded 'Bort 44', but no such aircraft has been seen.

Like the prototype Su-27IB, the pre-series Su-27IB (Su-34) has fixed-geometry intakes, with a single boundary layer spill slot in the underside, and with auxiliary suck-in intakes relocated to the inboard sides of the main intakes. Although the Su-27IB (Su-34) prototypes are all powered by standard AL-31F engines, the aircraft could accommodate the higher thrust AL-31FM or AL-35.

The aircraft also has a redesigned tail fairing projecting between the engines. This is of greater diameter than that of the standard Su-27, is mounted higher, and projects much further aft. The tailcone can house a small rearward-facing air-to-air radar, probably a derivative of the N-012 fitted to the Su-27M, with a similar 3/4-km (2/2.5-mile) range, or perhaps more. The aircraft is likely to use this radar in conjunction with a rearward-facing R-73 (AA-11 'Archer') AAM installation (already tested on an Su-27). The aircraft's twin braking parachutes were relocated to a compartment above the tailcone, between the tailfins. The nose has been slightly lengthened and reprofiled ahead of the windscreen and can now house a Leninets phased-array radar giving fully automatic terrain following and terrain avoidance. The Su-27IB (Su-34) also has a new navigation and attack system with a GLONASS satellite navigation set integrated with the standard INS, and with a 'principally new' computer.

For self-defence, the aircraft has a Pastel radar warning receiver and a Mak IR missile-warning system, as well as a laser-warning system and provision for wingtip-mounted Sorbtsiya ESM pods. The exact equipment fit of the T10V-2 is uncertain, the equipment above being specified for the production Su-27IB (Su-34), but not necessarily fitted to the prototype.

The Su-27IB (Su-34) can routinely carry up to 8000 kg (17,640 lb) of weapons on its 12 external hardpoints, which are similar to those fitted to the Su-27K, Su-30, Su-27M and Su-32FN. For the first time, the

Above: The side-by-side cockpit of the Su-27IB allows excellent crew co-operation. It is armoured and pressurised, and has a food heater and toilet for long-range flights.

Below: The production Su-27IB has a distinctive main undercarriage with tandem mainwheels, and a raised and recontoured tailcone. This was the first pre-production aircraft.

Sukhoi 'Flanker' Variants

The first pre-production Su-27IB sits at Kubinka, waiting for inspection by visiting VIPs. It carries a Kh-29 underwing, with a Kh-31 under the starboard intake.

Fully laden, an Su-27IB (Su-34) can easily be twice as heavy as an operational Su-27, making it a very different aircraft, despite sharing a common airframe. The increased weight of the Su-27IB (Su-34) airframe, and the increased weight of its air-to-ground warload, made the provision of a strengthened undercarriage essential. The aircraft was fitted with a new twin-wheel nosegear with KT-27 tyres, and with new main oleos with tandem KT-206 mainwheels. The nose gear unit was externally similar to that used by the Su-27IB aerodynamic prototype, but the redesigned main gear was entirely new. The main gear oleos were longer than on previous Su-27 variants, giving the type a more 'tail-up' position on the ground.

The aircraft's increased weight and fixed intakes impose some performance penalties by comparison with the basic Su-27 and variants like the Su-30MK. Mach number is limited to 1.8, and the aircraft has a maximum load limit of 7 g even at light weights. At low level, the Su-32FN is at least 70 km/h (44 mph) slower than the Su-27 (drag-limited at these heights) and is 480 km/h (300 mph) slower at altitude (where the intakes make it thrust-limited). Ceiling is reduced from about 18000 m (59,000 ft) to about 15000 m (9,320 ft). Static tests of the T10V were completed in November 1995, but flight tests continue, and reports suggest that an initial evaluation batch of 12 aircraft is under construction at Novosibirsk. Most observers expect the Su-27IB/34 to spawn a number of sub-variants for the reconnaissance and EW roles, and perhaps even for high-speed VIP transport and target towing. In the short term, however, funding makes even the evaluation batch of bombers uncertain. In May 1996 Colonel General Abrek Ayupov, air force deputy C-in-C for acquisition, acknowledged that during 1996 the air force would only be able to afford to pay for "one and a half of the Su-27IBs produced at Novosibirsk."

centreline and inboard underwing fuel tanks are 'plumbed' for the carriage of PTB external fuel tanks of various sizes, while the centreline hardpoint may also be used for the carriage of a UPAZ buddy pod.

The wingtip hardpoints are unchanged from those on previous 'Flanker' versions, and can carry a Sorbtsiya ESM pod or the combined anti-flutter weight/missile launch rail compatible with the R-73 or RVV-AE. Alternatively, a Sorbtsiya ESM pod can be carried on the aft centreline station. The outboard underwing pylons are unchanged and are stressed only for the carriage of a defensive AAM, usually an R-73 or possibly an RVV-AE. The remaining pylons (two more under each wing, two under the engine nacelles and two on the centreline) are used for the carriage of air-to-surface weapons or BVR missiles.

The Su-27IB (Su-34) will be cleared to carry virtually the full range of Russian air-to-surface ordnance. The aircraft can carry up to 34 AB-100 100-kg (220-lb) bombs, two

under the central underwing pylons, three under each centreline pylon and six (in tandem triple clusters) under the intakes and inboard underwing pylons. A triple cluster of 250-kg (550-lb) AB-250 bombs may be carried on each hardpoint, with pairs only under the central underwing pylon, for a total of 22 bombs. Alternatively, 12 AB-500 500-kg (1,100-lb) bombs may be carried, comprising pairs of bombs on the centreline and central underwing pylons and single bombs on the other stations. The stations which carry pairs of bombs can actually accommodate two tandem pairs of bombs, raising the total to 16 500-kg bombs in some circumstances.

The Su-27IB (Su-34) can carry up to seven KMGU cluster bomb dispensers, on the rear centreline pylon, under the engines and under the inboard pair of underwing pylons. The aircraft can carry a variety of unguided rockets, including B8M pods of 20 S8 80-mm rockets, B13 pods of five S13 130-mm rockets, or single S-25 or S-25L

(laser-guided) 250-mm rockets. Two pods can be carried on the central underwing pylons, with single pods inboard, giving a total of six. The aircraft can also carry up to six KAB-500 PGMs singly on the underwing and under-nacelle hardpoints, or three KAB-1500s on the centreline and inboard underwing pylons.

Although the Su-27IB (Su-34) will replace primarily the Su-24 in the tactical strike role, it may also replace the Tu-16 and Tu-22M in some roles, including the carriage of long-range stand-off missiles. The Su-27IB (Su-34) has already been proposed as a potential launch platform for the AFM-L Alpha cruise missile, for example. A May 1996 statement by the Russian air forces' chief of staff, Colonel General Peter Deinekin, that the Tu-22M and Su-24 would be replaced by a "multi-functional bomber with increased combat capabilities" was taken as confirming that the aircraft would eventually be replaced by the Sukhoi T-60S, but could equally be taken to confirm that the Su-27IB would replace both types. The Su-27IB (Su-34) can also carry the same air-to-surface weapons as the Su-32FN, which are detailed in that entry.

Left: The strengthened, redesigned nose gear retracts into a completely redesigned undercarriage bay, which also accommodates the cockpit access ladder.

Below: The tandem mainwheels of the Su-27IB spread the aircraft's footprint. They are not staggered, like those of the MiG-31, so the rear wheels do not cut fresh snow.

Only the tip of the white-painted area on the Su-27IB's nose will house the aircraft's attack radar, though this aircraft, 'Bort 43', has no radar fitted.

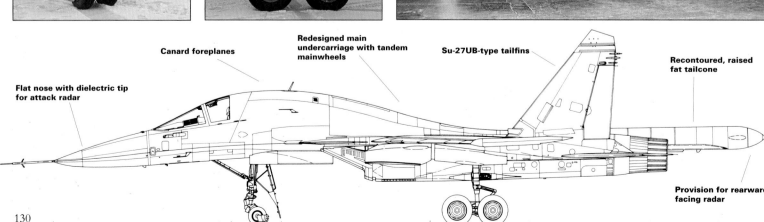

Flat nose with dielectric tip for attack radar

Canard foreplanes

Redesigned main undercarriage with tandem mainwheels

Su-27UB-type tailfins

Recontoured, raised fat tailcone

Provision for rearward-facing radar

Su-32FN (T10V)

The first Western public appearance by the side-by-side 'Flanker' was made by 'Bort 45' (T10V-5), which was displayed statically at Paris for the 1995 Air Salon at Le Bourget. The Su-27IB aerodynamic prototype had previously been shown at successive Mosaero show exhibitions at Zhukhovskii. The Su-32FN designation (applied to a turboprop-powered, tricycle-undercarriaged, tandem-seat military trainer derived from the Su-26/29 family) was revealed at the June 1995 Paris Air Salon. The designation was obviously new to many of the Sukhoi delegation at Paris, who confirmed that as far as they were concerned the aircraft had merely been one of the Su-34 prototypes until a day or two before they left for Paris.

It is unclear whether the Su-32FN designation has supplanted the Su-34 designation, or whether it applies only to the dedicated maritime strike version of the Su-27IB (Su-34). Most analysts believe that the Su-34 designation remains current within the OKB, and is applicable to the overland strike version under development for the Russian air forces as an Su-24 replacement, and which the Russian air forces still refer to as the Su-27IB.

Certainly, Sukhoi has emphasised the maritime role when describing the Su-32FN, whose stated avionics fit is optimised for maritime reconnaissance and maritime strike duties, and whose camouflage appears more suited to overwater operations than to overland duties. The aircraft is described as being suitable for maritime all-weather, round-the-clock operations against waterborne and submarine targets, which it can detect, classify, track and attack if necessary.

The Sea Dragon avionics complex integrated a Sea Snake coherent radar (claimed to be superior to the AN/APS-137 by a factor of between 25 and 30 per cent) with a MAD, a two-channel IR TV system, and a Hydrolocator. The aircraft used an Argon digital onboard computer and had a new display and control system compatible with the 72 sonobuoys which can be carried in an optional centreline pod. The buoys include passive and active, directional and non-directional buoys which are claimed to be superior to the American SSQ-53B,

SSQ-75 and SSQ-77A buoys.

The Su-32FN has 12 hardpoints, as do the Su-27K, Su-30M, Su-34 and Su-27M, and can carry a wide range of air-to-surface weapons including various anti-ship missiles. The aircraft can carry a single ASM-MSS (Kh-41) under the centreline, or two of these massive 4500-kg (9,920-lb) missiles on the centre underwing hardpoints, although development of the Kh-41 is reportedly under suspension.

The aircraft can carry up to three of the newer 250-km (155-mile), 1500-kg (3,300-lb) ASM-MS missiles under the centreline and under the central underwing pylons. These seldom-photographed weapons can be identified by the broad flat rectangular ventral intake immediately aft of the wing, in the pinched-in waist of the missile. Other weapons suitable for use in the maritime role include the Kh-25, the Kh-29 or the Kh-31 (six of which may be carried, on the inboard pair of underwing pylons and under the engine nacelles). Alternatively, three Kh-59M (AS-18 'Kazoo') ASMs can be carried, on the centreline and central underwing pylons, with the necessary

ARK-9 datalink pod carried on the rear centreline hardpoint.

A preliminary purchase agreement for 12 Su-32FNs has been signed (according to the OKB) at a unit price of $36 million. The identity of the 'unnamed country' which signed this agreement has not been revealed. Speculation that a carrier-capable variant of the Su-32 might be developed seems unlikely, since the aircraft is too heavy to operate from Russia's tiny carriers.

Specification
Su-32FN
Dimensions: fuselage length including probe 24.8 m (81 ft 4 in); length without probe 23.3 m (76 ft 5 in); canard span 6.4 m (21 ft); overall height 6.5 m (21 ft in); wheel track 4.4 m (14 ft 5 in); wheelbase 6.6 m (21 ft 7 in)
Powerplant: two AL-31F afterburning turbofans each rated at 74.53 kN (16,700 lb st) dry and 122.59 kN (27,500 lb st) with afterburning (production Su-32FN/Su-34 will have AL-31FM or AL-35 with augmented thrust rating of between 125.53 and 137.3 kN/28,200 and 30,860 lb)

Development of the Su-32FN was halted in early 1997 to allow Sukhoi to concentrate on the Indian Su-30II and Chinese Su-27 requests. When abandoned, the type was described as the export version of the Su-27IB rather than a dedicated maritime attack variant as was claimed at the type's Western debut at Paris in 1995.

Weights: normal take-off weight 42000 kg (92,600 lb); maximum take-off weight 44630 kg (98,000 lb)
Load: normal weapon load up to 8000 kg (17,600 lb)
g limits: +7 at basic design gross weight
Performance: maximum level speed 'clean' at sea level 702 kt (1300 km/h; 808 mph); maximum level speed 'clean' at altitude 972 kt (1800 km/h; 1,118 mph); limiting Mach No. 1.8; (estimated) service ceiling 15000 m (49,200 ft); range 2,160 nm (4000 km; 2,485 miles), or 3,777 nm (7000 km; 4,350 miles) with inflight-refuelling

Su-27LL-PS (T10U-16)

Although the advantages of thrust-vectoring engine nozzles (especially in improving take-off and landing characteristics) were made clear by the F-15 S/MTD, Sukhoi was slow to begin productive work on vectoring nozzles for the Su-27M. A single Su-27UB was modified to take a two-dimensional (pitch: up/down) nozzle, although early reports suggested that this would be used for trials in support of the Gulfstream/Sukhoi SSBJ (Supersonic Business Jet), and particularly for noise footprint measurements. It is now thought that this explanation was largely disinformation, and that the testbed was actually used for trials in support of the Su-27M project.

The Su-27UB testbed, reportedly designated as the T10U-16, or as the Su-27LL-PS, was fitted with a lengthened fairing aft of the port engine. This incorporated an articulated end-piece which allowed different flat-shaped nozzle

The Su-27LL-PS was a converted Su-27UB, and had a two-dimensional vectoring nozzle in a massive fairing at the end of the port engine nacelle. There is some doubt as to whether the nozzle had much freedom of movement, but it is believed that the results prompted development of the Su-37.

positions to be simulated, although it is unclear whether it could be actuated in flight, at least initially.

The aircraft (based at Zhukhovskii with the LII Gromov Flight Research Centre fleet) began trials in 1989 (a year after the S/MTD, although the US aircraft had two, fully vectoring nozzles which were so advanced they were almost good enough to be adopted there and then by a production

aircraft). Oleg Tsoi vectored the engine in flight for the first time on 31 March 1989, after the first flight with the new engine nozzle on 21 March. The Su-27LL-PS soon confirmed the advantages of thrust-vectoring previously demonstrated by the US aircraft. Steps were made to incorporate more advanced nozzles in the Su-27M, while the OKB also hoped that funding would be made available for similar nozzles

to be fitted to the Su-27K.

The thrust vectoring Su-27 flew much later than has previously been supposed. Simonov had claimed a first flight in 1988, and some Western authors had assumed the participation of a vectoring aircraft in the ski-jump trials at Saki in the mid-1980s after they were shown a cleverly edited film at the 1991 Paris Air Salon.

The size and crude simplicity of the first 'Flanker' vectoring nozzle is apparent in these views of the Su-27LL-PS. The airflow is vectored by moving the upper and lower plates.

Su-27LMK-2405

Although it may look like an ordinary Su-27 with canard foreplanes and a few detail differences, the Su-27M was viewed by the OKB as representing an entirely new generation, introducing major improvements in a variety of areas. It was preceded by a host of testbeds trialling and verifying different elements of the proposed Su-27M configuration. The canard-equipped T10-24 has already been described, as has the thrust-vectoring Su-27LL-PS (T10-16). Arguably more important to the project was the Su-27LMK-2405 ('red 05', based at the LII Gromov Flight Research Centre), which was externally identical to the basic Su-27 fighter, but whose cockpit contained a

single CRT display screen of the type developed for the Su-27M, and for the Su-27IB, and which also had an F-16-style sidestick controller mounted on the starboard side console. The aircraft retained its conventional central control column as a back-up, and was used first to evaluate, and then develop, the sidestick and its use. The aircraft was also used as a testbed for the Mak IR-based missile approach warning system. The LMK laboratory was subsequently used to test fly an early version of the axisymmetric nozzle developed for the Su-37 in place of its starboard nozzle.

The Su-27LMK-2405 was a dedicated cockpit development aircraft for the Su-27M.

Su-27M (T10M, OKB Su-35)

The Su-27M was developed as a multi-role derivative of the basic Su-27, intended to allow Frontal Aviation units to replace aircraft like the MiG-23ML, Su-17 and MiG-27 with a single aircraft type, and to also replace the first-generation MiG-29 and Su-27. Mikoyan developed the MiG-29M to meet broadly the same requirement. Although planned to meet an all-weather precision attack role, the MiG-29M and Su-27M were expected to fulfil this task without prejudicing their air-to-air capabilities. The aircraft were designed to take advantage of technological advances such as improved radar and flight control systems to actually enhance their proficiency as air combat fighters.

When asked about the Su-27M at the 1992 Farnborough SBAC show, project head Nikolai Nikitin described the primary aim as having been to give "better dogfighting characteristics, with higher Alpha limits (up to 30°), improved high-Alpha handling, 3.5 times greater instability and lighter weight." He said that these requirements drove the increased use of composites and advanced materials, and the adoption of canard foreplanes and heavy fuel tanks in the tailfins.

The second Su-27M, 'Bort 707', retained the standard Su-27 tailfin shape, with cropped tips. Red outline stars were applied as a low-visibility national insignia.

In addition to the usual Su-27 mix of R-73 (AA-11 'Archer') IR-homing AAMs (up to six) and longer range IR- and semi-active radar homing R-27 (AA-10 'Alamo') AAMs (up to eight, or six with R-73s), the Su-27M could also carry up to 10 of the new R-77 (AA-12) medium-range inertial and active homing AAMs, using all but the wingtip stations for the much-vaunted 'AMRAAMski'. There are persistent reports that the Su-27M can carry the R-33 (AA-9 'Amos') or the related R-37, which are normally associated with the MiG-31 and MiG-31M. This seems unlikely, since these weapons offer no improvement over other weapons that are carried, and do not figure in any Sukhoi literature.

Most impressive of the weapons to be carried by the Su-27M in the air-to-air role was the Novator KS-172, then known simply as the AAM-L. This massive weapon was 6 m (24 ft 3 in) long and had a range in

excess of 400 km (250 miles) with its optional solid fuel booster fitted. The missile was a fire-and-forget weapon, employing inertial mid-course guidance (with optional command updates) and active terminal radar homing. According to a brochure being shown (but not released) at Farnborough, the Su-27M could carry seven of these awesome weapons.

By 1996 Sukhoi was displaying the Su-27M with mock-ups of a number of other proposed long- and medium-range AAMs, many of them based on advanced SAMs designed by Fakel. These include an active radar seeker-equipped version of the naval 9M96 (resembling the 9M330 SA-15) which apparently is a competitor to the

The first Su-27M seen in the West was 'Bort 703' which was more representative of the intended production configuration. It eventually received a spectacular and gaudy splinter camouflage.

R-77. Another missile (perhaps based on the 9M100) has tail controls only. The Fakel bureau is also working on an imaging infra-red short-range dogfight AAM, which may eventually replace the R-73. The R-73 remains arguably the best short-range AAM in service today, but a requirement for a successor has already been issued. The importance of a short-range IR- or IIR-homing AAM to the Su-35 is limited. The aircraft is simply too big and too expensive to be routinely risked in deliberate close-in engagements. The IR-homing AAM represents a last-ditch final line of defence, and the aircraft would normally rely on its BVR kill capability (or, if rules of engagement prohibited this) on a screen of cheaper close-in dogfighters.

In addition to its improved armament, sensors and radar, the Su-35 was capable of a much higher degree of autonomy from ground control, even in conditions of heavy ECM jamming. The aircraft was intended for co-ordinated group operations using datalinks (transmitting data at up to 4,800 bytes per second) and with automated target allocation between aircraft in the formation.

Although Nikitin was keen to stress the Su-27M's air-to-air capabilities, Simonov and others within the bureau stressed the aircraft's ability to carry air-to-surface weapons and to operate as a multi-role strike fighter, although they acknowledged that air-to-ground capability was 'secondary'. Nevertheless, primary air-to-surface weapons compatible with the Su-27M were revealed as the passive radar homing Kh-31P (AS-17 'Krypton'), the similarly guided ASM-M, the TV-guided Kh-29T (AS-14 'Kedge'), or the KAB-500T TV-guided bomb (the Su-27M could carry six of any of these weapons, below the nacelles and under the inboard and centre underwing pylons). Up to four GBU-1500T TV-guided bombs or similarly guided AGM-TVS missile (now known to be the Kh-59M or AS-18 'Kazoo') could be carried underwing, there being insufficient ground clearance below the nacelles.

In addition to its offensive armament, the Su-27M had a comprehensive defensive/offensive EW suite. The ECM system was designed to give individual or mutual (formation) protection against a wide range of threats, many of which were pre-programmed (512 sample threats were

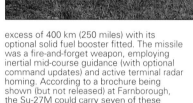

The Su-27M is intended to be a multi-role fighter, and when development is complete, the aircraft will have a formidable precision ground attack capability. 'Bort 703' is seen here carrying Kh-31 missiles and LGBs.

The Su-27M's primary role will be an air-to-air one, and this prototype is seen here carrying a load of dummy R-27, R-73 and R-77 air-to-air missiles. The type retains its internal 30-mm cannon.

carried onboard), including the ground-based Hawk, Patriot, Nike-Hercules, Roland, Crotale and Gepard, and air threats which included the F-14, F-15, F-16, F/A-18, B-1B and B-52. The passive RHAWS gave 360° coverage horizontally and 30° above and below the aircraft's flight path, covering the D-, E-, F-, G-, H-, I- and J-bands.

The internal directional EW jammer covered the H- and I- bands, in sectors through 45° on each side of the nose and tail horizontally, and through 30° horizontally. A supplementary ECM system covered the G- and J- bands, covering the same sectors horizontally, plus 30° below the aircraft and 5° above it. This also transmitted directional jamming signals. The onboard jammers could be augmented by either G- or J-band wingtip-mounted L-005 Sorbtsiya-S ECM pods. The aircraft has the usual mix of secure voice radios, scrambling and encoding equipment, with random frequency hopping for ECU.

The advanced 'Flanker' was formally redesignated Su-35 by the Sukhoi OKB during 1993, although they had been referring to the aircraft as the Su-35 since before the type's 1992 Western debut at Farnborough. The air force continues to designate the aircraft as the Su-27M.

The batch of Su-27M prototypes were preceded by an array of equipment and systems testbeds, some of which are described above. The first two prototypes were built in the bureau's own Moscow workshops and were followed by a batch of between five and nine aircraft built at Komsomolsk. The first prototype made its maiden flight on 28 June 1988, more than two years after the first MiG-29M, but still before the basic Su-27 was in really large-scale service.

When the Su-27M made its debut at Minsk Maschulische, Western observers were surprised at how similar the aircraft looked to the original Su-27. A contemporary RAF crew-room joke ran as follows: Question: "How do you tell the difference between the Su-27 and the Su-27M?" Answer: "If you see it before it shoots you down it's an Su-27, if you don't it's an Su-27M." In fact, the Su-27 was not as potent a threat as many feared. In a BVR engagement the Tornado ADV would probably even have enjoyed a slight edge, since the R-27 (AA-10 'Alamo') has proved to be less effective than was once predicted. Even at close range, the Su-27's much-vaunted agility is dependent on the aircraft being at low weight. Similarly, the Su-27M will not represent much of a threat until its weapons, radar and systems are properly integrated, and until the aircraft has been delivered to front-line units. There remains little prospect of a sufficient level of integration (let alone service deliveries) being achieved in the short term.

The first Su-27M prototype (T10M-1) was coded '706', and had standard Su-27-type tailfins and a single nosewheel. Despite the external similarities to the basic 'Flanker', it differed from the earlier Su-27 in a number of important respects. The increased use of

composites and of advanced welded aluminium-lithium alloy sub-assemblies was visible only from very close quarters and only in certain limited areas, although it was a very significant improvement. The combination of the tailfin tanks (on Komsomolsk-built prototypes) and the higher capacity offered by welded aluminium-lithium tanks gave the Su-27M a 1500-kg (3,300-lb) increase in internal fuel capacity, for example, while saving weight, reducing parts count and increasing the volume for avionics, systems and fuel.

Sukhoi's claims that the aircraft had a new digital quadruplex FBW flight control system were later proved to be less than accurate, reflecting intention rather than fact. Although signalling remained the same (analog), most of the Su-27M's control surfaces were modified in some way or other, with increased actuator power and on later aircraft with slight increases in control surface area. The aircraft also had canard foreplanes, although these were no different to those fitted to the Su-27K and Su-27IB.

Like most of the advanced 'Flanker' derivatives, the Su-35 has a retractable inflight-refuelling probe below the port side of the windscreen. Its installation necessitated the relocation of the electro-optical sensor ball from the centreline to the starboard side of the windscreen. The original simple IRST with collimated laser rangefinder was replaced by a new electro-optical sensor which also incorporated a TV channel and laser designation capability. This could cover an area ranging through 60° in azimuth, up to 60° in elevation above the nose, and 15° below. The new IRST can reportedly detect 'tail-on' jet targets at ranges of up to 50 km (30 miles), and 'head-on' subsonic targets at up to 10 km (6 miles). The laser channel is effective out to 3 km (2 miles). The Su-27M's ability to undertake extended-range/long-endurance flights was further enhanced by refinements to the ejection seat, which was raked back by 30° for increased *g* tolerance and improved comfort.

New sensors on the spine and wingtips serve the new IR-based Mak missile approach warning system, and the aircraft has Pastel RWRs in place of the Su-27's Beryoza. The Su-27M's new NIIP N-011 multi-mode radar necessitated the provision of a new nose radome, with no pitot probe. The N-011 radar uses a conventional (AN/APG-65 type) flat planar array antenna, rather than the dustbin-like twist cassegrain antenna used by the original 'Slot Back' radar. This allowed a more graceful radome shape, tapering more gently to the tip and being less bulbous further forward. The new radar had a claimed detection range of 216 nm (400 km; 249 miles) and offered the ability to simultaneously track up to 15 targets, engaging six of them at once. The radar also incorporated a host of useful air-to-ground modes.

The planned provision of an N-012 rear-facing radar (fitted to few of the Su-27M prototypes, if any) meant that the aircraft required a thicker tail sting, and the twin braking parachutes were relocated to a compartment above the spine. The N-012 can detect 3-m² (32-sq ft) targets out to between 30 and 50 km (18 and 31 miles), and the radar scans through 60° in azimuth and elevation.

It was expected that the Su-27M's wingtip hardpoints might be occupied by L-005 Sorbtsiya-S ECM pods, so the aircraft had an extra pair of hardpoints underwing. The same extra hardpoints were fitted to a number of other Su-27 sub-variants, including the Su-27K, the Su-27IB and the Su-30M. The increased number of pylons were apparent even on the first Su-27M prototype when it made its debut, although they were not loaded.

The second prototype Su-27M was almost certainly '707', which (like '706') has cropped Su-27-type fins and a single nosewheel. The first two aircraft were almost identically painted, with a red outline star on the fins and with the codes in dark blue outline form only. The second prototype was fitted with a modern glass cockpit, and had two MFDs on the

starboard side of the instrument panel only, with another on the starboard side console, and had a smaller CRT display on the port console. The first prototype may have had a 'glass' cockpit. In recent years, '707' has been one of a number of development workhorses flying from Akhtubinsk.

Subsequent Su-27M prototypes were built on production tooling at the Komsomolsk na Amur production plant and differed in detail to the two OKB-built prototypes. The first of these aircraft (T10M-3, coded '703') made its public debut at the 1992 Farnborough SBAC show. This aircraft was the first to feature the definitive Su-35 tailfin, with a square tip profile and an integral fuel tank in each fin box. The aircraft also introduced a new nose undercarriage unit, with twin nosewheels. This may well be derived from the nose gear fitted to the Su-27K, although it differs in detail, and reflects the Su-27M's higher operating weights. The new twin-wheel nose gear is not the same as that fitted to the Su-27IB, and retracts forward. The first Komsomolsk-built prototype's cockpit layout was initially similar to that of '707', but the main MFDs were later separated and were spaced widely to the left and right of the panel.

Some observers believe that there has been a total of 11 Su-27M prototypes, but this is believed to be a misconception based upon the '711' code of the latest prototype. As far as can be ascertained, the Komsomolsk prototype batch consisted of fewer than nine aircraft, and only '703', '707', '709', '710' and '711' have been seen in published photographs.

In February 1993 Major General Alexander Yanov, then director of operations and deputy chief of the Russian Federation Air Staff, announced that flight testing of the Su-27M was complete. This may have been true, insofar as basic aerodynamic testing was concerned, although the aircraft remained far from its intended production configuration, with delays still being experienced in many key systems. As late as 1996 there was no agreement as to which radar would be fitted

Intensive efforts to sell the Su-27M to the UAE saw some of the prototypes painted in an unusual desert splinter camouflage, seen here on 'Bort 709' during a demonstration at Zhukhovskii.

The Su-27M has an entirely new nose and radome shape, with no pitot on the radome tip, and with slightly more 'droop'.

to any production Su-27M.

When originally drawn up, the Su-27M was designed around the NIIP N-011 multi-mode radar, as described above. This radar was not (as has frequently been stated) an enlarged derivative of the Phazatron N-010 used by the MiG-29M, nor of the related Zhuk radar also produced by Phazatron. Originally proposed with a conventional planar-array antenna, the N-011 has subsequently gained a phased-array antenna, and performance figures have been revised upwards. The radar scans through 55° in elevation, and through 90° in azimuth. NIIP claims simultaneous tracking of up to 20 targets, and simultaneous engagement of up to eight targets. A target with a radar cross-section of 3 m² (32 sq ft) can now be detected at 140-160 km (90-100 miles).

The published performance figures of the N-011 are extremely impressive, but there have been suggestions that the radar has suffered development problems and that the figures represent something more akin to wishful thinking by NIIP marketeers than they do to reality. Whatever the truth,

Phazatron has proposed a Zhuk-27 radar for Su-27 upgrades and for the Su-27M, and has also submitted the new Zhuk PH, which offers an electronically scanned fixed phased-array antenna. Although its published performance figures are slightly lower than those given for the N-011, the Zhuk PH has attracted great support, and is believed to be closer to operational standards than the NIIP equipment. The Zhuk PH has wider scan limits than the phased array N-011, of 65° on each side of the aircraft centreline (though these could be further increased by mechanically moving the phased-array antenna). It also enjoys a claimed detection range of about 89-132 nm (165-245 km; 103-152 miles). The radar can track 24 targets simultaneously, and engage up to six or eight of them at once.

The competition offered by the Zhuk PH has reportedly prompted the NIIP to offer its own advanced alternative to the N-011. This radar (whose designation remains unknown) has a compound air-to-air/air-to-surface mode which allows the simultaneous search and tracking of airborne targets while

simultaneously undertaking ground mapping, allowing the presentation of a comprehensive air/surface target picture. The technical difficulties associated with such a system are huge, and it may be assumed that any radar with these capabilities remains a long way from service.

Radar was not the only definitive system still not flying in prototype Su-27Ms. It is now widely understood that most of the Su-27M prototypes were flying with an interim analog fly-by-wire control system,

and not with the MNPK Avionika digital control system intended for the production version. The definitive Su-27M flight control system had four longitudinal channels and three transverse, with the canard channel also available as a redundant channel if required. This more advanced system was fitted to at least one of the later Su-27M prototypes (perhaps by retrofit), but the aircraft using it was badly damaged in a landing accident during 1996. Oleg Tsoi experienced a yaw channel failure in flight, which led to severe banking oscillations. He was ordered to bail out, but instead flew the aircraft the 150 km (90 miles) to Akhtubinsk using the back-up rigid link FCS. The aircraft left the runway on landing and the left main gear collapsed. Damage was relatively minor, and the aircraft will be repaired and returned to flying status.

It was once believed that production Su-27Ms would be powered by AL-31FM or AL-35 turbofans, but the prototypes (apart from the single aircraft fitted with vectoring nozzles) are understood to have retained less powerful standard Su-27-type AL-31Fs. Despite the different designations, the engines are very similar, with extra thrust provided mainly by increased operating temperatures and small improvements in mass flow.

It is now apparently Simonov's intention that any production Su-27M will be fitted with vectoring engine nozzles (which are fitted to yet another version of the engine). Development of the thrust-vectoring version of the Su-27M began during the early 1990s, and by late 1993 Mikhail

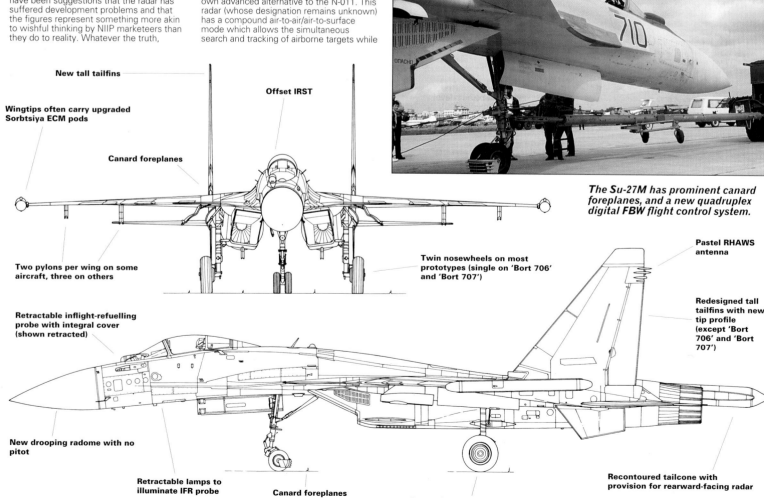

The Su-27M has prominent canard foreplanes, and a new quadruplex digital FBW flight control system.

New tall tailfins

Wingtips often carry upgraded Sorbtsiya ECM pods

Canard foreplanes

Offset IRST

Two pylons per wing on some aircraft, three on others

Twin nosewheels on most prototypes (single on 'Bort 706' and 'Bort 707')

Pastel RHAWS antenna

Retractable inflight-refuelling probe with integral cover (shown retracted)

Redesigned tall tailfins with new tip profile (except 'Bort 706' and 'Bort 707')

New drooping radome with no pitot

Retractable lamps to illuminate IFR probe

Canard foreplanes

Strengthened undercarriage

Recontoured tailcone with provision for rearward-facing radar

Simonov was optimistically promising that the thrust-vectoring prototype would be flying at Farnborough in 1994, to the obvious amazement of other senior figures within the OKB. The last Komsomolsk-built Su-35 (711) was chosen as the testbed for the new engine nozzles, and was soon redesignated (by the OKB at least) Su-37.

The Su-27M is now running very late, as a result of the many technical problems suffered and the slackening in funding following the end of the Cold War. Simonov's proud (1992) boast that the aircraft would "enter service in 1995" now has a terribly hollow ring to it, and it is unlikely that the aircraft will enter service before aircraft like the Eurofighter, if at all.

The Su-27M is now facing some competition from the resurrected MiG-29M (known to the MiG OKB as the MiG-33), which received funding for the completion of development during the summer of 1995. The smaller aircraft's low price tag, commonality with the existing MiG-29, strong export potential and apparent freedom from some of the problems plaguing the Su-27M have won it some powerful friends within the Russian air forces, while Mikoyan is now reportedly working on a further improved version with fully vectoring 3D nozzles (and perhaps also with canards, though some officials at Mikoyan have stated that these are probably unnecessary with a good thrust-vectoring system). This new aircraft (reportedly designated MiG-35) also has more powerful engines, a phased-array Zhuk PH radar and a longer-span, larger-area wing similar to that already flown on the MiG-29K. Some of the MiG-35's features may have been adopted from the stalled MiG 1-42, which awaits funding for its first flight, and which some expect to be too expensive to ever be procured.

Mikoyan and various suppliers have finally teamed together to form VPK MAPO (MIG MAPO or Military Industrial Group MAPO in English). This consortium is bigger than the original MiG-MAPO and forms a larger and more powerful organisation which enjoys greater influence and power, and which may challenge Sukhoi's domestic political pre-eminence during the late 1990s. While Sukhoi now faces increased political competition, its aircraft faces competition on technical grounds. The improvements to the MiG-35 give the aircraft better performance than the Su-27M (and a very similar level of capability), and the advanced

'Bort 710' was the penultimate Su-27M prototype, the last aircraft being converted to serve as the Su-37 testbed.

'Flanker' may finally find its position challenged by a derivative of its oldest rival.

Specification
Sukhoi Su-27M
Dimensions: fuselage length 22.183 m (72 ft 9 in); span over wingtip missile launch rails 14.7 m (48 ft 3 in); span over wingtip ESM pods 15.16 m (51 ft 2 in); overall height 6.340 m (20 ft 10 in)
Powerplant: two AL-31FM afterburning turbofans each rated at 130.43 kN (29,321 lb st) with afterburning, or thrust vectoring AL-37FUs with slightly lower ratings
Weights: normal take-off 26000 kg (57,320 lb); maximum take-off weight 34000 kg (74,955 lb)
Fuel and load: maximum internal fuel 13400 kg (29,541 lb); normal weapon load 1400 kg (3,068 lb) (air-to-air), or up to 8000 kg (17,640 lb) air-to-ground
g limits: +10 basic design gross weight
Performance: (estimated) maximum level speed 'clean' at high altitude 1,350 kt (2500 km/h; 1,550 mph); maximum level speed at sea level 790 kt (1450 km/h; 901 mph); limiting Mach No. 2.3; (estimated) service ceiling 18000 m (59,055 ft); range with 150 rounds of 30-mm ammunition, two R-73 and two R-27 missiles and internal fuel 2,280 nm (4200 km; 2,610 miles), 3,690 nm (6800 km; 4,225 miles) with same load and inflight-refuelling; radius with two wingtip R-73s and either three AAM-Ls or 10 RVV-AEs 760 nm (1400 km; 870 miles); lo-lo-lo radius with wingtip ESM pods, two R-73s

outboard and two AGM-TVS ASMs 400 nm (730 km; 454 miles); hi-lo-hi radius with the same load 710 nm (1310 km; 814 miles); hi-lo-hi radius of action, with two R-73s, two Kh-29Ts, two Kh-31Ps and two wingtip ESM pods 615 nm (1135 km; 705 miles); lo-lo-lo radius of action (same load) 340 nm (630 km; 391 miles); required runway length 1200 m (3,937 ft)

Above: Su-27M prototype 'Bort 709' is seen during a tour of Africa.

Below: Here '709' conducts a flying display, with local imitations of the 'Smokewinder' smoke generator on each wingtip being employed to highlight the type's agility.

Su-37

The latest Su-27 variant is a derivative of the Su-27M equipped with thrust-vectoring engine nozzles. The prototype was actually the last Su-27M prototype (which may already have flown quite extensively with 'standard' powerplants installed). This thrust-vectoring Su-27M may be nothing more than an ambitious private venture by the OKB, and there may be no Russian air force order for the thrust-vectoring model. It seems unlikely that any Russian air force designation has been allocated, though the Su-37 tag is probably appropriate for export aircraft.

Photographs of '711' with its new nozzles began appearing during 1995, the new engines having been installed in July that year. The nozzles were integral with the engines, which were modified versions of the standard Su-27's AL-31F powerplant and are designated as AL-37FUs. The nozzles are actuated by two pairs of hydraulic cylinders per engine, although a production engine would use pressurised fuel as an actuating fluid. The production engine installation is also expected to incorporate an emergency nozzle actuation system using pneumatics. In all versions of the AL-37FU, failure of a single hydraulic cylinder automatically returns the nozzle to its original position. Perhaps the most difficult design problem to overcome was the sealing of the junction between the fixed rear section of the jet pipe and the moving section of the nozzle, where temperatures reach 2000° C (3,630 °F), and where pressures can be as high as seven atmospheres.

The AL-37FU (FU standing for Forsazh Upravleniye, or afterburner-controlled) is not just an AL-31 with vectoring nozzles; it also has an entirely new fan and forward section. The new fan uses new blade technology, which reportedly reduces vibration. The AL-37FU has a four-stage LP compressor, a nine-stage HP compressor, an annular combustion chamber and single-stage HP and LP turbines, and is of modular design. New measures have been taken to reduce IR signature in dry thrust, and they can also be applied to the baseline AL-31F.

The AL-37FU has a claimed TBO of 1,000 hours, although the nozzle is cleared for only 250 hours. Nozzle lifetime will be increased to 500 hours after additional testing, and should then be increased further, not least when the steel circular turning unit is replaced by a titanium component in production versions of the engine. Thrust of the AL-37FU is reportedly 83.36 kN (18,740 lb) dry, and 142.2 kN (30,800 lb st) in afterburner. Specific fuel consumption is variously claimed as 0.685

Above: The Su-37 taxis out at Zhukhovskii for its first thrust vectoring tests, during April 1997.

Right: The Su-37 is based on the last Su-27M prototype, and has AL-37FU engines and a sidestick controller.

or 0.677 kg/kgf.hr. Only three of the new engines had been built by the start of 1997 (one for bench tests, the other two for the prototype), but design documents for the engine were available at the end of 1996.

The aircraft itself had been resprayed in a disruptive sand-and-brown splinter camouflage during its long lay-up, and bore the logos of Sukhoi, Saturn Lyul'ka, the NIIP, Avionika, RPKB and FPI below the port side of the cockpit canopy, with a red-edged blue star on the lower part of the fin, on which was superimposed the Sukhoi logo, and from which flowed a white, blue and red tricolour stripe. It is though that any production version willy have four CRT display screens in a 'T' on the main panel. They will display all major aircraft, weapon and navigation functions. If so, this will mark the first appearance of the definitive Su-35 cockpit, first illustrated in the 1992 Sukhoi brochure. Reports that the aircraft has colour LCD displays supplied by Sextant Avionique are certainly erroneous, although the inclusion of such equipment may be planned for the production variant.

As seen in a Sukhoi promotional video, the Su-37 prototype has a sidestick controller in place of the usual centre stick, and may also use a strain-gauge (pressure-to-throttle) non-moving engine controller. The aircraft has CRT display screens on each side of the main panel, with conventional flight instruments in the centre, above the third display screen. The thrust vectoring controls are fully integrated into the quadruplex digital flight control system, and operate in two modes. In the manual mode the pilot directly selects nozzle position, while in the automatic mode the nozzles are actuated to direct the thrust vector according to inputs to the flight control system.

The early photos showed the aircraft with its nozzles drooping downwards, but there was little evidence that the installation was complete, with no sign of the aircraft having operable nozzles. The aircraft's absence from the 1994 Farnborough SBAC show was suddenly less inexplicable. Even with the new nozzles fitted, it took months of intensive effort to integrate them with the flight control system.

The aircraft finally flew with its new nozzles on 2 April 1996, although they were almost certainly initially locked in position, fore and aft. There have been repeated claims that the Su-27M's vectored nozzles will eventually be actuated in both pitch and yaw, although this would seem to be ruled out by the close proximity of the central tail sting to the engine nozzles. Unless the nozzles can move differentially in yaw, any sideways movement would result in blast damage to this tailcone, which will supposedly house the Su-27M's N-012 rearward-facing radar. It may be that only one nozzle will operate in yaw at any one time, toeing out from the aircraft centreline, while both will move, symmetrically or differentially, in pitch.

At the June 1996 Moscow Aero and Industry Engine exhibition Victor Chepkin, the designer general of the Saturn Lyul'ka OKB, revealed that the engines fitted to the

The Su-37 made its public debut at Zhukhovskii, during the annual Mosaero show. The aircraft demonstrated extraordinary new manoeuvres which have yet to be emulated by any Western aircraft. It demonstrated an astonishing ability to 'point' the nose away from the direction of flight, for sustained periods.

Above: The Su-37's thrust vectoring nozzles have allowed it to imitate many of the manoeuvres flown by the X-31, as well as some unique moves of its own.

The Su-37's vectoring nozzles are understood to operate only in two dimensions (up/down), with the proximity of the tailcone and tailplanes preventing movement in yaw. Operation of the nozzles is integrated into the flight control system software.

first Su-37 had nozzles which moved only in pitch, due to the difficulty of integrating TVC (thrust vectoring control) with the FCS and due to the limited scope for movement in the yaw plane imposed by the tail sting. Chepkin claimed that a three-axis pitch and yaw nozzle had been developed and was already "in his pocket", presumably having been developed for the MiG 1-42. At the same exhibition, it was claimed that the Su-27M's nozzles (whose freedom of movement in pitch goes from -15° to +15°, at a rate of 30° per second, and not from +20° to -20° as hitherto claimed) had already been actuated in flight, and were fully integrated with the new digital fly-by-wire control system.

June 1996 also marked the first time that doubt was publicly stated regarding fitment of the series production Su-27M with TVC. There is reportedly no timetable for handing over '711' for Russian air force testing. There are suggestions that the thrust vectoring nozzle trials were funded by the OKB and by general research subsidies, rather than by the air force. This casts doubt on Mikhail Simonov's frequent assertions that production 'Su-35s' would 'definitely' feature vectoring engine nozzles.

Whatever doubts exist about the thrust-vectoring Su-27M's production prospects, the type made an impressive public debut at Tushino on 18 August 1996. Sukhoi had reportedly hoped to display the aircraft for the first time on 14 June at the Moscow Aeroengine show, but this event was only two days before Russia's elections and no VIPs were available to attend.

The aircraft completed 50 flights before its appearance at the 1996 Farnborough SBAC air show, mainly in the hands of Yevgeni Frolov and Igor Votintsev. Frolov worked up an impressive display routine (clearly influenced by that of the Rockwell X-31 at Paris in 1995) which he was able to

demonstrate at Farnborough. The manoeuvres were predictable and repeatable enough to be used in a low-level display routine, demonstrating Frolov's confidence in the aircraft's handling characteristics, and in the integration of the vectoring nozzles with the control system. Unfortunately, Frolov found it difficult to stay true to his display, occasionally descending below his minimum display height and sometimes straying over the crowd line; this might have indicated that handling was not quite as predictable as with the standard Su-27 or Su-27M. New manoeuvres demonstrated at Farnborough included the Kulbit (Circle), in which the aircraft rotated its nose through 360° after pitching up into the well-known Cobra, then recovering to straight and level flight. The aircraft was also able to recover from a tailslide by rolling into an entirely different plane, and performed a version of the X-31's remarkable Mongoose.

Saturn/Lyul'ka claims that the vectoring AL-37FU is fully interchangeable with the baseline AL-31, meaning that any Su-27 can be retrofitted with the new engine, although

it is uncertain how well the thrust vectoring can be incorporated in the old-style flight control system software. Two-seat Su-30MKs for India are scheduled to be the first early-generation Su-27s to be fitted with the new engine.

It is unknown if the vectoring nozzles are a feature of the aircraft which first used the Su-37 designation. In the West, the Su-37 tag was first (wrongly) assigned to the short-lived lightweight single-engined S-37 tactical fighter project (which never had an Su- series designator). It was later reported to have been assigned to an advanced Su-27M derivative offered to the UAE for use in the strike role. This was reportedly a dedicated strike version of the Su-35, but the ways in which it differed from the basic Su-27M or its Su-35 export version have not been specified. It is probable that the aircraft never got much further than a vague promise by the OKB to produce a ground attack dedicated version of the Su-35 for the UAE if required.

Specification
Dimensions: fuselage length 22.2 m (72 ft

10 in); span over wingtip missile launch rails 14.7 m (48 ft 3 in); span over wingtip ESM pods 15.16 m (49 ft 9 in); area 62 m² (667.4 sq ft); overall height 6.4 m (21 ft)
Powerplant: two AL-37FU each rated at 83.36 kN (18,739 lb st) dry and 142.2 kN (31,966 lb st) with afterburning
Weights: normal take-off 26000 kg (57,320 lb); maximum take-off weight 34000 kg (74,955 lb)
Fuel and load: normal weapon load 1400 kg (3,068 lb) (air-to-air), or up to 8000 kg (17,640 lb) air-to-ground
g limits: +9 at basic design gross weight
Performance: (estimated) maximum level speed 'clean' at altitude 1,350 kt (2500 km/h; 1,555 mph); maximum level speed at sea level 760 kt (1400 km/h; 870 mph); maximum rate of climb at sea level 230 m/sec (45,275 ft/min); service ceiling 18800 m (61,680 ft); range with 150 rounds of 30-mm ammunition, two R-73 and two R-27 missiles and internal fuel 2,100 nm (3880 km; 2,410 miles), 3,515 nm (6500 km; 4,040 miles) with same load and one inflight-refuelling; required runway length 1200 m (3,937 ft)

Undesignated two-seat Su-37 strike version

In late 1996 it was revealed that the Sukhoi OKB was developing a new two-seat strike version of the Su-37, which would be

entirely different from the thrust-vectoring, canard-equipped, two-seat strike derivative of the Su-30 being developed for India. The

core of the new variant lay in the NIIP-developed phased-array radar proposed for the single-seat Su-27M and Su-37 and

reportedly optimised for simultaneous operation in both air-to-air and air-to-ground modes. **Jon Lake**

Above: Originally to have retired in 1993, the Aéronavale's Crusaders soldier on as the service's only air defence assets. Also capable of carrying Sidewinders and MATRA R.530s, the Crusaders usually use R.550 Magic missiles.

Below: Deck crew prepare a Super Etendard for launch, attaching the catapult bridle to underwing hooks. The aircraft is from 59 Escadrille de Servitude, the Hyères-based training squadron recently moved to Landivisiau.

Above: Although hampered by a light weapon load, the Super Etendard can nevertheless carry a wide variety of stores. In addition to bombs and rockets, it can carry one AM39 Exocet anti-ship missile or an ASMP nuclear stand-off missile.

Below: 16 Flottille, shore-based at Landivisiau, maintains eight upgraded Etendard IVPMs. These elderly warriors continue to provide reconnaissance for the fleet. This aircraft carries mission marks from service over Bosnia.

Aéronautique Navale

French Naval Aviation

Presently getting by with a series of minor upgrades to its ancient aircraft, the Aéronautique Navale is a force in limbo. In the next century the capabilities of this professional and highly-motivated organisation will have been transformed beyond recognition following the introduction of Hawkeye, NH 90, Rafale M and new ships.

Below: Over 40 years after its first flight, the Br.1050 Alizé is still an important part of the Aéronavale fleet. Two flottilles operate 24 aircraft, these aircraft being from the Atlantic coast unit, 4 Flottille at Lann-Bihoué. This unit is scheduled to be the operator of the E-2C Hawkeye, receiving its first aircraft in 1998.

Left: France received 42 F-8E(FN) Crusaders in the mid-1960s, this variant featuring blown flaps to enable the aircraft to land safely on the small French carriers. Life extension and upgrade programmes have kept the Crusaders flying, including the fitment of parts taken from retired US Navy F-8Js. The current force numbers 17 aircraft, all of which have been through a recent upgrade programme devised by Dassault but undertaken by the navy's workshops at Cuers. Modernised aircraft are designated F-8P (P=prolonge).

Below: This busy deck scene on Clemenceau shows Alizés from 6F, a Crusader from 12F, Super Etendards from 59S and 17F, and an Etendard IVPM from 16F.

Above: The remaining Crusaders fly with 12F, which usually has 14 aircraft operational at any time. Until 1979 14F also flew the F-8, and it is this unit which will be the first to get Rafale M.

Below: A 'Sue' from 59S displays its A-frame arrester hook and ventral airbrake while trapping. Fast-jet pilots train in the US before joining 59S for French carrier training.

Above: With everything 'down and dirty', a Super Etendard approaches Clemenceau. The elevators are fully up, and the tailplane trimmed to the full nose-up position.

Right: The cross of Lorraine badge identifies 6 Flottille, based at Nîmes/Garons. This unit's Alizés have a dual operational and training tasking.

Below: All 'Sues' have undergone the SEM (Super Etendard Modernisé) programme. The current force numbers 53 aircraft.

Top: The F-8P upgrade
programme gave the
Crusader some new
avionics and structural
improvements. The most
obvious addition was that
of fin-tip radar warning
receiver antennas.

Above: In addition to its
primary strike/attack role,
the Super Etendard can be
used in an emergency as a
fighter (with R.550 Magic
missiles) or as a tanker,
equipped with a
centreline buddy pod. The
SEM upgrade programme
replaced the original
Agave radar with
Anemone, new avionics
and cockpit systems
(including new INS, wide-
angle HUD and NVG
compatibility), extra
fuselage stores pylon and
minor structural work for
service until at least 2005.

Above: SA 316B and SA 319
Alouette IIIs are used for a
variety of support and rescue
duties. This example flies with
23S from Saint Mandrier,
responsible for support of
carrier operations in the
Mediterranean. An Alouette is
attached to the carrier for
plane-guard duties. The badge
depicts a seagull dropping a
lifebuoy.

Right: 23 Escadrille also
operates the AS 365F Dauphin 2
on general support duties. The
aircraft are winch-equipped for
SAR duties. The Aéronavale
also flies the AS 565MA Panther
(with 35F and 36F).

Above and above right: The Alizé remains an effective ASW platform thanks to continuing updates. 6 Flottille will continue operations with 14 aircraft until Foch decommissions in 2005.

Land-based patrol assets consist of four flottilles. 23F and 24F at Lann-Bihoué, and 21F (right) at Nîmes/Garons fly the second-generation Atlantique 2, while 22F at Nîmes/Garons continues to operate the original Atlantic 1 (right). The Atlantique 2 is a new-build airframe with a new ASW suite, including a Tango FLIR in an undernose turret, Iguane retractable search radar, Arar 13 A ESM, and Mk 46 or Murène torpedoes.

Left: From 1990 the Alizé fleet was cycled through the Cuers workshop to receive new decoy systems, a new data processing system (with **SAGEM MTP16** microcomputer) and other mission avionics improvements. More recently the fleet has received the Thomson **TTD** Optronique Chlio system. This thermal imager was developed from the Atlantique's Tango unit, and will enhance surface detection capability at night or in bad weather.

Below: The elderly SA 321 Super Frelon has not performed its ASW design task for several years, but 17 are maintained for general transport and rescue duties. The fleet is split between Atlantic coast (32F at Lanvéoc-Poulmic, illustrated) and Mediterranean (33F at Saint Mandrier).

Above: ASW/ASV cover is provided by the 30-plus Westland Lynx **HAS.Mk 2(FN)/4(FN)** in service with 31F at Saint Mandrier and 34F at Lanvéoc. They all wear a two-tone light grey camouflage, and have been updated with **BERP** rotor blades.

Left: The Dauphin/Panther family is gradually replacing the Alouette III as the main support helicopter type, flying a variety of support and rescue tasks from Lanvéoc and Saint Mandrier. Variants in use are the AS 365F, AS 365N and AS 565MA. Two Dauphin 2s are flown on behalf of the coast guard.

Below left: The Aéronavale operates a number of **SOCATA MS.880B** Rallyes as grading trainers (alongside Mudry CAP 10Bs with 51S at Rochefort/Soubise) and for providing air experience. This aircraft performs the latter task, assigned to 50S at Lanvéoc. Additional light aircraft are flown on communications duties in support of the Cuers workshop.

Below: The Super Frelon's varied duties encompass SAR work, vertical replenishment of ships at sea and marine assault. The type will fly into the next century, its intended replacement being the NH 90. These are from 33F.

Above: Sixteen *EMBRAER EMB-121AN* Xingus are flown by *2S, 11S, 52S* and the *ERCE* (ferry squadron) on general liaison and multi-engine training duties.

Right: The Morane Saulnier *MS.760 Paris* has been used for many years as a trainer and liaison aircraft, but its days in service with *57S* are numbered, and it is to be withdrawn. The squadron will continue to fly the Mystère *10MER*.

Right: Fourteen Nord *262Es* are in service, used primarily to train future patrol crews (with *56S* at Nîmes/Garons). The aircraft are equipped with training consoles, *OMERA ORB* 32 search radar under the fuselage, Arar 12 *ESM* and Omega navigation. Additional 262Es fly with 2S at Lann-Bihoué and 3S at Hyères on coastal patrol duties.

Below: To counter the ravages of overwater flying, a 56S Nord 262E receives a washdown. In addition to the radar-equipped Nords, the Aéronavale flies 11 further Frégates for transport duties with 2S, 3S and the ferry unit.

Thailand

In recent years Thailand's multi-faceted military aviation forces have undergone a gradual, and continuing, overhaul. New aircraft and new capabilities have been introduced in response to growing security concerns and a rise in regional tensions. This *Air Power Analysis* charts the changes, both in the three armed forces and Thailand's substantial paramilitary aviation units.

Royal Thai AF (Kongtap Agard Thai)

Surrounded by the politically volatile countries of Burma, Laos, Cambodia and Vietnam, and in immediate proximity to China, the ancient Kingdom of Thailand – known as Siam until 1939 – is unenviably placed as the gateway to much of prosperous Southeast Asia. Its vulnerability has been emphasised by the supply of advanced weapons systems from Russia, including MiG-29s and Sukhoi Su-27s, to its neighbouring states of Malaysia, China and Vietnam; this in turn has required a new level of re-equipment and expansion of Thailand's already large armed forces. Thailand is the first Far Eastern country to acquire the multi-role F/A 18 Hornet and LTV's Corsair strike-fighter, as well as a V/STOL aircraft-carrier and its accompanying Harrierrs, as part of ambitious and correspondingly expensive long-term defence plans.

Unlike its neighbouring countries, with their British or French colonial histories, Thailand (Muang Thai), which straddles the gulf bearing its name, has a long tradition of independence. Remarkably, this did not prevent it from joining the Allied cause during World War I, to which the Royal Siamese Flying Corps contributed about 100 pilots for training in France from July 1917, although it was formed only on 23 March 1914. With subsequent mainly French and American equipment, the renamed Royal Aeronautical Service became the Royal Siamese Air Force when granted independent status by Royal decree in April 1937, and the RTAF in 1939.

Limited training and transport operations were allowed to continue following the largely unresisted Japanese occupation of Thailand from December 1941.

Post-war reconstruction and expansion achieved with the help of an RAF mission was followed by major reorganisation on US lines in the early 1950s with the arrival of an American Military Air Advisory Group, as part of the State Department's policies of countering Communist expansion in the Far East.

Initial US military aid included the supply of 100 Grumman F8F-1D Bearcats, plus 29 earlier -1B versions for use as spares, as well as 138 T-6s, and a small batch of Curtiss SB2C-5 Helldivers for the Thai navy. Ten Grumman U-2C/S-2F Trackers also delivered to the navy in 1952 were transferred to RTAF operation for the next 11 years because of a Thai naval mutiny. Cessna L-19s and Piper L-18s were provided for army use, together with substantial numbers of support aircraft and helicopters. As a pending partner in the Southeast Asia Treaty Organisation (SEATO),

Thailand received its first jet aircraft in February 1957, in the form of six Lockheed T-33As and 30 Republic F-84G Thunderjets.

These were followed in 1961-62 by 47 North American F-86F and 17 later F-86L Sabres, as well as three squadrons with 88 North American T-28D armed trainers for counter-insurgency (COIN) operations, plus eight Cessna T-37Bs and various support aircraft and helicopters. Among these were 22 Fairchild C-123B Provider tactical transports, later followed by 24 jet-boosted C-123Ks.

In the early 1970s, a few Helio U-10 Couriers were joined by 13 of the similar short-field but more potent Fairchild AU-23A Peacemaker (licence-built Pilatus PC-6s) with light armament for mini-gunship roles, supplemented by the first 16 of 32 OV-10C Bronco COIN aircraft delivered in 1971 and 1973. Now operated by 411 Squadron from Chiang Mai in northern Thailand, the 19 remaining heavily-armed OV-10s are popular with the RTAF, which was unable to buy more examples due to the end of production. AU-23A deliveries began in 1973 through the USAF Pave Coin programme to 202 Squadron, and were followed by 20 more, including some for the Police Air Wing, ordered in 1974 for $12 million and delivered from late 1975.

After the RTAF's 1977 reorganisation, the AU-23As equipped one of three squadrons in 2 Wing at Lop Buri, alongside Sikorsky S-58Ts and Bell UH-1Hs for COIN and heli-support roles, and are now operated by 202 and 531 Squadrons, replacing Cessna O-1s in the latter unit. COIN missions were also undertaken by 18 ex-South Vietnamese air force Cessna A-37B Dragonflys delivered at about the same time to 43 Squadron, before transferring to 211 Squadron at Ubon Ratchathani to replace NAA T-28Ds until their withdrawal in late 1993. Eighteen PT6T-3 Twin-Pac turboshaft-powered S-58Ts were operated by 201 Squadron after conversion from CH-34Cs by Thai-Am from September 1977, for continuous combat/SAR service to date.

In 1967-69, the RTAF began receiving its first Northrop F-5 fighter-bombers, comprising 11 F-5As, four RF-5As for tactical reconnaissance, and two two-seat F-5B combat trainers for 13 Squadron, followed by another seven F-5As (five as attrition replacements) and two F-5Bs from USAF sources in 1971-73. Air defence roles were allocated to the first 17 uprated F-5Es, with their short-range Emerson APQ-59(V)3 fire-control radar, and three F-5F trainers ordered for $80 million in 1976 for 102 Squadron, followed by

another similar batch delivered to equip 403 Squadron. Two more F-5Bs were acquired from Malaysian surplus stocks in September 1982.

Vietnam and after

At the height of its war with Vietnam in mid-1973, the US had about 45,000 military personnel and no fewer than 660 aircraft at Tha airbases in central and eastern Thailand, including Korat, U-Tapao, Ubon and Udon Thani. These bases were greatly expanded during this period, from runway extensions to improved infrastructures for the operations against Vietnam, and military aid was intensified to the Thai armed forces.

Of equal importance was the RTAF's adoption of the USAF's unit structures, tactical doctrines, training techniques and support organisation, which over the long term have led to its continued reliance on mainly American equipment, particularly for its combat elements. Following the US withdrawal from Vietnam and the Communist take-over of Cambodia, Thailand adopted a nominally neutral political stance. This resulted in the withdrawal of all but 100 US advisers by 1977, and the ending of American military aid in the following year. The RTAF disbanded its Tactical Air Command in October 1977, after which time all wings were administered from air force HQ.

Squadrons were redesignated with three-figure numbers, the first of which also identified its wing. Some squadrons were elevated to wing status. The squadron numbers also feature as the first three of the RTAF's five-digit aircraft serials, the remaining two comprising individual identities within their units. Each aircraft carries additional letter/number serials in Thai characters on the fuselage, indicating role function, type and individual identities, and the year of service entry in relation to the Buddhist calendar. For example, the Pilatus PC-9 01 of the RTAF's flying training school carries the Thai serial of T.19-1/34, which indicates that it is the first example of the 19th trainer type to enter service, which was in 2534, or 1995 in the Christian calendar. Role function prefix letters, which encompass virtually all types ever operated by the Thai military service, comprise BK for fighters (the F-16 being BK.19); BT for bombers; BF, BJF, BKF or BTF for trainers (J or K apparently indicating armament capabilities, and T, reconnaissance); BPT for aerial mapping aircraft; BT or BJT for utility/observation; BL, BJL or BTL for transports; BS for light aircraft; and H or HPT for helicopters.

More US equipment

Despite brief neutralism after the Communist take-over of Vietnam, some purchases of US equipment continued through FMS sources. Additional emergency aid was provided by the State Department when Vietnamese occupation troops crossed the Thai border from Cambodia in June 1980. US equipment received in that year included three C-130Hs (60101-3) to equip 601 Squadron at Don Muang. In April 1983 this unit received another C-130H, this time a stretched C-130H-30 (60104), and in late 1990 a delivery of four included three C-130H-30s (60105-8). Arms deliveries were accelerated in April 1983 after the Vietnamese continued pursuing Cambodian Khmer Rouge guerrillas into Thai territory, resulting in the resumption of US military aid programmes. Guerrilla activity within Thailand was then considerably reduced, although political

ove: This F-16A wears the red lightning bolt badge 103 Squadron, the RTAF's first Fighting Falcon uadron, which was established in 1988/89. wever, it was not until 1991 that 103 Sqn received full complement of F-16As.

Right: In 1995 Thailand began to take delivery of a second batch of F-16A/Bs, allowing the the formation of a second F-16 unit, 403 Squadron, in 1996. The unit's badge features a cobra.

e RTAF uses the Czech-built Aero L-39ZA Albatros as a d-in fighter trainer, with a secondary attack role. Three uadrons are equipped with the L-39, including 4 Squadron (as seen above) and 102 Squadron (right).

ove: The RTAF's F-5E aggressor rce, 904 Sqn, is based at Don Muang. tailcode is derived from Crown ince Vajirarongleon Mahidol's name.

Right: This F-5A carries the winged demon badge of 231 Squadron, Wing 23, which is based at Udon Thani in northeastern Thailand.

ove: These Surat Thani-based 5Es of 711 Sqn, Wing 71, wear the w-style RTAF three-tone mouflage and three-letter tailcodes erived from the base name).

Below: This specially-marked F-5E is the personal mount of the Crown Prince. It is stationed at Khon Kaen, as part of the RTAF Royal Flight.

Above: This camouflaged F-5A is one of those currently in service with 231 Squadron. All RTAF F-5As are allocated to this unit.

Below: The bulk of the RTAF's transport assets are based at RTAFAB Bangkok/Don Muang. C-130Hs (seen here) and C-130H-30s are operated by 601 Squadron.

instability continued during the 1980s with two unsuccessful coup attempts.

In other border clashes, an RTAF Northrop F-5 and a Thai army Cessna U-17 liaison aircraft were shot down by Cambodian forces in 1986-87, while another RTAF F-5 and an OV-10C were lost to Laotian SA-7s and ground fire in February 1988, before a ceasefire. Other guerrilla forces were active in northern Burma (Myanmar). It was therefore hardly surprising that in January 1987 Thailand finally abandoned any vestige of neutralism by agreeing to US proposals for the establishment over a five-year period of a $100 million stockpile for emergency use, mainly comprising small arms and mortar ammunition.

F-16 acquisition and modernisation

Earlier, Thailand had sought higher-performance combat aircraft from the US to match the threat from Mach 2 MiG-21s in the area, although initially the Pentagon was prepared to release only the J79-powered F-16/79 F-X for Third World sales. With no takers for this hybrid prototype, however, following its mid-1984 rejection by Thailand, the US then accepted the RTAF's intention to order 16 (of a required 20) F-16A/Bs, costing $475 million.

Because of funding restrictions, the RTAF's initial order through the FMS Peace Naresuan programme in April 1985 comprised only eight F100-PW-220-powered Block 15 F-16As and four F-16Bs in a Bht8.9 billion ($317.9 million) package. Delivery was scheduled between June 1988 and May 1989. Options for the remaining six F-16As were taken up in mid-1987 for a further cost of $115 million, to give 103 Squadron at Korat its full aircraft complement by May 1991. A further $20 million was allocated for infrastructure improvements at Korat, including the provision of hardened aircraft shelters. An Air Combat Manoeuvring Instrumentation System was built at Korat by the US Cubic Corporation from a $28 million contract in 1985, to maintain operational proficiencies.

Although they retain the original Westinghouse APG-66S fire-control radar for primary air defence roles, the Thai F-16s are being operated with several non-standard weapon systems, apart from Paveway II-equipped Mk 82 500-lb LGBs (GBU-10s). These include Rafael Python 3 AAMs, augmented from 1992 by four Thomson-TRT Defense ATLIS-II automatic TV-tracking laser designator/range-finding pods. In November 1993 six Rubis low-altitude night/bad-weather navigation pods were also ordered from Thomson-TRT for the RTAF F-16s. Originally developed for French air force Dassault Mirage F1CRs, Rubis was integrated into the F-16's weapons systems with assistance from Lockheed.

Air defence system build-up

Events in Southeast Asia increased the urgency of Thailand's plans for a comprehensive air defence organisation, particularly along the Cambodian border, for detection and interception of frequent Vietnamese incursions into Thai airspace. With US assistance, this was started in early 1985 with a $435 million 10-year programme, as a follow-on to the 1980 acquisition of two Westinghouse TPS-43 three-dimensional surveillance and tracking ground radars.

One of the first contracts was for $17 million with Sanders Associates in the US for a Thai army low-level air defence system (ThaiLLADS) using AN/MOQ-5 radars. 1985 also saw a $10 million order for the first of three planned Westinghouse TPS-70 radars for delivery by October 1986. Two General Electric AN/FPS-117 radars were then added from a late 1989 $43 million order, followed by two long-range GEC Marconi 743D Martello units in late 1990.

A contract worth $71 million was awarded to the US Systems Development Corporation in early 1986, for command, control and information installations linking the five radar stations in the central region to RTAF HQ, as the first phase of the Royal Thai Air Defence System (RTADS). Following 1990 completion by Unisys of an Air and Sector Operations Centre in Bangkok, and similar facilities at 11 other sites, the US company was awarded a $15 million contract for Thailand's Joint Air Defence Digital Information Network (JADDIN). Extending coverage mainly to northeast Thailand, along the borders with Laos and Cambodia, this integrated system for the exchange and display of digital data, air tracks, and C² information was completed between May 1991 and late 1993.

Westinghouse Electronic Systems Group was selected in September 1993 for the next phase of the Thai Air Defence System, known as RTADS III. This was to extend early warning and defence coverage 250 miles (400 km) to the south, from radar sites at Hat Yai, Koh Samui, Phuket and the HQ at Surat Thani, for which a Bht4.59 billion ($184 million) contract was eventually signed with Westinghouse in mid-1994. In addition to three Westinghouse ARSR-4-based W-2100 or FPS-130 long-range L-band radars, this included advanced data-processing equipment and C² ground stations, linked with Thailand's air defence missile batteries, for completion by 1999.

As an integral part of the RTADS network, 10-20 of Canada's Oerlikon Aerospace shelter-mounted eight-missile ADATS (air defence and anti-tank system) were ordered for the RTAF in late 1993. They were planned to operate in conjunction with two existing Oerlikon-Contraves SkyGuard fire-control radar units for target acquisition and tracking, each controlling four Arrow firing units with twin 30-mm Mauser F AA gun units on Kuka towed mounts, delivered from Germany in 1988.

SAM and AEW systems

Thailand's air defence missile system was augmented by a mid-1996 RTAF order from Ericsson Microwave Systems in Sweden for truck-mounted Giraffe 40 articulated ground search and C³I radars. This order was associated with another to Sweden in October 1996, from the RTAF to Bofors AB, of the Celsius Group, for RBS-70 Mk II man-portable SAM systems. An initial Bht98 million ($3.83 million) contract was placed for three launchers, 15 RBS-70 missiles and a training simulator, for air base defence, with deliveries to be completed in 1997.

In January 1991 the RTAF sought Cabinet approval to buy four Grumman E-2C aircraft for about $300 million, to extend coverage of its ground-based air defences, particularly in the south. Some $140 million more was required for building associated ground support facilities, communications and infrastructure between 1991 and 1996. No finance was available at that time, however, and although scaled-down proposals comprising three E-2Cs for overall costs of $382 million, for both air and ground components, were embodied in a Pentagon letter of offer and acceptance (LOA) in early 1992, even this exceeded RTAF resources. The requirement remains, consideration being given to acquiring a single C-130 converted for AWACS roles, but no funding has so far been forthcoming.

RTAF expansion sought

F-16 procurement marked the first stage of ambitious expansion plans in the mid-1980s to meet long-term acquisition targets, subject to fairly stringent funding restraints. At least 18 more multi-role fighters and two squadrons of long-range attack aircraft were the most immediate priority. Five new tactical-reconnaissance aircraft were also required to replace the ageing RT-33s, together with another four C-130Hs, increasing Thailand's total to 12, plus 16 transports to replace C-47s and C-123s.

Plans for new advanced trainers or surplus F-5Bs were deferred with the purchase from Singapore of 20 T-33As in 1986. They followed 12 T-33s acquired from France in 1982.

To meet the RTAF's new combat aircraft requirements, in 1987 China had offered Thailand the latest A-5C version of the Nanchang Q-5 'Fantan', plus the Chengdu F-7M Airguard, both at 'friendship prices' of only $3 million each. US procurement was complicated by Congressionally-mandated deletion of FY1987 FMS funding for such countries as Thailand and South Korea. In late 1988, however, the RTAF chief of air staff called for the purchase of 80 more fighters, including 18 F-7Ms, which underwent serious evaluation for a possible 'high/low' package with F-16s, as well as surplus USAF A-10s then due for retirement in the early 1990s.

By then, the RTAF had undergone major reorganisation in support of the army's four regional commands. Fighter modernisation plans had narrowed to the planned acquisition within a Bht12 billion ($452 million) budget of a squadron of 12 Tornado IDS and ECR aircraft, another F-16 squadron, and procurement of the AMX or Hawk 100/200 for attack roles, to replace its F-5E/Fs. Although credit assistance was offered through the UK's Overseas Development Administration for Tornado procurement, this was eventually deemed too costly and complex for RTAF operation.

F-5 upgrade programme

Thailand was one of the first countries to upgrade its F-5s. After some of its 34 F-5Es and six two-seat F-5Fs had been rewinged by Northrop, the RTAF signed a $38.2 million contract in June 1985 with SLI avionics, the US Grand Rapids Division of UK Smiths Industries, to modernise 39 of them. Formerly in the Lear Siegler group, SLI supplied new dual 1553B digitised avionics upgrade kits for supervised RTAF installation at Don Muang air base from February 1989, when eight F-5As, four RF-5As, six F-5Bs, and four F-5Es were also still being operated by 231 Squadron from Udon Thani.

These kits were based on a GEC Avionics Type 956 HUD/WAC, Litton AN/ASN-117(V)/LN-39 INS, Litton/General Instruments ALR-46(V) RWR, and Tracor AN/ALE-40 chaff/flare dispenser system. Only 20 RTAF F-5s required the defensive EW systems, already fitted to the

Above: Since 1977 201 Sqn's Twin-Pac conversion S-58Ts have served as armed combat SAR helicopters.

Below: This GAF N-22B Nomad is one of those in service with 605 Sqn, detached from 461 Sqn.

bove: Thailand is eager to acquire more V-10Cs, but the type is out of production nd the few remaining users are all qually keen to keep their existing fleets.

Below: The Lockheed T-33 remains in RTAF service as a lead-in fighter trainer, but its place is rapidly being taken by the L-39ZA. This is one of the ex-AA T-33As in service with 561 Squadron.

Above: Bell UH-1Hs are in RTAF service as trainers and SAR aircraft. This is one of 203 Squadron's aircraft.

Below: Thailand's last (two) C-123Ks are in use as rain-makers and are due to be replaced by CN.235s.

bove: Bell 412s operate longside UH-1Hs as part of 03 Sqn, based at RTAFAB okkathium/Lop Buri.

Below: Surviving AU-23A Peacemakers still fulfil the COIN role with 202 (seen here) and 531 Squadrons.

elow: Deliveries of the lenia G222 transport to 603 quadron began in May 1995, nd six are currently in use.

Below right: The RTAF's secretive IAI Aravas are used for Sigint-gathering missions by 605 Squadron.

other 19, and consideration was given to adding pulse-Doppler radar at a later stage. The LN-39 INS was fitted only to 12 F-5Es intended for ground/maritime-strike, for which gun pods containing the 30-mm GPU-5/A cannon were also acquired. Other armament sought included up to 200 Durandal anti-runway bombs from MATRA. Northrop also quoted around $3.3 million per aircraft for kits to convert six RTAF F-5Es to RF-5E Tigereye standard.

Following the loss of three F-5Es in a formation accident on 27 March 1987, five attrition replacements were sought from various F-5 operators through FMS funding. Ten F-5Es formerly operated by the USAF's Pacific Air Forces aggressor squadron were purchased for $5 million in late 1988 for 102 Squadron, but further attempts to acquire 16 from the US in 1990, as well as from Jordan and Saudi Arabia, proved unsuccessful. Talks with Taiwan in March 1991, to buy a squadron of 14 F-5Es and five two-seat F-5Fs, also failed, and Ethiopian offers of 12 F-5As, two F-5Bs and eight F-5Es were rejected because of the aircraft's poor condition. In early 1994, the RTAF discussed acquiring 10 F-5A/Bs from Korea for, to supplement its eight remaining F-5As and two F-5Bs in 231 Squadron, but no further progress has been reported. In fact, it was reported in early 1995 that the RTAF planned to sell 12 of its F-5s to Uruguay.

More combat aircraft orders

Mid-1990 negotiations with the AMX consortium culminated in a decision to procure 38 AMX ground-attack fighters, including 12 AMX-T combat trainers, for Bht19.7 billion ($774 million), with delivery from mid-1992. Of this total, Bht15.36 billion ($603.7 million) was for the aircraft, and the remainder for spares, support and training. Selected in preference to the Hawk 100/200, the AMXs were intended as A-37B replacements for maritime strike and coastal defence, to supplement the planned second squadron of F-16s. After Cabinet prevarication over programme costs, the RTAF renewed its AMX proposals by September 1991, only to be overruled on 12 February 1992 by a Presidential decision that there was no money to spare for this programme.

Most available funding had been allocated for the $607 million FMS order placed in late 1991 for the second squadron of 12 Block 15OCU F-16As and six F-16B two-seat combat trainers. This order was originally to comprise 14 F-16As and four F-16Bs, but the accompanying support equipment remained unchanged, including four spare uprated F100-PW-220 turbofans and six sets of LANTIRN systems.

Deliveries started with formal acceptance of the first F-16A (40310/USAF 90023) at Lockheed Martin Fort Worth on 10 September 1995, and were completed in February 1996. These aircraft replaced the F-5E/Fs in a second squadron (403 at Takhli), supplementing the 14 F-16As and four F-16Bs equipping 103 Sqn. 403 Squadron's F-5E/Fs then replaced the earlier F-5s of 231 Squadron at Udon Thani.

Funding was sought in the FY1996 defence budget, starting 1 October 1995, for another 18-20 fighters to equip a third combat squadron to supplement its current 36 F-16A/Bs. Against strong competition from the F-16C/D, as well as the Mirage 2000-5 and Su-35, McDonnell Douglas lowered its F/A-18 unit price below $25 million in an early 1996 LOA. This proposed a $578 million contract for four each F/A-18C/Ds, which also included four spare GE F404 turbofans and five AGM-84 missiles. Other additions were an ALQ-165 internal ECM suite, AAR-50 FLIR pods, and AAS-38 LTS pods.

A government-to-government contract was signed on 30 May 1996 for the Bht14.6 billion RTAF purchase, which was originally conditional on the supply of AIM-120s to counter Malaysia's anticipated R-77s (AA-12 'Adders') on its MiG-29s. Although AMRAAM had not then been released to the Far East, an option for 50 AIM-120s for the RTAF was made the subject of a separate LOA in early 1996 by the Pentagon. AIM-7M Sparrows will be used as interim AAMs, supplementing AIM-9L Sidewinders. Hornets will have inflight-refuelling probes, for which the RTAF has been actively seeking an air refuelling tanker. After unsuccessful requests to the US for the necessary kits to convert three Thai International DC-10-30ERs for this role, consideration is now being given to HDU installations in a C-130, by the time RTAF Hornet deliveries start in February 1999. Eight more F/A-18C/Ds are planned for procurement, for which funding is being sought in the FY1998 defence budget.

Transport and support aircraft

From its original equipment of Douglas C-47s and Fairchild C-123s, supplemented from 1980-90 by eight C-130H Hercules, 6 (Transport) Wing at Bangkok's Don Muang International Airport received two more pairs of C-130Hs and stretched C-130H-30s. They were delivered to 601 Squadron between April and December 1992, for an estimated cost of Bht3.6 billion, or about $143 million. This increased its total strength to six each C-130Hs and H-30s, and the RTAF has stated requirements for six more (C-130Js). 601 Squadron also operated three DC-8-62AFs until mid-1989, when all were sold.

Having been retired from service in 1990, the last two C-123Ks operating with 602 Squadron were brought back in 1992 after a severe drought to resume their rain-making role. This entails seeding clouds at about 5,000 ft (1525 m) with a silver iodide solution from rear-fuselage outlets. The RTAF's remaining four C-47s in 603 Squadron, operating alongside five BAe 748-208s from eight delivered in 1983-88, have been used for similar and general transport operations. The C-123s are being replaced by Alenia G222s, but three PT6A-powered Basler Turbo-67s were due for delivery from January 1997.

Although the RTAF received Cabinet approval in November 1993 to buy six G222s, agreement was only reached in July 1994 after the Italians accepted nearly 20 per cent of the programme costs as a barter deal, and reduced spares package prices. The first three G222s (s/n 60307, 08, 09) were delivered to 603 Squadron on 2 May 1995, and the last three in 1996. The RTAF has discussed buying at least six more G222s.

Also at Don Muang, 604 Squadron no longer operates Cessna O-1 Bird Dogs, while having taken over the army's Survey Department and its associated aircraft in 1986. 605 Squadron has a miscellany of light transports for reconnaissance, ECM and photographic survey roles. Among these are trios of Swearingen Merlin IVAs (60501-3); specially-equipped Learjet 35A light jet transports (60504-6); GAF N-22B Nomads (46111-3); IAI 201 Aravas (60509-11); and a Rockwell Commander 690 (81491).

Delivered to the RTAF in March 1988, the Learjets have some F-16 systems, including TACAN, INS, IFF and RWR, as well as oblique and vertical mapping cameras. Two underwing hardpoints carry IR and radar ECM systems, or target-towing equipment. 6 Wing's GAF Nomads are detached from 461 Squadron at Phitsanulok, where most of 20 N-22Bs delivered from 1982-84 from Australia, augmented by two more in 1987 from regional defence aid, are now employed on light transport roles. Initially, they operated in 402 Squadron from Takhli alongside AC-47D gunships on COIN missions, with underwing ordnance pods and a cabin-mounted 20-mm M60 cannon. Transferred from the disbanding 404 Squadron in 1993, the RTAF Aravas are equipped for EW/Sigint missions.

The final 6 Wing component is the RTAF's Royal Flight at Khon Kaen. It operates an Airbus A310-324, ordered in May 1990 and delivered in September 1991. Also on inventory is a single F-5E, maintained for the use of King Bhumibol Adulyadej's eldest son, who is now reported to have more than 1,000 hours on type. More conventional transports include two Boeing 737-3Z6s, from three procured in all; the other crashed during a test flight on 30 March 1993.

Two Royal Flight Bell 412ST helicopters were joined from October 1996 by three Eurocopter AS 332L2 Super Puma Mk 2s ordered in late 1995, after 1989 plans to buy four Sikorsky S-70Cs failed to materialise. Two Super Pumas have luxurious 10-seat cabin layouts for Royal use, while the third has 14 passenger seats in an executive layout, for use by government and other dignitaries.

RTAF trainer scene

In 1969 the Flying Training School (FTS) moved from Korat to custom-built facilities at Kamphaeng San. There, after five years at Armed Forces and RTAF Academies, students originally completed 20 hours on 24 NZAI CT-4As and 80 hours on 18 SIAI-Marchetti SF.260s. Primary training is undertaken by 1 'Chicken' FT Squadron, which now operates 17 CT-4As and six CT-4B Airtrainers, the latter completed in late 1991 by the Pacific Aerospace Corporation at Hamilton, New Zealand.

Students streamed for jets then flew 110 hours on 14 T-37B/Cs from MDAP deliveries of 16 (10 ex-USAF T-37Bs in 1961 and six new T-37Cs in 1970), with 2 'Twinny' Squadron for basic jet training. (The aircraft were later augmented by six attrition replacement T-37Bs from USAF sources in 1980.) Non-jet students remained on SF.260s for another 100 hours. Advanced jet training comprised 80-100 hours in about five months on R/T-33s of 561 Squadron, followed by 60 hours of operational conversion on F-5Bs and F-5Fs.

In anticipation of the 1983 abandonment of the indigenous RTAF-5 turboprop COIN/trainer programme, replacements for the CT-4s and SF.260s were sought in August 1982 with an order for 47 Rhein Flugzeugbau Fantrainers. They comprised 31 RFB Fantrainer 400s with the 420-shp (315-kW) Allison 250-C20B engines driving a centrally-mounted ducted fan, as well as 16 Fantrainer 600s with the more powerful

Above: The BAe 748-208s in service with 603 Squadron were delivered in 1983/88.

Below: Thailand was the second military A310 operator after the Luftwaffe.

Above: Two VIP-configured Boeing 737-3Z6s remain in use with the Royal Flight.

Below: RTAF Royal Flight helicopters include a pair of smartly-painted Bell 412STs.

Above: 605 Sqn is the RTAF's special missions unit and operates three grey Merlin IVAs.

Below: Three Learjet 35As are used by 605 Sqn for survey and ECM tasks.

Above: Cessna T-37B/Cs still serve with the Flying Training School (FTS) at Kamphang Saen, though the RTAF's A-37 Dragonflys have now been retired. This is a T-37B attached to 1 Flying Training Squadron.

Below: Thailand's procurement of the German-built RFB Fantrainer has not been a success. The RTAF had hoped to acquire and assemble over 40 Fantrainer 400/600s but only 16 Fantrainer 600s have entered service with the FTS.

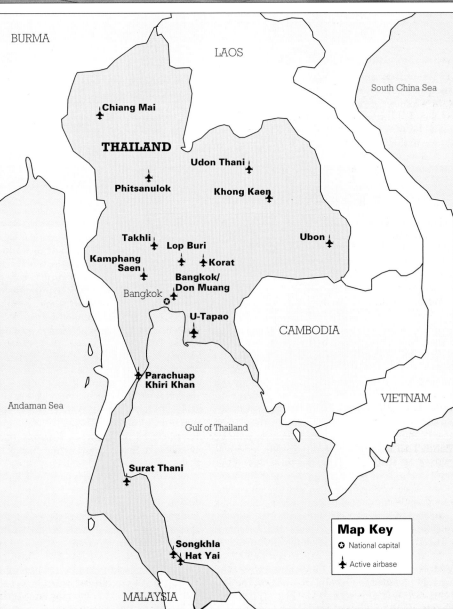

Map of Thailand showing neighbouring BURMA, LAOS, CAMBODIA, VIETNAM, MALAYSIA, the Andaman Sea, Gulf of Thailand and South China Sea.

Locations: Chiang Mai, Udon Thani, Phitsanulok, Khong Kaen, Takhli, Lop Buri, Kamphang Saen, Korat, Ubon, Bangkok/Don Muang, Bangkok, U-Tapao, Parachuap Khiri Khan, Surat Thani, Songkhla, Hat Yai.

Map Key

✪ National capital

✈ Active airbase

(650-shp/485-kW) -C30. Forty-three were scheduled for local assembly at Bangsue. To recoup some investment made in metal tooling and jigs for the RTAF-5, metal wings built by the RTAF Directorate of Aeronautical Engineering were adopted for the Thai Fantrainers instead of their original GRP mainplanes.

RFB supplied single examples of the Fantrainer 400 and higher-powered 600 series with GRP wings in October 1984 for flight test at Don Muang, and shipped 14 GRP fuselages to Thailand, where they awaited delivery of their metal wings for some time. To accelerate the programme, the RTAF accepted six sets of GRP wings from RFB for local assembly, from which the first aircraft was due in early 1985. The first locally-produced GRP fuselage shell was due for incorporation on the 17th aircraft off the Bangsue line, but the first metal wings were not shipped to RFB for German certification until early 1986. Only the 16 Fantrainer 600s were reported to be in service by 1988, when CT-4 replacement began, although all 31 kits of the Srs 400 had by then been supplied from Germany.

Apart from programme delays, serviceability problems with the Fantrainer resulted in negotiations being finalised in late 1990 for the RTAF purchase of 20 Pilatus PC-9s. A $90 million order, including spares, training and support equipment, was signed by April 1991, with delivery starting in October to 2 FT 'Mustang' Squadron. This was completed by March 1992, and the T-37s retired in 1994, but a later request for another 10 PC-9s was rejected for economic reasons. From the earlier training sequence of CT-4, SF.260M, Fantrainer 400/600, and T-37, RTAF pilots now fly 65 hours on the CT-4, and 135 hours on the PC-9, before jet conversion.

The remaining SF.260MTs were transferred to 604 Squadron, known locally as the 'Thai Flying Club', and are operated for continuation and refresher training alongside Cessna T-41Ds and a few Cessna 150Hs from Don Muang. The RTAF has a requirement for another 24 primary trainers, for which Pacific Aerospace in New Zealand was offering the CT-4E, with a 300-hp (235-kW) AEIO-540 piston engine, in late 1996.

PC-9 deliveries resulted in the transfer of the FTS FT-600s by September 1993 to 402 Squadron at Takhli for weapons training and light attack roles. Later RFB offers of modified Fantrainers were rejected by the RTAF; the aircraft, known as the Tiro-Trainer, featured a 1,900-lb (8.45-kN) FJ44 turbofan and had a 340-kt (630-km/h) maximum speed. It had been offered for the same DM3 million ($1.8 million) unit cost as its 225-kt (417-km/h) capable predecessors.

For advanced training, Cabinet approval was received in March 1992 for acquisition of 36 Czech Aero L-39ZA Albatros armed jet-trainers. The RTAF requirement was originally for 50, to replace 19 RTAF T-33As and three RT-33As, with secondary ground-attack roles, but four more were later ordered, increasing total Thai procurement to 40. Initial programme costs were estimated at about Bht5.3 billion ($210 million), including upgraded Elbit avionics, but funding is planned for another 10 L-39s in FY1998.

Formal hand over of the first L-39ZA at Vodochody occurred on 15 October 1993, and actually involved the second example off the line (c/n 365407), serialled 10112. The first (365404/10111) was delivered earlier to partici-

pate in the Thai International air show at Kamphaeng Saen air base in September 1993. Three RTAF squadrons have been equipped with the L-39s, comprising the reformed 101 (for jet conversion) and 102 at Korat, while 401 Squadron has replaced its Fantrainers for light attack/combat training roles from Takhli. The F-5E/Fs formerly operated by 102 Squadron were then transferred to 411 Squadron at Takhli, alongside Fantrainers of 402 Squadron, and to 711 Squadron at Surat Thani, replacing OV-10Cs.

Order of Battle, Royal Thai Air Force

1st Air Division	
Wing 2	**RTAFAB Kokkathium/Lop Buri**
201 Squadron	Sikorsky S-58T
202 Squadron	Fairchild AU-23A
203 Squadron	Bell UH-1H/Bell 412
Wing 6	**RTAFAB Bangkok/Don Muang**
601 Squadron	Lockheed C-130H/H-30
602 Squadron	Fairchild C-123K, Basler Turbo 67
603 Squadron	BAe 748, Aeritalia G222
604 Squadron	Cessna 150, Cessna T-41D, SF.260MT
605 Squadron	SA226AT, N-22B, Learjet 35A, IAI 201
904 Squadron	F-5E/aggressor unit
Royal Flight	**RTAFAB Khong Kaen**
	Airbus A310, Boeing 737, Bell 412, F-5E
2nd Air Division	
Wing 1	**RTAFAB Korat/Nakhon Ratchasima**
101 Squadron	Aero L-39ZA
102 Squadron	Aero L-39ZA
103 Squadron	Lockheed Martin F-16A/B
Wing 21	**RTAFAB Ubon Ratchathani**
211 Squadron	Northrop F-5E/F
Wing 23	**RTAFAB Udon Thani**
231 Squadron	Northrop R/F-5A/B/E/F

3rd Air Division	
Wing 4	**RTAFAB Takhli**
401 Squadron	Aero L-39ZA
402 Squadron	DASA/RFB Fantrainer 400/600
403 Squadron	Lockheed Martin F-16A/B
Wing 41	**RTAFAB Chiang Mai**
411 Squadron	Rockwell OV-10C
Wing 46	**RTAFAB Phitsanulok**
461 Squadron	GAF N-22B
4th Air Division	
Wing 53	**RTAFAB Prachuap Khiri Khan**
531 Squadron	Cessna O-1, Fairchild AU-23A
Wing 56	**RTAFAB Hat Yai**
561 Squadron	Lockheed R/T-33
Wing 71	**RTAFAB Surat Thani**
711 Squadron	Northrop F-5E/F
Flying Training School	**RTAFAB Kamphang Saen**
1 FT Sqn	NZAI CT-4A/B, Cessna T-37B/C
2 FT Sqn	Pilatus PC-9
Helicopter Flight	Bell 206B-3, Bell UH-1H

transferred to 411 Squadron. Although replaced by L-39s as lead-in fighter trainers, a few Lockheed T/RT-33As were still operated on support roles by 561 Squadron at Hat Yai in 1996.

For helicopter pilot training, the FTS has a small number of Bell UH-1Hs, although they were supplemented by five Bell 206B-3s from a Bht150 million ($5.85 million) contract signed in December 1993. About 30 RTAF UH-1s are operated in SAR roles by 203 Squadron with HQ at Lop Buri, with regional detachments.

RTNAD (Kongbin Tha Han Lur Thai)

Thai interest in naval aviation dates back to 1938, when six Watanabe (BTL.1) biplanes were delivered from Japan. In the late 1940s, equipment supplied from the UK and US included a dozen land-based Fairey Firefly FR.Mk 1s, followed by a small batch of Curtiss SB2C-5 Helldivers. Ten Grumman S-2Fs and two U-2C Trackers were acquired, but they and other aircraft were operated by the RTAF until 1963 because of RTN political instability.

The RTN Air Division (RTNAD) was then reformed to operate the Trackers and a couple of HU-16B Albatross amphibians to support surface vessels patrolling the Gulf of Thailand. Although the HU-16s have been retired for several years, seven U-2C/S-2F Trackers are still operated on training and utility roles by 101 Squadron within RTNAD's 1 Wing at U-Tapao/Sattahip, near Bangkok, which comprises the Naval Division's first-line element.

Most ASW roles were taken over in September 1984 by three Fokker F27MPA Maritime Enforcer Mk 1s (10663/1109, 10666/1110, 10676/1111). They have six weapons pylons, surveillance radars and are AGM-84 Harpoon-capable. The first six AGM-84s were delivered to Thailand in September 1988, supplementing RGM-84As already used by RTN corvettes. The F27MPAs can also carry Marconi Stingray torpedoes and depth charges. Following the early loss of a RTNAD F27MPA in February 1984, a fourth

example (10676) was ordered immediately, and delivered in April 1987.

For shorter-range coastal and border patrols, three Dornier Do 228-212s (121, 122, 123) were bought in early 1990, with mission equipment, including Bendix 1500 360° surveillance radar, FLIR, and provision for external stores. They were delivered for 101 Squadron from February 1991, and three more were ordered for RTNAD service from 1996.

Having abandoned 1990 plans to upgrade its Trackers because of corrosion, the RTNAD approached the US DoD for the supply of three surplus early-model P-3 Orions. After USN depot level maintenance, two P-3As were first delivered from the resulting $86.3 million contract in December 1993 and January 1994 for spares cannibalisation. They were followed in February 1995 by two P-3Ts (152142/152143), upgraded to approximate P-3B Plus standard with cockpit and powerplant updates, for operation by 101 Squadron. A single UP-3T (152184) for training followed in November 1995.

As the second element of 1 Wing at U-Tapao, 103 Squadron undertakes light attack and general support roles. Its small fleet of Cessna light aircraft mainly comprises 11 Cessna/Summit Aviation 337H-SP Sentry piston-engined tandem twins (327-337) supplied from the US in 1980-83. With underwing machine-gun and rocket pods, they are used for COIN and coastal anti-piracy

*ove: **To** cover for delays in the Fantrainer ogramme the **RTAF** acquired 20 Pilatus **PC-9** iners, now in service with **2 FT Squadron**.*

*Right: The **RTAF**'s surviving **SF.260MTs** serve with **604 Squadron**, the so-called '**Thai Flying Club**'.*

4 Squadron operates a handful of civilian-spec essna Model 150Hs from Don Muang.

*Alongside 604 Squadron's civilian **Cessnas** are a number of military-standard **Cessna T-41Ds**.*

*Thailand and Australia were the only export customers for the New Zealand-built **CT-4 Airtrainer**.*

*ove: '**Tango Squadron**', the **RTAF**'s istoric flight, maintains this nmaculate 1948-vintage de Havilland anada **DHC-1 Chipmunk T.Mk 30**.*

*Right: Thailand's last remaining North American **T-28Ds** are kept airworthy by '**Tango Squadron**', which also flies a **Cessna O-1**.*

*bove: The **RTAF**'s last Cessna **A-37 Dragonflys** were operated by 211 quadron, but were withdrawn from service in 1994/95. This shark mouthed -37B wore this special scheme to commemorate the retirement of the type.*

*Left: The Royal Thai Navy Air Division (RTNAD) flies two **CL-215-111** amphibians, which replaced **HU-16** **Albatrosses**. They operate as part of 202 Sqn, based at Songkhla.*

*Above: The **RTNAD** has gained a whole new combat capability through its 1995 acquisition of 14 ex-**US Navy A-7E** strike aircraft and four **TA-7E** trainers. The A-7s are all operated by **101 Squadron**.*

operations, and operate alongside the unit's four U-17A/B utility lightplanes (1438, 1442, 1455, 4423) and five O-1G Bird Dog liaison/trainers.

New equipment and organisation

Naval aviation expansion was planned from the late 1980s around an air attack wing, comprising 30 shore-based strike fighters, and the acquisition of an assault carrier for up to 12 helicopters and six V/STOL fighters. They were required for tactical support of the 16,000-strong Royal Thai Marine Corps, which included one amphibious assault battalion, and to defend Thailand's sea approaches. From 1992, the Thai Naval Aviation Division (TNAD) also became a key part of the newly-formed Air and Coastal Defence Command, which planned to double its assets, perhaps including a second helicopter-carrier. By late 1994, a major new naval base was also being built at Krabi for the RTN to become a two-ocean force – in the Gulf of Thailand, and the combined Andaman Sea/Straits of Malacca – these bodies of water being, separated by the Malaysian isthmus.

After evaluations of the Nanchang A-5 and upgraded A-4 Skyhawks, funding limitations were reflected in a Bht2.04 billion ($81.6 million) FMS contract placed with the US in early 1994 for 21 surplus Vought Corsair IIs. They comprised 14 A-7Es and four two-seat TA-7Es, plus three more for spares sourcing, compared with the original 1991 requirement for 24 A-7Es and six TA-7Es, plus eight for spares.

Following pilot and technician training in the US, at NAS Meridian, and Corsair refurbishment at the US Naval Air Depot, Jacksonville, Florida, the first Thai TA-7Es (156746, 156779) and A-7Es (158658, 159288, etc.) were delivered in late July 1995 to the newly-formed 104 Squadron at U-Tapao Naval Air Station at the Sattahip naval base. As an ex-USAF airfield of the Vietnam War era, U-Tapao was the only Thai naval air base with a sufficiently long runway (of 2000-2500 m/ 6,560-8,200 ft) to operate the A-7s. With a single 66.7-kN (15,000-lb) thrust Rolls-Royce/Allison TF41-A2 Spey turbofan, the A-7Es can carry up to 6800 kg (15,000 lb) of a wide range of external stores. (As a matter of historical record, the A-7 is technically the Corsair III, although it is the second Vought aircraft of this name to be operated by Thailand. The first was not the famous F4U 'bent-wing bird' of World War II, but a V93S Corsair two-seat biplane of the 1930s, still to be seen in the RTAF museum at Don Muang.)

The RTN's helicopter support ship, or V/STOL carrier, requirement was originally to be fulfilled by a DM325 million ($218.2 million) order in January 1991 to Bremer Vulkan AG Schiffbau und Maschinenfabrik in West Germany for a 7800-tonne vessel accommodating up to 10 helicopters. This order was cancelled by August of that year, probably because the ship was too small to operate a flight of V/STOL fighters, with their accompanying ski-ramp.

A contract worth Pts30 billion ($285 million) was then awarded in March 1992 to Empresa Nacional Bazan in Madrid for a new 11400-tonne V/STOL aircraft-/helicopter-carrier, to be known as the *Chakri Naruebet* and built in the El Ferrol shipyards. It was launched as scheduled on 20 January 1996 for delivery in April 1997. Basically a scaled-down version of the Spanish navy's similar carrier, *Principe de Asturias*, the Thai vessel was designed with a 175-m (570-ft) flight deck

and a 12° bow ramp to operate Harriers, and accommodate up to 12 utility helicopters or smaller numbers of CH-47 Chinooks. Bazan also received a $79 million follow-on contract in late 1995 for the carrier's command and control system.

For its primary RTN carrier complement, a contract for around $100 million was negotiated from October 1993 through the US as original suppliers for seven remaining Spanish AV-8S and two TAV-8S Harriers. Known in Spain as VA.1 Matadors, the AV-8s were formerly operated from Rota, and their supply also included some spares, support equipment, and training.

Twelve RTN pilots were sent to the US in early 1995 for basic naval flying training, followed by Harrier conversion for the eight graduates from 16 August 1996, via the simulator and TAV-8A training at Rota. Formal transfer of the Harriers to the TNAD's newly-formed 105 Squadron took place in Spain on the same date, for working-up training which would continue until embarkation on delivery and commissioning of the *Chakri Naruebet* at Rota in July 1997.

Delivery is also due at about the same time of six S-70B-7 Seahawks ordered through a $140 million RTNAD FMS contract placed with Sikorsky on 18 October 1993, for carrier-based SAR, maritime patrol, coastal surveillance and over-the-horizon targeting operations. These helicopters are reported to incorporate provision for Bendix AQS-13 dipping sonar, sonobuoys, ESM and Penguin missiles, none of which are initially being fitted.

RTNAD second-line units

All RTNAD air transport, utility and support activities are undertaken by 2 Wing from Naval Air Station Songkhla, in the extreme south of Thailand. As its fixed-wing element, 202 Squadron now operates two remaining C-47Bs from 13 received in 1978, for general transport roles. They were augmented from 1986-87 by two Fokker F27 Mk 400s (2211/12), used for SAR and target-towing, among other duties.

Four armed GAF N-24A Searchmaster Ls (2206, 212-214) are used for light transport, coastal patrol and limited ASW operations. The aircraft are equipped with nose-mounted Litton APS-504 search radar and SSQ-801 Barra

sonobuoy systems, and were delivered with Australian funding aid from July 1984. They were joined in 1985 by a fifth (215) UN-funded example with side-looking airborne radar, for anti-piracy roles. Two Canadair CL-215-111 amphibians (2204/5) which replaced the RTNAD's HU-16s in 1978 are used for SAR and fire-fighting.

Naval rotary-wing support is provided by 203 Squadron from Songkhla, which began operations with four Bell UH-1H (401-404) and eight ASW-equipped Bell 212 (405-412) helicopters in 1975-78. They were joined in March 1987 by five Bell 214ST utility helicopters (413-417) costing $33 million, which have wheel instead of skid undercarriages, but retain fittings for the latter.

Reported orders in 1990 have so far failed to materialise, for either six Kaman SH-2F Seasprites in a US weapons package costing $258 million, including 24 Honeywell Mk 46 torpedoes, Mk 12 tubes, and 16 AGM-84 Harpoons, or for nine Chinese-built HAMC Z-9A (Dauphin 2) utility helicopters, announced by the Chinese Aerospace Industry Ministry in March 1992.

203 Squadron is now expecting to undertake general transport, SAR and utility roles with six Sikorsky S-76Bs, for which an FMS contract was signed in September 1994. Formal acceptance of the first example took place in the US on 31 March 1996, and the S-76s were delivered to U-Tapao between June and September. The RTNAD was considering buying six more S-76s equipped for ASW/ASV missions, in early 1997, when it was also awaiting six S-70B-7 Seahawks.

Order of Battle, Royal Thai Navy Air Division

RTN Wing 1	Naval Air Station U -Tapao
101 Squadron	Grumman U/S-2C/F, Lockheed P-3A/UP-3T, Dornier Do 228-212, Fokker F27-200MPA
103 Squadron	Cessna O-1G, Cessna U-17B, Cessna 337H-SP
104 Squadron	Vought A-7E/TA-7E
105 Squadron	MDC/BAe AV-8A(S)/TVA-8A(S)
RTN Wing 2	**Naval Air Station Songkhla**
202 Squadron	Canadair CL-215-III, Douglas C-47, Fokker F27-400M, GAF N-24L
203 Squadron	Bell 212, Bell 214ST, Bell UH-1H

RTAAD (Kongbin Tha Han Bo)

Army aviation gained independence from the RTAF in 1952, with the transfer of a few L-4 Piper Cubs and Stinson L-5s. They were followed from 1956 by an eventual 60 or more Cessna L-19A/E/G (later redesignated O-1s) liaison and artillery-spotting aircraft. In addition to a dozen Bell 47G/OH-13 helicopters, they were supplemented in 1967 by 10 Cessna T-41Ds and a similar number of beefier U-17Bs in 1971, following earlier deliveries of DHC-2 (U-6A) Beavers.

In 1986, Cessna also provided the RTAAD with more substantial transports in the form of eight U-27As (Model 208 Caravan). These aircraft can carry an underfuselage GD reconnaissance pod with day/night optical and electronic sensors, plus underwing weapons or stores. Twenty five-seat Maule M-7-25 Super Rockets delivered in 1992 are used for training/liaison.

Fixed-wing army aircraft procurement also included a 17-seat Beech 99 in 1970, followed by two Model 200 Super King Airs in 1984, and two 19-seat Beech 1900C-1s in November 1991, all for senior personnel transport. Heavier army airlift missions originally performed by four Douglas C-47s were taken over from June 1984 by two Shorts SD330UTT utility tactical turboprop-twins (3098, 3102) for the RTAAD's Transport Division, followed in February 1996 by a pair of CASA C.212-300s (28053/4) for similar roles.

Orders for two 29-seat BAe Jetstream 41 light turboprop-twin transports were announced at the 1995 Paris air show for communications use by the RTAAD from late 1995-96. Both incorporated provision for a quick-change twin cabin layout, including one compartment with VIP accommodation.

...ve: The RTNAD abandoned plans to upgrade its ...ting Grumman Trackers in the early 1990, and ...ead began to acquire a fleet of P-3A and upgraded ...T Orions. The Orions are flown by 101 Squadron.

Right: The original RTAAD requirement for Bell 412s, to replace over 100 Bell UH-1s, has been met with 56 new aircraft, to date.

Above: The RTAAD's two C212-300 Aviocars are CASA-built aircraft, delivered from Spain in 1996. They are attached to the Air Division's Transport Division.

...ove: The RTAAD is unique ...a military operator of the ...stream International ...4e) Jetstream 41. Two are ...use as VIP transports.

Below: Another unique RTAAD type is the Shorts SD330 UTT (Utility Tactical Transport). The UTTs replaced C-47s in 1984.

Left: In 1967 the RTAAD took delivery of a number of Cessna T-41Ds to serve alongside the Cessna L-19s (O-1s) and remaining Piper L-4s and Stinson L-5s then in service.

Above: The RTAAD relies on the CH-47C/D Chinook, which has the ability to transport the Army's M198 155-mm howitzers as underslung loads. This is a CH-47D, delivered in 1989.

Left: Some veteran Cessna O-1A Bird Dogs still survive in RTAAD service, a few in three-tone camouflage.

Above: Schweizer Hughes TH-300Cs serve with earlier Hughes TH-55s as basic trainers for the RTAAD.

Apart from the O-1, the other RTAAD mainstay has been the Bell UH-1B/D/H, of which 139 were supplied between 1968 and 1991. Many O-1s and about half the UH-1s are still in service. Other early helicopter procurement included 25 ex-US Army Hughes TH-55As in 1974. They were withdrawn in the late 1980s, having been replaced from November 1986 by 24 Schweizer Hughes TH-300C light helicopters, and another 24 in 1988-89.

Four CH-47A Chinooks were acquired from 1972. Under a mid-1988 contract, two surviving CH-47s stored since withdrawal from service two or three years earlier, plus one ex-US Army CH-47B, were rebuilt to CH-47C standard for redelivery by March 1991. A parallel 1988 contract included orders for five CH-47Ds, delivered from 1989.

The Thai army's first attack helicopters were ordered in mid-1986 in the form of four Bell AH-1Ss (later AH-1F), armed with BGM-71A TOW. They arrived in November 1990, and funding was sought for eight more by 1991 to form an air cavalry regiment. The RTAAAD also looked into the potential of a turret-armed Bell 214ST for ground-attack/troop transport, having taken delivery of three in 1984. However, the Bell 214STs were disposed of within a few years.

Following delivery of six Bell 212s to the RTAAD's 3 Squadron in 1986, orders for five more planned for mid-1987 were held up until late 1988 because of Parliamentary opposition; the helicopters were intended for use by the Thai government and the Royal family. A 1987 armed forces requirement for more than 100 new utility helicopters, including up to 40 assault transports, then resulted in late 1989 orders for 25 more, costing $118.4 million including spares, for acceptance at the rate of one per month between 1989-92.

At that stage, the RTAAD still had 100 UH-1s in service. In 1990, Defence Ministry approval was expected for the purchase of 50 Bell 412s costing Bht8.3 billion ($330.7 million), in preference to surplus US Army UH-1s. Insufficient funds were then available, however, leading to prolonged consideration of low-cost CIS offers of Mil Mi-17s. Eventually, the Thai government decided to limit further procurement to another 20 Bell 212s for army use, for which a contract for $110.3 million was signed in late 1993. New Bell 212 deliveries were scheduled as six in 1994, and seven each in 1995 and 1996, increasing overall RTAAD totals of this type to 56.

Organisation and deployments

HQ of the Royal Thai Army Air Division at Lop Buri, north of Bangkok, which is also the location of the Army Aviation Centre, which undertakes most of the RTAAD's flying and technical training. For fixed-wing aircraft, Cessna T-41Ds, U-17Bs and O-1s, plus Maule M-7-235s are mainly used, while rotary-wing instruction is given on Schweizer/Hughes H-300Cs, Bell 206s, Bell UH-1Hs and 212s.

Operational and support tasks are the responsibility of the RTAAD's Air Battalion, comprising two regiments with 150 or more fixed-wing aircraft and helicopters. HQ of these units is also at Lop Buri, although detachments are widely deployed throughout Thailand at Don Muang, Chiang Mai, Kachanaburi and other bases.

From Lop Buri, the RTAAD's Transport Division operates BAe Jetstream 41, Beech 99, Beech 200, Beech 1900, CASA C.212 and Shorts SD330s, alongside a flight of AH-1Fs, and a large number of UH-1Hs, Bell 212s and CH-47Ds.

RTA SAM systems include a single Selenia SPADA SAM battery, including semi-active radar-homing Aspide missiles, ordered by the RTA in early 1987. Plans were revealed in September 1994 for the purchase of 10 Searcher UAVs from IAI for target surveillance in support of Thai army artillery units deployed along Thailand's northeastern borders with Cambodia and Laos. The Thai military previously operated Lear Astronics Skyeye UAVs, although apparently with a high crash and failure record.

Order of Battle, Royal Thai Air Aviation Division (RTAAD)

Army Aviation Centre   *Lop Buri*
Bell 206, Bell 212, Bell UH-1H, Cessna O-1G, Cessna U-17B, Cessna T-41D, Hughes H-300C

Army Aviation Battalion *Lop Buri, detachments at RTAF base*
BAe Jetstream 41, Beech 99, Beech 200, Beech 1900-C1, Bell 206A/B, Bell 212, Bell 214ST, UH-1H, Bell AH-1F, Boeing CH-47D, CASA C.212-300, Cessna O-1A, Cessna U-17B, Cessna T-41D, Cessna U-27A, Shorts 330UTT

Royal Thai Border Police Aviation

With 4800 km (2,980 miles) of land borders to patrol, the RTBP came into effective operation in 1954, with much assistance from the CIA. As a component of the civil police, it is funded by the Interior Ministry, but its operational control is exercised under the Supreme Command of the Thai Armed Forces, in liaison with the armed forces.

The Police Aviation wing is organised on similar lines to the RTAAD, from HQ at Ram Inthara, in Bangkok, with detachments at most RTAF bases and a dozen or more up-country strips. Apart from anti-smuggling and border patrols, its duties include medevac, anti-rebel, anti-piracy and drug interdiction/monitoring operations.

From its original 1960s equipment of a Beech 65 Queen Air, Cessna 310Fs and three Fletcher Fu-24As, plus a few Bell 47Js and Bell 204s, the RTBPA had grown to more than 20 fixed-wing aircraft and over 60 helicopters by 1995. Rotary-wing strength at that time, centred on Ram Inthara, comprised mostly Bell 205s and UH-1Hs, of which 18 and 26 had been delivered from 1970-76, plus 12 armed Bell 206B JetRanger IIIs received in 1982-86, and two 206Ls in 1987. Two Bell 412s also arrived in 1981, followed by 10 Hiller UH-12Es for training in January 1987, and two Aérospatiale SA 365s in 1990. Confirmation of five more SA 365s due for delivery in 1993 has not yet materialised.

In the RTBPA's fixed-wing fleet, which use Don Muang at its home base, the sole DHC-4 from three delivered in 1969 is still flying. Three Shorts SC.7-3M-400 Skyvans operated since 1972 and Dornier Do 28Ds received in 198. have now been retired; the Skyvans were replaced in 1984-85 by two Shorts 330UTTs. These, in turn, were supplemented on 13 March 1996 by a CASA CN.235-200, from an April 1995 order. Two more CN.235s are currently being considered as Caribou replacements. The RTBPA also took delivery of a Fokker 50 VIP/passenger transport on 15 December 1992.

For lighter transport, 10 STOL Pilatus PC-6B Turbo Porters have been in service since 1976, although only four are currently operational. Five armed Fairchild AU-23A versions from nine originally received for police use in 1973 were transferred to the RTAF in 1977.

Order of Battle, Royal Thai Border Police Aviation (RTBPA)

RTBPA centres at Don Muang, Hua Hin and numerous dets
Aérospatiale SA 365, Bell 205A/UH-H, 206B/L, 212, 412, DHC-4, Fokker 50, Pilatus PC-6B, Shorts 330UTT

Royal Thai Agricultural Aviation

With its HQ at Nakon Sawan, Royal Thai Agricultural Aviation (KASET) is administered by the Ministry of Interior, with responsibility for crop-spraying, top-dressing, rain-making and fire-fighting, among other roles. Aircraft, which carry military markings, are based at Takhli, with detachments deployed throughout Thailand.

KASET is mainly employed on crop-spraying roles, for which it has a fleet of 26 aircraft. They are spear-headed by 11 CASA C.212-100/-200/ -300 delivered in the 1990s, plus an additional four -300s ordered in 1995. Other aircraft include a BN-2 Islander, a Cessna 310Q, two Cessna 180s, three Cessna U-206s and two Cessna 208/U-27As. KASET's spraying/training helicopters include a Schweizer/Hughes H-300, two Enstrom F-28Fs, two MDH 500s, and an S-58T. Another 16 KASET multi-role aircraft include four Fletcher FU-24-954s (from six delivered in 1989), and seven PC-6s. Two new CN.235s are also being acquired by KASET in a $34 million barter deal agreed with IPTN in September 1996, to replace Thailand's last C-123Ks.

Until early 1992, only four Bell 206Bs were operated by this section of KASET, although they were then joined by the first of 10 AS 350Bs on order through Samaero in Singapore. However, no further AS 350 deliveries have been reported.

Royal Thai Agricultural Aviation (KASET)

HQ, Nakhon Sawan   *main base, Takhli*
Aérospatiale AS 350B, Airtech CN.212-100/200/300, Bell 206B, PBN BN-2, Cessna 180, U-206, 310Q, U-27A, Enstrom F-28, Fletcher FU-24-954, Hughes H-300, H-500, Pilatus PC-6B, Sikorsky S-58

John Fricker, with additional material by **René van Woezik**

Above: The RTBPA still uses [si]ngle DHC-4 Caribou, kept [al]ive by cannibalising one [o]f its predecessors.

Below: The DHC-4's replacement will likely come in the form of more CN.235s, two of which are now in use.

Above: The RTAAD's primary combat type is the TOW-armed AH-1F Hueycobra, which forms part of the Army's air cavalry division.

Below: The Army operates two 19-seat Beech Model 1900C-1s as part of its VIP transport fleet based at Lop Buri.

[Ab]ove: The RTBPA operates [wi]th armed Bell JetRangers [an]d unarmed LongRangers.

Below: A pair of Bell 412s operates alongside RTBPA Bell Model 212s and UH-1Hs.

Above: A single Fokker 50 serves as a VIP transport with the RTBPA. It was delivered in 1992.

Right: Four PC-6B Turbo Porters remain in use with the RTBPA.

Below: Eurocopter AS 350 Ecureuils have begun to join Bell 206Bs in KASET service.

[Ab]ove: The ungainly Fletcher [F]U-24 crop-sprayer is in both [R]TBPA and KASET (as seen [he]re) service.

Below: The STOL PC-6B is also in RTBPA and KASET service. KASET examples are based at Takhli.

INDEX

INDEX

Picture acknowledgments

Front cover: Robert Hewson. **4:** Westland, E.A. Sloot. **5:** Martin Salajka, Siegfried Wache, Robert F. Dorr. **6:** Robin Polderman, B. Fischer, E.A. Sloot. **7:** E. de Kruyff, McDonnell Douglas. **8:** Brane Lucovnik. **9:** Peter R. March, D. Eklund, Andrew P. March. **10:** E. de Kruyff (two). **11:** Yaso Niwa, E. de Kruyff. **12:** Robert Hewson (two), AVIC. **13:** C.P. Justo, E.A. Sloot. **14:** Robin Polderman, Matthew Olafsen. **15:** Henry B. Ham (two), Alec Fushi, A.A. Bayliss. **17:** D. Eklund, Ted Carlson (two). **18:** CATIC via Robert Hewson (RH), Chengdu via RH. **19:** Robert Hewson (two), AVIC via RH. **20:** Robert Hewson, AVIC via RH. **21:** AVIC via RH, Robert Hewson (five). **22:** Robert Hewson (two), Shenyang via RH. **23:** Shenyang via RH, LOEC via RH. **24:** Robert Hewson, Changhe via RH (four). **25:** Jose M. Ramos, US Navy via Jose M Ramos (two). **26:** Jose M. Ramos (three), US Navy via Jose M. Ramos. **27-29:** US Navy via Jose M. Ramos. **30-33:** René van Woezik. **34-47:** David Donald. **48-49:** Robert Hewson (two), Randy Jolly. **50:** Peter R. Foster. **51:** McDonnell Douglas (two). **52:** Lockheed (two), Boeing, Bell (two). **53-54:** Hughes. **55:** Hughes, US DoD, Aerospace. **56:** Hughes. **57:** Hughes (three), Randy Jolly, Hughes. **59:** Randy Jolly, Hughes. **60:** Hughes, US DoD. **61:** Greg Davis/FPI, McDonnell Douglas. **62:** Hughes, McDonnell Douglas (two). **63:** Rick Llinares/Dash 2. **64:** McDonnell Douglas. **65:** Jeremy Flack/API, McDonnell Douglas. **66:** McDonnell Douglas (two). **67:** Randy Jolly, McDonnell Douglas. **68-69:** Robert Hewson. **70:** Robert Hewson, David Donald (two). **75:** Robert Hewson (two), John Gourley (four), David Donald (two), Yves Debay, Aerospace. **91:** Aerospace (three). **92:** Rick Llinares/Dash 2, Yves Debay, Aerospace. **93:** Rick Llinares/Dash 2. **94:** John Gourley, Dougie Monk, Rick Llinares/Dash 2. **95:** McDonnell Douglas. **96:** Hughes, McDonnell Douglas (two), Ted Carlson/Fotodynamics. **97:** Yehuda Borovik/BIAF Magazine. **98:** Tim Ripley (two), McDonnell Douglas. **99:** Michael Stroud, McDonnell Douglas.

100: Ted Carlson/Fotodynamics, Westland. **101:** via Swedish Defence Forces. **102:** McDonnell Douglas (three). **103:** Westland (two). **104:** Peter R. Foster (three), Robert Hewson. **105:** David Donald, Tom Kaminski, Peter R. Foster (two), Robert Hewson. **106:** Robert Hewson, Doug Youngblood. **107:** Yves Debay, Yehuda Borovik/BIAF Magazine, McDonnell Douglas, Ted Carlson/Fotodynamics, K. Dimitropoulos via René van Woezik. **108:** McDonnell Douglas (two), Paul Van den Elsaker. **109:** Jeremy Flack/API. **110:** Dave West, Ian Malcolm (three). **111:** Ian Malcolm (three). **112:** Ian Malcolm (three), Dave West. **113:** Ian Malcolm (three), Dave West. **114:** Dave West, Ian Malcolm (three). **115:** Ian Malcolm (three). **116:** Ian Malcolm (three), Dave West. **117:** Ian Malcolm (three). **118:** Dave West (two), Ian Malcolm (four). **119:** Ian Malcolm (four). **120-122:** Yefim Gordon. **124:** Roman Kondrat'yev via Yefim Gordon, Steven Jacob. **125:** Sukhoi via Yefim Gordon, Yefim Gordon, Robert Hewson. **126:** Tim Senior, Andrew Thomas, Yefim Gordon (two). **127:** Peter J. Cooper, David Donald, Robin Polderman, Sukhoi. **128:** Simon Watson, Yefim Gordon, Gordon Upton. **129:** Fred Willemsen, Yefim Gordon (two). **130-131:** Jon Lake, Yefim Gordon, David Donald, Mick Jennings. **133:** Yefim Gordon, Peter J. Cooper, Gordon Upton. **134:** Marcus Fulber, René van Woezik. **135:** Herman Potgieter, Gordon Upton, Yefim Gordon. **136:** Yefim Gordon (two) Chris Ryan. **137:** Yefim Gordon, David Donald, Robert Hewson. **138:** Gert Kromhout (three). **139:** Gert Kromhout, A. Buonomo. **140-141:** Gert Kromhout. **142:** Gert Kromhout (two), John Blackman, A. Buonomo. **143:** Gert Kromhout (two), A. Buonomo (two). **145:** A. Buonomo (three), John Blackman (three), Gert Kromhout. **147:** Lockheed Martin, Henry B. Ham, René va Woezik (three), Roland van Maarseveen and Cees-Jan van der Ende (three), Dick Lohuis (two). **149:** Dick Lohuis (three), René van Woezik (three), Robert E. Kling. **155:** D. Reade M.J. Gerards, Roland van Maarseveen and Cees-Jan van der Ende (two), René van Woezik (four). **157:** René van Woezik (five), Roland van Maarseveen and Cees-Jan van der Ende (two M.J. Gerards (three). **151:** Dick Lohuis (eight). **153:** Dick Lohuis (five), René van Woezik (three), Robert E. Kling. **155:** D. Reade M.J. Gerards, Roland van Maarseveen and Cees-Jan van der Ende (two), René van Woezik (four). **157:** René van Woezik (five), Roland van Maarseveen and Cees-Jan van der Ende (two), M.J. Gerards (three).